# NEVER HAD IT SO GOOD

## Burnley's Incredible 1959/60 League Title Winning Triumph

Tim Quelch

Photograph sources (in order of appearance in book):
Burnley FC: 65a, 76, 84, 88
Charles Buchan's Football Monthly: 1, 26-29, 35-36, 39, 47, 52, 54, 72-73,75, 77, 80, 82-83
premier pictures: front image
Chix Bubble Gum: 12,
Geoff Bannister: 18, 24, 53, 67
Howard Talbot Photography: 22-23,32-34, 37-38, 43-45, 58-59, 61, 68, 70, 74, 79, 81, 86
Lancashire County Library & Information Service: Burnley Library: 17, 19, 48-49, 62, 66, 85
mirrorpix: 55-57
PA Photos: 25, 31, 40-41, 60, 64-65
Unknown: 2-7, 8-11, 13-16, 20-21, 30, 42, 46, 49a, 50-51, 52a, 63, 69, 71, 78, 87

Regrettably, the author has been unable to identify the copyright ownership of some photographs, listed under 'unknown' above. Therefore it has not been possible to seek permission before reproduction in this book. It is hoped that their usage here is not opposed. Should the owners identify their work they are asked to contact Know The Score Books.



Know The Score Books Limited
118 Alcester Road
Studley, Warwickshire B80 7NT
01527 454482
info@knowthescorebooks.com
www.knowthescorebooks.com

A CIP catalogue record is available for this book from the British Library
ISBN: 978 1 84818 600 2

Printed and bound in Great Britain
by Athenaeum Press, Gateshead, Tyne & Wear

# Contents

# Thanks

I would like to thank the large number of people who helped me so much in writing this book. If I have overlooked anyone inadvertently I hope they will accept my apology.

I am deeply grateful to the members of Burnley's title-winning side who gave me generous amounts of their time. These were: John Angus, Adam Blacklaw, Trevor Meredith, Jimmy McIlroy, Brian Pilkington, Ray Pointer, Jimmy Robson, and Bob Seith. Sheila Blacklaw, and Jean Seith also kindly told me about their lives as footballer's wives, while Ella Heap and her son, John told me so much about their father and grandfather, Billy Dougall. Bob and Jean Seith went well beyond the call of duty in reading an early draft of the book as did long-standing supporter and writer, Geoff Crambie, and local historian, Roger Frost. Burnley authors, Dave Thomas and Phil Whalley kindly gave their permission to use extracts of interviews they conducted with players I was unable to meet. A number of long-standing Burnley supporters came to my aid splendidly. Thank you to Frank Bailey, Stuart Barnes, Gerard Bradley, Peter Burch, Dave Cooper, Geoff Crambie, Lester Davidson, Frank Hill, David and Sandy Hird, Brian Hollinrake, former Burnley MP, Peter Pike, Gary Roberts, Donald Speak, Dave Thomas, Rev. David Wiseman and Rob Woodmore. I am greatly indebted to Ray Simpson, Burnley, FC historian, for access to his vast and brilliant array of historical and statistical information, to Tony Scholes of The Clarets Mad website, Tom Morton (Foreverclaret) at www.thelongside.co.uk and Phil Whalley at The Clarets Archive website for access to their excellent archive material. Thanks go to Burnley FC and to other League clubs for use of their programmes and to other fans' websites. Rival supporters came to my aid, too, including Dave Harris, Rod Robbins, Dave Wellbelove and Nigel Woodcock. National and local newspapers provided rich sources of material. Thanks go to the *Burnley Express, Daily Mirror, Daily Sketch, Sunday Pictorial, News of the World, The Times* and *Sunday Times* and *Charles Buchan's Football Monthly* magazines. I would like to thank Edward Lee formerly of *Burnley Express*, Anthony Fairclough at Burnley Football Club and the staff at Burnley Central Library for their great help accessing archive material and current and past photographs. Howard Talbot and Geoff Bannister provided me with some wonderfully atmospheric photographs of the period. Howard's treasure trove of team action shots was a godsend. 'Ashtonian's stunning colour photographs of present day Burnley was a bonus, too. Thanks are also due to mirrorpix, premier pictures and PA Photos who kindly granted permission for their superb team and action shots to be printed in this book. Finally, I would like to express my gratitude: to my wife, Liz, and to my daughter, Lydia for their support; to my friends, Andrew Hannon, Rob Woodmore, Dave Hird and cousin, Judy Edwards for proof-reading earlier drafts and suggesting helpful amendments; to my publishers for their experienced guidance throughout and to everyone who has supported me during the writing of this book. Great thanks go to fellow author, Dave Thomas for his invaluable advice and assistance.

# Introduction

*Back to the Future*

PROFESSIONAL football's major prizes are now the monopoly of a select few. If the biggest are not always the best, then the exceptions are few and far between. But in what now seems a faraway place in time, the smallest could still aspire to be great.

Join me now as we spin backwards in our rickety time machine. We are returning to a time when the recently-opened Preston by-pass (now part of the M6) heralded the start of the motorway age. But only a sparse parade of vehicles – Ford Anglias, Triumph Heralds and Morris Minors among them – can be seen on its 3-lane blacktop. It is also a time when Cliff Richard, our Elvis copyist, has just enjoyed his first number one hit with *Living Doll.*

So take note now as our machine emerges from the sulphurous mists, juddering to a halt in a cobbled, terraced street, its Pennine stone houses blackened by the fumes of so many mill chimneys. The place is Burnley. The time is August 1959. It's bright and hot. The sun is so strong it easily pierces the thin, yellowed industrial haze. There's hardly a breath of air. Craig Douglas is on the radio and the week's washing is on the clothes lines. Sheets and shirts hang limply from the pleated ropes that criss-cross the street. Young girls are playing hopscotch, others are clattering around in oversized shoes and their mothers' cast off dresses and hats – a grotesque sense of theatre. There are boys here, too, dressed in aertex shirts and short grey trousers that are held up by twisted elastic belts with snake clasps. Their twin-hooped grey socks have fallen carelessly, bunching around their ankles. One starts a card game, tossing a Chix bubblegum card onto the ground. A portrait of Jimmy Greaves stares up at them from the cobbles as another boy tries to claim the card by flicking one of his own, a picture of Tom Finney, in its direction, trying to cover it. He fails. Yet another boy joins the game sucking on a liquorice straw, thrust into his sherbet fountain.

Footballers are their icons. But it is The Clarets who monopolise local reverence. The boys all have portraits of their favourites pasted into their sugar paper scrapbooks or taped to their bedroom walls – Ray Pointer, Jimmy McIlroy, Jimmy Adamson and others – cut from their copies of *Charles Buchan's Football Monthly*, *Soccer Star* or *Reynold's News*. They have their League ladders as well – free gifts from the *The Tiger* comic. As the new Football League season is about to be unveiled, all Four Divisions have their t-cards in place, primed for the first round of results. The boys have dug out their flip flop autograph books, too, ready for when the first visiting team coach pulls up outside the club entrance in Brunshaw Road. Their *Ian Allan ABC* locospotter guides will then become of secondary importance.

Very soon now, these boys will resume their place among Turf Moor's 27,000 throng; a crowd that amounts to a third of the local population. This staggering proportion is twice that found at an average First Division club of the time. For these boys, the club is a barometer of their town's importance. They reason that because their team is a force in the land so must their town be also. They are unaware that no town as small as theirs now is has ever won the First Division. They are oblivious of the fact that Burnley has lost a fifth of the population it had when it previously won the First Division Championship. That was back in 1921 before the inter-war recession undermined the prosperity of the town's traditional industries – cotton and coal. They are unconcerned that the local mills and mines are continuing to decline. Their older brothers have already moved away in search of better job prospects, but they are happy with their lot. They know their team is among the best in Britain and maybe in Europe, too. With the club's totemic floodlight pylons shimmering in the glare of the day's sun, they are confident, perhaps complacent, too, that their club is forever blessed, destined always to be giants. This season they will be rewarded with a rare triumph, an incredible victory but these boys will take this herculean performance slightly for granted. Only when they become much, much older will they realise the enormity of what was achieved.

This book is an account of a remarkable club and an even more remarkable team, with the players who pulled off this improbable Championship telling a substantial part of the story. How good were that Burnley team which lifted the First Division championship in 1959/60? Listen to what a brilliant contemporary, Jimmy Greaves, had to say about them. In his book *The Sixties Revisited* Jimmy wrote: 'in the first season that took us into the sixties Burnley were writing poetry on their way to the First Division championship. They

*Ray Pointer*

*Jimmy Adamson*

*Jimmy McIlroy*

*Brian Pilkington [1]*

played smooth, skilled soccer that was a warming advertisement for all that was best about British football.'

Jimmy continued: 'Harry Potts was the manager of Burnley, inheriting a squad that had been shaped and fashioned by his predecessor, Alan Brown, who was mainly responsible for introducing the success-breeding tactics – particularly the quick, short corners and mesmerising variety of free-kick scams ... This Burnley team brimmed with outstanding individual players and they were encouraged to play with the emphasis more on skill than sweat and stamina. I loved playing against them because they put a smile on the face of football, and even in defeat I wanted to applaud their artistry. In an era when quite a few teams believed in the big boot, they were a league of gentlemen.'

Eamon Dunphy added in *A Strange Kind of Glory*, his bestselling book about Matt Busby and Manchester United: 'Burnley won the Championship in 1960 playing cultured Continental-style football under Jimmy Adamson, their captain, and Jimmy McIlroy, their gracious articulate schemer.

This apparently unfashionable and declining town boasted a team which delivered modern, tactically astute and enterprising football. Of all the First Division sides of 1959/60, probably only Burnley and Spurs were able to match the standard of the best Spanish and Italian sides of their day. Although Burnley's players demonstrated their tactical astuteness in a series of well rehearsed dead ball routines, tactics were never employed as a substitute for skill. A high premium was always placed upon improving ball skills, underpinned by fluidity of movement and by swiftness and sudden changes of pace. Unsurprisingly, the Burnley team acquitted itself well in the European Cup competition of 1960/61 and failed by the narrowest margins to qualify for the semi-finals. Perhaps significantly, Spurs, whose style of play was so similar to Burnley, would become the first English side to win a European trophy, when they lifted the European Cup Winners' Cup in 1963.

But this is also a book about a very different time, before global finance and the international power of television had any bearing on the strength of football clubs and their consequent fortunes. This was when the maximum wage was still in place and before the top clubs had encountered foreign oligarchies, satellite TV, pay-per-view, executive boxes, agents, 'tapping up', 'bungs', spread betting, drugs tests and 'simulation'. Sporting achievements are understood better when placed in the context of surrounding events. So, as well as considering the tactics, coaching and training techniques employed by clubs of the time and what it was like to be a professional footballer then, we shall also look at what life was like in Britain more generally and how the fortunes were changing for the town of Burnley while this heroic success was being achieved. The aim is to examine as well as celebrate a remarkable triumph and to evoke warmth of nostalgia among those who lived through these times and create a vivid sense of history for those who did not.

## Chapter One

# 'Absolute Beginners'

*The way we were before the Sixties swung*

IN THE immediate post war years, Britain seemed exhausted by the social and economic dislocation brought about by World War Two. The pound had been drastically devalued in relation to the dollar, losing 30% of its former value, as Britain struggled to regain economic sustainability. Rationing was not finally eliminated until 1954. Despite this, many leading politicians and military chiefs maintained that Britain was still a major power. It still held a world policing role and, despite the independence granted to India and Pakistan in 1947, its Empire was largely intact

*Harold Macmillan: '...Never had it so good' [2]*

As the fifties drew to a close, Conservative Prime Minister Harold Macmillan, who had succeeded Anthony Eden on his resignation in January 1957, insisted that most Britons had 'never had it so good'. But despite Britain's apparent economic recovery in the late fiftes, it was in fact regressing on the world stage. Its productivity had grown by just 21% during the decade, compared with the 84% growth achieved by West Germany and the 62% growth achieved by Italy. Moreover, the other defeated Axis power, Japan, realised an incredible 300% growth between 1951 and 1964, during which time Britain's growth was a comparatively paltry 40%. Exports showed a similar profile. Despite a claim, made in *The Economist* in 1954, that Britain's 'economic miracle' had been achieved without inflation, the average weekly wage in Britain had increased by almost 75% between 1950 and 1959, rising from £6/8 shillings (£6-40p) to £11/2 shillings 6 pence (£11-12p). As Margaret Thatcher would chide us twenty years later, Britons were paying themselves more for producing less. In this case, 'less' meant less than our rivals.

*Steamed powered Britain: Bank Hall Colliery where some Burnley players worked [3]*

In the face of the 'never had it so good' message, Britain's traditional industries – steel, shipbuilding, textiles, heavy manufacturing and coal mining – were being undermined increasingly by foreign competition and by outdated production methods and restrictive practices. Through increasing modernisation, greater innovation, better use of new technology and more efficient management of labour and material resources, growing numbers of developing countries, including our recent foes, were catching up with, or actually overtaking us.

In addition, the growing affluence of the late fifties did not bless all Britons. By 1962, 42% of employees still earned under £10 per week. Nevertheless, many more homes had improved amenities. Bathrooms had become more of a standard feature, dispensing with our need of the weekly fireside bath. Electricity had replaced both downstairs gas lighting and bedtime candles, although many of the older properties still had outside toilets. With our basic comforts in better shape, many found that there was greater scope for luxuries.

By 1960, 3.5 million Britons could afford a Mediterranean holiday. Private transport had become more affordable, too. A down payment of just £4/8 shillings (£4-40p) would secure a Ford Popular saloon on a hire-purchase agreement; only £1/5 shillings (£1-25p) more than was required for the first instalment on a fridge. With the introduction of the new Mini saloon in 1959, the range of affordable small cars expanded. Car ownership increased by 250% during the decade. As a consequence, rail patronage fell away sharply, causing the network to quiver in expectation of Beeching's axe. Nevertheless, *Hornby Dublo* and *Triang* electric train sets remained popular among schoolboys, at least for those whose families had progressed beyond gas power.

Irrespective what Imperial diehards like Viscount Montgomery of Alamein chose to think or say, by 1959, Britain was no longer a leading world power,

*The motorway age arrives: the opening of the M1 in 1959 [4]*

having been utterly humiliated at Suez in 1956. British troops did all that was asked of them, converting a poorly-co-ordinated operation into a certain military victory, but with the country's balance of payments in such a poor state, the United States were able to call, or more to the point, stop the shots. US support for Britain's bid for International Monetary Fund assistance was made conditional upon our prior military withdrawal, meaning the campaign ended less like the snarl of the British bulldog and more like the yap of a poodle. A contemporary US politician, Dean Acheson observed in 1962 that: "Great Britain has lost an empire and has not yet found a role."

Still, millions of pounds were wasted in developing an independent nuclear deterrent as if it was essential to demonstrate that Britain was still a global military *and* political power. Not even the growing Campaign for Nuclear Disarmament (CND) movement, led by the likes of Canon Collins, Bertrand Russell and Michael Foot, could shift Government thinking. CND made little impact upon most of the population. Seduced by the trappings of affluence and suspicious of 'a movement of eggheads for eggheads', when it came to marched protests the working classes largely voted with their feet up.

One potential way forward was to develop new continental markets with European partners, but the government was reluctant to forge new partnerships outside our existing circles. Despite joining the new, but decidedly 'second division', European Free Trade Association in November 1959, most politicians remained sceptical of the benefits of a pan-European trading alliance preferring to stick with our tried and trusted commonwealth ties. This reluctance was partly a product of suspicion, or plain fear of being taken over, invasion by the economic back door, well encapsulated in Attlee's acid remark about the European Economic Community (EEC): "very recently this country spent a great deal of blood and treasure, rescuing four of 'em from attacks by the other two." More far-sighted politicians such as the Labour Party's George Brown and the Conservative Party's Ted Heath were in a minority when it came to forging closer links with Europe. As for the wider British public, an opinion poll conducted in late 1957 suggested that most of the electorate were either indifferent or hostile to the prospect of joining the EEC.

Had Britain been quicker about varying and modernising its economy, the country might have put itself back sooner on a sounder footing. By 1959, traditional industries had a limited shelf life but the country seemed reluctant to explore possible alternatives. Instead heads were being firmly placed in the sand. By the end of the fifties Britain was complacently enjoying the benefits of a boom, as short-lived as this proved to be, assuring itself of 'greatness' with a succession of self-reverential war dramas, like *Reach for the Sky*, which celebrated pluck and indomitable strength against unappealing odds. The growing popularity of Ian Fleming's Bond novels reflected a similar determination to place Brits 'on top', through a fantasy of superior British wit and courage confounding all, underpinned, even more improbably, by superior British technology. Naturally, Soviet and American agents were compelled to give way. Ironically, our record in post-war espionage was pretty dismal, scarred as it was with the highly damaging defections of MacLean, Burgess and Philby. There were other national security disasters, too, involving the likes of George Blake, the Krogers, John Vassall, Greville Wynne and 'Buster' Crabbe. Far from being the slick, smooth, glitzy operations evoked by James Bond, life in the secret services seemed much more akin to the grimy, austere tales of chilly mistrust presented in the convoluted plots of John Le Carré. Even our rebellious youth of the fifties, as represented by the 'Teddy boys', seemed to be hankering for a time of lost glory, not only by adopting the fashion of a pre-First World War age, but also by attacking with parochial and jealous fervour London's growing cosmopolitanism, as demonstrated, for example, by their part in the 1958 Notting Hill Riots. As the fifties drew to a close, misty-eyed conservatism was rife in Britain.

There were indications that Britain recognised the days of Empire were passing. Macmillan's 'Winds of Change' speech in February 1960 conveyed that message forcibly, although its principal target seemed to be apartheid-obsessed South Africa. Empire Day had been retagged as Commonwealth Day in 1958 and, within the following five years, independence was granted to a majority of former colonies. Other improvements were made, such as educational prospects, particularly at the higher university level, although, arguably, insufficient emphasis was placed upon developing scientific skills. Greater efficiencies were sought, as in the railways and mines, for example. And yet it seemed as if Britain was being held back by parochial, staid and reactionary attitudes. Even some of the 'New Wave' authors and film makers, far from being the voices of a more liberated future, seemed stuck in a male, white-dominated, discriminative past. It was as if they, too, were reflecting male disquiet about the growing emancipation of women from household drudgery and 'Little Englander' concerns about increasing cosmopolitanism. Perhaps, though, the social and moral conservatism of the time is best symbolised by the Crown's decision to charge Penguin books with obscenity for daring to print *Lady Chatterley's Lover*. Although the prosecution was almost certainly guided by a need to limit the excesses of the existing obscenity laws, the arguments put forward in court surely highlighted the fustiness of Establishment thinking in 1960. This was no better exemplified than by the prosecuting counsel's summing up. He asked the members of the jury: 'Is it a book you would wish your wife or servants to read?'

Britain had undergone significant changes during the fifties, which affected what we ate, wore, watched, read, played at and listened to, and yet by 1959 the nation remained in the grip of a staid and snobbish class divide which impeded its growth – commercially, politically and on the sports field. In his assessment in *Anatomy of Britain*, a seminal analysis of the archaic, privileged political and social networks that dominated British life at the beginning of the 1960s, Anthony Sampson concluded: 'Britain is still the most civilised and humane country and the happiest to live in' but it is 'backward, inefficient, unambitious and nepotistic'. What happened during the sixties helped erode this crabby conservatism. Growing disenchantment with the 'old school tie' cartel operating at the heart of government would soon release a cascade of iconoclasm and satire ranging from *Beyond the Fringe* to *That Was the Week That Was* and from the ironic offerings of the *Establishment* club performers to the scrappy first editions of *Private Eye*. So, on the eve of the 'swinging sixties', were too many of us thinking that the only thing to look forward to was the past?

Without doubt a major external influence on British society was American culture. Its influence had been growing for decades. This is best illustrated by the case of popular music. Noel Coward and Ivor Novello had drawn heavily upon Broadway musicals during the 20s and 30s although it was American Big Band music which really turned the British public onto stateside sounds. This followed Benny Goodman's highly successful UK tour of 1935. War-time broadcasts only intensified British enthusiasm for swing and jazz. Nevertheless, in the immediate post war period there were serious misgivings about the prospect of American stars dominating our popular cultural life. The British Music Union even prevailed upon the BBC to limit the 'needletime' given to 'black', 'New York intellectual' and 'immoral' dance music. The censorious, ultra-conservative Music Union did not have it entirely their way, though. The new British dance bands were keen to give their audiences what they craved – more jazz and swing. Tentatively, BBC Radio began to follow suit although what was broadcasted hardly represented a full scale invasion. For much of post war radio music was an uninspiring mixture of brass bands, church choirs, Gilbert and Sullivan, light classics, novelty songs, folk ballads and romantic crooners. Essentially, this was anaemic music for a generic audience, one in which adult and younger tastes remained undifferentiated. It therefore made perfect sense for the BBC to call its record request show *Family Favourites*.

The emergence of rock 'n' roll changed all that. Prompted by a full-scale US invasion of pulsating, adrenaline-driven, rabble-rousing sounds, generational lines were quickly drawn. The increasing affluence enjoyed by 1950s youth created the market in which the music could prosper. With the medium adjusting to the message, this exciting new music was recorded on 45rpm rather than on the traditional 78rpm discs and these sold by the millions. In 1955, one year after Bill Haley had recorded *Shake, Rattle and Roll* four million 45 rpm records were sold in Britain. By 1960, that number had shot up to 52 million. But it would be entirely wrong to describe the impact of this as a 'Youthquake' in which the staid old order was overturned by the vibrancy of the new. Five years after *Rock Around The Clock* was released, BBC light entertainment was still dominated by a clutch of crooners, big band singers and show guys and dolls: American artists like Dean Martin, Nat King Cole, Perry Como and Doris Day plus British equivalents including Frankie Vaughan, Dickie Valentine, Michael Holliday, Alma Cogan and Ruby Murray. Even during the swinging sixties, the best selling albums included *The Sound of Music, West Side Story and South Pacific*.

In staid Britain, the new 'rip it up' music, performed by the likes of Elvis, Jerry Lee Lewis and Gene Vincent stirred up an unholy moral panic, just as The Sex Pistols would twenty years later. In early 1956, the *Daily Mail* reflected the unease of its more uptight readership in describing rock 'n' roll as 'tribal', 'which surely originated in the jungle', concluding that 'we sometimes wonder whether this is the Negro's revenge'. What the *Mail* was condemning here was 'pop' not popular music. It was clearly a time for taking sides. In defining its market, *Melody Maker* plumped for the breadth of popular music while the *New Musical Express* struck out for the brash, uniqueness of pop. Guess whose sales went up?

For Richard Hamilton, a British pop artist of the period, the term 'pop' encompassed that which was; 'designed for a mass audience; transient; easily forgotten; low cost; mass produced; aimed at youth; witty; sexy; gimmicky; glamorous; and big business.' Dave Marsh, the veteran rock critic, went further. He believed that it was a distinguishing feature of 'pop' music to give a 'voice and a face to the dispossessed'. For him, an essential ingredient of 'pop' is to grant visibility and audibility to voices often excluded from the mainstream – Blacks, gays and lesbians, women and outsiders of all types. Jeff Nuttall, author of *Bomb Culture* added a class dimension. He believed that in the late fifties and early sixties 'pop' music belonged primarily to the working classes while protest (such as the Campaign for Nuclear Disarmament), Beatnik folk music and trad jazz were more middle class passions. Certainly, on BBC radio, rock 'n' roll seemed treated as if it belonged to an alien or pariah culture, briefly given the light of day during *'Pick of the Pops'* then pushed back into a dark corner.

Television was not nearly as inhibited as its radio sibling. In February 1957, *Six-Five Special* began its two year run on BBC attracting up to ten million viewers. Here we had the bum-clenching embarrassment of DJ Pete Murray strafing us with catchphrases of the day – 'cool cats' 'having a ball'. If Grannie could take a trip then Auntie knew where it was at. Not to be outdone, the ITV launched its punchier *Oh Boy!* in June 1958 with Cliff Richard and Marty Wilde becoming its regular stars. Before the decade was out, there was the launch of *Juke Box Jury* in June 1959 with compere David Jacobs demonstrating the pop credentials of an anthropologist.

In these unpropitious times, we actually produced a performer who took the fight to the Americans, selling back to them a raucous stew of 'rent music' skiffle, snaffled from the US South, flavoured with Appalachian and Cajun folk, blues and black spirituals and garnished with some dumplings from the British music hall tradition. Lonnie Donegan was the first British performer to crack the US Charts. In 1959 he was one of our biggest selling artists but he was at pains to point out that he wasn't a rock 'n' roller.

Most of what Britain heard on BBC radio in 1959 wasn't rock 'n' roll either. It was mostly 'easy listening'. There were, of course, fine performers such as Frank Sinatra or Ella Fitzgerald who could invest deceptively simple songs with puzzling and unsettling emotions. Take Ella's *My Happiness* and Sinatra's *It Was A Very Good Year*. It wasn't all about the 'bland leading the bland'. But much of the airplay was given over to candy floss – light melodies with cloying lyrics. The worst of these, such as The Browns' *The Three Bells*, a 'hit' in September 1959, really should have carried a diabetic health warning.

If you listened to *Two-Way Family Favourites* on a typical Sunday lunchtime in 1959 you were much more likely to hear some anodyne swing from Rosemary Clooney or some bubbly banality from Alma Cogan than you were to hear the raunchy shrieks of Little Richard or the nasal hiccupping of Buddy Holly. If you were after Muddy Waters, Howlin' Wolf or Chuck Berry you had no chance. If you were after Ray Charles you might be lucky but if you were seeking Miles Davis or Billie Holiday you were bound to be disappointed. Most of the requests were dedicated to some relative doing military service in Germany. If these musical selections were anything to go by our squaddies didn't sound too red-blooded. Thank God the Russkies stayed at home. And, of course, we had *Children's Favourites* on a Saturday morning when 'Uncle Mac' trotted out a vast array of so-called novelty songs such as *The Runaway Train*, *Nellie the Elephant* and *I Tawt I Saw A Puddy Tat*. Pop music has another key attribute. It has a wonderful capacity for capturing the fleeting moment, helping impale a sensation and define a sense of time and place with greater immediacy than any photograph. What 'Uncle Mac' played for us, though, seemed as timeless as the weather.

So perhaps BBC radio was still exercising some form of class-based censorship in '59. If you wanted to listen to something 'cooler' or should I say, hotter, you needed to tune into Radio Luxembourg or make for the nearest Espresso coffee bar. Here, ensconced amidst the rubber plants and cane furniture but competing with the hissing Gaggia coffee machines, you could listen to some thumping Gene Vincent track on the juke box while sipping your frothy coffee from a glass cup. Not that 1959 was a vintage year for rock 'n' roll. After all, it had been the year in which 'the music died' after Buddy Holly lost his life in a plane crash. Fellow rockers Ritchie Valens and the Big Bopper perished with him.

Whether this was coincidental or not, rock' n' roll's rougher edges had almost disappeared by 1959. Jerry Lee Lewis had been ostracized after his marriage to his 13 year-old cousin. Chuck Berry had been arrested for an offence with an underage girl. Little Richard had turned to his church and Elvis had been conscripted only to emerge a year later as more of a crooner than a gyrating rocker. Larry Parnes had assembled his stable of British performers giving them 'stud-like' monikers such as 'Fury', 'Steele' and 'Wilde' to play upon and excite pubescent sexual fantasies but much of what was around was safe and sleekly packaged. Take the array of slickly dressed and coiffured US teen idols. Here we had Bobby Darrin, Paul Anka, Fabian, Edd 'Kookie' Byrnes (from *'77 Sunset Strip'*), Pat Boone and Frankie Avalon. This lot were never going to 'rip it up'. Pat Boone's insipid cover of Little Richard's combustible *Tutti Frutti* was as threatening as skimmed water. Apart from the rabid 'Sweet' Gene Vincent, Cliff Richard, with his plagiarised lip curl, was about as wild as they came. No wonder so many of us working class boys and girls ignored the class implications and turned to 'Trad. Jazz'. But pop is also about makeovers. Just as Reginald Smith became Marty Wilde and Terry Nelhams became Adam Faith, so our R'n'B bands became world beaters by nicking and re-inventing the black American blues. We no longer needed imported oldies like Johnny Ray or Bill Haley for our kids to wet their pants. We could rely upon our young Fab Four instead.

In 1959, in the face of rapidly-changing times, the town of Burnley was caught up in a dilemma about how it should sustain its future. Reflecting the misgivings we had as a nation, there were concerns about relinquishing that which had made the town successful – textiles and coal.

The industrial revolution had converted Burnley from a small, quiet, out-of-the-way market town into the world's largest producer of cotton cloth. Its typically damp atmosphere was conducive to the manufacture of cotton fibre, which quickly displaced wool as the number one textile when British colonial markets opened up a massive export trade for light cloth. Moreover, the ready availability of local coal – by 1800, there were a dozen pits in the centre of town alone – meant that Burnley was ripe for rapid industrialisation. Its population grew from 10,000 in 1801 to 21,000 in 1851 before expanding prodigiously to 106,322 by 1911.

The town's football fortunes reflected its increasing economic prosperity, with its premier team capable of attracting the best talent in the country in the early twentieth century. In 1914, Burnley won the FA Cup for the first and only time in its history, defeating Liverpool 1-0 at the Crystal Palace ground in the final. Shortly after the First World War, Burnley won the English First Division for the first time. However, the tide of prosperity had begun to ebb by the time that hostilities ended in 1918. With the textile trade and coal mining stuttering during the inter-war depression years, the town's population fell by almost 20% between 1921 and 1939.

Helped by post war modernisation in both the mills and the pits, there was a brief recovery during the early fifties, with almost full employment once again achieved, but even the introduction of cheap labour, recruited from the Indian sub-continent from the early fifties onwards, could only defer but not prevent the abdication of 'King Cotton'. Ultimately, there was no way of competing with low cost Far Eastern production. As a consequence, the town's population continued to decline, falling by a further 5% between 1951 and 1961.

With the sixties just around the corner, there were certain industrialists and local politicians who thought that the cotton trade could still be salvaged through new technology and increasing specialisation, while morale-boosting lectures were given about the continued importance of coal. There seemed to be a strong belief that alternative manufacturing (aircraft components, fridges, tyres etc.) could be made to work despite growing evidence that many items could be produced more cheaply abroad. When new employers were courted to replace the closing mills and mines, greater faith was placed in specialist manufacturing than in service industries.

But it wasn't all about local people being too rooted in their past. There were those who were looking to uncouple the town from its Victorian image and place it more firmly on a modern footing: a thoroughly modern mill town. Whatever view is taken about the value of those efforts now, the plans for the re-construction of the town centre, drafted in 1959-60, were an expression of a well-intentioned progressive desire.

*The abdication of 'King Cotton': A Burnley mill at the start of the 'weaving out' process [5]*

*'Homes fit for heroes': The post-war Woodbine estate, Burnley [6]*

It would be wrong to give the impression that the town was resting upon its laurels and not embracing change. A variety of new manufacturers had been successfully attracted to the area including Lucas (aerospace components), Mullards (electrical components), Belling (electric cookers), Michelin (tyres), Rolls Royce (at Barnoldswick) and Rover (at Clitheroe). Moreover, cotton manufacturers had consolidated, diversified and specialized to meet the new economic climate, also commencing production of man-made fibres.

In 1959, the arguments ranged back and forth about what should be done. Attempts were made to enlist Government assistance in attracting new industry to the town but the Government would not act while the employment figures were so high. However it was clear to local MPs that these figures falsified the true situation. Mills were closing rapidly but in order to honour outstanding orders a number of them would run double shifts staffed with temporary labour. The high rate of closure was encouraged by the Government's Cotton Industry Act which provided financial inducements to owners to scrap their looms and 'weave out'. New jobs were not being created at the speed at which old ones were being lost and the temporary employment arrangements were merely disguising that fact.

Seen from the heights of its surrounding moors, Burnley seemed to be thriving in 1959. As Burnley supporter, Lester Davidson recalled: "in 1960 you could still see at least 14 mill chimneys in Burnley in any direction you cared to look." This was no museum. An industrial pall still hung over the town with fumes belching from these chimneys. The new factories hummed and clattered with activity and hoppy aromas from Massey's Brewery still

*Another clanking coal train trundles over Burnley viaduct in the late fifties [7]*

scented the Burnley air. Meanwhile, panting, clanking coal trains continued to struggle up Copy Pit, their hoarse whistles echoing across the valley, just as they had done over the previous 100 years.

As much as the local paper talked up the brighter prospects of the future, there was difficulty in escaping the fact that the town's traditional industries were in various stages of retreat and its new ones stamped with a limited life span. With Burnley positioned precariously away from the main national transport networks, new trade was difficult to attract and many of the manufacturers which moved into Burnley after 1959, such as Michelin, would succumb to declining economic fortunes in the ensuing decades. Coal mining disappeared entirely when the last deep coal mine at Hapton Valley Colliery closed in February 1981. The last steam-powered cotton mill, Queen Street Mill, Briercliffe, shut down its looms for the final time in 1982 and Burnley's two largest manufacturers also have both closed their factories: Prestige in July 1997 and Michelin in April 2002.

*Prestige factory, Burnley [8]*

The town has struggled to recover: its employment statistics between 1995 and 2004 placed it 55th of England's 56 largest towns and cities and as of 2007 it was the 21st most deprived local authority (out of 354) in the United Kingdom.

If traditional industries were at the cusp of terminal decline by 1959, the news from the sports field was not much better. Having been given undemanding qualifying challenges, England's national team had failed to progress beyond the group stages in two out of the three World Cup competitions of the 1950s, and were eliminated by the injury-depleted reigning champions, Uruguay at the next hurdle, in the 1954 competition in Switzerland. Although the Munich disaster deprived our 1958 squad of at least three key players – Edwards, Taylor and Byrne – too often, perverse selection decisions made by unqualified FA selection committee members during the fifties deprived our national side of its best players – Matthews, Shackleton and Charlton were cases in point. Also, despite enjoying status-lifting victories over new World Champions, West Germany, and World Champions in waiting, Brazil, England were annihilated twice by Hungary and once by Yugoslavia in other friendlies and humiliated by the USA in a 1950 World Cup group game. Britain's 1956 Olympic medal haul was a meagre six golds, with only one coming in track and field, and England's aged Test cricketers were thrashed 4-0 in 1958/59 by the resurgent Aussies under Richie Benaud.

After the 1948/49 peak in football attendances, when an average English Football League game attracted an average 22,300 crowd, football had begun to lose popularity. By 1959/60, the average Football League gate had been reduced to 16,000, a fall of 28% over the decade. The English First Division was not immune. Top flight attendances fell by 20% over that period.

Cinemas were experiencing declining custom, too, with TV proving to be a huge counter-attraction. In 1946 there were 1,635 million cinema admissions, but by 1956 these had fallen to 1,101 million and by 1963 this figure had plummetted to just 357 million. By the end of the fifties, an average family watched 5 hours of TV a day during the winter. With rising prosperity, leisure options were widening, particularly for the working classes. There was also some disillusionment with the game of football on account of our failures against foreign opposition. Britons were adjusting slowly to the growing realisation that we could no longer kid ourselves we were a world power – politically, economically, militarily or as a leading football nation.

Around this time, there was much recrimination about Britain's, or more specifically, England's, international prowess. During the fifties Wolves won a series of status-lifting and telvised friendlies against the likes of Honved and Real Madrid under the lights of an invariably muddy Molineux. But neither Wolves nor the 'Busby's Babes' had managed to prevail against the superior Spanish sides in the newly established European Cup. Despite the promptings of the national coach, Walter Winterbottom, and the pioneering stands taken by club managers like Matt Busby and Stan Cullis, the FA had adopted that same lofty isolationism to European competition as they had to the fledgling World Cup before the War and were now paying for that disdain. On the disastrous South American tour in the summer of 1959, England, who took a number of young, inexperienced with them in their squad, lost all three internationals – against Brazil, Peru and Mexico – with the Peru defeat (1-4), reported to be the most embarrassing of the lot.

A chastened ex-Claret and England international, Tommy Lawton, commented: "we forgot that the Continentals were all the time perfecting the art of the game advancing the tactics and the moves. We didn't think that anyone had anything to teach us. We didn't want to learn that our tactics became out-of-date." The irony was that the emergence of two leading continental international sides during the fifties – Hungary and Sweden – owed much to the coaching skills of two Englishmen – Jimmy Hogan from Burnley and George Raynor from Barnsley. Talk about: 'a prophet is not without honour save in his own country'!

Hogan favoured the 'pass and move' game which often caught the opposing defenders ball watching and helped evade their crunching tackles. He championed the techniques which were employed so successfully by Arthur Rowe's 'push and run' Spurs side of the early fifties and practised by both Harry Potts' Burnley and Bill Nicholson's Spurs sides of the late fifties and early sixties. Hogan preached the advantage of the short corner to keep possession and to draw tall defenders out of the penalty area. He advocated the short free-kick to keep the momentum of the game going and prevent the opposition recovering the ball. He insisted goalkeepers should throw the ball out to a colleague rather than launching it down the centre. He would demonstrate the art of the 'drag back' with the sole of the boot, perfected and so exquisitely demonstrated to devastating effect by Puskas at Wembley in 1953. Hogan was frustrated by the 'Victorian ideas' impeding English football. He commented: "Our former intelligent ideas are gradually fading out. We have developed an 'up-in-the-air', 'get-the-ball-if-you-can' game. We are continuously kicking the ball down the middle to the marked centre forward, hoping for a defensive error and not exploiting the wing play as we used to."

*'Prophet without honour': Jimmy Hogan, the international master coach from Burnley [9]*

Scottish international, Tommy Docherty, took note. He was also a convert to Walter Winterbottom's new gospel of coaching, alongside the likes of Alan Brown of Burnley, Ron Greenwood of Arsenal, Bill Nicholson of Spurs,

Malcolm Allison of West Ham, Joe Mercer of Aston Villa, Don Revie of Leeds and Alf Ramsey of Ipswich. He could see clearly how Hogan's influence had manifested itself in Hungary's humiliating 6-3 victory at Wembley. It was small wonder that the Hungarian people dedicated their famous triumph to Hogan. Docherty remarked: "(Hungary's) passing movement made us British players feel as if they were from a different planet. They'd lull you into a false sense of security with a procession of quick, short passes that took them nowhere and then suddenly unleash a paralyzing long pass that would arrive in space a split second ahead of one of their tuned-in team mates. They realized the importance of supporting runs. Everytime they had possession they had between two and five men ready to receive the ball."

Just as Hogan helped revitalize post-war Hungarian football, George Raynor achieved similar results in Sweden. Goran Berger, the Swedish

*'Prophet without honour': George Raynor, the international master coach from Barnsley [10]*

national football museum's curator remarked: "it really seems amazing that England didn't want him when he came home. For us, he's simply the most successful national coach of all time. Incredibly popular, he changed the game here with his tactics and organisation. He taught himself how to coach, never took an exam in his life and yet he taught us how to win."

Raynor's roll of honour included; 1948, Olympic gold medal, won in England; 1950, third place in the World Cup competition (in which England experienced a humiliating 1-0 defeat by the United States); 1952, Olympic bronze medal, won in Helsinki, beaten only by the great Hungarians; 1958, World Cup Finalists in Sweden, after Pele's brace helped Brazil beat his side 5-2. Then, the following year, on a brief sabbatical from Skegness, where he worked as assistant storeman at Butlins, Raynor provided the tactical blueprint for Sweden's visit to Wembley, masterminding a 3-2 victory in October 1959, which was then England's only second home defeat to foreign opposition.

"I feel like a football fifth columnist," Raynor told the pressmen the night after Sweden's Wembley victory. "I got some sort of satisfaction out of the result, but not enough. I would much rather have been doing the same sort of thing for the country of my birth. All I consider is that the people in England have had their chance. I want to work in England – *for* England. They want me in Ghana, in Israel, in Mexico and in Sweden. I am a knight in Sweden and have a huge gold medal of thanks from King Gustaf. I have a letter of thanks and commendation from the Prime Minister of Iraq. My record as a coach is the best in the world. I don't smoke. I don't drink. I live for football."

*Walter Winterbottom, FA Director of Coaching 1946-1962 [11]*

Instructively, it was Raynor's tactical innovation to put a man on Hidegkuti, thus stalling the Hungarian supply line, which had helped Sweden achieve a highly creditable 2-2 draw in their friendly with Hungary in Budapest, just prior to the Magyars' 1953 Wembley triumph. Raynor was also astute enough to know that this would be an exhausting task and therefore detailed two Swedish players to undertake this task in turn, swapping over during the game to ensure that the marker always remained fresh.

Although Winterbottom watched this game, he did not follow Raynor's lead. It took both Alf Ramsey and Stanley Matthews to recognise the need to contain Hidegkuti once the Wembley game was underway. In fact, Matthews yelled at captain, Billy Wright, to assign someone to close down Hidegkuti, who was enjoying the freedom of the park. Ramsey was convinced that if the Hungarians had been allowed less room in midfield, the result would have been different, but England's preparations had not been good enough. Ramsey learned from this humiliation when he came to create a world-beating England side after assuming the full managerial duties over the national side in 1962.

After three World Cup failures and the South American fiasco, the hacks gathered with famished talons. In his *Empire News* column in 1959, the former England international, David Jack concluded: 'make no mistake this is crisis time for England. The game we gave to the world is no longer played with the required skill in these islands.' Jack blamed poor team selection, which to be fair to him, was not the sole responsibility of coach Winterbottom.

Nottingham Forest's 1959 FA Cup winning manager, Billy Walker, blamed the lack of craft in the inside-forward and wing half positions. Even Johnny Haynes, England captain following Billy Wright's retirement and an inside-forward of Wayne Rooney's stature, was not excused. Walker complained that English coaches were suppressing individual flair. The Burnley players were exempt from this criticism because none had been selected for England, although Young England's Ray Pointer had helped embarrass Walter Winterbottom's side in a warm up game at Highbury just prior to their departure for South America in 1959.

Walker, a former Aston Villa and England star, was right to place an accusing finger at English coaches. The evidence provided by the likes of Jackie Charlton, Jimmy Greaves, Noel Cantwell, Gordon Banks, Tommy Docherty and Alan Mullery suggested that the standard of preparation employed by many leading clubs was little better than 'shambolic'. With notable exceptions, such as at Spurs, West Ham and Burnley, there was little attention applied to developing ball skills or to honing tactical manoeuvres, such as dead ball routines. Training more often comprised perfunctory long distance running and weight lifting. Some 'coaches' held the view that depriving their players of the ball during training made them 'hungrier' for it on match days. Whilst the methods employed at Spurs, West Ham and Burnley were of a much more sophisticated order, there is little doubt that the prevailing amateurish approaches held back the development of English football.

The brilliance of Real Madrid's performance in the European Cup Final of 1960 emphasised the gulf in class between the top foreign performers and our own. Real's stunning 7-3 victory at Hampden Park over Eintracht Frankfurt was secured on the same bumpy surface that was blamed for the turgid

1-1 draw between Scotland and England nine days before. Charles Buchan, editor of *Football Monthly* blamed England's failure to compete at the highest level upon tactical intransigence. He wrote: 'we will not accept the facts that long wing-to-wing passes and long kicks upfield by full-backs are useless. And that players trying to run, or dribble, round opponents are doomed to failure.'

Burnley and Northern Ireland playmaker, Jimmy McIlroy, shared Buchan's frustration. In 1960 Jimmy, having just schemed Burnley to the League title victory said: "I wish I could interest every club in the country in FOOTBALL. I mean football, which doesn't include 'getting stuck in,' 'fighting' or 'belting the ball'. Before Burnley leave their dressing room, the final instructions from manager, Harry Potts, are nearly always the same: ''Play football but above all, enjoy your game'. What a pity other managers don't think the same way. Critics bewail the lack of ball players. So do I. Yet the blame rests entirely on the people who control the teams. What chance has a boy to concentrate on skill as he avoids crunching tackles and hard robust play? Why aren't defenders taught to win the ball in a tackle, instead of simply learning to stop an opponent? I believe skill and fight are opposites – the complete footballer possesses a blend of both – but the emphasis should be very much on skill. If we are to equal the best in Continental football the tough stuff must be erased from our game, to make way for more subtlety, delicacy and softness of touch. Like sheep, clubs follow the leader. When Wolves and Chelsea won the League the secret of their success was claimed to be hard, fighting soccer, which led to many copying this method. My wish for the coming season, is that Burnley's style of play becomes the fashion, because I'm certain English football will benefit from it." It didn't – even though Spurs would win the double in the 1960/61 season playing in a similar style.

Britain's major national sports, football and cricket, remained largely insulated from a world that was leaving Britain behind. Up until 1962, professional cricket still staged an annual representative contest between the 'Gentleman' and the 'Players'. The administration of the game epitomized the 'old school tie' ethos. We would not recover the Ashes until another ten years had passed and then, only after the appointment of a curmudgeonly professional tactical leader in Ray Illingworth. At national and club levels, professional football was little different from cricket. It was still gripped by what Anthony Sampson described as 'club-amateur' influences. Despite having a major say, the national coach, Walter Winterbottom, was not even entitled to pick his own team. International selections were made by an F.A. committee, made up of the 'great and the good' with no experience of managing professional football. Ultimately, we would look to another ultra professional tactician, Sir Alf Ramsey, to change that practice and restore our international prowess.

Manchester United's brilliant young team had threatened to turn the tide from 1956 to 1958, but they were snuffed out at Munich, so, it was left to others to pick up the early running. Emerging from the tactical vacuum of the late fifties were two British club sides who would lead the way in developing a more fluid style of play. It was an approach that would have greater prospects of success against continental opponents. Spurs would become the first British club side to secure European silverware, when they lifted the European Cup Winners' Cup in 1963, but little Burnley would demonstrate on national TV how illustrious European sides could be overturned in their impressive but frustratingly brief European Cup campaign of 1960/61. Both sides' approach was more modern than their First Division contemporaries. Alan Ridgill of *The Sunday Pictorial* described Burnley thus: 'Here was the almost perfect soccer machine – as smooth running as a Rolls Royce and yet packing the punch of a centurion tank'. At that time, protected by the mandatory wage cap and the feudal 'retain and transfer' system, it was then just possible that a talented, tactically astute David, like Burnley, could defeat a series of richer, more fancied Goliaths over the long, rugged haul of an English First Division football season. But even in at the time it was acknowledged that, as with Ipswich's League Championship in 1961/62, that theirs was a triumph against the odds.

Thereafter, those odds grew ever longer. Burnley's team, like the town, required more resources in order to thrive. The imminent abolition of the footballers' maximum wage not only disturbed the balance sheet, it also meant that the team could no longer rely upon attracting the best young talent. That talent would go increasingly to the highest bidder. As a small town club with limited means, greater efficiencies needed to be found in order to keep at bay the increasing competition from richer teams. There were also other leisure attractions to contend with. The club was forced to consider how it should market itself within the confines of a declining local economy. The 'sell to survive' policy was born in this climate. Regrettably that policy could only work whilst the club remained a force in the top flight and seen to give its talented youngsters a potentially earlier opportunity to shine on the big stage. By so doing, Burnley could still hope to compete with and confound the more lucrative enticements offered by larger clubs. However, it needed its youth policy to deliver at a high rate of productivity to plug the gaps left by its departing stars. Once the harvest began to fail, the team fell away, and, as a result, the law of diminishing returns began to bite deeper and deeper into its prospects.

The legacy of an illustrious past is often to breed expansive and sometimes unrealistic expectations. Some past glories become rods with which to punish present failures rather than remaining as sources of pride and occasions for commemorative celebration. Perhaps selective interpretation of Britain's past has left succeeding generations with a preposterous burden, leading to expectations of glory irrespective of the type, size or quality of competition they face in business or on the sporting field. A number of ex-England managers might have something to say about that. To have ambition and belief is obviously positive. Burnley's 1959/60 achievement set a daunting standard for the Clarets and whilst new goals need to be stretching, they also need tempering with realism. As with the town's modern economic struggles, all of that is for today. This story is about yesterday: a triumph of small over big. In a world dominated by increasingly flawed global conglomerates, let's celebrate that for now.

*The top clubs of the 1950s – Wolves and pre-Munich Manchester United [12]*

## Chapter Two

# 'This Sporting Life':

## *The life of a Burnley footballer in the Fifties*

BEING one of the less glamorous clubs of the era, lacking the pull and clout of a Manchester United, Wolves or Spurs, Burnley set huge store by its youth recruitment, development and retention policy. It was a proud record which saw the vast majority of the title-winning squad come through the ranks. Describing the policy, which was designed to retain and nurture young starlets, Burnley's inspirational captain Jimmy Adamson wrote in 1962: 'as soon as a youngster arrives at Turf Moor he is made to feel part of the Burnley Football Club. And, just as important, he knows he is not going to be tossed out after a short spell. Every young player arriving at Turf Moor is guaranteed four or five years on the staff. In that time he gets the chance to learn the game. He is not tossed out if he fails to live up to expectations in one season. The only reason he may go is if he doesn't measure up OFF THE FIELD. If he wants, the lad can be apprenticed to a trade. Or he usually goes on to the ground staff, doing all the odd jobs around the ground. For instance, there is always one ground staff lad with the first team – looking after the kit.'

Right-back John Angus, one of those youngsters, who joined the club in 1954 aged nearly 16, recalled his introduction to the life of a professional footballer: 'Charlie Ferguson, the Burnley scout, spotted me while I was playing for Amble. Newcastle was the nearest league team but I knew I had no chance there because they bought so many of their players. So, off I went to Burnley. It was quite a journey in those days, involving a change of train at Newcastle, York and Leeds and two bus journeys. It took ages. I remember finally getting off the train at Manchester Road Station in Burnley. That's the station half way up the hill above Burnley town centre. I looked down on this town with its many mill chimneys and smoggy atmosphere. It was quite unlike anything I had experienced – coming from a small Northumbrian seaside village. When my wife and I were first married we lived on the hill overlooking Turf Moor and on matchdays we'd frequently look down on this thick smog engulfing the town and ground and think "there's no chance of the game being played today". But usually we'd be wrong. Once you got down there it'd be OK to play, though it was very murky.

I started off in digs in Brierfield with Jimmy Robson, who later became my best man. Although we were made to feel welcome there I was always pleased to get home. As soon as the season ended, I would return to Northumberland. That's where I met my wife. Most of my team mates married Burnley girls. Perhaps that's why so many stayed there after they finished playing.'

Jimmy Robson, who made his Burnley debut in 1956 aged just 17, added: 'When I first came down to Burnley I was dreadfully home sick. Remember, I came from a small mining village. I hadn't seen much life outside. A lot of us were like that. But those first three months here were hard. The digs were good but I knew that the big test would come after I went home for the first time. Anyway I came back and stayed here since – apart from a spell when we moved to Blackpool, which was nice. A lot of us stayed here because we married Burnley women. It really isn't as bad as Jimmy Greaves made out. He must have arrived here from the wrong direction. There is so much lovely countryside around. Life in Burnley has been good.'

Tommy Cummings, who joined the club at 18 after appearing for Great Britain in a junior international tournament in Strasbourg in 1948, recalled: 'I arrived by train in a place called Todmorden and I hadn't been on many train journeys before. I was like a little boy looking out of the window and taking everything in. There was somebody from the club to meet me and we caught the bus to Burnley where they had arranged digs for me. There was another lodger, a Pole, who was working at the pit, but when the landlady proposed taking in a third, it would have been too cramped, so I was moved to lodgings near the ground.'

The top clubs of today ensure their players maintain a healthy, well-balanced diet, with only a light pre-match meal. However, the received wisdom in the fifties and early sixties was that a player needed a substantial meal before a game to build up his energy levels. Gordon Banks recalled that as a Leicester City player in the early sixties a typical pre-match nosh would comprise a large steak, boiled and roast potatoes plus peas to be followed by a large bowl of rice pudding. Jimmy Greaves remembered that he would often eat a pre-match meal of roast beef and Yorkshire pudding 'with all the trimmings' or pie and mash followed by blackcurrant crumble and custard. Steak was the Holy Grail, though. No-one knew then that it took as much as 36 hours to digest steak and that its benefits – protein, strength and energy – would only be experienced after a few days.

Jimmy McIlroy commented: "in those days a different view was taken about the ideal diet. A typical pre-match lunch consisted of steak, chips and peas. I used to find this a bit much although I would often have quite a large breakfast. I would watch Ray Pointer tuck into a large steak lunch and point out to him that I would be sick after 5 minutes of the game starting if I had eaten as much as him. Ray would retort that he wouldn't get through the game without it!

When you were travelling with the club, eating in those days could be very regimented. I recall a player at another club telling me that their manager had told the coach driver to pull into this café on the way home from a match and, without consulting with the team, ordered fish and chips for all of them. Apparently, one member of his team had requested double helpings of fish, to be told in no uncertain terms by his manager that he would have the same as everyone else!"

Jimmy Robson added: "we were well managed and well supported. Bob Lord did a lot of good for the club whatever people say. We were well looked after. They would lay on these three-course meals with steak at the Sparrowhawk Hotel for us. Of course, there wasn't the attention given to diets then as there is now. It was left largely up to you what you ate. On match days I would normally have a regular English breakfast but would only eat toast before a game. I remember Willie Irvine getting stick for eating fish 'n' chips before a game but then he went on to score a hat trick, so I wondered then whether I should do the same."

Equally the treatment of injuries and what we know as sports science was in its infancy. As former Burnley winger, Trevor Meredith, recalled, fractures generally took longer to heal in the fifties than they do now. Cartilage injuries were much more serious too. Medial or cruciate injuries were generally terminal to a footballer's career as was the case with Burnley's wing half, Brian Miller and Bolton's centre-forward, Nat Lofthouse, although Burnley's Tommy Cummings eventually returned to the fray after his cruciate injury in 1956.

But new innovations, practices and equipment were in use at forward-thinking Burnley at that time. Trevor remembered that Billy Dougall, the club physio, used ultra sound to help heal muscle and ligament damage. He added that Billy also used a hot waxing machine to boost the healing process. He said: 'It was an earlier version of the heat and ice treatment. Billy would use this waxing machine to apply a heated mould around the injury and then you would take it off and apply ice.' The ever-innovative Billy Dougall explored how he might develop his physiotherapeutic skills, often experimenting with new electrical equipment.

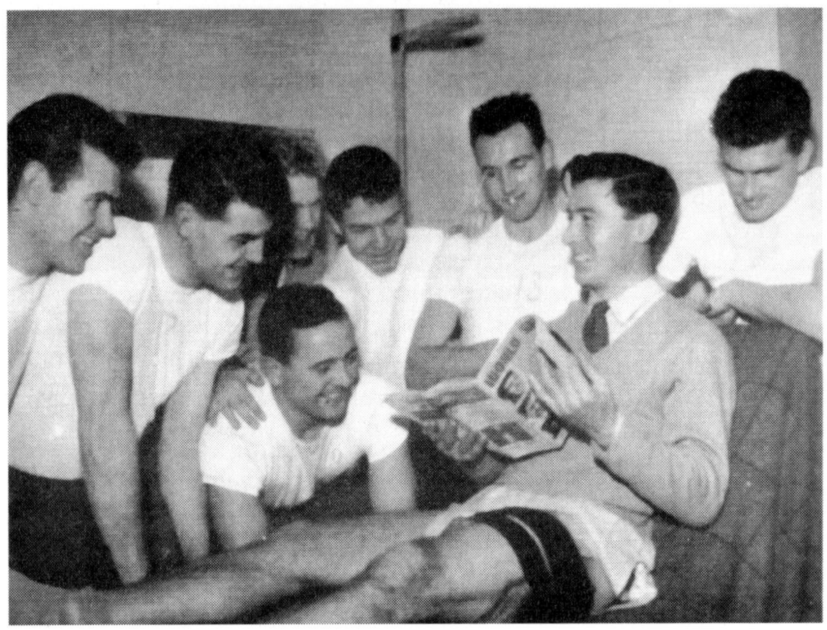

*Jimmy McIlroy on the Turf Moor treatment table during the 1959/60 season [13]*

During the 1959-60 season, Jimmy McIlroy kept Billy very busy indeed. Jimmy added: 'in those days, injured players often had to play on. There were no substitutes, so you had to get on with it as best you could. In December 1959, we were playing at Arsenal and during the first half my groin went. Instead of being taken off, I played deeper, virtually standing on one leg but I still managed to dominate the game, fanning passes out to each wing.' Jimmy explained that he was rarely fit during that season, with either shoulder, groin or thigh problems troubling him, although he only missed 11 games and three of these were because of international commitments. He did point out, though, that he had never been troubled by a metatarsal injury! He attributed his good attendance record to the skills of trainer and physiotherapist, Billy Dougall. Reflecting upon the depth of Billy's experience, Jimmy said: 'Billy could tell you to the day when you would be fit to play again.'

Jimmy Robson thought: "the medical back-up was good, too. We had quick access to a consultant surgeon at Colne Clinic if someone had a serious problem with a doctor on call, as well. I had reason to be grateful for this because once I bent my large toenail back having kicked a stake on the Longside when we were playing this impromptu game up there. It hurt like hell but I kept playing. You did in those days. When I'd finished I could feel this horrible squelching sensation. The boot was full of blood. Billy Dougall suggested taking the nail off but Dr Iven came in and bent it back into position. Had he not done so, I would have been out of the team for the important game on the Saturday. Yes, things were good that way. If I was to make one reservation about the medical care – I suppose we were propped up too often with Cortisone injections. It was the same everywhere. That couldn't have done us much good."

John Angus agreed with his best man, commenting: "for the most part I stayed pretty fit, although I did have trouble with my knee ligaments. That's what brought my career to an end in 1972. There were many occasions when they'd pump cortisone into you just to get you going. I'm sure that hasn't helped in the long run. I still get a bit of soreness around my knees. But that was the way it was back then – you'd often play when not completely fit. There were many times when I found I couldn't stretch because my muscle injury hadn't healed properly. Billy Dougall had his heat treatment and ultra sound appliances. It was rest that we needed to clear these problems up. Of course, back in the fifties and early sixties we had no substitutes so you had to play on if injured. There was one time when they pushed me up front at Arsenal after I suffered a knock. I scored twice, too, though both goals were tap-ins really. I only scored two more in my entire career."

Goalkeeper Adam Blacklaw added: "I was quite lucky with injuries while at Burnley – just the odd broken finger, that's all. However, I wasn't so lucky at Blackburn, where I developed this hiatus hernia. You were looked after at Burnley when it came to injuries. You got to see the club doctor or surgeon pretty quickly if there was something more seriously wrong although once the problem was diagnosed you would then have to wait your turn."

There was a world of difference between the pay and conditions on offer in 1959 and the lot of a modern footballer. The maximum wage of £20 per week (raised from £17 per week only the previous summer) was in force, yet to be tested by Newcastle inside-forward George Eastham's court case, although that seminal change in the footballing landscape, akin to the Jean-marc Bosman ruling in the 1990s, was only four years away.

Young Burnley prospects were ordered to get themselves a second trade as a back up to either injury or lack of development stunting their footballing careers. John Angus recalled: "Soon after I started at Burnley I was apprenticed as a joiner. One of the Burnley directors sorted that out for me. We were all encouraged to take up a trade. It was hard going in those early years. I trained during the day and had night school in the evenings. It was particularly tough when I started doing my national service at Bank Hall Colliery. I was employed as a joiner there, too. Although the Coal Board were good about letting us have time off for football we still did almost a full day's work with training and night school to fit in during the evenings. It was slower getting around then as well. It took around an hour to get from my digs in Brierfield to Gawthorpe on the bus. Then there was a tidy walk from the bus stop down the long drive to the training ground. There wasn't much time to yourself.'

In those days I was earning around £7-8 per week as a part-timer with Burnley. That compared well with what most working people were getting, but it wasn't a huge sum. I didn't get my first second hand car, an Austin Somerset, until I was 19 or 20. By that time I was established in the first team and earning around £15 per week with a win bonus of £2 and a draw bonus of £1. Once I got the car I could drive to Gawthorpe or Turf Moor. On match days I would park further up Brunshaw Road and walk down the hill to the ground. Having the car cut the journey times but I didn't mind mixing with the supporters on the bus. They would chat away to you and ask you how you thought the last game went or how the next game might go. It kept you in touch and helped keep your feet on the ground."

To put this into context, in 1959 the average weekly wage in Britain was £11/2 shillings/6 pence or to give this its modern equivalent, £11.12p. Consequently, the maximum weekly wage of a professional footballer was 80% higher than average earnings, although considerably lower than what top entertainers might gain. For example, Fulham's Chairman, comedian Tommy Trinder was paid around £100 per week as the compere of ITV's *Sunday Night at the London Palladium*.

Also, £20 per week would only be paid to the very top performers. Stewart Imlach, Nottingham Forest's Scottish international winger and 'man of the match' at the 1959 FA Cup Final, was offered £20 per week for the 1959/60 season, but only whilst he remained a first team regular. This figure fell to £15 per week if he was dropped. As was the custom then, summer season wages were paid at a lower rate. For him, the close season offer was also £15 per week.

Jimmy McIlroy recalled: "You were at the club's mercy over what you could earn. There was always the possibility of doing a bit of coaching on the side or some summer work, like helping out the groundsman, but it didn't add up to much. Some of the team had work with the National Coal Board, but that was part of their National Service. Those on National Service often received preferential treatment, as did Brian Pilkington during his period with the RAF. As a professional footballer on a full-time contract you were committed to the club. Your freedom to earn more was limited. It was made clear to me that if I wanted to increase my income I would need to join one of the London clubs, where I could use the higher profile to secure advertising deals. Dennis Compton, of Arsenal and Middlesex, was one of the first top sportsman to cash in on this opportunity when he advertised Brylcreem. Jimmy Greaves of Chelsea advertised Bovril. But Burnley would not let me go. I wasn't resentful, though. After all, I was getting £20 per week while local tradesmen were earning around £7.

In 1957, I was sufficiently well off to buy my first car – an Austin 7. Not many players had cars then. A few had second hand ones, like mine, but most of us were still reliant upon public transport or upon lifts given by better off supporters. A son of a local businessman would drive me to some of the local games, such as at Blackburn. I can also remember shelling out for our first continental holiday – a week in Ibiza for £52! That seemed quite an outlay then.

We were helped also by the club housing policy. As a married couple we were allocated a Club house in 1954 for which we paid a rent of £1 per week. At that time my earnings would have been around £15 per week. We were also given an allowance for decorating the house and I recall one of the Burnley directors creating a bit of a fuss when he thought we had been a bit too extravagant."

Trevor Meredith agreed that it was then very difficult for players to supplement their income. He said that during the summer months while he was at Shrewsbury Town he had worked in a Nursery and hoed sugar beet, but at Burnley opportunities were more limited. He agreed with Jimmy McIlroy that there was the possibility of helping the groundsman out, but these jobs were not very lucrative.

One benefit of having a less high-profile status than the modern footballer was that players then were not continually being preyed upon by the media. Jimmy McIlroy remarked upon how the relationship between the top players and the press had changed since his playing days. Despite Bob Lord's criticisms of press intrusions Jimmy said: "In the late fifties and early sixties, the relationship we had with the press was very different from how it is today. In those days they were primarily sports writers. Their main interest was what was happening on the field of play. They were often our friends, too, regularly coming out with us – playing snooker together or going out on the town. We wouldn't be worried whether we would be exposed or misquoted. You could trust them more. They would respect confidences. From that point of view, it was better then. We may not have earned as much as modern players but we had more freedom."

A very important aspect of the club's success was the family atmosphere at Burnley. Jimmy Robson recalled: "We were a close bunch. We got on well with one another. We would be pleased for one another when success came. Similarly, we would look out for one another during the difficult times. I don't think we were 'clannish' (*this was in response to a remark made by Bobby Charlton in his autobiography*). I just think we stuck together because we were such good mates – that's natural isn't it? Mind you, this team bond did occasionally cause us a bit of difficulty. Because we were so close we all wanted to stick with the same team. So, if one of us was injured and it wasn't immediately obvious that it was really serious the rest would try to get him to play. That's what happened with me in the Blackburn FA Cup replay in 1960. We'd been staying at this hotel in Blackpool beforehand. I'd got food poisoning and was sick for most of the day. I shouldn't have played, but when I got into the dressing room, the team tried to jolly me along. It seemed to work in that I did feel a bit better for a time but as soon as I was out on the pitch I knew I didn't have the legs."

*A family club: Burnley Football Club Christmas party 1959 [14]*

Bob Seith agreed, observing, "it was a caring, family club. We were very close. The wives would go to the games. My wife, Jean, and Joy Cummings would travel together. The Club were good at organizing events for the whole staff and their families. Each Christmas we would have these dinner dances in Clitheroe and in the summer there would be these trips to Blackpool or Morecambe where we'd see a show and have a slap-up dinner. Everyone would go – the groundsmen, the laundry women, the lot. Mind you, one year Bob Lord had this idea that it would be good to go to the Isle of Man. The day we travelled across was foul – blowing a fierce gale. The ship was pitching and rolling. Most of us felt sick as dogs. I was determined not to be the first to be sick, though. When I finally conceded and clambered up to the deck, there I found Peter McKay clinging onto the railings. Bob Lord was up there, too, but Peter didn't mince his words. He let Bob Lord know in no uncertain terms what he thought of this."

Jean Seith recalled: "Every Christmas all of the staff and their spouses would be treated to a dinner-dance at the Swan and Royal in Clitheroe. It was a very posh hotel in those days. I have no idea what it is like today or whether it still exists. Those evenings were really special with everyone dressed up to the nines. All the wives would be presented with a gift. I had some lovely pieces of china for my dressing table. We'd also receive a turkey at Christmas, which was so big you could barely get it into your oven. The club looked after us on match days, too. We had the billiard room set aside for us where we could wait for our husbands. Tea and cakes were provided. Yes, we had to watch the pennies but we were better off than most local people. Bob and I bought a three-bedroomed house in Burnley for £1,400 at the end of the fifties.

Like Adam and Sheila Blacklaw we used to go to the Imperial in Nelson. I loved the dance bands that played there in the fifties. There was Joe Loss, Ted Heath and Jack Parnell fronted by singers like Dickie Valentine and Dennis Lotus. I had no idea that Frank Sinatra was due to play there. I would have loved to have seen him. Sadly, the place burnt down but the wonderful memories remain."

Adam Blacklaw confirmed: "yes, it was a very close-knit club. Everyone looked out for one another. If someone was struggling with their game and so on, others in the team would help out. We were a team in the true sense. That's why we were successful. I don't think we ever lost that closeness. Whenever we get together it is as if we'd never parted. As good as it was, it would have been nice to play today with the kind of money you can earn at the top. We were paid nowt really. Mind you, the Club looked after us pretty well. Bob Lord sent each player a steak every Wednesday – just us, not our wives or family, though!"

Burnley's approach was very much to look after the home and therefore have a happy footballer turning up for training and on match days. Sheila Blacklaw, Adam's wife recalled: "when we married in 1956, Adam was earning £9 a week. In the first team he got £4 extra if the team won and £2 more if they drew. The wages went down in summer, too. There was no other income coming in. We had small children and we'd only Adam's Burnley wages. We had to be really careful with our money. We made the children's clothes and baked our own cakes. It was difficult to afford the clothes you saw in the shops. One of us used to make her own clothes copying the designs she saw in the shops. You had to work hard to make the money stretch, especially looking after three young children as we were. The Sunday joint would last for three days – the roast on Sunday, cold meat and chips on the Monday and shepherd's pie with the remains on Tuesday. So, you can imagine what a big thing it was when I was given £100 by Adam to buy a special outfit for the 1962 FA Cup Final. That was an awful lot of money in those days. We didn't go out too much once we had the children. I didn't make it to Maine Road for the Championship decider because I had no babysitter. As odd as it might sound now, but when we had enough money to afford a second hand car, we hand painted it ourselves. I remember the first decent car we got was after we sold some Wembley tickets in 1962. That enabled us to have a summer holiday in Cornwall.

It wasn't just the players who were close. The wives were, too. When we all went down to Wembley in 1962, the wives of the Spurs players remarked upon that. We have remained close friends and still keep in touch. As families, we lived near one another in the Worsthorne part of Burnley. We bought our first house in 1959 off Billy Morris, who was a former Burnley player. I remember we paid £1,500 for it. I was particularly close to Mary Miller (Brian's widow) but all the wives stuck together. We would help one another out – share recipes and the like. We used to go to the Saturday afternoon games together with our kids when they were old enough. They didn't have the refreshment bars as they do now. Life was simpler then than it is now.

Before we got married and had kids we used to go out a lot. We'd go dancing at the Astoria in Rawtenstall or at the Empress in Burnley which doubled as a skating rink. A number of the Burnley footballers got to know their future wives through going dancing. John Connelly met his wife Sandra that way. We'd also go to the Imperial in Nelson sometimes. They'd have these big name performers there like Frank Sinatra. They would have dance bands, too. When Adam was in his digs we had to make sure that he got home before the 11pm curfew. It was only then that we'd get a taxi. Otherwise it was often a case of walking. I lived over the other side of town so it was quite a hike – about 4 miles or so.

It was very disciplined at the club. They took their parental-like responsibilities very seriously. When we started courting, the club informed Adam's father. They wanted to assure themselves that I was responsible and trustworthy. That was the thing at Burnley, as wives or girlfriends you were expected to be sensible, dependable and down-to-earth. I remember when Alan Shackleton started courting a beauty queen. That didn't seem to fit the general expectation. The club made sure the players got home on time. It was a club rule that there was no drinking after Thursday and when you were married, no sex on Fridays before a game!"

*'We Are Family': Burnley wives at Wembley, 1962 [15]*

Under the management of Cliff Britton and Alan Brown strict disciplinary standards were maintained at the club. Bob Seith remembered: "Cliff Britton was tight on discipline. I recall visiting a snooker hall in town once with a few other young players. It only happened the once before Cliff Britton had us in insisting that we never go to such places again – I suppose they had a bit of a reputation as being the haunts of ne're-do-wells in those days. Cliff pointed out that if we wanted to play snooker, we could do so at the Club. Burnley was so small – you couldn't get away with anything without the whole town knowing. Everyone knew if you broke the rules, so there was no point in trying."

Jimmy Robson agreed: "life here was settled and pretty well disciplined, too. The discipline was mostly self-imposed. We knew the rules. Nobody had to read the riot act to us. We knew how to behave. We went out but rarely drank much. We were in at sensible times. We looked after ourselves. It was a good club to be at."

Taking account of the recollections of many leading players of the time – not only at Burnley but at other top clubs also – stronger standards of personal conduct seemed to apply at Turf Moor. Even under the avuncular guidance of Harry Potts, the Burnley sides of the 50s and 60s maintained high standards of personal conduct on and off the field.

Without doubt footballers in the late fiftes were heroes to many, but they were not separated from their fans in the same way as the modern player. Jimmy Robson remembered: "There wasn't any of this celebrity thing then.

We would mix with the Burnley public on the bus or in the shops. We didn't think we were that special except that we were being paid to do something we loved. Working with miners at Bank Hall helped keep your feet on the ground. They'd give you some stick if you hadn't come up to scratch and rightly so – they'd paid their money and were entitled to their opinions."

Both Brian Pilkington and Trevor Meredith remembered that life as a footballer in the late fifties and sixties was very different from the remote, celebrity life of their modern counterparts. Brian said: "we just blended in. We would travel on the buses alongside other local people. I remained living in Leyland, so I would catch the 8am bus to Burnley each day to get to training. So, supporters would come up to you for a chat and that was fine. There were some days when you wanted a bit of peace and quiet. Some days I would be riding home on the top of the bus just as one of the local shifts was ending and because may be I felt a bit tired and didn't fancy talking I would hide myself behind my paper. But that was rare. You just got on with your life just like everyone else.' Trevor added: 'Burnley had a reputation for being an accessible team. When the first team traveled to London, the autograph hunters made a bee-line for us because they knew we would sign. They would be waiting at the platform as we boarded the train home."

Although top footballers of this time were better off than local tradesmen, their greater purchasing power was often inhibited by a mistrust of credit. This suspicion was forged within the working class communities in which most of them had grown up, during the more austere years of the late forties and early fifties. Many working class people, particularly those living in small, labouring communities, considered all forms of credit, including mortgages, to be unbecoming. These people tended to regard payments in cash as the hallmark of integrity and financial independence. Consequently, those holding these suspicions often used the derogatory term 'never-never' when referring to credit, reflecting their fear of unrelenting financial servitude.

Unsurprisingly, footballers' increasing middle-class aspirations from 1961 onwards were a product of greater affluence. In 1960, though, before the wage cap was removed, the expectations and mode of life of most top professionals and their families were largely shaped by their class origins. While a majority of top professionals are still drawn from the working classes, their expectations and way of life are no longer bound by their formative years. For example, let us compare two footballer weddings of the late fifties with one of modern times to illustrate this point.

Jimmy and Irene Greaves married quietly at Romford register office in 1958 when Jimmy was earning £8 per week as Chelsea's leading goal scorer. Their first home was a flat in a clubhouse inside Wimbledon's old football ground and they supplemented their income by weeding the Wimbledon stadium terraces.

England captain, Billy Wright married pop star, Joy Beverley, at Poole register office, also in 1958. Joy was working in Bournemouth and Billy took a day out from pre-season training with Wolves to travel down on the train. It was described by one of Joy's sisters as "a very quiet affair".

By stark contrast, Chelsea and England player, Ashley Cole and *Girls Aloud* pop star, Cheryl Tweedy, agreed to have their 2006 marriage blessed at a Berkshire castle surrounded by a gospel choir and angel harpists with copious supplies of pink champagne on tap. Even the couple's pet Chihuahua, Buster, wore a special wedding suit. This 'quiet affair' cost a cool £1 million with the tab picked up by a celebrity magazine.

What was evident from Adam and Sheila Blacklaw's and Bob and Jean Seith's accounts was that Burnley's triumph in 1959/60 was not just due to the collective achievements of some remarkable football men but also to the love, care and help provided by a group of loyal, resourceful, mutually supportive women. This was a close-knit community who ensured that the members of this team enjoyed both security and stability in their home lives. As Sheila remarked "we were not pretentious, but happy".

Whilst the Burnley players remembered the strong family atmosphere at the club with great fondness, they were very aware of their status as hired hands with a limited shelf life. Ray Pointer spoke of his sadness about leaving, saying that he would have accepted reserve football in order to stay, but ultimately accepted moving on with equanimity. Trevor Meredith spoke in similar terms. Jimmy Robson added: "when it came to it, I didn't really want to leave. I was prepared to play in the reserves but the club was right. They had other players coming through like Willie Irvine. That was often the case then, if you were replaced, it was because younger players were coming through the ranks."

Although his chances of progression were restricted on account of the strength of the first team squad, Trevor said that he always felt an integral part of the Burnley team, whilst accepting that there was always going to be tough competition for first team places. He said that it was only when he reached his late twenties and when new stars like Willie Morgan and Ralph Coates were beginning to come through that he decided he would move on. Trevor was satisfied with his transfer in April 1964. He explained:"'Shrewsbury was a bit like going home. You see, I grew up on a farm in Shropshire, so this was very familiar territory. I knew I was coming to the end of my career so I was quite prepared to move down a couple of Divisions. I was happy to be offered a contract by player-manager, Arthur Rowley (brother of

Manchester United's Jack Rowley and scorer of a record 434 goals in 619 league games). This contract determined that my wage would increase according to the size of the crowd at Gay Meadow. Not that there was too much scope for major increases at Shrewsbury."

Brian Pilkington had greater misgivings about his departure though. He commented: "I had chances to move on before I was transferred to Bolton in February 1961. Manchester United were interested in me after the Munich crash but the club wouldn't let me go. So, it came as a big surprise when Harry Potts told me that I was going to Bolton, particularly after I had just scored two goals in our European Cup win over Hamburg. Before we played the second leg in Germany I was gone. It didn't really make sense at the time. I was in the first team, I was playing well, I was scoring, I was doing everything right. However, Harry Potts called me in to the office. He says at first: 'there's some teams interested in you.' There was Everton, Preston North End, Blackpool, Bolton Wanderers – he said I had a choice where to go. I replied: 'Oh, well no, I'm alright. Everything's okay here. But do you want me to go or what?' He then said, making it clear there was no choice, 'well put it this way, the Chairman's agreed terms with Bolton. It's out of my hands. You'll have to speak with him.' So, I tried to get hold of Bob Lord but every time I attempted to contact him I was told he wasn't available. In the end I had no choice. I had to go to Bolton.

With hindsight, I should have called his bluff and said 'I'm not moving,' but at that time there wasn't the player power that there is now. There was no freedom of contract. In those days they could just retain you and you could do nothing about it. I was only 26 or 27 at the time. I'd probably another six or seven years in me. I honestly think I should have stopped here and both Bob Lord and Harry Potts said, 'We should never have let you go'. But they had Gordon Harris coming through. He was a good player. So I ended up at Bolton. I wasn't very happy there, though. They played a different game to what I had been used to at Burnley. They kept pumping long balls over the top of you. My head was forever swiveling back and forth."

There was little security for a professional footballer at this time. Contracts were for one season only and clubs dictated terms. Gordon Banks wrote in his autobiography *Banksy*: 'if a club decided to sell a player, he had to uproot and move home and family to wherever he'd been sold. If the club didn't want the services of a player any more, he was never told in person. He simply received the dreaded 'Not retained' letter at the end of the season – the signal for him to pack his bags and leave. Even if we'd had a voice in matters, no one would have listened. Players were seen by the clubs as commodities, to be hired and fired, bought or sold. There were no agents or personal advisers to look after our interests, no heart-to-heart chats with the manager and certainly no mollycoddling.'

Moreover, under the 'retain and transfer' system, a football club could also exercise the right to retain a player irrespective of his or his family's wishes. If a player refused to comply and continued to push for a transfer, as was the case with George Eastham at Newcastle in 1960, the club could prevent him from playing with an alternative club by simply refusing to relinquish his registration. It was small wonder that the PFA complained that the system was tantamount to 'soccer slavery'. But, as George Eastham famously found, a club's powers in this regard could be contested sucessfully.

George was not alone. Although his case received no publicity at the time, Bob Seith's dispute with Burnley resembled Eastham's situation. Both players asserted their right to go to the club of their choice once their playing contracts had concluded. And both players told their employers: 'if you refuse to let me go to the club of my choice then I will seek alternative employment outside football'. In George's case, Ernie Clay, later to become Fulham's chairman, was prepared to employ him as a salesman in Reigate. In Bob's case he had chiropody to fall back on. However, Bob's and George's situations were unusual. In those days, few players felt they could challenge a club's power, particularly those who had no financially viable alternative employment to fall back upon.

See Appendix 2 *What the ''Soccer Slaves' Earned in 1959* for more detail.

## Training at Burnley

During the summer of 1954, Burnley invested £200,000 in roofing the popular Longside terraces. A year later, the Club turned its attentions to developing its training facilities. Bob Lord, soon to become Burnley's chairman, explained in his book My Fight for Football: 'in January 1955 came events which were to prove one of the finest developments in Burnley's club history. Mr Hopkinson (a fellow director) and I had agreed about a definite youth policy. Earlier, Tom Clegg (also a fellow director) was probably the instigator of such a policy in first class football; about the same time Mr James Taylor was working along similar lines for Preston North End. This pair were pioneers. In January 1955, Alan Brown told me of a wonderful site on the borders of Burnley, adjacent to the National Trust property of Gawthorpe Hall in Padiham.'

The 79-acre site was duly purchased, although not without Board member misgivings about the price. During June and July 1955, manager, Alan Brown set about turning the plan into reality, converting the farm land into a training ground with three full-sized playing fields, a converted barn for a gym plus dressing rooms. Typically, Brown led from the front. He recruited a volunteer labour force comprising trainers, Billy Dougall, Ray Bennion and George Bray; centre forwards, Peter Mackay and Alan Shackleton; wing halves Bob Seith and Walter Joyce, full back David Smith and young apprentice, John Calvert. The collective effort shown by this group epitomised the Club's 'all for one and one for all' spirit. Of course, the extra income came in useful as well as players' wages were reduced substantially during the summer.

As for Alan Brown, he had previous experience to call upon, having dug ditches for 'days on end' while keeping observations on a disorderly house. This was when he was a young police officer. Brown was impressed with his players' attitude. He recalled to the journalist Arthur Hopcraft that the training centre was 'literally dug out of the ground. The players got down to it and dug ditches with me. And remember this was at a time when professional footballers were supposed to be the most grasping people in the world.' As Hopcraft observed, 'there was nothing aloof or over-theorizing about Brown; he led from among the players, not from his office. He was one of the first tracksuit managers. Alan Brown died in 1996. Fortunately, he was spared the worst excesses of today's cult of celebrity.

Bob Seith recalled: 'we had some brickies in to help us but we had some experience among our team of volunteers, too. Peter McKay had worked as a steeplejack. He'd done groundsman duties as well. It was a real team effort. By the end of that summer we had created two full size pitches, a five-a-side area, two dressing rooms with baths and a gym. By the time we had completed our task I was so fit I was dangerous!'

Bob continued: 'we were paid 2/- an hour for an average 8 hour day's work. We worked five and half days per week, including Saturday morning, earning what is now £4.10p for our weekly labour. This was enough to bring our lower summer earnings up to the basic season's wage of £14 per week.'

In 1960 Jimmy McIlroy wrote: 'at Gawthorpe, a few miles out of Burnley, we have our training headquarters set in delightful rural surroundings, the sort of spot to make even the most reluctant-to-train footballers feel good to be alive with possibly the only 'all-weather' pitch owned by a League club'.

Five years later a BBC reporter made a visit to Gawthorpe and observed: 'perhaps one of the major attractions at Burnley has been the marvelous training facilities provided by the club. The visitor, who might be forgiven for expecting something primitive at such a small club, is always amazed by the magnificent training grounds, two miles out of town. At Turf Moor itself, an extra training pitch has been provided, and the superbly equipped gymnasium is as big as the playing area, and full scale practice matches can be staged there.'

Bob Seith, who helped create those facilities in 1955, remembered: 'before we developed the training facilities at Gawthorpe we would use the so-called 'Gym' at Turf Moor. It was tucked away underneath the stand. There were the turnstiles on one side, a toilet on the other, some tarmac and a sandpit. There were three iron pillars as well. It was quite dangerous playing our competitive 5-a-side games there. Team mate, Harold Mather once broke his nose when he crashed into the turnstile.'

The first-class facilities created at Gawthorpe, augmented by a high quality scouting network, advanced coaching methods and innovative tactical ideas, provided the bedrock for Burnley's success during the sixties and early seventies. Bob Lord's and Alan Brown's ambitions became progressively realised as a stream of young Burnley starlets began to make the grade at the highest level in the land.

Coaching in the 1950s in English football generally amounted to nothing more than a few jogs around the perimiter of the pitch, some sprints up hills and 'gym' sessions with medicine balls. While players were fit enough, they were nowhere near the toned athletes of today. Burnley were one of the few clubs to pioneer a different approach to preparing their players for the intensity of top flight football physically, mentally and tactically. Ray Pointer was enthusiastic about the quality of coaching at Burnley. He recalled some of the training routines practised at their training ground at Gawthorpe. He believed that the hallmark fluidity, bite and flair of the Burnley side of this period were forged at Gawthorpe: "we prepared well for games taking into matches what we had done in training. Manager Harry Potts encouraged us to go forward and play football. Everybody wanted to be in the game but we had to work for one another. We were encouraged to exchange positions and not to be too tied to tight patterns. The full-backs would practise overlapping, but we needed to ensure that there was cover. Jimmy Adamson frequently stayed back when others pushed forward. We, forwards, regularly practised decoy runs in training, trying to draw defenders aside and create space for others. We had a series of very well rehearsed moves. These were sorted out in training."

Innovation in training had begun in the reign of Alan Brown. Brian Pilkington recalled that Brown "had these unusual ideas about how we should develop our momentum going forward. For example, he would sometimes start us off in training by playing our forward line against no defenders – 'shadow training' it was called. We would just move up the field as a unit, to help us get our rhythm right. Then he would start introducing defenders, one or two at a time."

Former England manager, Walter Winterbottom, introduced the 'shadow training' routine with the national squad during the mid-fifties. The value of the exercise was lost on the so-called 'Clown Prince of Soccer', Len Shackleton, who asked Walter, with weary sarcasm, which side of the goal wished the unmolested attack to score in. However, this was at a time when many leading players thought that they should be left to develop their own game, free of coaching instruction. Stanley Matthews was a strong case in point. When former England cricket captain, David Gower, adopted this philosophy during the late-eighties, he and his faltering team were condemned as 'unprofessional' by the unforgiving British press. But in these times professionalism was more conspicuous by its absence.

Winterbottom saw more value in gearing training to the coming match by choosing specific opposition for practice matches. If he wanted to practise against a hard tackling side he would organize a game against a side like Chelsea. If he wanted to practise against a faster, more fluid style of play he might enlist the help of Spurs. But of course, he could use his position as the national coach to encourage such support from certain club sides. He had in any event, much less time to mould his team than a club manager so he had to be judicious in his use of the limited time he had with a constantly changing group of players.

However, Walter was not sold on the value of five-a-side routines. He told Bob Ferrier author of *Soccer Partnership: Walter Winterbottom and Billy Wright* in 1960: "another clear lesson was the danger of five-a-side play in training. It involves almost no tackling and it can develop a leisurely, almost dilettante, attitude in the minds of players. Although it is good fun, it can degenerate into pointless larking."

This was totally contrary to the way the five-a-side games were organised at Burnley. Jimmy McIlroy said: "Every footballer likes to have a ball at his feet. That is why I have always regarded five-a-side practice games as the finest form of soccer training ever devised…"

Jimmy Robson was with Mac on this saying: "we did most of our training with the ball (as was the case at the top Italian and Spanish clubs at the time). I'm sure this helped a lot. Like other clubs we had our sprints and longer distance running but a lot of time was spent in five-a-side games. That helped keep our ball skills sharp – developing instant control and quick passing. There was this theory still circulating then that if you deprived players of the ball during the week it made them hungrier for it on a Saturday. We didn't go with that. We all wanted to play. Harry Potts, our manager, always made sure we had odd numbered sides so he could join in, too. They were very competitive affairs – everyone got stuck in."

Spurs trainer, Cecil Poynton, sided with the Burnley lads. saying: "I consider that five-a-side games have tremendous value. Because they are played on a field which is less than half the size of a real pitch, the boys have to run, think and act twice as fast as they normally would and this helps to give them a fine edge when they transfer their activity to a full-time pitch…mastery of the ball is the first thing that you must achieve if you want to be a professional footballer. Fitness and knowledge of tactics can always be instilled later."

Specialist training for goalkeepers had yet to truly emerge. Indeed, even in 1960, it was clear that little thought had been given by any of the professional clubs to how to best to prepare their goalkeepers for action. Even clubs with advanced coaching ideas like Burnley and Spurs seemed deficient in this respect. Leading custodians, like Leicester and England's Gordon Banks, had to organise their own specialist training, prevailing upon colleagues to give them Sunday morning workouts. In his autobiography *Banksy*, Gordon described his self-designed supplementary training regime. He wrote: 'sometimes I'd ask these young lads to ping shots at my goal from a variety of angles (heights or distances) or to chip or lob the ball towards goal (so I was) constantly running backwards (thereby improving my positioning). I worked hard at improving my footwork, my handling, punching, positioning, reflex saves, clearances out of both hands, building my stamina and strength, body suppleness and ability to ride a challenge. I studied angles, the flight of the ball and how to organise defences in front of me.' Even as a novice 'keeper, Banks was the consummate professional – setting a benchmark of excellence for the new breed of top goalkeepers. By contrast the then current England goalkeeper, Ron Springett, simply threw himself into 5-a-side games as an outfield player. Whilst there was no goalkeeping coach as such in Adam Blacklaw's Burnley playing days, he did not feel deprived of practice in team training sessions. Adam explained: "I didn't need special training. I would get the boys to belt balls at me. That was enough to keep me on my toes."

What went for the first team was replicated in the youth team. Jimmy Adamson described the approach taken with the training of Burnley's youth team players. In 1962 he wrote: 'While Joe Brown is in charge of these youngsters the first team players help by example. Boys will always copy the senior players. An inside-forward will watch Jimmy McIlroy; study Jimmy's positional play, his ability to find the open space, his pacing of a game. Training at Turf Moor generally takes the same pattern. The idea is to have all players thinking along similar lines. Then, if a reserve player has to be introduced to the No. 1 side, he slots into the pattern without too much effort. Obviously as far as the younger players are concerned there is a bigger emphasis on basic skills. The first team is more concerned with tactics.'

The major difference between modern training and that of the period with which we are concerned was the attention given to match fitness. Preparation in this regard was so deficient that several leading First Division players of the time were critical of their clubs' focus upon long distance running and weight training. Jimmy Greaves remarked in his autobiography *Greavsie*: 'I didn't like long-distance running because I didn't think I benefited from it. Where I did apply myself was in sprinting and shuttle runs'. Indeed for years Stanley Matthews had prepared himself for matches by sprinting repeatedly over five to ten yards and no more as this was the distance in which he had to beat his man and get a cross into the penalty area.

In his 1960 book *Right Inside Soccer* Jimmy McIlroy agreed. He wrote: 'pressure training, and by that I mean the really strenuous stuff, is good propaganda for clubs, but quite unnecessary. Once an athlete has reached peak fitness, he finds it a simple matter to remain in that desirable state by simply doing routine lapping and sprinting...When I tried my hand at (weight training) I noticed nothing more beneficial than an ache in my limbs and a loss of balance. Also my nippiness was suffering and I was losing my speed off the mark.'

Much later McIlroy conceded: "we did do a lot of jogging and sprinting, too. But the fitness regimes at Burnley served me well. I remember playing later in my career in Spain. We were opening the new stadium in Barcelona. The Argentinian President couldn't believe that I was then over 30 years old. He remarked to Charlie Mitten, the former Manchester United star and ex-Newcastle manager: 'He runs so much,' to which Charlie replied, tapping his chest: 'ah, Rolls Royce engine!.' They were so perplexed by my athleticism that they thought that I was the father of the player that 'runs so much when I later opened their stadium."

Whilst Walter Winterbottom took issue with both Jimmy McIlroy's view of weight training, he shared Jimmy's scepticism about the value of long distance running. He concluded in *Training for Soccer*: 'Soccer is not rhythmical and therefore it is important that the footballer should practise the kind of running needed in a game. He must break-up his running into short bursts of sprinting, jogging and walking, moving off at different angles.'

Ray Pointer agreed: "For us up front, the emphasis was placed upon speed. We didn't do the long distance running in training so much as some of the others at the club. We used to do more sprints. But as the youngsters in the side, we were expected to do most of the running. If we couldn't pick up the ball we would run back to gain possession."

Jimmy Robson added: "We were very fit. Even when several of us did our one-year National Service at Bank Hall Colliery we stayed fit. I guess we were all naturally fit. That may have something to do with the way we were brought up. I remember playing football for hours on end as a kid, growing up in a mining community. I don't think today's kids are as well prepared in that respect."

The biographies of leading players of this period – Denis Law, Jimmy Greaves, Jack Charlton, Bert Trautmann and Alan Mullery, for example – carry a litany of tales of how training routines were practised in a perfunctory fashion, at best, with long-distance runs punctuated with visits to the pub, shammed sweat, bus rides and hitched lifts. Even a prestigious club like Manchester United was not exempt. Both Denis Law and Noel Cantwell were highly critical of the apparently shambolic and lax training regime adopted at Old Trafford in the years immediately following the Munich tragedy. Meanwhile the apprentices at many other clubs seemed to be little more than ground staff skivvies. Life was much more dedicated and disciplined at Burnley, it seems, as indeed it was at Spurs, Wolves and West Ham. Ultimately that would show on the pitch.

## Chapter Three

# 'The Not So Beautiful Game'

*Football in the 1950s*

DURING the fifties, a football's uncoated leather exterior would easily absorb surface moisture from the often sodden, poorly irrigated mudbaths which passed for mid-season pitches, doubling its weight so that as the game progressed it became more akin to a medicine ball. Using the modern, lighter ball, one shot by David Beckham was recorded as having attained a speed of 100mph. However, David Herd, the Arsenal, Manchester United and Stoke City centre-forward, who played in the late fifties and sixties, managed to hit the much heavier ball of his day at a speed of almost 75mph. Given the greater heaviness of the ball in Herd's day, it is probable that Herd's shooting was the fiercer of the two. Although more difficult to strike with as much force as the lighter present day ball, Brian Pilkington commented: "you could master it with practice. It was all a matter of timing."

Jimmy McIlroy remembered: "in our day the ball was so heavy, particularly when wet. No-one was expected to score from outside the penalty area. In fact, the goalkeeper would get a right rollicking if anyone did. Today, it is so different. The ball is so much lighter. It bends and dips, too. The first player to bend a ball in my day was Newcastle and Sunderland inside-forward, Len Shackleton also known as the 'Clown Prince' of football for his showy skills and his forthright views on football's inadequacies, notably that of directors. He could make the heavier ball swerve by as much as four feet. It was amazing." Jimmy recognised that the heavier ball of the fifties posed a health hazard for those who were required to head it frequently, notably the centre-forwards and centre-halves. He added with an ironic smile, "not that it caused me a problem because I rarely produced a header." Brian Pilkington remembered one time when Jimmy did steam into one of his crosses, sending a bullet header into the back of the net. "It was a pure fluke," Brian said. "I recently said to Jimmy. 'There's not much chance of you getting Alzheimer's, Jimmy. You hardly ever headed the ball.' Early onset dementia has recently been identified as a possible health hazard of playing professional football before the introduction of the lighter, moisture-resistant balls.

With regard to the state of pitches at the time, Jimmy McIlroy observed: "the pitches are so different today. I regret not playing on such pitches. I remember walking on to the Turf Moor playing surface a few years ago after a period of heavy rain. I was astonished to find how firm it was. I was listening to the Arsenal groundsman recently. He reckoned that the quality of the modern grass surfaces and the lighter weight of today's footballs accounted for the biggest changes in the present game. I'm sure these factors also contribute to the greater number of injuries experienced today, too. The bounce of the modern ball is so much steeper. You see more players clashing heads as they converge on the higher bouncing ball, their eyes focused upwards rather than upon one another. When we played, referees would allow games to go ahead on surfaces that would cause them to postpone or abandon fixtures now."

Both Trevor Meredith and Brian Pilkington agreed that the standard of football pitches has improved enormously since their playing days. Brian said: "we were at our best in the early season games, before the winter rain. The pitches were firm and smooth. We could play our passing game better then." Trevor added: "by winter most of the pitches had become ploughed fields and once they began to dry out in the early Spring they were horribly bumpy."

Jimmy McIlroy continued: "it wasn't just the muddy pitches which were a problem then. We played on some icy surfaces, too, that would not have been allowed today. We once played against Swansea. Well, it had been wet but with a sudden change in the weather, there had been a sharp frost, causing the pools of water on the pitch to ice over. It was going to be very difficult for us to keep on our feet. So, Billy Dougall, our trainer, came up with this idea to help us retain our balance. He replaced our normal studs with ones he had fashioned himself. He tipped the nail with a narrow strip of soft leather that would easily rub off once we were on the pitch. This left us with small spikes which helped us to keep our footing. It might be seen as dangerous now although I don't remember this causing any harm."

Bob Seith recalled arriving at Stamford Bridge prior to an FA Cup replay – one of four replays in the marathon sequence of 1956. "When we arrived at the ground it was clear that we were poorly equipped. Our heavy boots and full-sized studs would not enable us to keep our footing. Seeing this, Jimmy

McIlroy gets on the phone to his Northern Ireland team mate and friend, Danny Blanchflower. In next to no time a taxi arrives with a consignment of rubber boots – courtesy of Spurs' bootroom."

Ray attributed a significant part of Burnley's success to the quality of the Turf Moor pitch. He said: "we weren't very good players in heavy conditions (*although they performed brilliantly against Hamburg SV on a very muddy surface the following season during the European Cup campaign*). We were much better on a good pitch and that's why the ground staff worked so hard to maintain Turf Moor in decent order.'

The other major barrier to playing the style of football, which Burnley sought to impose on otherwise dour opponents, was the way in which the Laws of the Game were implemented. In the last 15 years FIFA has ordered numerous clampdowns on violent and dangerous play, such that many observers feel that the lawmakers have gone too far. However, perhaps for highly skilful players, such as Jimmy McIlroy, who were trying to pit their wits against the 'hard men' of the fifties, nothing could have been further from the truth.

Burnley play-maker Jimmy McIlroy recalled: "typically, the opposition's most dangerous attacking players, like Haynes and Stanley Matthews, were closely marked. I recall that Alex Elder, our young left-back, was once asked to stick to Stan like glue. He followed him all over the park. Talk about 'Me and My Shadow'! Anyway, as we came off at half-time, Stan said to Alex, 'Since we've spent so much time together this afternoon, are you coming in for a cup of tea?' Alas, Alex's efforts were in vain. Burnley lost 2-1 and Matthews set up the winning goal!"

Brian Pilkington and Trevor Meredith identified Jimmy Armfield, Don Howe and Ray Wilson as their most skilful opponents and were also clear about which full-backs stood out as their top hard men. Brian said: "Don Megson, the Sheffield Wednesday full-back and father of current Bolton manager, Gary, was one chap I disliked playing against. He could be really tough. Another was John Sillett, the Chelsea right-back and later manager of FA Cup-winning Coventry. You didn't get much protection in those days."

Trevor agreed: "You had to use your skills to evade the punishment these players dished out. If you were quick, you were mostly okay because these full backs would dive in and you could nip around them. But there were always a few who would hurt you if they caught you. Roy Hartle of Bolton, for example, would whack you down."

John Connelly recalls Hartle had a team-mate who was just as fearsome: "Tommy Banks was never particularly fast and when I played against him he was even slower. Mind you there was one game when I thought I'll switch

*Hard men: Don Megson of Sheffield Wednesday, Roy Hartle of Bolton and 'Snozz' Sillett of Chelsea [16]*

wings with Brian Pilkington to get away from him. Then I looked across and saw it was Roy Hartle on the other side so I stayed where I was. You knew you were going to get wellied, but you just got up and got on with it. And the boots we wore in those days were like concrete. They were so stiff, you had to break them in and wear them a few times at Gawthorpe to soften them, before you could ever wear them for 90 minutes in a game. And we didn't get a new pair every couple of weeks. They were repaired over and over again at Cockers in Burnley."

Jimmy Robson added: "We didn't play with a target man as they do today. There was no point trying to play with your back to goal, trying to screen the ball. You'd just get one those hefty centre halves come clattering through the back of you, sending both you and the ball back as far as you'd come. There was little protection from referees. They allowed tackles from behind. No, you had to learn to lay the ball off first time before you got hit. That wasn't easy, though. The pitches were generally poor – they were either thick with mud or, like at Easter-time, when they were often bone hard and bobbly. Either way, the ball bounced erratically giving defenders a big advantage, so you had to perfect your technique in these difficult conditions.

I remember when I first started at Burnley as a kid. I had this big guy up against me – Eric Binns. He went straight through me soon as I got the ball – totally flattened me. There I was lying in the mud thinking 'this isn't right,' but there was no-one to protect me. You had to look after yourself."

It wasn't just the outfield players who took the hard knocks, goalkeepers were often charged by opposing forwards, so needed to be hardy souls. Adam Blacklaw confirmed this: "You had to look after yourself as a goalkeeper. They'd shoulder charge you so you had to be prepared. I was a big lad about 15 stone so I always reckoned I could give as good as I got. The funny thing was that one of the worst opponents in this respect was Jimmy Greaves. He was such a gentleman off the pitch, such an amusing man, but he'd scrape you across your shins if you didn't look out. I used to warn these fellas – 'any funny stuff and you'll get more than you bargained for'. I took smelling salts out with me along with my string gloves and flat cap. You had to be prepared."

An article in the *1959 Big Book of Football Champions* posed the question: 'Is Football Too Rough?' after eight keepers, including Burnley's Colin McDonald, Arsenal's Jack Kelsey and Spurs' Bill Brown, suffered serious injuries and Accrington was forced to field right-back Bob McNichol in goal after all three of their keepers had been injured as a result of over-robust challenges.

Jimmy McIlroy was less sanguine about the standards of fairness: "I was playing [for Northern ireland] against an England Under 23 defender. I anticipated a hard match against a skilful adversary but my illusions were soon shattered. In the first minute, this future England ambassador had whipped my legs from me! Later, as the two of us went up to head a centre, he hit me, by no means accidentally, across the face and sent me reeling. I was livid as I struggled off the ground, but the referee, an experienced official, took me on one side and said: 'keep cool, Mac. I saw what he did.' Coming off at half-time, considerably bruised, I said to the referee: 'what chance has England of ever winning anything when clowns like that are honoured?' He said simply: 'I've thought that for some time now.'

Nevertheless, Ray Pointer remembered his clashes with Spurs, the other purveyors of push and run football, with affection. "We knew how they would play and vice versa. So we knew we had to do something different if we were to get the better of them. Maurice Norman, the Spurs centre half, was probably the most difficult defender I faced during my career. He was a hard player but not dirty. To be honest I don't think there were outright dirty players although there were certainly many hard tacklers. There wasn't any nastiness that I can recall. After all, they were your mates. We would talk to one another, sometimes during the game, too.'"

In support of Ray's statement the 1962 FA Cup final with Spurs was a good exhibition of fast, cut and thrust attacking football, played with skill and determination but entirely devoid of niggling fouls or mutual antagonism that sully so many games today. The sportsmanship displayed at the end of this fine contest, particularly by the Burnley players, was exemplary. Given the intense disappointment that the Burnley team must have felt in failing to secure a 'Double' triumph which had previously seemed well within their grasp, their demeanour in defeat was truly impressive, setting a challenging standard for so many of our pampered and petulant stars.

The other main team to beat in 1959/60 were Stan Cullis's league title holders of the last two season Wolves. Matches against Wolves were physically tougher than against Spurs, though. Brian Pilkington recalled: "Wolves were difficult to break down. They played to a strict plan. Stan Cullis, their manager, was as much of a disciplinarian as our Alan Brown had been. They had these powerful six foot defenders, too. When we played them at Molineux in March 1960, they hammered us 6-1. I'm not sure what happened. I think they'd just caught us on one of those off days, really. It didn't shake us up too much.

Bob Seith added: "at Burnley we didn't fear anyone really. Wolves were difficult to beat. They weren't necessarily the most skilful side we faced but they played to their strengths. Their wing halves, Flowers and Clamp would hit balls into the corners for their wingers to chase. Peter Broadbent, their inside left, had skill but their success relied heavily upon a physical direct style of play. As for individual tough opponents, Jimmy Scoular, the Scottish wing half, was about as tough as they came. Blackburn Rovers had this Scots' winger called Alistair MacLeod. He was certainly one for shooting a line as he did prior to taking Scotland to the World Cup finals in Argentina in 1978. MacLeod reckoned that he was a bit of hard case himself and claimed that he'd sorted out Scoular. When Bob told this story to Alex Ferguson, Fergy was withering in his contempt. "Oh aye,' Fergy said. 'I never saw Scoular play but I believe if he had been at the OK Corral then Wyatt Earp wouldn't have turned up.'"

Bob reckoned that among the most skilful players he faced while at Burnley were Tom Finney, Jimmy Greaves, then of Chelsea, Bobby Charlton and Jimmy Hagan of Sheffield United. He thought Charlton was the most complete player, though: "Bobby had two great feet and, boy, did he have a fierce shot on him. I recall Billy Dougall telling me that it was better to make a clearing header in two stages – the ball was so heavy in those days. He told me to head the ball up in the air and then complete the clearance with a volley. Billy was always bringing you down a peg or two – he was loathe to give you any credit. Anyway I followed his advice. The trouble was that my partial header reached Charlton before I could hack the ball clear. Without hesitating, Charlton unleashed this volley. It caught me square on my left thigh. The shot was so powerful that an imprint of the ball's panel remained on that thigh for a week. Had the shot been slightly to my right, I'd have been turned into a soprano."

## Chapter Four

# Managing To Win:

*Management and tactics in the 1950s*

FOOTBALL management in the 1950s was dominated by the figures of Matt Busby and Stan Cullis. The managers of Manchester United and Wolves were both the most successful in terms of winning trophies and developing teams during the era and also the most charismatic and in demand from the football press, which, although nowhere near as news-hungry as the modern 24-hour TV and internet led media, was just as influential. But both were also strong tacticians, albeit with entirely different approaches to the game.

Busby prioritised skill over power and fluency over method and whilst he had a pattern which he expected his team to follow, this was kept commendably simple, allowing opportunities for his talented players to express themselves. As John Connelly later pointed out, with players like Herd, Charlton, Best, Law and Stiles (*and also with the pre-Munich generation before them*), Matt Busby's simple instruction "just make sure you pass to a red shirt" was probably sufficient as the victories piled up.

However, Busby was more tactically shrewd than this description suggests. Stan Matthews recalled how his Blackpool side was outwitted during the second half of the 1948 FA Cup final against Manchester United after having bossed the first period. He attributed this turnaround to Matt Busby's tactical acumen. While Matthews' manager, Joe Smith, was enjoying his 'reet good' half-time cigar, Busby was busy reorganising his side, instructing his defenders to push up to harry and hustle their opposing half-backs, Johnston and Kelly, thereby cutting off the supply lines to wingers Matthews and Rickett. According to Stan, Busby's instruction worked like a dream and enabled United to turn a 2-1 deficit into a 4-2 victory. Stan told

Jimmy Greaves: 'at the time it was very unusual to encounter a manager who paid so much attention to tactics as Matt Busby did during that final. It completely flummoxed Blackpool.'

By contrast, Stan Cullis at Wolves adopted a more direct, physical, schooled style of play. His goalkeeper was instructed to launch the ball quickly forwards and his wing-halves were told to hit the corners giving the wingers something to chase. This was not simply the application of brute, ill-considered force for Cullis was a thinking manager who fashioned a game plan based upon what he believed to be irrefutable statistics. The infamous Wing Commander Charles Reep's analyses had revealed to him that 50% of goals came from no more than one pass and 80% from not more than three passes. So convinced was Cullis by the greater efficacy of the long-ball game that it was this aspect of the Hungarians' play which impressed him most whilst he sat watching their mauling of England at Wembley in 1953.

National coach Walter Winterbottom said of Cullis in 1960: "his theories of playing the long ball, of pouring incessantly into the opposing penalty area, have produced a specialised type of player. Cullis himself would be the first to tell you that there are certain types of player – highly talented though they may be – that he simply does not want and cannot use at his club. He 'type-casts' his players. They must be physically strong; they must be prepared to accept severe training; they must be fearless; they must be mentally indomitable; they must be prepared to fight and chase and harry and tackle, to snap at the merest crumb in front of goal, to defend remorselessly in front of their own goal."

Jimmy McIlroy recognised the extent of Stan Cullis's achievements whilst firing off at 'fighting soccer', epitomised by Wolves style of play. Jimmy wrote in 1960: 'Artistry with the ball is not all-important with Wolverhampton Wanderers: therefore it is now treated as something of an expendable luxury by managers all over the country. These managers to their eternal shame are breeding a race of footballers who would be more at home in a wrestling stadium than on a playing field.' There were several football journalists who agreed, citing Wolves alleged spoiling tactics against Red Star of Belgrade in the European Cup of 1959/60 and against Leicester in the quarter-final FA Cup during the same season.

Although both Alan Brown and Harry Potts, Burnley's two managers of the second half of the decade, favoured skill over power, placing them closer to Matt Busby, their tactical preparations, such as their dead ball routines, had a greater affinity with Cullis. Spurs' manager, Bill Nicholson, was in the same camp. Nicholson was formerly a member of the Arthur Rowe's title-winning 'push and run' side, whose fluid, creative, short-passing style mirrored the principles of international master-coach, Jimmy Hogan. And yet Nicholson, like Cullis, was not averse to employing negative tactics. For example, he helped Walter Winterbottom devise a successful plan to stop the fluent Brazilians from expressing their talents against England in the 1958 World Cup final group game in Gothenburg. The game was drawn 0-0.

Although the arguments may range back and forth as to who were the 'New Wave' innovators and who were the disciples, it is undeniable that a new breed of tactically astute coaches and managers were emerging during the late fifties, typified by Alan Brown, Bill Nicholson, Ron Greenwood at Arsenal, Vic Buckingham at West Bromwich, and Joe Mercer at Aston Villa. Others such as Tommy Docherty and Don Revie would soon join them. The time of the 'track suit manager' was almost nigh.

In the late-fifties managers varied greatly in how much license they were prepared to grant their teams in deciding their pattern of play once the game was underway. Stan Cullis was not in favour of delegation, neither was Sheffield Wednesday manager Harry Catterick – they worked to a pre-set plan – whereas Bill Nicholson was content that Danny Blanchflower should be the leader on the pitch, as was Harry Potts with his captain, Jimmy Adamson. The freedom they granted was crucial to their teams' success.

Whether managers led from the front or not, they had to be an arch diplomat in dealing with their board of directors. Many directors liked to play an active part in the proceedings – sometimes venturing into the dressing room at half-time to present their advice or, as was the case at Newcastle, attempting to select the team. Some club chairman considered it was their responsibility to recruit new players. Luton manager Syd Owen fell out with his board of directors because of this. We were still in the days of the club amateur – in football, in business and in politics. Whilst Bob Lord understood his limitations in relation to football matters he was still too much of an autocrat to allow his managers a totally free hand, as Alan Brown and succeeding Burnley managers found.

More than tactical ruses and innovation, the degree to which boards of directors invested in their club and not simply in their team separated out the best from the rest. The simple footballing truth that good players will more often than not beat less good players has never changed, although thankfully there will always be enough variables in a game of football, such as the state of the pitch, fitness, belief and passion which avert results being utterly inevitable leaving fans room for surprise, joy and disappointment which still binds them to the game in huge numbers. Whatever view is taken of Bob Lord's abrasive and sometimes offensive manner, he and his board gave Burnley the calibre of support which it needed to thrive as Jimmy

Adamson indicated. Probably what marked Burnley out as the top English side of 1959/60 was the degree of balance the club secured between its various assets and here the board of directors made an important contribution – it was a family club but an ambitious one; it was disciplined outfit but a generally caring one; it was close knit but also modern and outward-looking; it imposed routines but allowed individual expression and improvisation; it was focused on success but promoted fun, too; it was a thrifty club but one prepared to invest strongly in its future – a comprehensive scouting network, advanced coaching, modern training facilities, a strong youth policy.

Despite the marked differences in approach to the game, in terms of formation, most teams lined up in a similar way. Jimmy McIlroy observed: "That's why Don Revie's 'plan' caused so much confusion. This tactic took defenders some time to twig." This tactic was based upon the deep-lying centre-forward role adopted by Nandor Hidegkuti under coach Gusztav Sebes in Hungary's startling victory over England in 1953. "Normally each team would have two wingers. Ideally, one would be tricky like Stanley Matthews and one more direct, with pace like John Connelly or Tom Finney. Alongside the centre-forward there would be two inside-forwards – one would be a midfielder, like me, and the other a striker like Jimmy Robson. One of the wing halves would be an attacking midfielder. In our case, this role was undertaken by Jimmy Adamson, our captain. The other wing-half was more like a second centre-half. Brian Miller frequently played here although he would bomb forward, too, at times. Bobby Seith also played in the more defensive role, too. There would be two full-backs. Often one would be a hard man and one more of a ball player, although everyone had to be a capable footballer. It wasn't enough just to be a tough guy. You had to be able to play. Burnley's full-backs, John Angus and Alex Elder combined both qualities. In fact, Angus should have played more often for England. He had the ability. I think the trouble was that John was a bit of a home bird. He would frequently cry off with an injury when he was selected for one of the representative sides – the Football League or the Under-23s, if it meant staying over in a distant place."

Jimmy Robson added: "We still had a version of the W formation, then, although – going from back to front – it was more like a 3 (two backs and centre-half) – 2 (two half-backs) – 2 (two inside-forwards) – 2 (two wingers) – 1 (centre-forward) formation. There was no detailed game plan as such – not in the way there is today. But we knew broadly what was expected of each and everyone of us. We didn't adopt a way of playing to deal with different opponents, either. Had we done so, say in Hamburg, when they knocked us out of the European Cup, we might have done better. But generally speaking we played what we considered to be our natural game. It was based on the

W formation except we played it with pace and mobility. It was something which we built up over years of playing together. A lot of it seemed common-sense. For example, if Jimmy Adamson moved forward, one of us would cover the gap. We didn't need to be told, it was almost instinctive. As inside-forwards we knew we had to funnel back when we were under attack. The wing-halves – Jimmy Adamson and Brian Miller or Bobby Seith – would pull back to reinforce the defence and we, inside-forwards, needed to stay in touch with them."

But it would be wrong to interpret these comments as suggesting that club football formations in the 1950s were uniformly similar. Both Jimmys emphasised the scope they were given for improvisation on the field of play. Another Jimmy – captain, Jimmy Adamson – went even further, suggesting, in his 1962 article for the *Topical Times Annual* that Burnley played an early version of what came to be known as 'Total Football'. This flexible system of play is commonly, but wrongly, regarded as a Dutch innovation of the early 1970s. Arguably, the playing patterns adopted by Sebes' Hungarian teams and the Burnley sides of the early sixties pre-dated them by more than a decade. Jimmy Adamson explained: 'we like to keep our game fluid. We don't believe in sticking to numbers on our backs. If the full back suddenly finds himself in the momentary role of a winger, then he gets on with it, and someone else takes over his job in the rear. Burnley play their football "off the cuff". That best describes the Burnley style. There are few hard and fast rules. Obviously we try to vary our tactics according to the opposition and state of the pitch. But "off the cuff" fluid football is the aim.'

Not that this innovation found universal favour among the Burnley supporters. The *Burnley Express* reported that after the 4-1 home defeat by Blackpool in October 1959, a number of disgruntled home fans voiced their objections to a 'confusing' system of play which was blamed for The Clarets' heavy loss. Bert Trautmann recalled similar disquiet at Manchester City when their prototype deep-lying centre-forward system was introduced with Don Revie undertaking Hidegkuti's role, which resulted in a gush of goals – all at the wrong end. Of course, experimentation is fraught with risks, but as Tommy Docherty observed, even in these cautious, conservative times these setbacks did not halt the march of progress. Helped by increasing continental club competition and wider television coverage, British clubs began to look at tactical ideas being developed abroad.

The Italians had introduced the Catenaccio (the 'bolt') system of defence, based upon a 4-4-2 formation as early as the late 1940s. Its principal aim was to defend the scoring zone in and around the box by employing tight man-to-man marking of the opposing forwards supplemented by a sweeper who would seal off any gaps and pick up opposing players breaking from a deep position. Joe Mercer's Second Division Sheffield United began experimenting with a Catenaccio style system during the 1958/59 season. Mercer employed the immaculate Joe Shaw as a sweeper operating behind a back four of Cec Coldwell, Tommy Hoyland, Gerry Summers and Graham Shaw. Over seventeen Second Division league games bridging the 1958/59 and 1959/60 seasons, the Blades conceded a stingy seven goals. At the other end of the spectrum Les McDowall's 'gung ho' Manchester City were scoring and conceding goals in copious quantities, grossing 90 goals in their first twenty League games of the 1959/60 season.

Cliff Britton, the Preston manager, was a kindred spirit with Mercer. Britton said in June 1960: "I have long held the belief that all team work has to start from defence. Unless you have a workable defensive system, the mere scoring of goals can be futile". His success with Burnley during the 1946/47 season in which they reached the FA Cup final, only to lose to Charlton late in extra-time, bears testimony to that philosophy. Britton observed that "the Brazilians proved themselves better at what can be called defence in depth and in being equally adept at gaining a quick advantage on seizing the initiative."

The experimenters were not just the perceived leading edge tacticians, however. Although not given to trenchant tactical analyses, the Blackpool side under Joe Smith extemporised with a 4-4-2 type formation en route to their Wembley triumph in 1953. Stan Matthews explained in his autobiography *The Way It Was*: 'managers realised there were different systems to play... we played what was in many respects a 4-4-2 system with myself and Bill Perry playing wide on the wings but coming up from deep.' Although regarded as a conventional winger, Stan was quite prepared to go a-roaming rather than hugging the touchlines if the game merited it. Stan demonstrated this vividly at Turf Moor in October 1960 when a young Alex Elder gamely tried to shackle him. But as Walter Winterbottom found Stan was less keen on tracking back. Perhaps a violin maestro is less prepared to do the washing up?

As the 1950s were coming to a close, a wider and more informed debate was taking place about team formations and styles of play, encouraged by the work of the FA School of Coaching at Lilleshall. Once that centurion of English caps, Billy Wright, had retired at the beginning of the 1959/60 season he was free to express his reservations about the 'hit the corners' dictum of Stan Cullis, his former manager, despite Wolves' obvious success in employing this approach in domestic competitions. In advocating the 4-2-4 formation adopted loosely by the Hungarians of 1953 and Brazilians of 1958, Wright attacked 'our standard tactic (which) is to transfer the ball from the centre of the field to a winger who makes as much ground as he can before crossing into the heart of an overcrowded penalty area. That such an obvious drill can produce goals regularly is one of the fallacies of our modern game. Such centres are a barb only when there is a forward of the huge ability of a Lawton or a Dean in the centre…' Wright claimed that 'even for more imaginative sides the problem of beating a well-drilled defence employing a 4-2-4 system is considerable. The four-man defence drop back, allowing their opponents unchallenged possession in midfield. Then they take up position on the edge of the penalty area, where, with space between the last line of defence and the goalkeeper minimised, they will be joined in seconds by the two link men. And six men who know what they are doing should be able to bolt and bar the penalty area to all-comers.'

Whilst Wright indicated that the 4-2-4 system was not 'a golden panacea for all ailments', his unbridled enthusiasm for it suggested otherwise. Meanwhile, Gusztav Sebes, architect of Hungary's 1953 victory at Wembley, was about to break new ground. Whilst addressing British football's cognescenti – Cullis, Shankly, Mercer, Nicholson, Stein and others – at Lilleshall in the summer of 1960, Sebes said that at his Ujpest club he was experimenting with a 'circular system'. Within this system attackers became defenders and vice versa so that during the course of a game each outfield player fulfilled every position. Just as we were coming up to speed with the Brazilian's 4-2-4 approach, the goalposts were being moved once more.

Sebes placed skill ahead of method, though. He insisted that more attention should be given to raising the quality of coaching at all levels. He recommended that British clubs should involve young people at an earlier age, dedicating more time to improving ball skills. As testament to the success of his recipe, he explained that his deep-lying centre-forward, Hidegkuti, practised ball control for two hours or more every other day. The groundwork Sebes undertook prior to his Wembley victory had been meticulous. Beforehand, his team had practised extensively on Wembley-type surface using a British ball, with their playing style informed by detailed intelligence of the English approach.

The legacy of his influential address was to stir the pot of ideas among top managers of English clubs, who were left to ponder whether they had better chances of prevailing at home *and* abroad by employing: skill more than power; fluency as much as strength; patience as well as pace; short passes as much as long ones – working the ball rather than the player; short, accurate clearances rather than long, hopeful ones; play to feet rather than going aerial and so on.

The ways that both Burnley and Spurs played their football at the very beginning of the sixties suggested that they, at least, were on the right path.

Their styles were moulded partly through the new innovation of European competition. Jimmy Robson said: "The European Cup had a big bearing upon how the game came to be played in the mid and later sixties. Up until then, our teams played to win. It didn't matter whether the team you were playing were any good or not. After exposure to the continental style of play, teams gradually became more cautious. By the time I had moved to Blackpool in 1965, the English game had changed a lot. It was much harder scoring goals as defences became more packed. Mind you, I don't think the Bloomfield Road pitch helped. It was quite narrow, giving opposition defences greater opportunity to snuff out attacks. The season we went down, we couldn't win at home for neither love nor money. We had just one victory – a 6-1 thrashing of Newcastle, whereas on the road we won several times.

I think we benefited at Burnley from our summer tours taking on foreign opposition. It gave us early experience of continental styles like the sweeper system. We used to try to combat this by putting a man on the sweeper, reducing his freedom to play. We did pretty well. In seven games we played one summer against some good European sides (Atletico Madrid, Charleroi, Sevette) we won four and drew three. Those seven games were crammed into seven days, too! We also took on the Polish, Czechoslovakian and Austrian national teams and only lost each of these games by a solitary goal. They liked playing us because it gave them the opportunity to practice against the British style of football."

In assessing the strength of Burnley's style of play, Ray Pointer remarked: "we were helped so much by Jimmy McIlroy. He would constantly put himself in great positions. You could find him just like that. He would always be there for you. When Jimmy got the ball he'd keep it for quite a while. He would only release the ball if you had a chance of running on to it. We were the runners. He was the brains. If you couldn't pick up a pass he would turn back. If Jimmy Mac was heavily marked then Jimmy Adamson would move up to help find the wingers. Jimmy Mac hardly ever gave the ball away even though opposing sides would try to put a man on him. He was difficult to tie down, though. He was so quick from a standing start. He would create so much space for the rest of us.

But our success was based upon a lot of practice. There were a lot of times in a game that we would be already moving into position just as Jimmy Mac was releasing the ball. We didn't wait for him to find us. We knew instinctively where he would place the ball. But that was done through lots of practice in training and playing with one another over a number of years. Every time Jimmy ran at a defence with the ball, I would try and nip around the back of the defenders. Jimmy Robson was the best in the air, so we used to look to him to nod the ball on to set up chances that way."

In his 1961 book *Striking for Soccer* Jimmy Hill implored the English teams to adopt the approach that Ray was describing here. Hill maintained: 'the refinement of positional play is the fundamental lesson we must learn from the Continentals. The reason we shall have difficulty in digesting the lesson is that it is always the man who makes the pass and fails who is blamed; whereas very often it is the idiotic position his colleague takes up that brings out the bad pass.'

Jimmy Robson added: "If Ray and I were preparing for a corner we would have a quick word about who would go to the near post and who would position themselves at the far one. Mostly, I would go to the back post because I was taller. Many of these matters were sorted out on the pitch. With the understanding we'd built up over playing together for several years that approach usually worked well. Of course, we were well aware of what attacking ploys worked best. We knew that our right winger, John Connelly, liked to cut in a make for goal. This move would often drag the opposing full back in with him, creating space on the right, so when John cut the ball back to the right wing, as he often did, we were prepared to take advantage of this."

Ray Pointer thought that in retrospect Burnley were perhaps over-committed to attack. He said: "As a team we probably pushed up too much. We conceded quite a lot of goals. Thinking about the Hamburg defeat in the European Cup, maybe we should have played more defensively, having gained that lead in the first leg. But it was probably not in our make up. It was not really our style to go on the defensive. However, we did try to score early in our games – home and away – to try to draw other sides onto us more. If we could score early we would reinforce our defence a bit but we knew that because our forwards were quite quick, we could hit sides on the break. We relied on raiding tactics based on breakaways – usually on the wings. John Connelly and 'Pilky' were very fast. They could outrun most full-backs. When the first player on our side got through, we'd all move into position. We knew where to go so when the centre came across there was a good chance of someone being there to put the ball in the net.

If we were playing a good side, maybe we would ask the wingers to drop back a bit. These sorts of things were decided by the manager although the senior players would contribute their ideas, too. Quite often we would play with only two forwards up if we managed to get that early goal. If we were in the lead our defenders wouldn't go forward as much but generally speaking we pushed forward as a team and went back as a team. When I played for England, it wasn't so very different really. How we were expected to play for England then was similar to the way we would play at the club."

This underlines how modern Burnley's approach was. When Ray began his short international career, Walter Winterbottom had successfully introduced the 4-2-4 formation, which had served the Hungarians and Brazilians so well, although their success was probably based more upon the quality of their singers than the merits of their song. However, the quality of their singing owed much to concentrated practice plus astute coaching. It was not all about innate talent.

In the FA Cup Final of 1962 it was clear that Burnley and Spurs played in a very similar way. Smith, Jones and Medwin exchanged positions as fluently as Pointer, Connelly and Harris had done. The principal difference between the sides was the greater sturdiness of Spurs' defence. They employed a zonal defensive cover meaning that Ray's characteristic runs across the line were picked up by either of the Spurs full backs, Peter Baker or Ron Henry, when he ventured to the flanks and by Maurice Norman or Dave Mackay, when he moved inside. With Jimmy McIlroy below his best and often caught in possession, Ray was unable to create the customary space in which Robson and Connelly could thrive.

For all that, Walter Winterbottom, the FA Director of Coaching and England team manager, was still experiencing difficulties in getting his ideas widely accepted. He remarked in his book *Training for Soccer* (published in 1960): 'Forwards frequently interchanging functions and positions require an all-round skill and ability in each forward, as well as a clear understanding of each other's movements. At its best it provides the most devastating form of attack because of the confusion it can create amongst opposing defenders'. This was stated as if it was newly-found wisdom.

This was the style of play which not only characterised the great Hungarian side of 1953-54 and the World Cup winning Brazilian side of 1958, but also Real Madrid during their unprecedented run of European Cup triumphs between 1956 and 1960. Real's 7-3 victory over Eintracht Frankfurt at Hampden Park in May 1960 showcased their talents to an amazed British public. Helped by the addition of Ferenc Puskas (one of Ray Pointer's heroes), Real had learnt their Hungarian lessons well. But in Britain, by the early sixties, only the pre-Munich Manchester United side, Harry Potts' Burnley and the Double-winning Spurs had really followed suit, although Manchester City's success in the 1956 FA Cup Final owed much to Don Revie's adoption of the Hungarian deep-lying centre forward ploy.

Writing in 1961, Billy Wright made the following observations about leading English club's playing styles: 'Wolves, for example, come very quickly out of defence once they have won possession, and the result is that their opponents often find themselves in an off-side position. Note how they use the long ball to launch lightning attacks along the wings. West Bromwich Albion, when they are playing well, mix the long ball with the short superbly (so did the Hungarians); Spurs great confidence and ability enable them to start their attacks deep in defence; Burnley progress by nicely controlled patterns with every man searching hungrily for space.'

During the 1950s the role of the goalkeeper was beginning to change, inspired by ideas developed on the continent. For example, Billy Wright noticed how the Hungarian keeper, Grosics, operated as a 'sweeper', frequently sprinting from his area to intercept through balls when his back four pushed up. He was also aware of the offensive role adopted by Grosics, helping to start an attack by bowling the ball out to the unmarked backs or retreating wingers.

This was a ploy advocated by that respected nomadic coach from Burnley, Jimmy Hogan.

Grosics said: "I have learned a lot from the game: the running out, the starting by hand, which is very important for a goalkeeper because a quick and precise hand-thrown ball can gain time and space from the opponent. [In the fifties] this was not very widespread but I thought it was safer than kicking the ball, which might or might not reach its aim. I would add that my team mates had to adapt to my style. Those who got near to the goal were told to move in such a way so that I could easily throw them the ball. Puskas and Hidegkuti very often came back, approaching our goal to 20-25 metres, so the possibility to throw to them was very obvious."

Goalkeepers in England, like Bert Trautmann, a very proficient handball player, and Gordon Banks began to follow suit, preferring the greater accuracy of a throw to the lottery of the kick. Trautmann said that he began using this approach when Manchester City adopted the deep-lying centre-forward tactic – the Revie Plan. He explained: "I probably played a big part in it because, after having caught a ball, the ball was already on its way. This was my handball experience. People were running into space and I delivered the ball with my hand, eliminating three, four or five opponents. We were like a military machine. Unfortunately, later on, when a lot of players had left … we struggled. That proved to me that you had to have good players, intelligent players, to play anything."

Adam Blacklaw confirmed that he was expected to play this way, too, although he also kicked from hand as well. Adam said: "fortunately, I have big hands. You need big hands as a goalkeeper. It helps with bowling the ball out as I was encouraged to do – to help get an attack going."

The instructions given to Bert, Gordon and Adam were different from those given by Stan Cullis to his giant goalkeeper, Malcolm Finlayson. Finlayson was told to launch the ball long towards the opposition's penalty area. That was where Stan Cullis wanted his side to play and he wanted the ball to arrive there with the minimum of fuss. However, it seems that not even Cullis's men were bound by an unswerving rule here, for there were times when their brilliant innovator, Peter Broadbent, would drop back to collect a short ball from Finlayson, before prompting a Wolves' attack.

In the fifties, pre-match preparations rarely comprised forensic examination of the strengths and weaknesses of the opposition. At Burnley, for example, opponents were discussed but not minutely scrutinised, certainly nowhere near as much as Don Revie's Leeds did with their rigorous scouting and elaborate dossiers.

John Angus recalled: "when we had our weekly discussions about our next opponents we would examine their particular strengths and weaknesses. We'd know which goalkeepers were confident about high crosses and which weren't. We'd know which players were good in the air and which were better on the ground. We'd identify the danger men. We wouldn't alter our basic style of play as a team to combat these threats but as individuals we would prepare to make adjustments to our own game. I cannot remember ever being told to change the way I played whether at club level or when playing for England, either at Under-23 or at the senior level. The national coaches, Walter Winterbottom and Ron Greenwood would attempt to build upon your strengths, making some suggestions about how you might improve your game. There was never any attempt made to alter the basic way you played. With Alan Brown and Harry Potts, at Burnley, it was the same."

But Brian Miller added: "at Gawthorpe we didn't spend hours looking at blackboards and discussing tactics. Jimmy Adamson confirmed Brian's view. He wrote in 1962: 'we don't do a lot of talking at Turf Moor. Of course we hold team talks but these last only five or ten minutes. They are a free-for-all with every player saying his piece. We prefer to concentrate our tactics and team work on the field.

As indicated by Jimmy Greaves, Burnley were renowned for their free-kick 'scams'. Jimmy Robson confirmed: 'Tuesday and Thursday afternoons were dedicated to set play practice. During Alan Brown's time we had the smallest forward line in the country. This is where the short corner came in. We had this routine in which Jimmy Mac and the corner taker would start a mock argument over how the kick should be taken. Typically, Jimmy would stomp off in disgust fooling the marking defender into thinking that he was being ignored but then Jimmy would dart behind the defender's back to a pick up a short kick pushed along the by-line. Similar deceptions were employed at throw-ins'. Jimmy McIlroy insisted that although Burnley were often labeled 'the gimmick team', to make progress in their set plays months of monotonous practice were required.

The second leg of the European Cup tie with Rheims, played in Paris on 30th November 1960, featured a brilliant free-kick routine. In the 32nd minute Burnley were awarded a free-kick just outside the Rheims penalty area. McIlroy and Adamson, the architects of so many of Burnley's set plays, positioned themselves five yards from the ball. Both sprinted forward but at the last moment Adamson peeled away leaving McIlroy to slide the ball to Ray Pointer who had slyly moved into a position on the right of the Rheims' wall. Unhesitatingly, Ray deflected the pass behind the wall and into the path of Brian Miller who made a late blind side run on the left side of the French defensive line. Miller's first time shot hit the bar but the ever-alert Jimmy Robson nipped in to score from the rebound and put Burnley 3-0 ahead on aggregate

Chapter Five

# 'Among My Souvenirs'

*A diary of Burnley's title-winning season*

## AUGUST 1959

THE MARILYN MONROE and Tony Curtis film *Some Like It Hot* was showing at the Burnley Odeon as preparations for the new season were being finalised. Fittingly so, for apart from the torrential June rain, the summer had been Riviera-like. Huddled in their narrow valley on the

*A scorching summer but not everyone trusts the forecast – Burnley town centre, August 1959 [17]*

Pennine's western fringes, Burnley folk are accustomed to rain. Here they are directly in the Atlantic front line, so their air often comes mossy and moist and, before the Clean Air regulations, it often came sulphurous and sooty, too, particularly during the winter months. It was that characteristic moistness which helped establish their cotton industry. So when the high summer of 1959 delivered day after day of unrelenting sunshine and shimmering heat, it came as bit of a foreign experience.

Not that many residents had yet sampled a holiday abroad. Local travel agents, Althams, were beginning to drum up interest, though, at least among the better off. Cruises to Madeira, Tenerife and Casablanca were on offer from £75. That amounted to almost seven times the national average weekly wage in 1959. Converted into current values a £75 cruise would now cost around £3,500. Unsurprisingly then, most local holidaymakers plumped for the Costa Fylde with ranks of Yelloway coaches ready to pick up the staggered Lancashire 'Wakes' traffic. British Railways competed strongly in the day trip market, advertising their steam hauled Sunday excursions to Blackpool at 7/3 (36p) and Windermere at 11/6 (57p).

That roasting summer the roads melted, the clay cracked and 'down, down, down' went the water in Burnley's few and inadequate reservoirs. The *Burnley Express* raised the alarm on 15 August, indicating that commercial water usage should reduce by 25%. An appeal was made to the townsfolk that they, too, should cut their domestic water usage. There was a warning that water pressure may need to reduce at night while temperatures remained in the upper 70s. Rather belatedly, the Council put forward a plan to construct a new reservoir at Crown Point. This was to improve water supplies for households in the Manchester Road area, on the lofty south side of town.

More folk were concerned with the cotton mill closures, though. In the Burnley area 6,000 looms had been scrapped under the Government Concentration Plan with 1,000 workers placed under notice of redundancy. By 1959, Lancashire had lost two-thirds of its looms. On 26 August, just four days into the new football season, it was announced that the Benjamin Thornber and Sons Mill would

*No escape from the thicket of mill chimneys: Thompson Park, Burnley August 1959 [18]*

close after 100 years of operation. 320 redundancies would follow. The *Burnley Express* concluded: 'Burnley is no longer a cotton town as engineering and allied workers now outnumber the textile operatives'. Nevertheless, there was still a place for niche textile production such as at the Jacqmar – Hebe factory where fashion items were being produced or at Haythornthwaite's where 'fashionable waterproof windcheaters' and ski outfits were being manufactured. Ironically, the shortage of skilled labour was said to be slowing production. Perhaps that was why Lomeshaye Mill in Nelson (owned by Southalls) continued to advertise for skilled textile operatives in the *Burnley Express*, insisting that this was a 'factory with a future'.

Greater hope focused on the growth of new manufacturing industries moving into the area. As if to reinforce this point, the *Burnley Express* announced in that month the local unemployment figures had fallen below the national average. It was stated that these figures were the best since the 1957 credit squeeze. The *Express* added: 'Nelson and Colne are beginning to get a share of the new industry projects. There are good prospects of absorbing any future redundancy when local firms take advantage of Government proposals for the shrinkage of the cotton industry.' This was the 'weaving out' provision which compensated owners for the scrapping of their looms.

The local employment situation was not the only pressing concern for the local trade unions, though. On 19th August, the Burnley Branch Committee of the National Union of General and Municipal Workers called for the 'unilateral renunciation of the H-Bomb by the Labour Party.' With the US and USSR bullishly opposed, many of us were left shivering in the 'shadow of the bomb'. Nuclear disarmament had become a hot national issue, although perhaps more among the middle classes, with the much publicised CND movement prodding consciences. *Look Back In Anger* was then showing at the Burnley Empire. The 'Angry' Jimmy Porter reflected something of the angst and recrimination about class credentials, social mobility and socialist commitments that were fermenting within Hugh Gaitskell's Labour Party. Not that Labour was anymore unified when it came to nuclear disarmament. The gaping cracks were there for all to see and Gaitskell would duly pay for that disunity at the October polls, just as Michael Foot and Neil Kinnock would do during the Thatcher years.

It is said that the height of new buildings is a barometer of public optimism. Coinciding neatly with the Majestic's showing of *Room At The Top*, the Burnley's town planners unveiled their blueprint for a new high-rise luxury hotel. The Keirby Hotel was intended to become the 'Claridges of the North'. A model of the new hotel was showcased proudly to the visitors from

*Thoroughly modern mill town: the construction of the showpiece Keirby Hotel in 1959 [19]*

the twinned French town of Vitry-sur- Seine. The Keirby was to be the centre-piece in the £5 million town centre revitalisation project. That makeover also included a new shopping centre, a new bus station and a ring road. The municipal leaders seemed determined to uncouple Burnley from its brooding Victorian image. By embracing a new concrete and steel vision, they felt they were making a bold claim for modernity. Too bold, it seems. As commendable as their intentions were, few things fade as quickly as today's fads.

Home modernisation was on the agenda, too, as the *Burnley Express* gave notice of a new Act of Parliament which would provide financial assistance for the installation of household bathrooms. Five million British homes were still without a bathroom in 1959 with the outside 'lavvy' and fireside zinc bath about to greet the 'swinging sixties'. Music hall entertainment was clinging on, too, despite being counted out in *The Entertainer*, a sour satirical drama about Britain's post war decline. Hylda *'She Knows You Know'* Baker proved to be more resilient than Archie Rice, the *Entertainer*'s sleazy compere. Indeed, Hylda was top of the bill at the Burnley Palace during August. There was no place for Frank Sinatra, though, at least, not on his originally planned date in October. The fault wasn't Frank's. Apparently the Imperial Ballroom, Nelson had been double-booked and precedence was given to the Colne Swimming Club. Sorry, Frank, it's strictly first come, first served here.

Other revolutions were happening too. The Austin and Morris versions of the Mini were launched on 18 August, bringing cars into ever more affordable brackets for the masses. The first transistor radios appeared, too, costing a hefty £23 (around £1,000 in today's value) for a handbag-sized model. Meanwhile, in the US the first microchip was being produced. So was the first Barbie Doll.

As has been previously discussed, America featured heavily in British lives. While their music was beginning to make major inroads into popular culture influencing lives on a daily basis, so were their politicians. At the end of August US President, Dwight Eisenhower, arrived in England for talks with Harold Macmillan. These ranged from world peace to Britain's beleaguered textile industry. In an unprecedented development, the talks were televised live as 'Mac the Knife' sought to gain maximum capital in the run up to the impending General Election.

Elsewhere on the political front, tension between India and China was mounting in relation to the disputed territories in Bhutan and Sikkim. In the face of Chinese oppression, the Dalai Lama fled Tibet to find refuge in India. Back in the USA, the Civil Rights Movement was gaining momentum but it was a bloody battle. In Little Rock, Arkansas a 1,000 strong crowd gathered to protest against educational de-segregation.

## 22 August 1959

Arsenal 0 Sheffield Wednesday 1
Birmingham City 0 Wolverhampton Wanderers 1
Blackburn Rovers 4 Fulham 0
Blackpool 3 Bolton Wanderers 2
Chelsea 4 Preston North End 4
Everton 2 Luton Town 2
Leeds United 2 Burnley 3
Manchester City 2 Nottingham Forest 1
Newcastle United 1 Tottenham Hotspur 5
West Bromwich Albion 3 Manchester United 2
West Ham United 3 Leicester City 0

## Leeds United 2 v 3 Burnley

*'Living Doll'*

It was like an oven inside Elland Road. The sun beat down mercilessly. Inside the corrugated 'scratching shed' the heat was stifling. Even with their sports jackets discarded and their shirtsleeves turned up, all the men were perspiring heavily. Surely you couldn't play football in these conditions? But

Leeds could, it seemed. Making light of their lacklustre preparations they turned up the heat a notch or two on Burnley's frequently wrong-footed defenders. Much to the home crowd's delight the muscular Wilbur Cush and the deft Jimmy McIlroy, fellow Northern Irish internationals, started engaging in a right bumping and boring battle. Less to their delight, Leeds failed to make their darting attacks pay; missing three easy chances in the opening twenty minutes, with young inside left, Chris Crowe, the main culprit. Up front for Leeds was ex-Claret centre forward, Alan Shackleton. He was determined to put himself about among his former team mates, downing the impressive Tommy Cummings and also tangling with Burnley left-winger, Brian Pilkington, much to Jimmy McIlroy's amusement but much to 'Pilky''s annoyance. 'Pilky' was quick to make Leeds pay. Taking advantage of a deflected pass from Jimmy Robson he accelerated into the box and proceeded to thump the ball past 'keeper Ted Burgin to put Burnley into a 23rd minute lead. Eleven minutes later, John Connelly doubled Burnley's advantage, netting at the second attempt after a bewildering exchange of passes between Ray Pointer and arch playmaker, Jimmy McIlroy. The heat was now beginning to get to the Leeds players and particularly to their centre-half, Jackie Charlton. Suffering from heat exhaustion, Charlton had to be removed, hosed down and restored as a shaky left winger. By this time, Tommy Cummings had sorted out his defence. Brian Miller had taken care of Shackleton and Leeds weren't getting so much as a sniff of a chance. At half-time, The Clarets were well in command with a 2-0 lead.

*Elland Road in 1962 with the 'scratching shed' in bottom left of picture [20]*

Twenty minutes after half-time there was a change of fortunes. Bobby Seith mistimed his tackle on winger George Meek – a stonewall penalty. Midfielder, Cush strode forward purposefully. He placed the ball carefully on the spot then walked back slowly to his distant mark, licking his right hand as he did so. Turning sharply at the end of his long run, he thundered in and smacked the ball past Blacklaw. Burnley weren't going to let their advantage slip, though. All afternoon, the nippy and compact Pilkington had the beating of his marker, Jimmy Ashall. With six minutes remaining, 'Pilky' flashed past Ashall once again and crossed perfectly for Pointer to convert confidently. That seemed to be that. But just two minutes later, the previously subdued

Don Revie found Charlton with a precise pass. Making light of his exhaustion, Charlton went on a mazy run weaving around the bemused Burnley defenders to set up an easy scoring opportunity which he took. John Angus was furious claiming that at the start of his run Charlton had taken the ball out of play. It was to no avail. The goal stood. But Leeds were now down on their knees. It proved to be their last shot in anger. Burnley were home, if exceedingly dry.

## 25 August 1959

Birmingham City 4 Newcastle United 3
Bolton Wanderers 0 Blackburn Rovers 3
Burnley 5 Everton 2
Fulham 5 Manchester City 2
Leicester City 3 Leeds United 2
Luton Town 0 Blackpool 1
Manchester United 0 Chelsea 1
Nottingham Forest 0 Arsenal 3
Preston North End 1 West Ham United 1
Tottenham Hotspur 2 West Bromwich Albion 2
Wolverhampton Wanderers 3 Sheffield Wednesday 1

## Burnley 5 v 2 Everton

*'Battle of New Orleans'*

In the programme for this evening's game (priced three pence or 1p in modern currency), Burnley manager, Harry Potts, garnished his notes with Churchillian rhetoric. He urged the supporters 'to stand in with us for all you are worth', committing himself to providing high quality football. He wrote, 'we pride ourselves on being a footballing team and no club can be more eager to meet the demand for better play. That being so strongly ingrained in our intentions we confidently anticipate providing you with good displays'.

*Everton's Dave Hickson – the 'Cannonball Kid' [21]*

In this programme, season tickets were on offer starting at £2/2/- (£2.10p in modern currency) for adults and £1/15/- (£1.75p) for boys and girls.

In balmy Burnley the wilting heat continued but 29,000 were still drawn to Turf Moor for this evening's local derby. Not that the temperature appeared to restrain Burnley. They were three-up within 20 minutes. Left winger, Brian

Pilkington, was again the star performer. His cross was headed home by John Connelly in the 14th minute and then he then scored himself with a diving header four minutes later. He even supplied the pass from a miscued clearance which allowed centre-forward Ray Pointer to score a simple third. However, prompted by the diminutive, dynamic Scottish midfielder, Bobby Collins, Everton began to assert theirselves and Eddie Thomas's fierce 35th minute drive pulled them back into the game. But up until half-time Burnley had the better of the exchanges with play flowing frantically from one end to the other. In order to protect their goal, both 'keepers, Blacklaw and Dunlop, had to be at their very best.

After the interval, Burnley had to resist early pressure but the siege was lifted in the 72nd minute. Jimmy McIlroy's sudden burst along the left flank set up Jimmy Robson to volley Burnley's fourth. Even then Everton were not to be subdued. Dave Hickson, their 'Cannonball Kid' centre-forward, was finding Brian Miller's attentions too stifling so he moved out to the right wing. This did the trick. From here he produced a cross which Miller miscued. The ball skewed off Miller's forehead and smacked against the crossbar. Everton's Eddie O'Hara was quickest to react, although Burnley defenders claimed his 78th minute shot had not crossed the goal line. It did not matter. With three minutes to go, Burnley's free-scoring right winger, John Connelly, fired home after running onto Robson's pass.

## 29 AUGUST 1959

Bolton Wanderers 2 Everton 1
Burnley 1 West Ham United 3
Fulham 1 Blackpool 0
Leicester City 3 Chelsea 1
Luton Town 0 Leeds United 1
Manchester United 3 Newcastle United 2
Nottingham Forest 2 Blackburn Rovers 2
Preston North End 1 West Bromwich Albion 1
Sheffield Wednesday 1 Manchester City 0
Tottenham Hotspur 0 Birmingham City 0
Wolverhampton Wanderers 3 Arsenal 3

## Burnley 1 v 3 West Ham United

*'Roulette'*

West Ham's Scottish international, John Dick, and Vic Keeble had scored 47 League goals between them in the previous campaign lifting the newly-promoted Hammers to sixth place in the First Division, one place above

*Here comes summer and here comes Ray Pointer but with West Ham 'keeper, Noel Dwyer diving at his feet, Ray misses the target [22]*

Burnley. In that previous season they had taken three points off the League Champions, Wolves, and had thrashed Villa 7-2, Portsmouth 6-0, Blackburn 6-3 and Manchester City 5-1. This Division held no terrors for them and they had opened up their new campaign confidently. At a blisteringly hot Turf Moor not even John Connelly third minute opening goal disconcerted them. Future US Soccer supremo, Phil Woosnam, equalised six minutes later. Thereafter, with Jimmy McIlroy subdued and left back, Tommy Cummings, having a poor game, West Ham dominated the proceedings. Their cause was assisted by some magical wing-play from Michael Grice. Andy Smillie, a replacement for John Dick, put the Hammers ahead in the 63rd minute and Grice secured both points after Burnley's goalkeeper, Blacklaw, had misjudged his swirling 76th minute cross.

*Noel Dwyer saves from Jimmy Robson as Burnley stutter to defeat [23]*

## First Division

| **29 August 1959** | *P* | *W* | *D* | *L* | *F* | *A* | *Pts* | *Goal average* |
|---|---|---|---|---|---|---|---|---|
| 1. Blackburn Rovers | 3 | 2 | 1 | 0 | 9 | 2 | 5 | 4.50 |
| 2. West Ham United | 3 | 2 | 1 | 0 | 7 | 2 | 5 | 3.50 |
| 3. Wolverhampton Wanderers | 3 | 2 | 1 | 0 | 7 | 4 | 5 | 1.75 |
| 4. Tottenham Hotspur | 3 | 1 | 2 | 0 | 7 | 3 | 4 | 2.33 |
| 5. Blackpool | 3 | 2 | 0 | 1 | 4 | 3 | 4 | 1.33 |
| 6. BURNLEY | 3 | 2 | 0 | 1 | 9 | 7 | 4 | 1.29 |
| 7. West Bromwich Albion | 3 | 1 | 2 | 0 | 6 | 5 | 4 | 1.20 |

| | *P* | *W* | *D* | *L* | *F* | *A* | *Pts* | *Goal average* |
|---|---|---|---|---|---|---|---|---|
| 8. Fulham | 3 | 2 | 0 | 1 | 6 | 6 | 4 | 1.00 |
| 9. Leicester City | 3 | 2 | 0 | 1 | 6 | 6 | 4 | 1.00 |
| 10. Sheffield Wednesday | 3 | 2 | 0 | 1 | 3 | 3 | 4 | 1.00 |
| 11. Arsenal | 3 | 1 | 1 | 1 | 6 | 4 | 3 | 1.50 |
| 12. Preston North End | 3 | 0 | 3 | 0 | 6 | 6 | 3 | 1.00 |
| 13. Birmingham City | 3 | 1 | 1 | 1 | 4 | 4 | 3 | 1.00 |
| 14. Chelsea | 3 | 1 | 1 | 1 | 6 | 7 | 3 | 0.86 |
| 15. Leeds United | 3 | 1 | 0 | 2 | 5 | 6 | 2 | 0.83 |
| 16. Manchester United | 3 | 1 | 0 | 2 | 5 | 6 | 2 | 0.83 |
| 17. Bolton Wanderers | 3 | 1 | 0 | 2 | 4 | 7 | 2 | 0.57 |
| 18. Manchester City | 3 | 1 | 0 | 2 | 4 | 7 | 2 | 0.57 |
| 19. Everton | 3 | 0 | 1 | 2 | 5 | 9 | 1 | 0.56 |
| 20. Luton Town | 3 | 0 | 1 | 2 | 2 | 4 | 1 | 0.50 |
| 21. Nottingham Forest | 3 | 0 | 1 | 2 | 3 | 7 | 1 | 0.43 |
| 22. Newcastle United | 3 | 0 | 0 | 3 | 6 | 12 | 0 | 0.50 |

# SEPTEMBER 1959

Temperatures were rising in Britain's car industry. An unofficial strike at the British Motor Corporation in Birmingham on 1 September halted production of the newly developed Mini. Despite the declining fortunes of British industries, UK citizens were enjoying more disposable income. This was reflected in the increased number of young people going to University. Entrants had doubled in the two decades between 1939 and 1959.

The Cold War was a frantic tussle of technological supremacy, ultimately ruinous in the Soviets' case. For around twenty-five years the Space Race provided a global scorecard of reputations. It was hardly a coincidence, then, that USSR rocket Lunik II was launched at the moon on the 12th September just as Soviet Premier, Khrushchev, was about to embark on a tour of the US. The Americans retaliated by refusing Khrushchev permission to visit Disneyland. Britons had to content themselves with Formula One, rather than global, supremacy, as Stirling Moss won the Italian Grand Prix on 13 September. But, sadly, West Indian Test cricketer and former Burnley professional, Collie Smith, died in a car crash.

In a dramatic national TV address on 16 September, French President De Gaulle offered Algeria the opportunity to choose its political future via a referendum. This choice even included the possibility of secession from France. Around 200 people were dying each year in Algeria as a result of terrorist acivity. Not that De Gaulle's offer did anything to appease the warring factions: the Algerian rebels; the resentful French Army officers in occupation of the colony; the French settlers and their strident supporters in France. The 'Battle of Algiers' was about to intensify.

On 17 September the BBC announced the purchase of 20 American feature films to be shown on TV. This move had been prompted after viewing figures had revealed that the BBC was losing the ratings war with ITV. At the same time the Rank Organisation revealed details of plummeting cinema attendances, with a 14% fall in the last year. 91 cinemas had been closed by Rank alone since 1956, with a further 57 ear-marked for closure. Greater prosperity was allowing working families wider leisure options and the increasing range of TV programmes provided tougher competition with the cinema.

On 25 September Khrushchev and Eisenhower began talks in Berlin, with the volatile Soviet premier in a sunnier mood having met some 'real Americans: as good and kind as our Soviet people' during his Californian walkabout. In Britain, Rolls Royce launched its new £9,000 Phantom V just a few days after the last Spitfire, flying in a Battle of Britain remembrance display, crashed.

How persuasive it proved to be is uncertain but the *Burnley Express* carried a half page advert for tripe. Underneath a pirouetting, zero-sized female skater the message ran: 'UCP tripe – easily digested and nourishing, light as a feather and full of energy'. For women whose digestion was more (or alternatively less) robust and who struggled more with their diets, the Burnley Co-op offered the Model 100 'natural figure control' corset from 57/6 (£2-87p). This corset promised to 'support weak muscles – as recommended by the medical profession.' Not wishing to appeal solely to starchy medics or unashamed frumps, a hint of salaciousness was introduced with a curvaceous, slinky model sketched in just her Model 100 and her stripper-like long sleeved gloves. There were no sexy trappings with the 'NEW Beasley Appliance', though. The advert barked interrogatively: 'Are you ruptured? You don't know what REAL COMFORT is until you have tried (one)'. We were also told about the 'new way to shrink piles without surgery' with a drawing of a white-coated lab boffin staring into a microscope just to assure us this was no quack remedy.

With the school holidays almost at an end, parental thoughts were turning to autumn school wear, not that the scorching weather provided any hints. Duffle coats, the standard issue for the Aldermaston marchers and *Cruel Sea* generation, were on offer at 41/3 (£2.06p) while the de rigueur Gabedine raincoat, manufactured quite aptly by Stoic Ltd. of Leeds, came in at a much more expensive 70/6 (£3.52p). Demand was obviously falling for the all seasons, all weather, all purpose, all horrible black Gabedine mac, since Burnley's specialist Gabedine cloth manufacturers, at the Vale Street Mill, had announced its impending closure. The cheaper option available at the Northern Raincoat of St. James Street was a 'slightly substandard' nylon coat at 39/6 (£1.97p). How refreshingly candid seemed these advertisements! Obviously, Vance Packard's seminal work on the power of advertising *the Hidden Persuaders* (published in 1957) hadn't yet made it to Burnley.

*Church Street, Burnley September 1959 [24]*

With the General Election just around the corner local politicians started declaring their hands. Predictably, employment generally, and the textile industry in particular, were at the top of their agendas. Things got off to a sticky start. On 5 September, 2,500 textile operatives were told that their employers planned to 'weave out towards the end of the year'. By 16 September, that figure rose to 3,290. To make matters worse a recently published report on the state of the local economy poured icy water on hopes for a swift recovery. Although new manufacturers were appearing, the report's authors at the Economic Intelligence Unit, were unconvinced by the speed of change. In Stoneyholme, the Scottish Aluminium Ware Ltd. started producing Venetian blinds, to the *Burnley Express*'s fanfare: 'Another new industry for Burnley!' but inadequate rail communications and poor quality industrial land sites were reported to be hampering overall progress in transforming the local economy. Although the report's authors considered that the Burnley area was 'relatively well placed in relation to markets for consumer goods', they predicted that workers, particularly those living in the Colne and Nelson localities, would have to travel farther to work.

The continuing migration of male workers was seen as almost inevitable, noting that 'textile closures affect mainly women.' This came as small comfort to older workers, particularly those laid off from mills in the surrounding villages where there was no other local employment immediately available. However, in Worsthorne, one of the villages to lose its mills, some relief was soon at hand. On 13 November it was announced that its closed Gorple Mill would be turned over to the manufacture of refrigerators. 'There's no deserted village look about enterprising Worsthorne', declared the *Burnley Express.*

It was reckoned that the mill closures in the Burnley area would cost the national government around £500,000 with the textile operatives collectively receiving around £200,000 to help soften the financial blow. However, the Economic Intelligence Unit report indicated that North East Lancashire was not benefiting from national development funding in the same proportion as the North West region was as a whole. With the first wave of 'baby boomer' school leavers expected in 1962, adding around 2,000 young people to the declining job market, the report writers insisted that there was an urgent need for an inter-authority strategy on economic regeneration.

These were the fault lines around which the politicians mounted their campaigns. In Burnley, the Tory prospective parliamentary candidate, Alderman Brooks, accused his opposite number, Labour's Daniel Jones, of scaremongering, of 'making wild and unrealistic claims' and of issuing (misplaced) 'dire threats'. Basing his campaign upon the 'Peace and Prosperity' theme, Alderman Brooks asserted: 'you only need to look at all the television aerials on the chimneys, the many motor cars, motor cycles and scooters which people own to see that the benefits of good government have been passed onto the workers. An average family now has 20% more purchasing power than it did in 1951 under a Socialist Government. Unemployment benefits have risen by 44%. Industrial and disablement benefits have risen by 40%' The reference to the rise in industrial and disablement benefits reminds us of the relatively primitive state of health and safety regulations in British industry in 1959.

There was no getting away from the drought problems, though. On 9 September the usage of stand pipes was first considered by the Town Council in the bid to save 1 million gallons of water per day. Rain actually fell on 23 September, but the yield was a meagre third of an inch, which quickly evaporated on the hard, dry surfaces. Emergency plans were put in place to pump water from the Lake District and a letter was sent to all local households listing 12 ways of conserving water. To add to the woes, a burst water main on 30 September cut off the supply to 6,000 homes.

During the lo-tech fifties comics provided a major distraction for many school children and particularly among the 'slacker' circles in which some of us moved. When it came to demonstrating a passing knowledge of literary characters and plots, *Classics Illustrated'* versions of *Henry V, Barnaby Rudge and Hamlet* lifted the aspiring slackers off the hook effortlessly, offering the shortest cuts to the chase. 'Get me behind this Arras – aarghhh!!'

Then there were *Movie Classics*. These introduced us to a series of fine films of the time such as John Ford's complex and controversial western, *The Searchers*. But *Movie Classics* provided to be a less reliable information source when it came to bluffing. Let's take *Solomon and Sheba,* for example. Sunday school teachers were generally less impressed with its Biblical credentials. A slightly prissy, but ever-so-nice, Joyce Grenfell type once said: "No, I don't think the Old Testament describes the meeting of King Solomon and the Queen of Sheba quite like that". Having later seen the scantily-clad Gina Lollobrigida 'strut her stuff' that teacher certainly had a point. Apparently, the film's orgy scene alone cost the Hollywood producers $100,000 to stage. They must have had a lot of fun.

*War Picture Library* was a particular favourite among pre-pubescent boys. The garish glossy covers of enraged combat were strictly 'dime store' fare with the titles such as *Fight Back to Dunkirk*, *The Gallant Few* and *Bomb Alley* slashed across the cover page. Inside, crew-cut, square-head Germans fought unequal contests with blond, craggy Brits with their inevitable defeats punctuated with anguished cries of 'achtung' and 'donner und blitzen' (*Expressions yet to be heard in a modern German hotel or airport*). When it came to a superior gene pool, *War Picture Library* suggested this was a British monopoly. Despite the growing moral panic about comics, the likes of *War Picture Library* were exempt. After all, this was patriotic, heroic 'Brits on top' stuff. It was a library, too, so of course it had gravitas.

The American comics had a much rougher ride. The Comics Campaign Council and the National Union of Teachers lobbied successfully for legal restraint. Their efforts resulted in the Children & Young Persons (Harmful Publications) Act of 1955. This immediately curbed the traffic in US horror comics with their shocking tales of grave robbers, monsters and flesh eaters. In the fifties, being a spoilsport helped ensure rapid career advancement.

Political, class and religious prejudice underpinned this Salem-like pursuit of folk devils. British Communists and conservatives were united in their Canute-like denunciation of American cultural influences. The middle-classes were deeply distrustful of comics, with many parents attempting to guide their children away from such 'common' (*in other words, working class*), 'corrupting' material. In dour, depleted post-war Britain, American influence swamped everything: films, TV, music, fashion, food, drink and home comforts. So how could their brash, bold, exciting alternatives fail?

*The Eagle* represented the Christian backlash. Slick, colourful and smartly turned out, it replicated the American production values. The difference was that it carried an overt moral message, a Christian one, with its creator being Rev. Marcus Morris, an Anglican vicar. *Dan Dare* started out as Lex Christian, not a devout Ford dealer but a fighting East End parson. Even in *Dan Dare*'s makeover space crusading role the emphasis was always placed upon compassion and conciliation – to boldly go and love thy alien.

With *The Eagle* covering constructive hobbies, eulogizing the patriotic virtues of the likes of Nelson and Montgomery (more 'Brits on top') or the moral virtues of St. Paul (*The Great Adventurer*), this was the comic to appease the middle classes. In 1959, the Eagle covered the life of Churchill (*The Happy Warrior* – a case of topper on Brit) and the biblical chronicle of King David. Even the vagabond French Foreign Legion, the brutal enforcers of the morally dubious French colonialists, was given an anodyne wash with the tales of *Luck of the Legion*.

*The Eagle*'s sister magazine, *The Girl*, brought similar respectability to the female comic market, alongside *Girl's Crystal* and *School Friend*. From 1958, *Bunty*, followed suit with its stories of jolly school escapades, intrepid girl investigators, brave policewomen, dependable air nurses, and historic heroines, like Helen Keller (*a perverse case of Yank on top*). With males generally dismissed as a pointless irrelevance, the *Female Eunuch* generation was nurtured here.

But all was not lost. Comics needn't be earnest. They could still be funny. They could still fly the flag of working class rebellion and anarchy, too. The *Beano* and *Dandy* were probably the most controversial of these. Here were tales of unruly children subverting effete adult authority. However, even with the later introduction of *Dennis the Menace*'s dog *Gnasher*, it was mostly bark and little bite. *Dennis* and his like always ended up outwitted and humiliated by their adult adversaries. However, things were different for the sisterhood. *The Beano*'s *Minnie the Minx* could get away with murder. Of course, it's always different for girls.

There was no stopping *Roy of the Rovers*, though. The *Tiger* allowed Melchester Rovers just one inexplicable slump, obviously anticipating the fortunes of clubs at the top of today's Premiership. In this distressing phase, Roy Race, who looked as if he had just jumped out of a Spitfire cockpit, had lost his scoring knack, so, had his colleague, 'Blackie' Gray. For all of two weeks they were being bounced by rubbish teams. It was far too good to last. Normal service was restored quickly with Melchester Rovers putting everyone to the sword. They even crushed the American Super Bowl winners, beating them at their own game and thrashing them at ours on Melchester Rovers' 1959 summer tour. How we missed the days of our gunboat policy.

## 2 September 1959

Arsenal 1 Nottingham Forest 1
Blackburn Rovers 1 Bolton Wanderers 0
Blackpool 0 Luton Town 0
Chelsea 3 Manchester United 6
Everton 1 Burnley 2
Leeds United 1 Leicester City 1

Manchester City 3 Fulham 1
Newcastle United 1 Birmingham City 0
Sheffield Wednesday 2 Wolverhampton Wanderers 2
West Bromwich Albion 1 Tottenham Hotspur 2
West Ham United 2 Preston North End 1

## Everton 1 v 2 Burnley

*'Lipstick on Your Collar'*

While Everton Football Club was about to enter an age of greater prosperity with new director, John Moores, using his Littlewoods fortune to bankroll the club, the prospects for the city of Liverpool were seen by some as less rosy. Philip Norman, author of *Shout: the true story of the Beatles* described Liverpool in 1959 thus: 'a gloomy, fog-bound city of docks, ships and crumbling Victorian splendour. It was an imperial port in terminal decline with a famous tradition of salty music-hall comedy, an impenetrable dialect and a distinctive working class flavour.' Although the searing September heat made nonsense of Norman's caricature Everton's relegation struggles had greater resonance with his lugubrious view. Unlike Melchester Rovers, Everton laboured to score on their travels. They were much more Melchester-like at home, though. During this season they would score 50 goals in 21 home League fixtures, the fourth highest return in the Division. Nottingham Forest, Leicester City and Chelsea would all return from Goodison with their tails between their legs having each suffered a 6-1 defeat. With John Carey in charge of 'The Toffees' and ex-Claret, Les Shannon, as his chief coach, Everton invested heavily in team strengthening. However, it would be left to a greater disciplinarian, Harry Catterick, to steer them to the First Division championship in 1963.

With Everton out for blood after their stinging defeat at Turf Moor, frugality had to be the order of the day for Burnley's defence. Thanks to Adam Blacklaw's stupendous agility, Burnley narrowly survived an Alamo-like siege, and then, to rub salt into their hosts' wounds, they managed to break away decisively on two occasions to seal both points. Not that the start of the game gave any hint of what was to follow. With winger John Connelly providing Burnley's only attacking prospect, The Clarets struggled to get going. Urged on by a 39,000 crowd, Everton mounted a succession of furious early assaults upon Burnley's goal. Something had to give and sure enough, young inside right, Frank Wignall, slammed home a drive from a 20th minute corner, which Blacklaw hardly saw. Miller had to hold on tenaciously to the fiery Dave Hickson, sometimes illegally, in an attempt to stem the Everton tide. Then, in the 36th minute, and completely out of the blue, the course of the game was changed. Jimmy McIlroy's astute pass pierced the Everton defence allowing the previously shackled Pointer to seize upon the chance and crack the ball home via the underside of the bar.

After the break, Everton had to contend with an injury to their Scottish international full back, Alex Parker. Despite the promptings of brilliant midfielder, Bobby Collins, eventually Everton's attack ran out of steam. With their defence depleted by Parker's injury, Brian Pilkington finally took advantage. Benefiting from Jimmy McIlroy's exquisitely placed pass, it was 'Pilky''s powerful run and cross, which set up Pointer for a precisely headed winner with just four minutes remaining. Now the boot was on the other foot. Having been subdued successfully by Miller, Dave Hickson resorted to strong arm tactics in a forlorn attempt to recover lost ground. Miller and his fellow defenders proved too resolute, though. This victory lifted Burnley back into fifth place, level on six points with Spurs and Wolves. Blackburn continued to lead the pack with West Ham hard on their heels. At the other end, Everton slumped into bottom place.

## 5 September 1959

Arsenal 1 Tottenham Hotspur 1
Birmingham City 1 Manchester United 1
Blackburn Rovers 3 Sheffield Wednesday 1
Blackpool 0 Nottingham Forest 1
Chelsea 4 Burnley 1
Everton 0 Fulham 0
Luton Town 0 Bolton Wanderers 0
Manchester City 4 Wolverhampton Wanderers 6
Newcastle United 1 Preston North End 2
West Bromwich Albion 5 Leicester City 0
West Ham United 1 Leeds United 2

## Chelsea 4 v 1 Burnley

*'Lonely Boy'*

Profligacy replaced frugality at Stamford Bridge, as Burnley blew their chances with a catalogue of defensive errors. Chelsea seemed there for the taking. Their vulnerability at the back was well-known. This had been underlined in their heavy midweek defeat by a brilliant Manchester United. Chelsea would concede 91 goals during this season: 50 of these at home. On the other hand, they failed to score in just four games, notching 76 goals over the season. Only physically robust Bolton had them firing blanks. According to Jimmy Greaves' accounts, fun would often prevail over professionalism.

*Chelsea's England keeper, Reg Matthews beats Ray Pointer to the punch at Stamford Bridge [25]*

For example, a farcical own goal conceded at Everton had the team helpless with laughter. With Tommy Docherty's later arrival as coach, greater professionalism and discipline would be installed but for now they would play with the spirit of a 'pub team'.

Chelsea certainly had an abundance of youthful talent including the prodigiously gifted Greaves. 12 months previously Chelsea had put Wolves to the sword winning by 6-2, having given the Champions an early goal start. Greaves had roasted his illustrious markers – Billy Wright and Bill Slater – on that baking afternoon, scoring five of the six goals himself. Today, Burnley failed to heed that warning. Again, The Clarets had the best possible start with Connelly beating goalkeeper, Reg Matthews with a fierce cross shot in the 21st minute but a mistake by defensive wing half, Bobby Seith, allowed England right winger, Peter Brabrook to set up Charlie Livesey for the equalizer 13 minutes later. With half-time beckoning, Brabrook then fired Chelsea ahead.

After the break, Greaves shredded the Burnley defence. With his instinct for goal, his quick feet and his probing mobility he ran The Clarets' defence ragged. There were few strikers and fewer defenders who could match

Greaves' speed off the mark. He scored a controversial goal himself in the 61st minute, when he appeared to be in an offside position. He then put Livesey through to record Chelsea's fourth six minutes later. With Burnley throwing caution to the wind and Greaves in irrepressible form, the scale of the defeat could have been more humiliating.

## 8 September 1959

Birmingham City 1 Chelsea 1
Bolton Wanderers 0 Arsenal 1
Burnley 2 Preston North End 1
Fulham 3 Wolverhampton Wanderers 1
Leicester City 1 Blackpool 1
Luton Town 1 Manchester City 2
Manchester United 6 Leeds United 0
Nottingham Forest 2 Sheffield Wednesday 1
Tottenham Hotspur 2 West Ham United 2
West Bromwich Albion 2 Newcastle United 2

## Burnley 2 v 1 Preston North End

*'Here Comes Summer'*

Jerry Keller was storming up the charts on both sides of the Atlantic with his debut single. Not that there was any evidence of the summer passing as temperatures continued to hover around the 25°C mark. Despite the heat 29,175 turned up tonight. Certainly, there was passion aplenty but in the first half Burnley spluttered, being guilty of over-elaboration. With Pilkington's fizz flattened by the rugged Cunningham, Burnley were deprived of their customary thrust on the left flank. Connelly was enjoying greater freedom on the right but his colleagues were having difficulty in imposing themselves against Preston's well-organised defence. Although John Angus and Tommy Cummings were having more success in containing Tom Finney, Preston grasped a 15th minute lead after breaking quickly. Taylor's pass sent inside left Sneddon through on goal and he coolly lobbed the ball over the advancing Blacklaw.

*Preston's hard man: Willie Cunningham [26]*

After the interval, Preston's defenders continued to hold the Burnley forwards at bay. With Finney shaking off his markers' attentions and creating a succession of chances, Preston should have increased their lead. Only Blacklaw's brilliance denied them. The Burnley 'keeper pulled off some remarkable saves from Hatsell, O'Farrell and Sneddon. With time running out, manager, Harry Potts, urged Adamson and Seith to move up. This did the trick. Bowing to the greater pressure, Preston's defenders started to lose their poise. In the final 20 minutes, Preston 'keeper, Fred Else, was under constant siege. But it took two precise crosses from Connelly to turn the game. First, Ray Pointer headed a 71st minute equalizer and then 15 minutes later, Jimmy Robson headed in the winner from Connelly's gold tap service. This last gasp victory pushed Burnley back into third place just one point behind Blackburn.

In his programme notes, Harry Potts referred to the Football Association's instructions to all League Clubs asking that they tell their players 'to cut out poor gamesmanship and other unsavoury practices that bring discredit to the game of football.' Harry Potts felt that his own players already complied with this code of behaviour but expressed the hope that great progress would be made in improving standards. He thought this would help 'raise our international standing'. Perhaps Harry chose to overlook his past reputation as 'a diver'.

## 12 September 1959

Arsenal 3 Manchester City 1
Bolton Wanderers 5 West Ham United 1
Burnley 2 West Bromwich Albion 1
Fulham 4 Luton Town 2
Leeds United 2 Chelsea 1
Leicester City 0 Newcastle United 2
Manchester United 1 Tottenham Hotspur 5
Nottingham Forest 1 Everton 1
Preston North End 3 Birmingham City 2
Sheffield Wednesday 5 Blackpool 0
Wolverhampton Wanderers 3 Blackburn Rovers 1

## Burnley 2 v 1 West Bromwich Albion

*'Mona Lisa'*

At Turf Moor, the summer heat was unrelenting. There had been no rain for a month. Consequently, the pitch was bone hard. Manager, Harry Potts, blamed the concrete-like playing surfaces for the leg fractures sustained by

*West Bromwich Albion's hard man: Maurice Setters [27]*

reserve right winger, Trevor Meredith and deputy left full back, Dave Smith. Perhaps the weather was too hot for the Burnley supporters with under 24,000 attending, two thousand fewer than for the West Ham home game. West Bromwich came to Turf Moor with an excellent away record having won 10 games on their travels during the 1958/59 season. Only Champions, Wolves, had a better return. Bustling England centre-forward, Derek Kevan, was their danger man having netted 27 goals in the previous campaign. Kevan was supported by the deep-lying veteran former international striker, Ronnie Allen. In midfield, West Bromwich had the, then, current England wing half, (Sir) Bobby Robson, and the scheming inside forward, David Burnside. At the back they had the creative Don Howe and 'hard man' Maurice Setters. Setters would leave his mark upon this game, or to be more precise, upon Jimmy McIlroy. Despite an abundance of talent West Bromwich trainer, Dick Graham, remained unimpressed. Graham remarked: 'too many players, once they have gained a regular first team place, are content to jog along at the same level. They are receiving top wages and there is no incentive to improve.' How little things change in 50 years!

With players on both sides gasping in the desiccating sun, it was little surprise that the game's quality suffered. Referee Holland's leniency hardly helped as a series of petulant tackles went unpunished. West Bromwich's Joe Kennedy and David Burnside were both forced to leave the field temporarily as a result of rough treatment but Jimmy McIlroy came off worse following a reckless challenge from Setters.

Jimmy McIlroy recalled: "we were still in a heat wave and the pitch was rock hard. Maurice was up against me that day. He was just up from Devon and as strong as an Ox. As I tried to get past him, early in the game, he came in at me with a clattering shoulder charge causing me to somersault and land awkwardly on the concrete-like surface. My right shoulder felt the full force of my fall. It hurt like blazes. I thought I must have broken it. What with that and a sensation of paralysis below the waist, I thought I was in a bad way. The West Bromwich centre half, Joe Kennedy, picked me up joking, 'count yourself lucky. You only have to play against him twice a season. We have to play against him every day!' It would never be allowed today but our trainer,

Billy Dougall, patched me up with a sling and on I went. Setters was unrepentant though. He kept sniping away to his colleagues: 'break the little one arm b*****d'."

As a result of his injury, Jimmy was forced to play for all but ten minutes of the game on the right wing with one arm strapped to his side. With so few chances created at either end, it was fitting that the stalemate should be broken by a freak effort. On the stroke of half-time Bobby Robson's speculative, long-range shot somehow eluded Blacklaw's attention and the ball looped gently into the unguarded net.

Whatever Harry Potts said to his team at half-time, it certainly worked as they re-appeared for the second half with warrior-like fervour. The ailing Jimmy McIlroy was transformed into an avenging *El Cid*, tormenting West Brom's wilting defenders with twinkling wing play and rapacious crossing. But it was Burnley's other wing commander, Pilkington, who set up Robson to guide a 55th minute equalizer past West Bromwich keeper, Ray Potter. Now Burnley poured forward and, with sweet justice, Jimmy McIlroy's 64th minute centre enabled Pilkington to seal the game. The two points gained here enabled Burnley to hold onto third place, equal on 10 points with Wolves and Spurs.

## 15 September 1959

Arsenal 2 Bolton Wanderers 1
Blackpool 3 Leicester City 3
Chelsea 4 Birmingham City 2
Everton 2 Blackburn Rovers 0
Leeds United 2 Manchester United 2
Manchester City 1 Luton Town 2
Newcastle United 0 West Bromwich Albion 0
Preston North End 1 Burnley 0
Sheffield Wednesday 0 Nottingham Forest 1
West Ham United 1 Tottenham Hotspur 2
Wolverhampton Wanderers 9 Fulham 0

## Preston North End 1 v 0 Burnley

*'Only Sixteen'*

On the morning of the game, Bobby Seith rang in to say he had contracted Giant Urticaria, a form of poisoning which caused his body to swell. Bobby remembered: "it was quite frightening as there was a danger that my throat would close completely". Jean Seith added: "though Bob travelled with the team to Deepdale, his feet were so swollen he couldn't get his boots on."

*The legendary Tom Finney of Preston and England [28]*

Debutante Alex Elder was drafted in at left back with Cummings moving to right half to cover for Bob. Billy White deputised for the injured McIlroy at inside right. Poor Alex made a disastrous start, losing his winger, Tom Finney, at a 6th minute corner. The 'Preston Plumber' took full advantage, heading in Sammy Taylor's high cross. It was enough to win the game but Elder proved he was a tough competitor, emerging as Burnley's undisputed 'man-of-the match'. Finney hardly had a look in after his early gift. Elder's hold on Finney was so tight that the great man was forced to roam. But wherever Finney went, Elder was sure to follow. However, Preston were equally resolute at the back and, without McIlroy's guile, Burnley struggled to make any impression upon the Preston rear guard. With their frustrations mounting, the game slid into a flurry of wild confrontations with Pilkington booked as he sought retribution for Cunningham's rough treatment.

## 19 September 1959

Birmingham City 3 Leicester City 4
Blackburn Rovers 1 Arsenal 1
Blackpool 3 Wolverhampton Wanderers 1
Bolton Wanderers 3 Fulham 2
Chelsea 2 West Ham United 4
Everton 2 Sheffield Wednesday 1
Luton Town 1 Nottingham Forest 0
Manchester City 3 Manchester United 0
Newcastle United 1 Burnley 3
Tottenham Hotspur 5 Preston North End 1
West Bromwich Albion 3 Leeds United 0

## Newcastle United 1 v 3 Burnley

*'40 Miles of Bad Road'*

Newcastle is still a place of insurgent cold. In the 1950s, it was even less hospitable. Blackened back-to-back streets fell away sharply to the iridescently tar-struck Tyne, perforating any protection from the grey sea wind. If you were a stranger you came heavily clad. But on this day there was no relief from the burning drought. The massive shipyard cranes oscillated in the hazy heat. The St. James' Park pitch was so parched it needed to be moistened with Tyne water.

During the early fifties, Newcastle were among the strongest sides in the country. They won the FA Cup three times between 1951 and 1955 assisted by 'Wor' Jackie Milburn's pace and power up front. Subsequent boardroom squabbles had undermined their progress. In 1958, the Board decided to appoint a full-time manager, Charlie Mitten, initially on a 12-month contract. He introduced gymnastics and highland dancing into their training regime and launched a new continental kit. He also began to invest in younger players, such as the brilliant play maker, George Eastham, supplementing youthful vigour with wily experience in the form of Welsh international inside forward, Ivor Allchurch, who was signed from Swansea. However, Newcastle started the 1959/60 season in poor shape. After the opening three games they were pointless and bottom. Mitten had steadily instilled greater confidence, though. Results had started to improve, although coming into this game Newcastle were in 18th position, just one point above the relegation places.

*Hard man: Jimmy Scoular of Newcastle [29]*

Nevertheless, the Magpies were up for this contest. In front of a vociferously partisan crowd of 38,600 they flew at Burnley. Prompted by the spectral shimmying of George Eastham and Ivor Allchurch's wily scheming, the Burnley defenders were sorely stretched. Burnley centre-half, Tommy Cummings, had a particularly torrid afternoon although The Clarets' young full-backs, Angus and Elder, stood firm largely halting the advances of United's wingers, Bobby Mitchell and Gordon Hughes. But Eastham was uncontainable and in the 27th minute, he slipped a precise pass between Cummings and Angus for deputy centre-forward, Alex Tait, to nip in and put Newcastle ahead.

With McIlroy and Connelly both carrying injuries, Burnley made little early impact upon the home defence, which was solidified by the thumping aggression of Jimmy Scoular and Bob Stokoe. Few forgot their encounters with Scoular. Jimmy Greaves described him thus: 'he was built like a coke machine with a bald head and at the sides, thick wedges of unkempt dark hair. The most striking parts of Jimmy's visage were a forehead hammered flat through contact with a thousand muddy leather balls, and a nose that made Karl Malden's look like Kylie Minogue's. If Tom Waits' voice could ever be turned into a face it would look exactly like Jimmy. He was like a bag of hammers; in addition to his Exocet tackling, every part of Jimmy's body appeared to jut out whenever necessary to inflict maximum pain'.

Jimmy McIlroy had good cause to remember Scoular, too. He recalled: "we were once playing Portsmouth at Fratton Park. My marker that day was the tough, dour Glaswegian, Jimmy Scoular. Jimmy made sure to mark my card nice and early. Just as I was reaching top speed, he lunged into me venomously, catapulting me over the cinder running track, over the fenced wall and into the crowded, sunken terracing. There I collided with one of the Portsmouth supporters, causing him to be taken off to hospital. As I clambered back onto the pitch, bruised and shaken, Scoular snarled at me: 'Take that you little Fenian b*****d, that's nothing compared to what I'll do to you next time.' I was still a bit naïve about religious sectarianism and protested with bewilderment: 'But I'm a Protestant!', whereupon Scoular's attitude softened immediately. Putting his arm around my shoulders, he soothed: 'Sorry son, I didn't realise.' Jimmy Scoular never troubled me after that."

So Jimmy had no reason to fear Scoular now and stung by Newcastle's goal, neither had his team mates. Within six minutes of going behind, Burnley won a free-kick inside the Newcastle half. The alert Jimmy Robson released Ray Pointer immediately and Ray's speed proved too much for the burly home defenders. Stokoe was forced to bring him down. Although the infringement appeared to have happened inside the box, referee Windle thought otherwise. Not that it mattered. A slick exchange between wing half Jimmy Adamson and Brian Pilkington set up Jimmy McIlroy to drill home the equaliser. It was a delightful way for Adamson to celebrate his 300th League game for Burnley. Thereafter, Burnley defended with stout determination, despite having to concede a series of free-kicks as they sought to contain the dangerous Eastham and Allchurch. But once John Connelly had slammed The Clarets into the lead soon after the break, Newcastle's spirit began to evaporate and it was Connelly again, Burnley's international Bank Hall collier, who sealed the game with an outrageous acute-angled shot in the 85th minute – another late goal to confirm victory.

Almost 50 years later left-back Alex Elder told Geoff Crambie and Nathan Lee Burnley, co-authors of *'The Greatest Burnley Team of All'*: 'this was my second game. Almost 40,000 fans saw a strong Newcastle side with star players Jimmy Scoular, Bob Stokoe, Ivor Allchurch, George Eastham and

Bobby Mitchell outplayed by our team. I played as well that day as I've ever done in my career.'

This would be George Eastham's final season with the Magpies. His landmark High Court victory opened up the prospect of huge financial benefits for the better players but arguably helped create a widening gulf – socially and financially – between them and many of those who supported them.

## 26 September 1959

Arsenal 2 Blackpool 1
Blackburn Rovers 3 Everton 1
Burnley 3 Birmingham City 1
Fulham 1 Chelsea 3
Leeds United 2 Newcastle United 3
Leicester City 1 Tottenham Hotspur 1
Manchester City 2 Blackburn Rovers 1
Nottingham Forest 2 Bolton Wanderers 0
Preston North End 4 Manchester United 0
Sheffield Wednesday 2 Luton Town 0
West Ham United 4 West Bromwich Albion 1
Wolverhampton Wanderers 2 Everton 0

## Burnley 3 v 1 Birmingham City

*'Just A Little Too Much'*

Burnley made hard work of this. Birmingham were in bottom place and initially posed little threat. When Ray Pointer headed Burnley into a 9th minute lead a routine victory seemed probable. Not so. For the remainder of the first half, ex-England keeper, Gil Merrick, was hardly troubled in the Birmingham goal. While Burnley faltered The Blues regrouped. At the start of the second half, only Blacklaw's sharp save stopped 'Bunny' Larkin from putting a rejuvenated City on terms. The lesson was not heeded. 12 minutes later, with the Burnley defenders still dozing, Bryan Orritt

*Hold the front page: Jimmy Mac heads for goal [30]*

latched onto a long clearance and scored easily. Orritt was then given time and space to drill a shot against a post. However, this let off finally galvanized The Clarets into action. McIlroy began to exert more influence in midfield and Connelly started to get the better of full back, Farmer. As a result Burnley's attacks gathered momentum and menace. Whilst there was an increasing air of predictability about Burnley scoring, the manner in which their goal came about was quite unexpected. Jimmy McIlroy scored with a 69th minute header.

Jimmy explained: "Heading was my main weakness. It was apparent before my teens. I have always had a problem if anything comes too close to my eyes. It can be as innocuous as the movement of a baby's arm. I always blink. Managers and coaches worked on this failing with praiseworthy diligence, the result was that I was able to jump higher. Yet having jumped, I still couldn't head the ball. If I ever managed to head the ball my Burnley team mates would make cracks like, 'McIlroy will have to wash his hair tonight'. I once scored with a bullet header from Brian Pilkington's cross. He couldn't believe what happened. The truth was I couldn't get out of the way in time."

This goal against Birmingham was quite different. Lest Jimmy dismisses this as a fabrication, the proof lies in a photograph from his own book *Right Inside Soccer* published in 1960. Here we see Jimmy jumping unchallenged at the far post, rising with perfect timing to meet Robson's thumped cross and heading the ball past the despairing arms of England centre half, Trevor Smith. Heaven knows where Gil Merrick was. Whether Jimmy's eyes remained opened or not cannot be determined. It hardly matters. With Burnley in command, John Connelly's added a flattering 89th minute third goal, for in truth this was a complacent, below-par showing.

Long-time Burnley supporter, Dave Cooper, said that this game has stuck in his memory, recalling: "I've always been a Burnley supporter, ever since I can remember. I had the full strip for my 7th birthday (or Christmas) and loved it. My dad too was a Burnley supporter and I guess that was the reason. Born in Stacksteads, Bacup in the Rossendale Valley, Burnley was the natural choice in the 50s and 60s. No longer so though; when I visit my mum now in Rossendale there is a preference for the red and white of a certain Stretford team.

Anyway, on Saturday 26 September 1959, just five weeks before my 9th birthday, I was to be taken by my dad to see my heroes. Birmingham City was the opposition. We always went in 'The Stand' or 'The Enclosure'. Stands didn't have names then as you only had one. The Enclosure' was a standing area in front of 'The Stand' and was more salubrious than the other standing sections. Here you could engage with rival supporters in friendly banter. I think this was half the enjoyment for my dad. Little boys were normally ushered to the front for a better view as indeed was I but being a 'mardy' kid I had to keep looking back to make sure my dad was still there – he always was. I think 'The Enclosure' became our normal choice but initially we went in 'The Stand' and most frequently my dad would say to the 'ticketing man', "You're not going to make me pay for the little one(me) are you". After some discussion, I was normally let in free with dad having to lift me over the turnstile to keep the numbers correct. If the attendance figures were ever announced I always secretly added on one. So, there I was watching Burnley versus Birmingham City from 'The Stand'. I think Burnley scored first but it was 1-1 by half time. In the second half, I remember seeing a lot of wing play and we went on to win 3-1. Jimmy McIlroy and Ray Pointer became my heroes overnight. I remember dad explaining to me how Jimmy McIlroy used to take penalties; making to send it to the keeper's right but hitting the ball with the outside of his right boot so it went in to the keeper's left. I tried this many times later but never perfected it. I still have the programme from this game (and many, many more) priced 3d. On the back of the programme it suggested you should enjoy a pint in a Massey House. Dad was only too happy to take up this suggestion on the way home. Pop and crisps in the car were fine by me.'

## First Division

| **26 September 1959** | *P* | *W* | *D* | *L* | *F* | *A* | *Pts* | *Goal average* |
|---|---|---|---|---|---|---|---|---|
| 1. Tottenham Hotspur | 10 | 5 | 5 | 0 | 25 | 11 | 15 | 2.27 |
| 2. Wolverhampton Wanderers | 10 | 6 | 2 | 2 | 31 | 17 | 14 | 1.82 |
| 3. Arsenal | 10 | 5 | 4 | 1 | 17 | 10 | 14 | 1.70 |
| 4. BURNLEY | 10 | 7 | 0 | 3 | 22 | 17 | 14 | 1.29 |
| 5. Blackburn Rovers | 10 | 5 | 2 | 3 | 19 | 12 | 12 | 1.58 |
| 6. West Ham United | 10 | 5 | 2 | 3 | 22 | 17 | 12 | 1.29 |
| 7. Preston North End | 10 | 4 | 3 | 3 | 19 | 18 | 11 | 1.06 |
| 8. Nottingham Forest | 10 | 4 | 3 | 3 | 11 | 11 | 11 | 1.00 |
| 9. West Bromwich Albion | 10 | 3 | 4 | 3 | 19 | 15 | 10 | 1.27 |
| 10. Chelsea | 10 | 4 | 2 | 4 | 24 | 24 | 10 | 1.00 |
| 11. Manchester City | 10 | 5 | 0 | 5 | 20 | 21 | 10 | 0.95 |
| 12. Leicester City | 10 | 3 | 4 | 3 | 16 | 22 | 10 | 0.73 |
| 13. Sheffield Wednesday | 10 | 4 | 1 | 5 | 15 | 13 | 9 | 1.15 |
| 14. Blackpool | 10 | 3 | 3 | 4 | 12 | 16 | 9 | 0.75 |
| 15. Fulham | 10 | 4 | 1 | 5 | 17 | 27 | 9 | 0.63 |
| 16. Manchester United | 10 | 3 | 2 | 5 | 21 | 24 | 8 | 0.88 |

| | *P* | *W* | *D* | *L* | *F* | *A* | *Pts* | *Goal average* |
|---|---|---|---|---|---|---|---|---|
| 17. Newcastle United | 10 | 3 | 2 | 5 | 16 | 21 | 8 | 0.76 |
| 18. Leeds United | 10 | 3 | 2 | 5 | 14 | 23 | 8 | 0.61 |
| 19. Bolton Wanderers | 10 | 3 | 1 | 6 | 13 | 16 | 7 | 0.81 |
| 20. Everton | 10 | 2 | 3 | 5 | 12 | 18 | 7 | 0.67 |
| 21. Luton Town | 10 | 2 | 3 | 5 | 8 | 13 | 7 | 0.62 |
| 22. Birmingham City | 10 | 1 | 3 | 6 | 14 | 21 | 5 | 0.67 |

# OCTOBER 1959

With a General Election imminent, the Labour Party under Hugh Gaitskell promised to abolish purchase tax if elected: a far cry from New Labour's obsession with VAT. The USSR's space race was turning into a sprint with their latest space craft, Lunik III, now managing to orbit the moon and send back first pictures of the 'dark side of the moon' to the underwhelmed Soviet scientists. But where the Soviet boffins found monotony, Pink Floyd found creative inspiration. Here in Britain, we refused to be left behind by the technological revolution. Bird's Eye launched their frozen peas, remaining mindful that many British families prided themselves on their gardening skills. 'Only peas as sweet as you grow in your garden are good enough to be Bird's Eye Peas', soothed the slogan, belying the advert's somewhat jaundiced colouring of the nation's favourite vegetable.

Macmillan's Government was re-elected with a thumping majority. It was the Tories third victory on the bounce. 'Super Mac' had campaigned on the slogan of 'Never Had It So Good'. While Mac passed off the triumph with a nonchalant 'It has gone off rather well', Gaitskell attributed his party's defeat to internal bickering. Both Macmillan and Gaitskell shared the surprising belief that the 'class war is now obsolete' and within days of the defeat a Labour spokesman announced that 'nationalisation plans will win no votes'. In Sao Paulo, the polls had a wilder flavour as a rhinoceros was elected to the local council. The week also represented a parting of the ways with Errol Flynn, a hell-raiser on and off screen. Just prior to his death Flynn announced with due solemnity: 'the rest of my life will be devoted to women and litigation.'

A UK survey revealed that a third of 15-year-old boys were regular smokers proving *'You're never alone with a Strand'*. Meanwhile, the Health minister pledged a 20 million pound investment for new hospitals. Almost 10 years ahead of its time, a Royal Mint report discussed decimalisation and the possibility of introducing five and ten shillings coins.

Elvis, Connie Francis and The Everly Brothers swept to victory in the World sections of this year's New Musical Express Readers' Poll, just as they had done in 1958. However, in the British categories, there were new winners: Cliff Richard; Shirley Bassey and Russ 'teeth and smiles' Conway. Craig Douglas headed the 'New Singer' list, followed closely by Billy Fury and Anthony Newley, then the husband of Joan Collins.

Just as a LSE study recommended the replacement of the London County Council with a Greater London authority, a London housing official revealed that slum clearances were not as successful as had been expected. He said: "re-housing causes misery for residents who are moved." The tower blocks were not the answer: so much for high hopes. Macmillan pledged his new Government to a policy of de-colonisation. In this week's Queen's speech, political freedom was promised for troubled Cyprus and Nigeria. But imperial ambitions were not a thing of the past for in Kashmir, the Indian troops were forced to stubbornly resist Chinese expansionism.

In July 1957, when Macmillan made his famous remark: "most of our people have never had it so good", he was referring to the rising prosperity enjoyed by British citizens. The array of advertisements in the thrice weekly editions of the *Burnley Express* reflected the consumer boom of the late fifties. Increasing numbers of families, and housewives, in particular, were now enjoying greater relief from domestic drudgery. As a result of rising wages, reduced income tax and the re-introduction of hire purchase agreements, a growing range of labour-saving appliances had become more affordable. There were copious advertisements for electric cookers, washing machines, spin dryers, fridges and vacuum cleaners. Between September 1957 and November 1959 ownership of washing machines and refrigerators had increased by 54% and 58% respectively. With expectations rising exponentially the standard of quality products was continually lifting. For example, Burnley families no longer had to risk the uncertain elements in drying their laundry if they could afford the 'Luxury' drying and airing cabinets that were available at £10/19/6 (£10.98p) from Dorman and Smith of Preston.

The new consumerism ushered in a more customer-focused approach. For example, a *Belling Electric cooker* was paraded with the claim that '10,000 women designed this exciting new (cooker)', even if this seems like an extravagant take on the contemporary quip: 'how many council workers does it take to change a light bulb?' The significance of this advertisement lay in its target. This was not picking out the 'man of the house', the traditional breadwinner, even if he still held the purse strings. Instead, it was making a direct appeal to housewives who, in the new marketing world, were being reframed as the 'dynamic', 'efficient' and 'glamorous' managers of the new domestic technology. Judging by the observations of Willmott and Young in their 1959 study of family attitudes in a London suburb, these sort of advertisements were not only playing upon housewives' hopes of material success, but were also exploiting their fears of social inferiority.

A new *Hoover Junior* vacuum cleaner was also available on hire purchase at Currys with the claim that: 'it BEATS as it sweeps as it cleans'. Their advertisement comprised a sketch of a pensive housewife with her husband leaving for work. The accompanying strap line read: 'will you be alone in the house all day today?' Hoover and Hotpoint struck at the heart of the matter. Hoover proclaimed that their products were 'saving millions of housewives from hard, wearisome drudgery', reinforcing their point with pictures of smiling young housewives in glamorous dresses and high heels contentedly vacuuming or washing. In a similar vein, Hotpoint named their new washing machine 'The Liberator'. Bendix displayed a young woman out on the town with her underlying indemnity clause: 'Bendix is doing my weekly wash at this very moment'. In 1959, a new Bendix cost £83.50p. This price was seven times more than the national average weekly wage, but with hire purchase available, these commodities became more affordable. English Electric depicted a housewife dressed like a dinner party hostess blithely demonstrating the contents of her bulging fridge and although her 'pinny' hinted that the culinary treats were the fruits of labour, it didn't look as if she had sweated too much over them. It seemed as if these devices were being sold as much for their lifestyle benefits as for their utility. Perhaps the *Hidden Persuaders* had negotiated the A6 after all.

The immediate question in Burnley was whether the local economy was robust enough to support these aspirations. The politicians were left with an invidious dilemma. Should they emphasise how bad things appeared to be in the hope of securing greater Government financial support? This risked an escalation of constituents' anxieties. That might prompt yet further migration away and it might also scupper their Party's chances at the polls. But if they played up the prospects of growth and diversification in the hope of attracting incoming business, there was a danger of appearing out of touch with local folk's concerns.

Prospective Tory Parliamentary candidate for Nelson and Colne, Councillor John Crabtree stuck with the 'peace and prosperity' theme. He stated: "New industries are coming. I assure you within the next twelve months there will be a shortage of labour not jobs in this area. When expansion and reorganisation are complete there will be more than enough jobs for local people…Cotton is in my blood. The new schemes will provide a rebirth of the industry which even now was beginning at certain mills.'"

Councillor Crabtree may well have been encouraged by the report of John Cockcroft's speech at the Burnley Textile Society at the beginning of October. John Cockcroft of Cockcroft and Sons, Todmorden, spoke enthusiastically about the 'fine new machines' he had seen at the Milan Textile Exhibition which he believed 'could boost cotton's future'. Others were less sure.

Sydney Silverman, the existing Labour MP for Nelson and Colne, took issue with the reorganisation process pointing out that some mills with closing notices still had full order books for the next 18 months, concluding that the compensation scheme was an 'example of the Tories looking after their own. The manufacturers lose nothing – they gain.'

Local political leaders sought further assistance from the Board of Trade for the introduction of new industries. A wide advertising campaign was initiated – on the radio, television and on posters at railway stations – drawing attention to the industrial potential available in Burnley. Representations were also made to Government about improving road communications.

On the upside there was news of a new factory, to be opened by Michelin on the Heasandford Industrial Estate in June 1960. Corrugated board was to be produced by a Middlesex-based company at a former Nelson Mill. Jobs were also being advertised at Alma Mill in Padiham where prospective employees would 'learn velvet weaving'. On the downside, the National Coal Board announced the closure of 'many Lancashire mines nearing the end of their useful lives'. This would result in 10,000 job losses. Among the pits identified for closure were the Burnley pits at Reedley and Salterford.

Meanwhile the water crisis was intensifying. On 14 October standpipes were introduced with 33,000 Burnley households cut off from normal supplies. Burnley was the first Northern town to resort to standpipes. Many local residents angrily accused members of the Burnley's Chamber of Trade of 'gross mismanagement'. There were growing health worries, too, with a number of residents stating that the water 'did not taste nice'. Burnley's Medical Officer of Health had to assure residents quickly that the water posed no threat to their health. However, tempers were not improved after a 24-hour deluge on 27 October poured millions of gallons into the local reservoirs and yet thousands of families still had to line up in the rain grumpily awaiting their turn at the standpipes. Although normal supplies were restored to all homes within the following two weeks, at the Burnley Council Meeting on the 7th November it was moved that there should be an enquiry into how the water crisis came about. With councillors and officers anxious to defend their reputations, 'fireworks' ensued.

The electoral war of words over the local employment situation was finally settled in Labour's favour on the 8 October. Daniel Jones won the Burnley seat with an increased majority while Sydney Silverman was returned to Parliament in Nelson and Colne, albeit with a reduced share of the poll. Silverman attributed this apparent loss of popularity to the fact that 4,000 Labour voters had left his constituency since the previous General Election of 1955.

Judged by Hollywood accolades, the films of the year included William Wyler's bloated Judeo-Roman spectacle, *Ben Hur*; Billy Wilder's drag farce *Some Like It Hot*; Otto Preminger's tense courtroom drama *Anatomy of Murder*; Howard Hawks' last stand western *Rio Bravo* and Hitchcock's iconic thriller *North by Northwest.* Although *Ben Hur* netted a record 11 Oscars, only equalled 40 years later by *Titanic,* helping save MGM studios from bankruptcy, this blockbuster has possibly travelled less well than its contemporaries, notwithstanding its epic chariot race. After *Monty Python's Life of Brian* it has become almost impossible to take such pseudo Biblical pomp seriously. In this respect we should be truly grateful to *Biggus Diccus* and his friends. Meanwhile, as the fifties drew to a close a series of British films were released which had greater relevance to contemporary issues at home.

By 1959, there was increasing disquiet among the middle classes about the power of the British trade unions. These anxieties were played out in two major British films of the time: *The Angry Silence* and the satirical *I'm Alright Jack* both of which represented shop stewards as petty, militant shop floor Napoleons. It was true that shop steward rebelliousness had increased. The growing number of 'wildcat' strikes, most notably in the car industry, was testament to that. With consumer demand increasing and employment levels high, trade union militants had better opportunities to flex their muscles. However, middle class fears of manual worker insurrection were overblown. During the fifties, Britain had a comparatively good record in terms of working days lost to strike action. Among the World's top ten 'free' industrial nations, only West Germany and Sweden had better figures.

In December 1959 the film *Yesterday's Enemy* was being shown at the Burnley Palace. This sardonic, gritty anti-war drama was billed in the *Burnley Express* as 'the most outspoken film of our time', principally because it suggested that the British were not always honourable in combat. Almost certainly influenced by the Suez fiasco, this message struck at the heart of strongly held beliefs about British courage and integrity. After all, had we not demonstrated these qualities so amply during the Battle of Britain? Had we not stood alone in 1940 in defying the evil of Nazism while our continental allies had capitulated so feebly? Our brave stand against Hitler's Armada remained central to the myth of the new Elizabethan age. The associated belief that 'British is best' underpinned both our complacent isolationism on the sports field and our excessive confidence in our expanding economy. Besides, if we were no longer a world power we could console ourselves that we had greater resourcefulness, courage and integrity allied to our commitment to fair play. Against almost overwhelming odds, this proud myth was championed by many, as if the size of the fight in the bulldog was more important than its physique. Metaphorically, the myth was played out in a catalogue of plucky, self-reverential Brit war dramas of the mid and late fifties – *The Dambusters, Battle of the River Plate, The Desert Rats, Dunkirk, The Cockleshell Heroes* and *Reach for the Sky,* – in which outstanding acts of courage were demonstrated with a stiff upper lip or jaunty conviction. And yet there was an ever-growing list of sporting insults to add to our Suez-inflicted injuries and economic frailties. But still the myth of British supremacy tottered on, albeit confined within a diminishing comfort zone.

The central theme of Tony Richardson's 1960 film *The Entertainer*, based on John Osborne's play, was one of terminal national decline. Historian Dominic Sandbrook observed: 'just as Archie Rice's desperate routines fail to mask the decline of music hall, so the country's leaders, off stage, drag a decaying Britain into the Suez crisis to defend national honour' and in so doing, kill Archie's son during the ill-judged landings. The nation's obsession with hardy jingoism only began to be exposed to public ridicule in the early sixties, prodded by the new boom in satirical humour. But as the *Beyond the Fringe* mob found frequently, scoffing at Second World War heroics was considered to be a no-go area, by a provincial older generation who insisted that Britain should be ever great and grateful.

As the Second World War began to recede from view a new form of conflict began to take centre stage at our local Odeons and ABCs – this was the 'class war'. Not only was the 'trade union' films evidence of this, for we also had the cinematic versions of the 'New Wave' books and plays. Probably, the most feted of these was *Room at the Top*, Jack Clayton's big screen version of John Braine's steamy novel. With advertisements promising 'a savage story of lust and ambition' the film did very good business, helping make the author, a former librarian a very wealthy man. The story plotted the rise of Joe Lampton, an aggressively materialistic and ambitious young man from a working class West Riding background who treated middle-class women as disposable commodities, much like his fashionable Vantella shirts. Mimicking his anti-hero, middle class Braine explained: 'what I want to do is drive through Bradford in a Rolls-Royce with two naked women on either side of me covered in jewels.' Either this limousine had strangely placed controls or one of his jewel-encrusted 'Godivas' had to be prepared to brave the Northern cold.

In contrast, Arthur Seaton, the central working-class character of Alan Sillitoe's *Saturday Night and Sunday Morning* was not ruthlessly ambitious, just callously hedonistic. In the 1960 film version, Albert Finney, playing the part of Arthur, insisted: 'what I'm after is a good time. All the rest is propaganda.' Neither Seaton nor Lampton were interested in revolution. They were neither class warriors nor 'angry young men' but simply determined to be free of moral strictures or social barriers in attaining what they wanted. It was left to Jimmy Porter, in *Look Back in Anger* – a 1959 film of Osborne's controversial play – to actually express his contempt for the middle classes, not sparing the two women who loved him. Disenfranchised by higher education from his working class roots, Porter bemoans the lack of worthwhile causes. But his invective is issued purely from the safe confines of his nuptial bed-sitter. He is no more than a pathetic grumpy young man, who cannot keep his toys in the pram; hardly a sturdy combatant in the British class war – a sure case of 'all mouth and no trousers'.

## 3 October 1959

Birmingham City 2 Leeds United 0
Blackburn Rovers 1 Preston North End 4
Blackpool 1 Manchester City 3
Bolton Wanderers 1 Sheffield Wednesday 0
Everton 3 Arsenal 1
Fulham 3 Nottingham Forest 1
Luton Town 1 Wolverhampton Wanderers 5
Manchester United 4 Leicester City 1
Newcastle United 0 West Ham United 0
Tottenham Hotspur 1 Burnley 1
West Bromwich Albion 1 Chelsea 3

## Spurs 1 v 1 Burnley

*'High Hopes'*

Only an 87th minute equaliser from Brian Miller enabled Burnley to snatch a point from table-topping Spurs on the hottest October day on record. Both sides were without their most influential players. Spurs had lost keeper, Bill Brown, left-half, Dave Mackay, and right-half, Danny Blanchflower, to the Northern Ireland versus Scotland international. For their part, Burnley were forced to play without their Northern Ireland schemer, Jimmy McIlroy.

Initially, Burnley seemed indisposed, uncertain of how to adjust to McIlroy's absence. In the opening 20 minutes, Spurs' sharp one-touch football bewildered them and it was no surprise when, after seven minutes of

*Billy White miscues badly on the hottest October Saturday on record [31]*

pressure, Welsh right winger, Terry Medwin, put Spurs ahead. The frail but deft Tommy Harmer combined with bustling Bobby Smith to set up the chance.

After Harry Potts had directed John Connelly and Billy White to swap positions, Burnley began to make more impact. Also Adamson and Miller began to neutralise Harmer's influence. Deprived of their playmaker's influence, Spurs began to splutter although Burnley's increasing pressure made little impact until Miller's late salvation. The draw proved of greater value to Burnley who leap-frogged defeated Arsenal to take third place, whereas Spurs had to concede top spot to victorious Wolves.

## 10 October 1959

Birmingham City 0 Sheffield Wednesday 0
Burnley 1 Blackpool 4
Chelsea 0 Bolton Wanderers 2
Leeds United 3 Everton 3
Leicester City 2 Blackburn Rovers 3
Manchester United 4 Arsenal 2
Newcastle United 2 Nottingham Forest 1
Preston North End 1 Manchester City 5
Tottenham Hotspur 5 Wolverhampton Wanderers 1

West Bromwich Albion 2 Fulham 4
West Ham United 3 Luton Town 1

## Burnley 1 v 4 Blackpool

*'Mack the Knife'*

This game should have been a home banker. It was not. Despite forcing nineteen corners Burnley could score once only. This was in the 5th minute when Jimmy Robson latched onto Connelly's pass and netted at the second time of asking. Lowly Blackpool were expected to disintegrate. They did not. They did not even need the wily skills of Stan Matthews to prevail. Within six minutes of going behind, Blackpool's left winger, Kaye waltzed through Burnley's inattentive defence to equalize. Two minutes later, the visitors were in front. With the Burnley defenders expecting an offside decision, inside left Dave Durie, left in acres of space, calmly lobbed the ball over Blacklaw. Had Blackpool's Scottish keeper, George Farm, not been in such superb form, Burnley might have salvaged something for time and time again he produced magnificent last ditch saves. He was well supported by his redoubtable defence, in which Hugh and Jim Kelly were outstanding. With Burnley pushing more men forward, gaps began to appear which Dave Durie exploited ruthlessly. His 48th and 73rd minute strikes earned him a prestigious hat-trick and his side a magnificent 4-1 victory. As a result of this unexpected reverse, Burnley fell back to fourth place, three points behind Spurs.

*George Farm denies Burnley again tipping over a shot from Robson [32]*

Manager, Harry Potts, might have rued his generosity. Between the Spurs and Blackpool fixtures, he had agreed to fit in two friendly games: at Folkestone, to open the Southern League side's new floodlights and at Plymouth, in a testimonial game for the son of the Burnley physiotherapist, Billy Dougall. Harry fielded strong sides in both games. He appeared not to have had second thoughts. For on 19 October he arranged for Burnley to play the Great Britain Olympic Team. Harry took his ambassadorial duties very seriously. He commented: 'we can look back upon (the games at Folkestone and Plymouth) with the greatest of pleasure: firstly, because each of these games brought us high commendations from our opponents and their supporters. That is a very nice recollection to come home with. Now I want to pay my own tribute in this public manner to our players for the splendid way in which they embraced these additional matches coming, as they did, right on the heels of the strenuous six weeks opening to the football season.'

## 17 October 1959

Arsenal 0 Preston North End 3
Blackburn Rovers 3 Burnley 2
Blackpool 3 Leeds United 3
Bolton Wanderers 0 West Bromwich Albion 0
Everton 0 West Ham United 1
Fulham 4 Newcastle United 3
Luton Town 1 Chelsea 2
Manchester City 3 Leicester City 2
Nottingham Forest 0 Birmingham City 2
Sheffield Wednesday 2 Tottenham Hotspur 1
Wolverhampton Wanderers 3 Manchester United 2

## Blackburn Rovers 3 v 2 Burnley

*'Broken-Hearted Melody'*

As with any heavy home defeat, there were the usual recriminations. This time goalkeeper, Adam Blacklaw, was in the firing line, with sniping supporters comparing him unfavourably with the injured Colin McDonald. Harry Potts' received his fair share of criticism, too. A number of supporters were unhappy about the Burnley defenders switching positions during a game, citing the defensive catastrophes against Blackpool. It seemed that they were not yet ready for 'Total Football'.

With John Connelly making his full England debut in the Home International against Wales, Harry chose to replace him with Brian Pilkington who was switched from the left wing. Gordon Harris was drafted in as Pilky's replacement. Jimmy Robson had been struggling with his form, as some carping supporters had pointed out, so Harry brought in Billy White to take his place. Bobby Seith also took over from Tommy Cummings, having finally recovered from his Giant Urticaria illness. As for Blackburn, tough right half, Ronnie Clayton was on England duty, too, as skipper. Bill Smith was selected in his place.

Blackburn were tough competitors. They had a dependable keeper in Harry Leyland and a robust half-back line of Clayton, Woods and McGrath. But it was up front where they had an abundance of talent. Their forward line today read: Bryan Douglas, Peter Dobing, Derek 'Cheyenne' Dougan, Roy Vernon and Alastair MacLeod. Interestingly, Fred Pickering was selected as their left back in place of the current Wigan Chairman, Dave Whelan. Pickering was an indifferent full-back but he proved to be a potent centre forward with Rovers, Everton and Blackpool, also representing England in that position.

As expected, this was a rough and tumble contest in the best traditions of Burnley-Rovers derbies. 33,600 piled into Ewood Park to watch an absorbing, uncompromising if error-strewn game. Had Adam Blacklaw not made two calamitous errors, Burnley might have come away with something. However, he was not at fault for Rovers' 2nd minute opener.

*With the Rovers defence at sixes and sevens Ray Pointer narrowly fails to score [33]*

Derek Dougan was nicknamed 'Cheyenne' because of his supposed similarity to Clint Walker, the TV Western star. Dougan was certainly a consummate showman and lapped up the attention he courted. He could play a bit, too. True to form his opening goal was something of a show piece. After taking on and beating three Burnley defenders, Dougan let fly with the cracking shot that gave Blacklaw no chance. The lead did not last long. Brian Pilkington tied things up in the 14th minute, turning in Jimmy McIroy's left wing cross at the far post. Parity lasted for thirteen minutes before Adam Blacklaw made the first of his howlers, inexplicably allowing Peter Dobing's acute-angled drive to slip out of his hands, over his shoulder and into the goal. Despite Elder's excellent containment of the dangerous Douglas, Rovers deserved their half-time lead.

After the break Burnley turned the screw. Within three minutes of the restart they were level. Under pressure in his own box, Douglas panicked, scything the ball over his 'keeper, Leyland. With Burnley's midfielders and full-backs moving up to support their forwards, the Rovers' defence was at full stretch. Although the game was more notable for its speed and robustness than its quality, Burnley did produce a five-man move that resulted in Harris flashing a drive inches wide of Rovers' left hand post. It seemed as if Burnley would take the points. Leyland was by far the busier keeper but Blacklaw was the more jittery. The game turned on a defensive error. In the 81st minute, Blackburn won a free kick just outside the Burnley box. Roy Vernon proceeded to lob the ball gently over the wall. It was not clear whether Blacklaw was distracted by Douglas's presence or he was unsighted since he failed to move as Vernon's gentle chip looped into the net.

*Blacklaw dives at the feet of Welsh inside forward, Roy Vernon [34]*

Apart from the rough tackling and Burnley's boobs, the other main talking point was Elder's tight marking of Bryan Douglas. One older supporter was overheard as saying: "when Douglas sits down for breakfast tomorrow I wonder whether he'll find Elder alongside him?" At this point few Burnley supporters gave their team much of a chance of seizing the League Championship from Wolves. They had fallen to 7th position, their lowest placing so far. It is easy to forget that few triumphant seasons feature uninterrupted success. A startling revival was just around the corner.

## 24 October 1959

Birmingham City 2 Fulham 4
Burnley 4 Manchester City 3
Chelsea 1 Everton 0
Leeds United 0 Blackburn Rovers 1
Leicester City 2 Arsenal 2
Manchester United 3 Sheffield Wednesday 1
Newcastle United 0 Bolton Wanderers 2
Preston North End 4 Wolverhampton Wanderers 3
Tottenham Hotspur 2 Nottingham Forest 1
West Bromwich Albion 4 Luton Town 0
West Ham United 1 Blackpool 0

## Burnley 4 v 3 Manchester City

*'Sea of Love'*

On the morning of 24 October the dry, warm weather finally broke. The rain swished down all day and throughout the following week, finally bringing about the removal of the hated standpipes. Burnley's indifferent run finally broke too, against the form team from Maine Road. City's five wins on the bounce had lifted them thirteen places from 18th spot to 5th.

Significantly, Jimmy McIlroy was back to full fitness and, despite being double marked, he made things happen all around him. Burnley's 15th minute goal was scored by Pilkington but McIlroy was the architect. Having drawn two City defenders out of position McIlroy slipped the ball through the inviting gap for 'Pilky' to score simply. McIlroy seemed to be everywhere. The second goal, guided in by Pointer three minutes later, was his creation, too. It came from Jimmy's left wing cross, after he had mesmerised City full back, Cliff Sear. Blacklaw was back at his best, too, saving brilliantly from Colin Barlow's fierce drive.

Veteran play maker, George Hannah, was City's version of Jimmy Mac. After a ragged start to the second half, Hannah imposed himself on the game with a succession of incisive runs and deft passes. He could score, too, as he proved in the 78th minute after a slick exchange with City's creative captain, Ken Barnes. This reverse stung Burnley into action once more with deputy inside forward, Billy White, snatching two close range goals in the 85th and 86th minute. This should have sealed the game but Burnley's frailty at the back had not been resolved. A minute later Hannah reduced the deficit with his second and then with two minutes left Colbridge shook off Angus's close attention to score City's third. A nervous finish followed. On City's last visit, they overturned Burnley's first half three-goal lead to win 4-3 but despite some heart stopping moments there was to be no repetition. Burnley's victory lifted them up to 6th position.

*Les McDowall's Manchester City side, charging up the table in October 1959 [35]*

Reverend David Wiseman recalled that Ray Pointer's performance drew particular praise. "(Ray epitomised) total commitment, which involved him in difficult and sometimes dangerous situations." As reported by the *Burnley Express*: 'Ray and City centre half, McTavish chased a long pass and disputed possession wide of the goal on the dead ball line. Pointer trying to turn at speed, crashed into the boundary wall hurting the back of his neck. (Club doctor) Dr. Iven and (trainer) Ray Bennion rushed round and ambulance men were on the scene with a stretcher. The doctor and trainer half-carried him between them towards the dressing room. It looked like a permanent retirement for Pointer, but to everyone's astonishment, he came out again after a few minutes and played better than before.' As David concluded: "such was Ray!"

## 31 October 1959

Arsenal 3 Birmingham City 0
Blackburn Rovers 1 Manchester United 1
Blackpool 0 Preston North End 2
Bolton Wanderers 1 Leeds United 1
Everton 6 Leicester City 1
Fulham 1 West Ham United 0
Luton Town 1 Burnley 1
Manchester City 1 Tottenham Hotspur 2
Nottingham Forest 3 Chelsea 1
Sheffield Wednesday 2 West Bromwich Albion 0
Wolverhampton Wanderers 2 Newcastle United 0

## Luton Town 1 v 1 Burnley

*'Three Bells'*

*Bottom club Luton proved a stiff test [36]*

Burnley Chairman, Bob Lord was up against it. The Burnley butcher had been fined after a dirty finger bandage was found in one of his stews. As usual, he didn't go down without a fight. Regrettably, Burnley came to Luton with little of their Chairman's combative spirit. What should have been a regulation victory against the bottom side turned into a sluggish struggle. It could have been worse, too. Both Northern Irish international winger, Billy Bingham and inside forward, Dave Pacey, spurned good chances of building upon Scottish international, Allan Brown's 9th minute lead. Burnley's only note of quality came from Pointer's blistering left-footed equalizer after 25 minutes. As a result of this disappointing draw, Burnley fell back one place to 7th position, four points adrift of leaders, Spurs. The Clarets' defence remained a cause for concern, having conceded 29 goals in their first 15 games, twelve more than Spurs.

Harry Potts explained the below par performance thus: 'No doubt many of our supporters were counting on a win for our League side at Luton. I would remind you that it is always regarded as a good point for an opposing side to get one here because the comparative smallness of the pitch is a very disturbing factor to visiting sides. In my experience I cannot recall playing in, or seeing, a good football match at Luton's headquarters, which I feel sure is accounted for by the dimensions of the pitch.'

In reflecting upon this season almost fifty years on, Jimmy Robson remarked: "it was never a push-over taking on these struggling teams on their own turf. It didn't matter whether they were any good or not, they would start by battering you. Teams would play to win in those days but just because we all adopted a more attacking style, there was still a fair share of defending to do."

The Luton Town programme notes extended a special welcome to Herr Liesengang, Mayor of Spandau who was reported to be especially interested in 'youth development'. Don't mention the score. The programme also told us that the Butlin Young Ladies would provide the half-time entertainment. Cue Ruth Madoc. The programme carried an advertisement for a Murphy's VHF radio, which at 14 pounds, three shillings and sixpence seems extraordinarily expensive. That translates to around £650 in today's values!

## First Division

| **31 October 1959** | *P* | *W* | *D* | *L* | *F* | *A* | *Pts* | *Goal average* |
|---|---|---|---|---|---|---|---|---|
| 1. Tottenham Hotspur | 15 | 8 | 6 | 1 | 36 | 17 | 22 | 2.12 |
| 2. Wolverhampton Wanderers | 15 | 9 | 2 | 4 | 45 | 29 | 20 | 1.55 |
| 3. West Ham United | 15 | 8 | 3 | 4 | 27 | 19 | 19 | 1.42 |
| 4. Blackburn Rovers | 15 | 8 | 3 | 4 | 28 | 21 | 19 | 1.33 |
| 5. Preston North End | 15 | 8 | 3 | 4 | 33 | 27 | 19 | 1.22 |
| 6. Fulham | 15 | 9 | 1 | 5 | 33 | 35 | 19 | 0.94 |
| 7. BURNLEY | 15 | 8 | 2 | 5 | 31 | 29 | 18 | 1.07 |
| 8. Arsenal | 15 | 6 | 5 | 4 | 25 | 22 | 17 | 1.14 |
| 9. Manchester City | 15 | 8 | 0 | 7 | 35 | 31 | 16 | 1.13 |
| 10. Chelsea | 15 | 7 | 2 | 6 | 31 | 31 | 16 | 1.00 |
| 11. Bolton Wanderers | 15 | 6 | 3 | 6 | 19 | 17 | 15 | 1.12 |
| 12. Manchester United | 15 | 6 | 3 | 6 | 35 | 32 | 15 | 1.09 |
| 13. Sheffield Wednesday | 15 | 6 | 2 | 7 | 20 | 18 | 14 | 1.11 |
| 14. West Bromwich Albion | 15 | 4 | 5 | 6 | 26 | 24 | 13 | 1.08 |
| 15. Nottingham Forest | 15 | 5 | 3 | 7 | 17 | 21 | 13 | 0.81 |
| 16. Everton | 15 | 4 | 4 | 7 | 24 | 25 | 12 | 0.96 |
| 17. Blackpool | 15 | 4 | 4 | 7 | 20 | 26 | 12 | 0.77 |
| 18. Newcastle United | 15 | 4 | 3 | 8 | 21 | 30 | 11 | 0.70 |
| 19. Leeds United | 15 | 3 | 5 | 7 | 21 | 33 | 11 | 0.64 |
| 20. Leicester City | 15 | 3 | 5 | 7 | 24 | 40 | 11 | 0.60 |
| 21. Birmingham City | 15 | 3 | 4 | 8 | 20 | 28 | 10 | 0.71 |
| 22. Luton Town | 15 | 2 | 4 | 9 | 12 | 28 | 8 | 0.43 |

# NOVEMBER 1959

The M1 opened and crowds flocked to witness the spectacle, picnicking on the approach roads. Five police chiefs were less impressed, claiming that the road's design and operation were 'unsatisfactory'. With the nascent M6 emerging from the Preston by-pass, the motorway age was born, though.

The European Free Trade Association was agreed this month. It represented a loose alliance between Britain, Sweden, Norway, Denmark, Austria, Switzerland and Portugal based on a common aim of promoting economic growth and eliminating non-agricultural tariffs. Harold Macmillan gave his Paymaster General, Reginald Maudling the responsibility of negotiating the deal. There were those in the Conservative Party who remained unconvinced about a European trading alliance, particularly if this meant subjecting British agricultural policy to French – led dictates. However, Maudling was alert to the danger of Britain's economic isolation within Europe particularly with Commonwealth trade declining so greatly. Although Macmillan considered that EFTA was a poor substitute for EEC membership, because EFTA markets were much smaller, this apparently inferior deal was seen as a necessary compromise. He feared that the EEC might attempt to exclude Britain from European markets and consultation on European policy, thereby presenting themselves as a more attractive ally to the US than Britain. West Germany and France, the two most powerful members of the EEC, did little to allay his fears. West German Chancellor, Konrad Adenauer quipped to De Gaulle: 'Britain is like a rich man who has lost his property but does not realize it.'

Following the successful Cuban revolution in January, Fidel Castro's close associate, Major Ernesto 'Che' Guevara was appointed as head of the Cuban National Bank. The first lesson to emerge from the Cuban revolution was that a small group of resolute men unafraid of death and supported by the people, could take on a disciplined regular army and completely defeat it. The lesson would be re-emphasized in Vietnam, Afghanistan, Somalia and elsewhere in the ensuing decades. However, for those Latin American revolutionaries who immediately followed Castro's lead, their experience would prove less rewarding. The American response was to strengthen its counter-revolutionary and global policing role in the attempt to contain the perceived threat of communist expansion, a policy which would have disastrous consequences in both the Cuban Bay of Pigs operation and subsequently in Vietnam.

With its traditional industries of coal and textiles waning, Burnley trade unionists had less 'muscle' to flex than their union brothers in car manufacturing or the railways. Nevertheless, two local strikes took place during

November. The first was in response to the NCB's decision to close the Reedley and Salterford pits but this proved to be a token gesture only with the 'manner of the announcement' cited as the principal cause of contention. The second concerned home help assistants. Just as the town was experiencing its first snow of the winter on 13 November, the home helps' trade union sought to revise their conditions of service. This included a bid to have Saturday mornings off. The Burnley Council Health Committee was not impressed. They reacted by accusing the home helps of depriving older people of their services and threatened to end all part-time contracts despite the necessity of part-time working to cover 'unsocial' hours. As low-paid employees in a less publicly visible occupation, the home help staff had even less industrial muscle to exercise than the coal or textile workers and their dispute subsided quickly.

The co-ordination of mill closures had become an increasingly vexed issue. Owners were anxious to maximise the financial benefits to be gained through 'weaving out' but were reluctant to lose business and goodwill through not fulfilling orders. In order to meet their outstanding commitments, a number of mills took on temporary operatives. Meanwhile the permanent operatives were concerned to secure their future employment prospects but did not want to deprive themselves of the compensation payment. Also, local manufacturers remained dependent upon mill supplies until such time as they could secure alternative sources. A precipitant mill closure could therefore threaten their commercial viability. On top of this, there was a range of small local businesses which drew significant custom from the mills – cafés, newsagents, stationers, engineers, joiners, electricians, plumbers etc. Mill closures could leave a number of these high and dry.

At Westminster, new Burnley MP, Daniel Jones spoke out during the second reading of the Local Employment Bill, stating that it did not offer enough inducement for firms to move into areas of high unemployment. He was also concerned that the Bill did not do enough to protect vulnerable employees from 'unscrupulous' employers who wished to hold a gun to their heads over employment rights.

Moral panics about teenage 'folk devilry' provide good copy in any age. It was no different in Burnley in November 1959. The cause celebre here was the allegedly rowdy behaviour of local 'Teddy Boys' with disgusted local residents writing to the *Burnley Express,* holding the boys' parents as responsible for these unwanted disturbances.

Perhaps 'outraged of Burnley' turned to the BBC for succour. In 1959, radio listeners were presented with just three choices of BBC programmes. There was the Home Service, a precursor of today's Radio Four; the Light

Programme, a legacy of General Forces broadcasts, which offered middle-of-the-road popular music, comedies and soap operas; and there was the Third Programme, which, with an almost unchanged format of classical music and 'high' culture, has now become Radio Three. Apart from Radio Luxembourg with its crackling array of leading edge pop music, there were no other choices available. The format of BBC radio broadcasts had been set in the 1940s and changed very little until the late 1960s, when, with the enforced closure of off-shore pirate radio stations, the BBC launched its own pop facsimile in the form of Radio One.

The Light Programme was the opiate of the housewife, supplying the balm as the 'little woman' busied herself with the daily household chores. First up was *Housewives Choice* an anodyne record request programme that started at nine each weekday morning and which was sufficiently stirring to prompt fifties housewives to pick up their mops, buckets and vacuum cleaners. After lunch, more commonly called dinner-time by working class families, there was the pre-school interlude. 'The time is a quarter to two. This is the BBC Home Service for mothers and children at home. Are you ready for the music? When it stops, Catherine Edwards will be here to speak to you. Ding-de-dong. Ding-de-dong, Ding, Ding! Are you sitting comfortably? Then I'll begin!' So began *Listen with Mother* every afternoon at 1:45pm, a 15 minute programme of stories, songs and nursery rhymes for children under five. Educational value was instilled through counting rhymes such as 'One, two, three, four, five; once I caught a fish alive; six, seven, eight, nine, ten; then I let it go again'. The enlightened audience was over one million at its peak.

*Woman's Hour* followed *Listen with Mother*. This was, and still remains, a magazine-style programme, although the range of topical issues it covers is now much wider and of interest to both sexes. In 1959, when the programme was presented by Marjorie Anderson, a thousand letters were received by the programme's organizers each week, asking for advice on such matters as children's feeding, shyness and menstrual problems. The programme developed as a forum for the voices and views of its listeners, gaining a reputation as a 'sisterhood of the airwaves' and a lifeline to those who were housebound. Early items ranged from the instructive advice, such as, surreally, how to 'knit your own stair carpet', to controversial social and educational issues. *Woman's Hour* was the first programme to tackle subjects such the menopause (in 1947), cancer (1950) and contraception (1962). Early broadcasts were mostly live. The subsequent widening of the programme's content reflects the enormous changes that have taken place in our society over the last fifty years, with many more married women spared much of the domestic drudgery of the 1950s.

In many fifties households, the great institution of the Sunday dinner was always accompanied by BBC radio. With steam hissing from pans of boiling cabbage and spuds, converting our normally arctic kitchens into tropical infernos, at the appointed hour we would hear: 'the time in Britain is twelve noon, in Germany it's one o'clock, but home and away it's time for "Two-Way Family Favourites". *Two-Way (later Three-Way) Family Favourites* presented by Jean Metcalfe provided a series of musical dedications for our squaddies esconced on the Rhine at BFPO something or other. The musical theme would continue with the *Billy Cotton* ('Wakey Wa-a-a-key') *Band Show*, a desperate collection of brassy swing, hamfisted comedy ('hey you down there with the glasses') and Kathy Kay's insipid covers of already bland popular songs. With the traditional apple pie nestling indigestibly on top of the greasy joint, we would then be regaled by one of the Light Programme's dispiriting Sunday sitcoms such as *Life with the Lyons*, *A Life of Bliss* or *Ray's a Laugh* although the advent of the farcical *Navy Lark* and the gently mocking *Beyond our Ken* signalled a welcome upturn in quality. These were not the golden years of radio comedy but there were other exceptions to the dross. The anarchic *Goons* made fun of imperialist Britain and its officer class, drawing particularly upon the war-time experiences of Spike Milligan. Meanwhile, the lugubrious Tony Hancock continually poked fun at the gulf between his own pretensions and the glum reality of living in a simple terraced house in Railway Cuttings, East Cheam. The aggressively ambitious Joe Lampton types were something of an exception in fifties Britain. Most ordinary folk knew how to keep their feet on the ground and hold their expectations in check. This probably explains why Hancock's humour had so much resonance. But probably the most bizarre comic offering on the radio was *Educating Archie.* The show featured a radio ventriloquist. Surely, only radio ballet could be as senseless, although radio darts runs it close. However, Peter Brough, the man with the golden arm was finally made to zip his lip and earn his corn after the show transferred to television in the late fifties.

Sunday represented a purgatorial interlude between the proper weekend (Friday night and Saturday) and the working week. Everything shut down on a Sunday – notably hope and joy. It was not so much a day of rest as one of suspended animation – at least for those who did not have to slave in the kitchen. The utter desolation of the day was well encapsulated by the Sunday evening music show *Sing Something Simple.* Here the Cliff Adams singers treated us to 'songs simply sung for song lovers'. It ostensibly offered 'warm, cosy, sentimental' entertainment but in truth it was an embalment, as doleful as the solitary church bell rung for Evensong. Even God was screaming at us to lighten up.

One of the most popular radio shows of the time was *The Archers*, an everyday story of country folk which of course is still running today. At its peak in the mid-fifties an incredible 20 million people tuned in. The popularity of the series owed something to romantic rural longings, notably among urban listeners. Laurie Lee's semi-autobiographical novel *Cider with Rosie*, which was published in 1959, capitalises upon similar sentiments albeit in a less rosy vein. The BBC's publicity for *The Archers* described Ambridge as 'a gentle relic of Old England, nostalgic, generous, incorruptible, and above all valiant. In other words, it is the sort of British community that the rootless townsman would like to live in and can involve himself in vicariously'. The attractiveness of this wheat-tinted myth appeared to be as great as that of the brave and righteous British warrior. Certainly there was little similarity between the BBC's prettified portrait of country life, as reflected in the early episodes of *The Archers* and that presented by the polemical contemporary playwright, Arnold Wesker. He saw the agricultural workers of the time, embroiled in a class struggle, which they were losing. In his dramas *Roots* and *I'm Talking About Jerusalem*, both written in the late fifties, Wesker emphasised the tough, hand-to-mouth existence that many rural labourers had to contend with, much more in keeping with the Ambridge strugglers of today.

The overriding impression left by BBC radio in the fifties was that it was aimed principally at a white, middle class, Home Counties audience. No programme epitomised this better than the long-running plummy saga, *Mrs Dale's Diary*. Each day, the ever-earnest 'Mary', wife of GP 'Jim', reflected upon her lot at suburban Virginia Lodge, telling us about her sophisticated sister, *'Selly'* and her cat, *'Kepton'* (captain). The nearest we came to radicalised insurgency was when the 'common', cockney 'Mrs Leathers' occasionally upset the privileged calm.

## 7 November 1959

Birmingham City 1 Luton Town 1
Burnley 4 Wolverhampton Wanderers 1
Chelsea 3 Blackburn Rovers 1
Leeds United 3 Arsenal 2
Leicester City 2 Sheffield Wednesday 0
Manchester United 3 Fulham 3
Newcastle United 8 Everton 2
Preston North End 1 Nottingham Forest 0
Tottenham Hotspur 0 Bolton Wanderers 2
West Bromwich Albion 2 Blackpool 1
West Ham United 4 Manchester City 1

## Burnley 4 v 1 Wolves

*'Oh! Carol'*

There was some trepidation about this one. Wolves' average strike rate stood at an incredible three goals per game. This was even better than their 1958/59 scoring record. Then, they galloped to their second Championship title on the bounce, scoring 110 goals. They had become more vulnerable at the back, though. Nevertheless, they had a formidable record of overpowering opponents. But on this sparkling afternoon, style triumphed over substance.

*Ray Pointer opens the scoring against Wolves [37]*

Prompted by Jimmy McIlroy's brilliance, Burnley won the opening exchanges hands down. Rattled by the incessant barrage of mortar-like crosses into their area, the Wolves' defence finally cracked, and with Flowers and Stuart dithering over a loose ball Pointer nipped in to score on 22 minutes. The lead lasted a matter of seconds. In familiar Wolves' fashion, Flowers pumped a long pass forward for inside right Mason to sprint through Burnley's yielding defence and smash the ball past Blacklaw. It was then Burnley's turn to be stung into action and Jimmy Robson restored Burnley's lead, three minutes later, after Wolves 'keeper, Finlayson, was unable to hold Connelly's powerful drive. Then, with the half-time whistle imminent, Pilkington beat Flowers on the left and centred for Pointer to score from close range.

Although play flowed from one end to the other throughout an equally vibrant second half, Burnley's defenders had clearly drawn inspiration from their forwards' brilliant display. As a consequence, they managed to contain Wolves' later raids with assurance, whereas the visitors' defenders remained under the cosh and Connelly duly gilded this scintillating performance with a fourth in the 72nd minute, having benefited from yet another incisive McIlroy pass. The result was doubled in value after it became known that leaders, Spurs, had lost 0-2 at home to Bolton. Burnley were now in 5th position just behind Wolves, on goal difference, and West Ham.

In his programme notes, Harry Potts congratulated John Connelly, Brian Miller and Alex Elder on being selected for international honours. Even then, there was some debate over the club versus country issue. Both Bill Nicholson and Stan Cullis had raised their concerns here. But Harry remarked: 'different people have different ideas about whether it is an advantage or a disadvantage for clubs to have their players called away for representative engagements. My personal opinion is that if the players are considered good enough to be chosen, both their clubs and theirselves benefit by the experience it affords them: that more than makes up for their absence from routine club training entailed on such occasions. We certainly are always proud to find our players recognised and will always be pleased to release any that are invited for such engagements.' This is a remarkably sanguine view from a manager in pursuit of the League Championship with one of the smallest squads in the First Division.

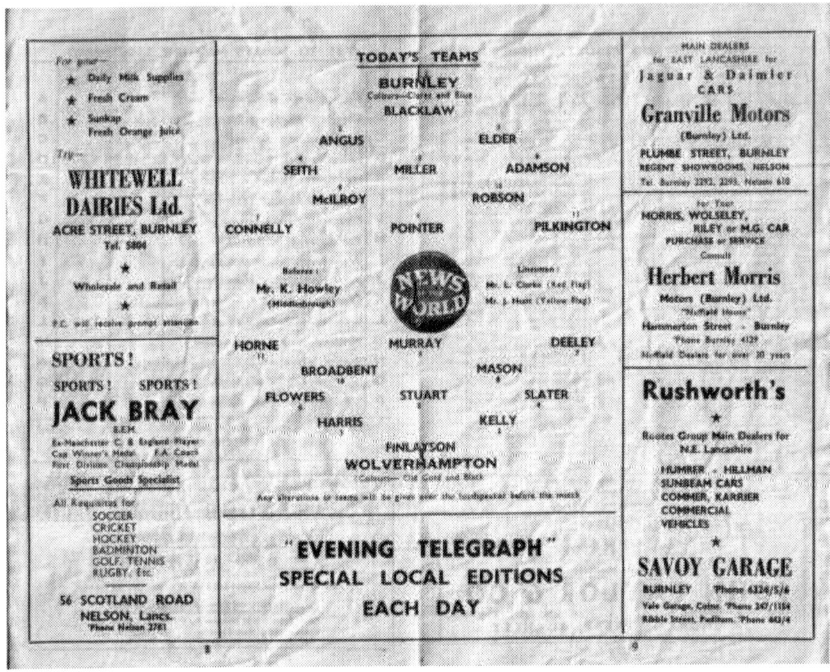

For your—
★ Daily Milk Supplies
★ Fresh Cream
★ Sunkap Fresh Orange Juice

Try—

WHITEWELL DAIRIES Ltd.
ACRE STREET, BURNLEY
Tel. 5804
★
Wholesale and Retail
★

SPORTS!
SPORTS! SPORTS!
JACK BRAY
B.E.M.
Ex-Manchester C. & England Player
Cup Winner's Medal F.A. Coach
First Division Championship Medal
Sports Goods Specialist
All Requisites for
SOCCER
CRICKET
HOCKEY
BADMINTON
GOLF, TENNIS
RUGBY, Etc.
56 SCOTLAND ROAD
NELSON, Lancs.
'Phone Nelson 2781

TODAY'S TEAMS
BURNLEY
BLACKLAW
ANGUS ELDER
SEITH MILLER ADAMSON
McILROY ROBSON
CONNELLY POINTER PILKINGTON

Referee: Mr. K. Howley (Middlesbrough)

NEWS OF THE WORLD

Linesmen: Mr. L. Clarke (Red Flag) Mr. J. Hunt (Yellow Flag)

HORNE MURRAY DEELEY
BROADBENT MASON
FLOWERS STUART SLATER
HARRIS KELLY
FINLAYSON
WOLVERHAMPTON
(Colours— Old Gold and Black)

Any alterations to teams will be given over the loudspeaker before the match

"EVENING TELEGRAPH"
SPECIAL LOCAL EDITIONS
EACH DAY

MAIN DEALERS for EAST LANCASHIRE for
Jaguar & Daimler CARS
Granville Motors
(Burnley) Ltd.
PLUMBE STREET, BURNLEY
REGENT SHOWROOMS, NELSON

for Your
MORRIS, WOLSELEY, RILEY or M.G. CAR
PURCHASE or SERVICE
Consult
Herbert Morris
Motors (Burnley) Ltd.
"Nuffield House"
Hammerton Street - Burnley
'Phone Burnley 4129
Nuffield Dealers for over 30 years

Rushworth's
★
Rootes Group Main Dealers for N.E. Lancashire
HUMBER - HILLMAN
SUNBEAM CARS
COMMER, KARRIER
COMMERCIAL
VEHICLES
★
SAVOY GARAGE
BURNLEY 'Phone 6324/5/6
Vale Garage, Colne. 'Phone 347/1154
Ribble Street, Padiham. 'Phone 443/4

8 9

## Going to the Wolves match: a vivid memory

Reminded by his 1959 diary, Geoff Crambie, a Burnley supporter since 1950, has vivid memories of the day. Geoff recalled: "I was sixteen when Burnley won the Championship. I still hold sharp memories of that season. It was a time of great players and magnificent football. But the home game with Wolves stands out. My three mates and I had a set routine each match day. We'd leave our homes in Colne after midday and saunter down the hill to the station, singing our favourite pop songs of the time like Adam Faith's *What Do You Want* and Marty Wilde's *Sea of Love*. On this day I remember that the song we were singing was Neil Sedaka's *Oh! Carol*. It's the one he dedicated to fellow singer / songwriter, Carole King.'

'I remember the day was bright and warm. The summer of '59 seemed to go on forever. We had those water shortages and standpipes, of course. On this day there was this lovely tingling sunshine, with a lingering haze softening the outlines of the massive Pendle Hill and the surrounding moors. I had this zipped up corduroy jerkin, and, of course, my ancient Burnley scarf, but felt a bit overdressed on this sparkling afternoon.

At the station we'd buy our 1/6 return tickets to Burnley Central (that's around 7p in today's money). In those days you would get a thick, stubby cardboard ticket which the ticket collector would clip cutting out a V-shaped wedge. It was still the age of steam so we'd know if we had to get a move on because you could see the plume of steam in the distance. They'd put on four special trains on a match day. These would come down from Skipton, about 11 miles away. The trains would also pick up supporters from further down the Aire Valley line – Keighley and so on. In those days, the Yorkshire teams weren't doing so well, so Burnley nabbed a bit of support from the rival county. After Skipton, the train would stop at Earby, which was still a small mill town out in the country and also take on supporters from the nearby village of Barnoldswick where there was a Rolls Royce factory. These trains were well-used by supporters when Burnley were at home so they'd often be headed by a bigger locomotive like a Stanier 'Jubilee'. We were keen train spotters with our *Ian Allan* books, so we'd always look out for an engine we hadn't copped. Mostly it was one we'd seen plenty of times before like *South Africa* or *India*.

Anyway, our train would pull in headed by a clanking 'Jubilee' with its roaring fire, its rampant lion insignia on the coal tender and its characteristic blend of smells; the sooty, sulphurous exhaust, the scorching oil and the coal tar scent, reminiscent of the soap some of us used. Wispy steam would coil carelessly around the locomotives valves and the carriage braking system. The carriages would usually be a mixture of the maroon and 'blood and custard' types. In the separate apartments on the corridor versions you would often find these pallid watercolours pinned under the netted luggage racks. There would be these hazy images of Ullswater or the Clyde with may be a paddle steamer progressing serenely across the mirror like water. The windows were strapped with a leather belt. On a warm day like this we would pull them down, often leaning out to catch sight of the snorting engine but getting an eyeful of smuts for our efforts.

When we reached Burnley, the old Victorian Station was packed. It was always pretty full but this was a big game against the current League Champions. Around 28,000 turned up for this one. With trains arriving from the Accrington and the Skipton directions, it was quite a squeeze getting out of the station. Most of the adult supporters – it was almost exclusively men in those days – would make for the Reindeer pub or the Adelphi Hotel, which was just opposite the station but now closed and derelict. The pubs would be heaving. We couldn't get in though – we were too young.

At the bottom of the hill from the station you had to cross this old iron bridge. With so many of us wearing clogs or boots it was quite a racket. It was also quite a crush so we'd be pressed up against these chaps who had may be just finished a shift at the local mills or at the pit. Some of the mill workers would still have traces of the cotton fluff on their clothing, although in those days most dressed up to go to a game. A lot of the men wore ties. In this churn, you'd pick up snatches of conversations. Some talk would have been about the game – Wolves danger men such as Norman Deeley or Peter Broadbent, their recent run of results like their 4-3 defeat at Preston a couple of weeks ago or what side Harry Potts would put out. Some talk would have been about England's lamentable home defeat by Sweden, although John Connelly scored our opening goal. Some would have been talking about the previous night's TV – may be how fit *Emergency Ward Ten* nurse Carole Young was or how some *Take Your Pick* contestant had ended up with a clothes prop after refusing the money and pinning everything on the key to 'Box Thirteen'. There may have even been some mimicry of gormless Bernard *'I only asked'* Bresslaw from *The Army Game*.

While the men made for the pub, we made for, what we called, the 'blood drink shop', officially *Fitzpatrick's* the herbalists, at the end of Yorkshire Street. Here we would down this bright red sarsaparilla. I guess it was a bit like *Red Bull*. It would give you a hell of a buzz. Maybe we would then go into the pie shop. They would also serve you tripe or black pudding for 3d (Remember the three penny bits with sharp-edged collars? They had a thrift plant on one side or a portcullis). Some chaps would eat strips of tripe from a greaseproof bag as they walked up to the ground – it was quite disgusting! I remember that there was this old guy who was always outside Turf Moor on match days with his cart. He would sell these 2d claret and blue balloons.

We'd always aim to get to the ground around 1.30pm so we could get the players' autographs. A couple of the Burnley players – Jimmy Robson and Trevor Meredith – came by bike. I think Brian Pilkington was one of the first to have a car. We'd get Jimmy McIlroy, a true gent, to sign his picture in *Charles Buchan's Football Monthly*. I remember the Wolves players arriving. 75% of them were smoking as they clambered out of their coach. It was so different then. I managed to get Ron Flowers and Eddie Clamp. My friend got

Norman Deeley. I recall Wolves 'keeper, Malcolm Finlayson, signing with a flourish. He was a big lad! He seemed about six foot – seven tall although I don't suppose he was. If you were around at this time you'd also pick up some ex-players who were doing turns as journalists – players like Frank Swift although he died at Munich. You would also get the reserves if they didn't have a game. We would then move down to the small car park to pick up the opposing manager. Stan Cullis, the Wolves manager, had a reputation of being a hard man but he was a real gent. He would always sign. He was friendly too, much like Harry Potts.

After that, we would make for the Bee Hole End, the open terracing behind the goal at the East end of the ground. There we would mix with the Wolves supporters with their flat, lugubrious accents and clad in their old gold and black scarves. They were very confident that day. They kept insisting they were going to whip us, reckoning we'd no chance. Judging by their record here over the years they were right to be confident. But on this day they were badly mistaken. One chap in his fifties was wearing a huge top hat painted in gold with all the names of the Wolves' famous star players of the era written on it. I saw spelt out in black ink, Billy Wright, Bert Williams, Jimmy Mullen, Johnny Hancocks, Dennis Wilshaw and Bill Slater. When John Connelly scored our fourth goal, the old chap whipped off the hat and hid it in a massive paper carrier bag that he pulled out of his pocket.

It was a fantastic game. The quality of passing was amazing. It was so fast and accurate, too. Burnley dominated from start to finish. True, Wolves got this breakaway goal that they were so good at taking but it didn't change the course of the game. Burnley were 3-1 up at half-time having scored three great goals. They added another good'n in the second half and Bobby Seith played a blinder. The noise inside the ground was incredible. In those days you could take in those huge gas warning rattles. They didn't 'arf make a din. We had this massive school bell which I'd painted in claret and blue. I suppose these would be considered offensive weapons now but they really added to the atmosphere. Just to add to the volume of sound there was also a brass band playing on this day, too. The game was over so quickly. Jimmy McIlroy said afterwards: 'the ball was on our side'. For me, it was one of the finest games I have seen. The fans lingered after the final whistle. Bob Lord stood on the pitch waving to the fans. None of us wanted to leave. It was that good.

The four of us left after lingering for around 15 minutes and at the same time we saw coming out into a busy Brunshaw Road journalists Frank McGhee of the Daily Mirror and Henry Rose of the Daily Express. We all said hello to Frank who waved back. As for Henry Rose we ignored him with his

*Jimmy Robson restores Burnley's lead [38]*

bow tie and homburg hat, a true snob: when we asked for his autograph, around three seasons before, he had told us to 'bugger off'."

## 14 November 1959

Arsenal 1 West Ham United 3
Blackburn Rovers 3 West Bromwich Abion 2
Blackpool 2 Newcastle United 0
Bolton Wanderers 1 Manchester United 1
Everton 4 Birmingham City 0
Fulham 1 Preston North End 2
Luton Town 1 Tottenham Hotspur 0
Manchester City 1 Chelsea 1
Nottingham Forest 1 Leicester City 0
Sheffield Wednesday 1 Burnley 1
Wolverhampton Wanderers 4 Leeds United 2

## Sheffield Wednesday 1 v 1 Burnley

*'Red River Rock'*

Today, Sheffield, with its motorways, ring roads, shopping precincts and high rise buildings is almost indistinguishable from many of our cities. But in 1959, it had a distinct identity. Sheffield was still Britain's 'steel city'. Its foundries growled, roared, stamped and hissed with the leaping furnace flames illuminating the carriages of passing commuter trains on dark winter mornings. Its production of the nation's cutlery was celebrated by the name of its crack London express – '*The Master Cutler*'. The Don may have flowed quietly but

*Keith Ellis, the rugged Sheffield Wednesday centre-forward [39]*

little else did for the city was also in the process of modernization. Wrecking balls were flattening the slums while rooms with a view were being created at the perched Park Hill flats. The Castle Market shopping centre was opened and a new inner ring road built with the original tram system about to be torn up. Although still a centre of heavy industry, the Clean Air legislation had done much to reduce the level of pollution. Until 1956, Sheffield was one of the dirtiest cities in England. As was the case in other large urban areas, Sheffield was becoming increasingly cosmopolitan with an influx of immigrants from the Caribbean and the Indian sub continent. Although the city's cinemas were coming under greater threat from television, a feature of the times, the crowds were flocking in to see the faux Biblical epic *Ben Hur*. By contrast, up at Hillsborough eye candy was in short supply for this was a brutal, ugly game.

During the fifties Wednesday had been the ultimate 'trampoline' artists. They had been promoted to the First Division four times but their longest stay had lasted for just three campaigns. Having been promoted yet again in May 1959 under the shrewd, authoritarian management of Harry Catterick, they were determined to scrap for success. On this grim day at Hillsborough the marks of their rugged intent were left all over Harry Potts' side. Jimmy McIlroy, Brian Pilkington and John Connelly were the craggy 'Owls' main targets but even the sturdy 'keeper Adam Blacklaw took a battering from forwards Keith Ellis and John Fantham. With experienced referee, Reg Leafe, showing considerable leniency, the home side had little compunction about employing such naked aggression. Amusingly, Blacklaw niftily evaded one reckless challenge from John Fantham by swinging on the crossbar. Unable to restrain his charge the 'Owls' forward proceeded to crash into the netting, in which he became hopelessly entangled. It was catch of the day.

The game started in a peculiar fashion. Kick-off had to be delayed for several minutes after a black dog invaded the pitch. With a series of sinuous twists and turns he initially defied all attempts at capturing him. Perhaps the Burnley's defenders had been distracted by the dog show for they began uncertainly, letting Wednesday off the leash. Home right winger, Wilkinson, duly cashed in, crossing quickly and crisply for centre forward, Ellis to nod in a 3rd minute opener via the underside of the bar. 'The Owls' tried to compound their advantage by clamping down on their opponents, denying them the space to exercise their characteristic flair. But, even whilst spluttering Burnley could usually conjure up a gem of sublime skill and once again it paid off. Following an exhilarating 14th minute exchange between Pilkington and McIlroy, Robson equalized. The build up was better than the execution for England 'keeper, Ron Springett, really should have stopped Robson's tame shot. Thereafter, it became an artillery offensive with Burnley humping the ball forward while Wednesday remained intent upon a manhunt. The long ball did little to help Burnley's cause with Wednesday's burly centre-half, Peter Swan, lapping up the aerial service. However, late in the game Pilkington nearly broke the deadlock. Having got the better of his crunching marker, Norman Curtis, he managed to cross for Jimmy Robson to crack a volley against the bar.

The game ended with Adam Blacklaw prostrate after yet another heavy challenge from Keith Ellis. Although this was not immediately recognized, Adam was concussed. His wife Sheila recalls: "although he seemed okay at first, Adam did not follow the rest of the team to the dressing room after the final whistle had blown. Once they realized this they went out to find him and there he was in the goalmouth mistakenly believing that the game hadn't finished. Seeing that he wasn't right, his manager, Harry Potts arranged for him to be taken to hospital straight away. He also took me with him in his car. It's funny what goes through your head when something worrying like this happens. I recall that what seemed to preoccupy me was the knowledge that Adam was wearing his Little Miss Muffett underpants which might have caused him some embarrassment when the hospital staff undressed him!" Fortunately, Adam made a quick recovery. So did his team mates. Whilst bruised they were certainly not beaten.

## 21 November 1959

Birmingham City 2 Blackpool 1
Burnley 8 Nottingham Forest 0
Chelsea 1 Arsenal 3
Leeds United 1 Sheffield Wednesday 3
Leicester City 0 Fulham 1
Manchester United 4 Luton Town 1
Newcastle United 3 Blackburn Rovers 1
Preston North End 1 Bolton Wanderers 0
Tottenham Hotspur 3 Everton 0
West Bromwich Albion 2 Manchester City 0
West Ham United 3 Wolverhampton Wanderers 2

## Burnley 8 v 0 Nottingham Forest

*'What Do You Want To Make Those Eyes At Me For'*

One Burnley supporter recalled: "I was ten when we played Nottingham Forest. Despite it being November it was still quite warm and very dry; the area was suffering from a drought but despite this my mum made me wear my scarf and balaclava to the match!" Others remembered the heat generated on the pitch. Having struggled against the beaten FA Cup finalists a few weeks before, Burnley's performance on this grey, misty day against the Cup winners, Forest, was of a different order. The *Daily Mirror* reported: 'it was a display of the high-geared soccer that left Forest floundering'. Ironically, some home fans had groaned on hearing that Jimmy Robson had been selected. Jimmy had been criticised by them because his ball control was considered inferior to that of Jimmy McIlroy. However, the young Geordie striker would silence those doubters in the most convincing way possible, notching a hat-trick before half-time.

WHITEWELL DAIRIES Ltd.
ACRE STREET, BURNLEY
Wholesale and Retail

SPORTS!
SPORTS! SPORTS!
JACK BRAY
Sports Goods Specialist
SOCCER
CRICKET
HOCKEY
BADMINTON
GOLF, TENNIS
RUGBY, Etc.
56 SCOTLAND ROAD
NELSON, Lancs.

TODAY'S TEAMS
BURNLEY
BLACKLAW
ANGUS ELDER
SEITH MILLER ADAMSON
McILROY ROBSON
CONNELLY POINTER PILKINGTON
Referee—
Mr. H. P. Hackney
IMLACH WILSON GRAY
QUIGLEY BOOTH
ILEY McKINLAY WHITEFOOT
PATRICK WHARE
THOMSON
NOTTS FOREST

"EVENING TELEGRAPH"
SPECIAL LOCAL EDITIONS
EACH DAY

Jaguar & Daimler
CARS
Granville Motors
(Burnley) Ltd.
PLUMBE STREET, BURNLEY

MORRIS, WOLSELEY,
RILEY or M.G. CAR
Herbert Morris
Motors (Burnley) Ltd.

Rushworth's
HUMBER - HILLMAN
SUNBEAM CARS
COMMER, KARRIER
COMMERCIAL
VEHICLES

SAVOY GARAGE
BURNLEY

Jimmy McIlroy was the main architect of Forest's annihilation, though. The *Daily Mirror* reporter endorsed this view headlining his piece with 'Mac the Knife carves way for goal riot'.

As was often the case, Jimmy had little difficulty in evading the attentions of his dual markers. His cause was helped when Forest's right back, Bill Whare tore a muscle in the 20th minute, reducing Forest to ten men. For the last 6 minutes depleted Forest were down to nine fit players after losing right half, Jeff Whitefoot, too. McIlroy and John Connelly compounded their opponent's confusion by continuously swapping positions. With Brian Pilkington totally outwitting and outrunning Forest's makeshift full-back, their fragile defence fragmented quickly. But as the *Daily Mirror* reporter concluded: 'even a well-drilled army could have hardly held out against this Burnley's brilliance'.

Jimmy Robson commented: "our mobility and fitness were two of our major strengths. There were plenty of tough defenders who were happiest if you gave them a physical battle. We weren't like that. We tried to pull them around with our running off the ball – creating gaps. Ray Pointer wasn't the type of centre forward who was looking to mix it. He was going to work the defenders, by being constantly on the move. Jimmy McIlroy did not need much space in which to produce penetrative passes but our mobility certainly helped him crack open a defence."

Forest's use of the offside trap proved disastrous as McIlroy kept threading exquisitely timed balls through the visitors' porous back line for his fellow forwards to latch onto. By half-time, Burnley were 5-0 up! As early as the 3rd minute, Jimmy Robson seized upon a loose ball after John Connelly's shot had been palmed away. Brian Pilkington then scored in the 13th minute with a magnificent solo effort. A stunning combination of passes allowed Jimmy Robson to thump in a third after 35 minutes and with the Forest defence in disarray; Robson scored two more in the 40th and 44th minutes putting Burnley well out of sight.

To Forest's credit they never resorted to spoiling tactics and constantly attempted to play attractive, open football. But they packed little punch and only former Claret, Billy Gray, caused the Burnley defenders any discomfort.

After the break there was no let up. Within eight minutes of the restart, Pointer's speed of thought and movement were too much for the visitors' hesitant defenders, allowing him to capitalise on Angus's long ball and head over the slowly advancing 'keeper, Chic Thomson. Jimmy Robson then added another to his bulging tally in the 60th minute, to set a post-war individual scoring record for the club. Ray Pointer tucked into second helpings, converting Brian Pilkington's cross in the 82nd minute, leaving the ravaged Forest defence with pieces of eight. This massacre enabled Burnley to climb two places into fourth spot.

Reflecting upon his achievement 50 years later Jimmy Robson commented: "to be honest I don't remember too much about the game apart from the fact that I scored with two volleys, which was fairly unusual for me. The injury to right back, Bill Whare certainly helped us, though. I'm not sure that we would have scored as many if he had managed to stay fit. In those days a team going down to ten left them at a greater disadvantage than appears to be the case today. I suppose team organization has improved. In those days an injured player was often told to play on and asked to try making a nuisance of himself up front."

Jimmy told Geoff Crambie and his grandson, Nathan Lee: "I didn't receive the match ball. However, I saw a 1950s leather case ball in an antiques shop in York and purchased it to remind me of that marvellous championship game."

## 28 November 1959

Arsenal 2 West Bromwich Albion 4
Blackburn Rovers 2 Birmingham City 1
Blackpool 2 Tottenham Hotspur 2
Bolton Wanderers 3 Leicester City 1
Everton 2 Manchester United 1
Fulham 1 Burnley 0
Luton Town 1 Preston North End 3
Manchester City 3 Newcastle United 4
Nottingham Forest 4 Leeds United 1
Sheffield Wednesday 7 West Ham United 0
Wolverhampton Wanderers 3 Chelsea 1

## Fulham 1 v 0 Burnley

*'Travellin' Light'*

In Cuba, the revolutionary government was establishing itself. Much closer to home, an English football revolution was also taking shape, to be led by today's bearded marksmen, Jimmy Hill. Hill would adroitly negotiate the abolition of the professional footballer's maximum wage. With the ending of this feudal financial restraint, the bigger clubs would begin to seize control of English football, signaling the decline of small town clubs like Burnley. But that still lay ahead.

*With Fulham keeper Macedo out of position Jimmy Robson screws his shot wide [40]*

As far as this match was concerned, it promised to be an interesting tussle involving, arguably, the two best playmakers in the First Division at that time: Jimmy Mac for Burnley and Johnny Haynes for Fulham. Burnley's hosts had other stars, though, including Scots international winger, Graham Leggat, former England full back, Jim Langley and future English World Cup stalwarts, George Cohen and Alan Mullery. London Palladium comedian, Tommy Trinder, was then Fulham's Chairman. His favourite catch phrase: 'you lucky people!' should have been targeted at his team today as they rode an ocean breaker of fortune to steal both points. Jimmy McIlroy did all he could to secure a deserved Burnley victory. Unfortunately, his colleagues left their shooting sharpness at the Forest game, whereas Fulham made the most of the one clear opportunity that came their way, with Jimmy Hill scoring with a soft, looping header after 32 minutes. This result enabled Fulham to leapfrog Burnley, who dropped to sixth place, while Preston North End took over in top spot.

The Fulham programme contained an advert for Bubble cars including the Heinkel and Messerschmitt models. Bubble cars became popular in Europe to meet the emerging demand for cheap personal motorised transport at a time when fuel prices were high due in part to the 1956 Suez Crisis. Most of these light cars were three-wheelers. This made them still cheaper to run in many places, since they were considered to be motorcycles for tax and licensing purposes. A vast majority of these were built in Germany by the former military aircraft manufacturers using the cockpit canopy designs for their World War Two bombers and fighters.

*Macedo punches clear from Robson [41]*

## First Division

| 30 November 1959 | *P* | *W* | *D* | *L* | *F* | *A* | *Pts* | *Goal average* |
|---|---|---|---|---|---|---|---|---|
| 1. Preston North End | 19 | 12 | 3 | 4 | 40 | 29 | 27 | 1.38 |
| 2. Tottenham Hotspur | 19 | 9 | 7 | 3 | 41 | 22 | 25 | 1.86 |
| 3. West Ham United | 19 | 11 | 3 | 5 | 37 | 30 | 25 | 1.23 |
| 4. Wolverhampton Wanderers | 19 | 11 | 2 | 6 | 55 | 39 | 24 | 1.41 |
| 5. Fulham | 19 | 11 | 2 | 6 | 39 | 40 | 24 | 0.98 |
| 6. BURNLEY | 19 | 10 | 3 | 6 | 44 | 32 | 23 | 1.38 |
| 7. Blackburn Rovers | 19 | 10 | 3 | 6 | 35 | 30 | 23 | 1.17 |
| 8. Bolton Wanderers | 19 | 8 | 4 | 7 | 25 | 20 | 20 | 1.25 |
| 9. Sheffield Wednesday | 19 | 8 | 3 | 8 | 31 | 22 | 19 | 1.41 |
| 10.West Bromwich Albion | 19 | 7 | 5 | 7 | 36 | 30 | 19 | 1.20 |
| 11. Manchester United | 19 | 7 | 5 | 7 | 44 | 39 | 19 | 1.13 |
| 12. Arsenal | 19 | 7 | 5 | 7 | 33 | 33 | 19 | 1.00 |
| 13. Chelsea | 19 | 8 | 3 | 8 | 37 | 39 | 19 | 0.95 |
| 14. Manchester City | 19 | 8 | 1 | 10 | 40 | 42 | 17 | 0.95 |
| 15. Newcastle United | 19 | 7 | 3 | 9 | 36 | 38 | 17 | 0.95 |
| 16. Nottingham Forest | 19 | 7 | 3 | 9 | 22 | 31 | 17 | 0.71 |
| 17. Everton | 19 | 6 | 4 | 9 | 32 | 37 | 16 | 0.86 |
| 18. Blackpool | 19 | 5 | 5 | 9 | 26 | 32 | 15 | 0.81 |
| 19. Birmingham City | 19 | 4 | 5 | 10 | 24 | 36 | 13 | 0.67 |
| 20. Leeds United | 19 | 4 | 5 | 10 | 28 | 46 | 13 | 0.61 |
| 21. Leicester City | 19 | 4 | 5 | 10 | 27 | 45 | 13 | 0.60 |
| 22. Luton Town | 19 | 3 | 5 | 11 | 16 | 36 | 11 | 0.44 |

# DECEMBER 1959

With the wounds of Suez beginning to heal, Britain started diplomatic talks with Egypt's President Nasser. Ironically, these talks started just before Archbishop Makarios was elected as the first President of the new Republic of Cyprus. Back in the dark days of Suez, Prime Minister Anthony Eden banished Makarios to the Seychelles for his part in the EOKA terrorism. It was as if Makarios had become Eden's Napoleon just as Nasser had become his 'Moslem Mussolini'. The banishment only served to aggravate nationalist tensions between the Greek and Turkish Cypriots fighting for supremacy with the British Army struggling to contain the conflict. In his inaugural presidential address, Makarios praised the 'heroes and martyrs' of the liberation struggle, mentioning Colonel Grivas, the EOKA Greek guerilla leader. He then insisted that antagonism and fanaticism must cease and that Greeks and Turks must work together 'in a spirit of great sincerity with great respect for the natural rights of one another'. Cyprus was granted full independence as a single entity in August 1960. However, one result of Makarios's ameliorating efforts was that the former EOKA activists launched several assassination attempts against him, although none succeeded. It would be some time before peace broke out.

The Royal Art Commission voiced its concern about the state of British architecture with John Betjeman and Henry Moore leading the charge. They indicted planners nationwide for permitting the construction of ugly new nuclear power stations in areas of natural beauty, for allowing the suburbs to swallow up the countryside and for approving the building of 'drab', 'mediocre' and 'low standard' inner city buildings. The future Prince of Wales would later follow their lead. It was symptomatic of the nation's growing ambivalence about the legacy of greater affluence. The success of contemporary ruralist literature like *Cider with Rosie* and the popularity of the radio soap *The Archers* were indicative of the fears about increasing urbanization.

With Christmas reputedly being a time of good will the *Burnley Express* covered the upbeat assessment of the local economy as reported to the Burnley Council General Purposes Committee at the end of November. The latest employment figures put Burnley ahead of the national and regional averages. 98.3% of working age adults were currently employed in the Burnley area compared with 97.7% within the North West region and 98.1% across the nation. It was said that fears about the prospective employment opportunities for school leavers had, so far, proved groundless. A list of good news stories was provided about future work opportunities. Michelin was expected to offer 200 jobs once production started in 1960. Lucas was expanding its aircraft components business with 300 more jobs being created. Mullard's, a company specialising in the production of electrical parts (including television tubes), was building a new factory which would begin operation in 1961. 600 jobs were expected to arise. Burnley Aircraft Productions was also expanding its operation to include the manufacture of liquid containers. 100 new jobs were to be offered there, also. During December news of other planned developments were announced, such as a 'huge new factory at Lowerhouse for the production of boiler houses and compressors.' Although, mills due to close in March 1960, were expected to lay off around 1,700 employees, there was a belief that all of these operatives would secure other work. In its confident New Year message, the *Burnley Express* reminded its 34,000 readers how far they had come in the previous ten years, first taking them back to the 'dark days of rationing' in 1950 before propelling them forward to this present time of relative plenty.

Glad tidings were extended on the water front, too, with the Yuletide news that the Council planned to make good the current deficit in the town's water supply by extending its reservoir capacity by 56 million gallons. The message to local residents was that the lessons of the 'long, hot summer' had been learnt.

Responding to the positive messages a Christmas shopping spree followed with a record two million cards posted during the festive season. The Burnley Express included pages of advertisements for Christmas goods, including Chanel No.5 from 30/- (£1.50p); a 'gay shortie dressing gown' at 82/- (£4.10p); vulcanised football boots designed by Stanley Matthews at 32/11 (£1.64p); and a Hi Fi tape recorder at 39 guineas (£40.90p).

For those children who had gained entrance to their local Grammar School by passing their 11-plus examinations, their Christmas reward was often a new bike. In 1959, a Raleigh Tourist Bicycle could be bought from H. Fitzpatrick in St. James Street for £20/5/6 (£20.27p).

Television was increasingly taking care of the Christmas entertainment. Nationwide, around 10 million households had their own TV with ownership having expanded by around a third during the previous two years. 'Ownership' had also been boosted by the introduction of rental agreements. In Burnley, Ardal in St. James Street offered TV rentals from 7/6 (37p) weekly. With television audiences continuing to grow, the fall in cinema attendances was unabated. But by way of boosting interest in his stirring new adventure film *North West Frontier*, Kenneth More made an appearance at the Burnley Odeon Cinema Club on the 9th December. He was hailed by the *Burnley Express* as being the star of *Night To Remember*, the original Titanic movie.

Having received such comforting messages about the local economy, Burnley folk were invited to move up the housing ladder. New bungalows were on offer in Brierfield from £2,150 and 3-bedroomed semi-detached houses available from £2,375. The message was: 'have confidence and invest in your Burnley roots'. 'This is a place with a future'. The demographics gave a different account, though, with the town's population having fallen by 5% in the previous ten years.

Car ownership had increased rapidly over the previous two years. By November 1959, 25% more British households had a car of their own compared with the September 1957 figure, when sales had stalled temporarily on account of the Suez-related petrol rationing. Skippers of Burnley now offered the 'New sensational performance-packed Ford Prefect' with a speed of up to 75mph and a fuel consumption of 50 miles per gallon. Fuel consumption was a major selling point after the sharp rise in the price of petrol. This £600 car could have been yours with a £62 down payment with the

*Turf Moor Garage, Burnley in 1959 [42]*

outstanding account settled over a four year period. Alternatively, the new chic Morris Mini was also on sale for £350 plus £146/19/2 purchase tax (£497 in total) with 12 months BMC warranty –'the most comprehensive in Europe'. This safety net proved to be very necessary because the early Minis proved to be as notoriously unreliable as the early washing machines.

It was left to the North East Lancashire Development Committee to play the role of 'party poopers'. They predicted that during 1960 there would be 5,300 redundancies as a result of mill closures and 400 fewer jobs at Burnley coal pits. Meanwhile, 1,000 school leavers would also be seeking work. They were less impressed with the current employment figures since they believed that these were artificially high having been disguised by the recruitment of temporary textile operatives in mills which were looking to clear their outstanding orders before closure in March 1960. They urged Government assistance in providing better road connections with Manchester and improved rail links with Yorkshire. They re-emphasised that without improved road and rail communications Burnley's relatively isolated location would hamper its prospects of diversification and growth.

With New Year nigh the fifties also came to a close. A decade, which started in Britain with rationing and bleak austerity had ended with a promise of greater prosperity and social freedoms. But the economic cracks would grow over the next twenty years, eventually resulting in the impoverishment of parts of the North, particularly within its small former mill towns. It was as if the cradle of the industrial revolution was being recast as its casket.

## 5 December 1959

Birmingham City 4 Manchester City 2
Burnley 4 Bolton Wanderers 0
Chelsea 0 Sheffield Wednesday 4
Leeds United 1 Fulham 4
Leicester City 3 Luton Town 3
Manchester United 3 Blackpool 1
Newcastle United 4 Arsenal 1
Preston North End 0 Everton 0
Tottenham Hotspur 2 Blackburn Rovers 1
West Bromwich Albion 0 Wolverhampton Wanderers 1
West Ham United 4 Nottingham Forest 1

## Burnley 4 v 0 Bolton Wanderers

*'What Do You Want?'*

Bill Ridding's Bolton came with a tough reputation. In defence they had the rugged Hartle, Higgins and Edwards. Going forward, they packed a punch, too. The rampaging warhorse, Nat Lofthouse, had been forced into premature retirement on account of an ankle injury suffered on a pre-season South African tour. He would reverse that decision in the following August. However, Bolton had a mobile deputy in Dennis Stevens. They also had the gifted young inside forward, Freddie Hill, to complement the subtle skills of internationals Doug Holden and Ray Parry. As if this was a frontier winter shoot-out, the game was played on an ominous, brooding afternoon, in which the wisps of the players' vaporizing breath could be seen against the background of the dark stands.

*Blacklaw grasps Holden's cross in front of Bolton centre-forward Stevens and Burnley centre-half, Brian Miller [43]*

Bolton performed as billed but it was Burnley who had the greater thrust. Ray Pointer headed the opener in the 22nd minute after Connelly's drive had come back off the post and proceeded to hold their narrow advantage resolutely until the interval. Afterwards, they expressed themselves more. Within eight minutes of the restart, Jimmy McIlroy's right

*Hopkinson punches over as the Bolton defence comes under severe pressure [44]*

wing sortie pulled the Bolton defenders out of position, creating sufficient space for Connelly to stab home his centre. Man-of-the-match McIlroy then ended the contest with a savage shot in the 74th minute. The 89th minute penalty kick, which Jimmy McIlroy blasted past England keeper, Eddie Hopkinson was pure garnish. McIlroy was uncontainable. Bolton tried to subdue him with three rugged markers assigned to block his runs and bruise his heels but to no avail. Jimmy Mac simply used this surfeit of attention to his advantage as his team mates revelled in the extra space around him. It was a triumph of brain over brawn. But Burnley remained in 6th position.

With the festive season almost upon us, today's programme carried an advertisement for a pantomime in Blackpool. One of the perks was the availability of 'hot chicken tea'. When it came to a Christmas feast, those pantomime dames sure knew which buttons to push.

## 12 December 1959

Arsenal 2 Burnley 4
Blackburn Rovers 6 West Ham United 2
Blackpool 3 Chelsea 1
Bolton Wanderers 4 Birmingham City 1
Everton 2 West Bromwich Abion 2
Fulham 1 Tottenham Hotspur 1
Luton Town 3 Newcastle United 4
Manchester City 3 Leeds United 3
Nottingham Forest 1 Manchester United 5
Sheffield Wednesday 2 Preston North End 2
Wolverhampton Wanderers 0 Leicester City 3

## Arsenal 2 v 4 Burnley

*'Rawhide'*

League championships are won not just by superior technique and fluency, but also by greater physical and mental toughness. On this dark, raw day in North London, Burnley proved this most emphatically in what must rate as their most courageous victory of the season. At half-time, Burnley were two down and, with Jimmy McIlroy a limping passenger, they appeared dead and buried. The Clarets were discomforted by Arsenal's 'push and run' tactics and gifted the Gunners the lead when Adam Blacklaw allowed Joe Haverty's hopeful effort to slip through his fingers in the 38th minute. Adding insult to self-inflicted injury, Arsenal's second goal, scored two minutes before half-time, was a disgrace. Having been awarded a free-kick on the edge of Burnley's box, Jackie Henderson barged into the Burnley wall, creating enough of a chink for Jimmy Bloomfield to thread his shot past the unsighted Blacklaw. The Clarets' vociferous protests made no impact upon referee, Sparling.

For the second half, necessity became the mother of invention as Harry Potts instructed the injured McIlroy to adopt a deeper midfield role alongside Adamson and pushed young Brian Miller further forward. It was a master-stroke. From his rear turret, McIlroy defied his deep-seated groin strain, by pinging incisive passes in all directions, while the released Miller created havoc in the Arsenal defence. Nevertheless, with just 23 minutes remaining, Arsenal's two-goal advantage was still intact.

It was Miller's piercing run in the 66th minute that forced the Gunners to concede a crucial corner. Brian Pilkington's flag-kick then picked out Miller perfectly and with the goal at the centre half's mercy, only keeper Kelsey's lunging foul denied him. With McIlroy indisposed, Jimmy Adamson converted the spot-kick with aplomb.

Now it was all Burnley. Arsenal were pushed further and further back and with both Adamson and Miller joining The Clarets' front line, the visitors swarmed all over the besieged 'Gunners'. John Connelly duly brought them level in the 72nd minute with a stinging shot and then bundled Burnley into the lead six minutes later following a scintillating six-man move that had sliced the hosts' defence apart. Not content with this, the England right winger seized his hat trick with two minutes left after capitalising upon Ray Pointer's pass. By this time, Arsenal's frail morale had collapsed. They were taking hits from all directions in what had become a 'turkey shoot'. One local paper would read: 'McIlroy did enough on one leg to make observers wonder to what depths of humiliation Arsenal would have sank if he had been able to bewilder them on two!'

This was Arsenal's third four-goal defeat on the bounce. Their next opponents would go one better. But now the national press started to sit up and pay attention to Burnley. With The Clarets rising three places to third spot, the pundits finally started picking out The Clarets as potential Championship contenders, alongside Wolves and Spurs. This sort of praise rarely bodes well as many 'manager of the month' winners will testify.

The Arsenal programme carried a warning about polio, which still represented a high health risk in 1959, particularly to residents of big cities. In March, Jeff Hall, the ex-Birmingham and England full-back had died of the disease aged 29 years. The polio warning urged those aged 26 years or under who had not protected themselves against polio to visit the London County Council mobile clinic, which was situated in a single-decker bus parked outside the ground.

## 19 December 1959

Bolton Wanderers 0 Blackpool 3
Burnley 0 Leeds United 1
Fulham 0 Blackburn Rovers 1
Leicester City 2 West Ham United 1
Luton Town 2 Everton 1
Manchester United 2 West Bromwich Albion 3
Nottingham Forest 1 Manchester City 2
Preston North End 4 Chelsea 5
Sheffield Wednesday 5 Arsenal 1
Tottenham Hotspur 4 Newcastle United 0
Wolverhampton Wanderers 2 Birmingham City 0

## Burnley 0 v 1 Leeds United

*'Little Donkey'*

The conditions were appalling. The whistling gale and cloying mud robbed Burnley of their customary speed. Without the injured Jimmy McIlroy to pull the strings Burnley lacked their customary sharpness. With their wings clipped and inside forwards, White and Robson, ineffective, Ray Pointer was marooned. Lowly Leeds' muscular defence, ably marshalled by Jack Charlton, contained the tamed Clarets with comfort. Making light of the absence of their playmaker, Don Revie, Leeds grew in confidence and took the game to Burnley. However, their decisive 39th minute goal was another controversial affair. Referee, Sant, inexplicably ignored George Meek's blatant foul upon Alex Elder allowing the Leeds right winger to run unhindered to the by-line from whence he sent in a fizzing, low cross which 'oppo' wide-

*Jack Charlton to the rescue as Burnley fail to break down the Leeds defence [45]*

man, Jackie Overfield steered past Blacklaw. Overfield was delighted, silencing both the Burnley faithful and the Leeds' 'boo boys' at a stroke. His joy was short-lived, though, as he sustained a season-ending cartilage injury later in the game. As much as Burnley huffed and puffed the occupants of the Leeds house were uncharacteristically piggy-like. Their only consolations were the defeats suffered by rivals, Preston and West Ham. Burnley fell one place to fourth spot, one point behind Wolves and three points adrift of Spurs.

## 26 December 1959

Arsenal 0 Luton Town 3
Birmingham City 2 West Ham United 0
Blackpool 1 Blackburn Rovers 0
Bolton Wanderers 2 Wolverhampton Wanderers 1
Chelsea 2 Newcastle United 2
Everton 2 Manchester City 1
Leeds United 2 Tottenham Hotspur 4
Leicester City 2 Preston North End 2
Manchester United 1 Burnley 2
Sheffield Wednesday 1 Fulham 1
West Bromwich Abion 2 Nottingham Forest 3

## Manchester United 1 v 2 Burnley

*'Seven Little Girls Sitting In the Back Seat'*

The Old Trafford of today is situated in an area of modern development. The nearby dockland area has been cleared of its giant cranes, warehouses, flour mills and sprawling sidings. In their place stand chic waterside properties, glass and chrome offices, retail outlets and cultural centres, like the Lowry and Imperial War Museum. A sense of light and space now pervades the area, which was once grimy, rusted, barren and oily, inhabited in *A Taste of Honey* by a gawky Rita Tushingham and her black seaman boyfriend. In 1959, Manchester was struggling to divest itself of its Lowryesque past. It was a place of clattering machinery with tall chimneys releasing serpentine trails of smoke. Black canals turned purple with ill-smelling dye. Although the slum clearance programme had begun, 68,000 of Manchester houses were still considered unfit for habitation. According to Michel Butor author of the contemporary novel *Passing Time*, the city was bleak and soot-laden, often enveloped in a spectral fog with startling neon-lit amusement arcades and cinemas contrasting sharply with the dark pubs and stark monuments. Warming to the experience, Butor felt the city 'swathed his soul like a wet shroud'. The early episodes of *Coronation Street* did little to correct this bleak image, personified by the glaring, hair-netted Ena Sharples as she held court in the inaptly named 'snug' of the *The Rover's Return* – her black looks matching her attire.

United were struggling to divest themselves of their past, too. The Munich tragedy had left them traumatized and short of cash and numbers. Matt Busby had been forced to shell out for replacements and with the coffers almost bare, he flew to Spain to persuade Real Madrid's president into playing two money-spinning friendlies with his team. However, United were still dangerous opponents. During this season they would score over 100 goals with the lithe, stealthy, Dennis Viollet netting a third of these in just 36 appearances. They even had enough strength in depth to consign their troubled England international, Bobby Charlton, to the reserves, although he was recalled at inside left for this fixture on a damp, grey Boxing Day. Unfortunately, Jimmy McIlroy was still unfit, so Ian Lawson was drafted in to replace the previous deputy, Billy White. Again, the conditions were atrocious, but here the heavy pitch disadvantaged United as much as it did Burnley. United's forward momentum was continually blocked by Jimmy Adamson, Bobby Seith and Brian Miller, who were resolute at the back. By contrast, Burnley found greater opportunities on the break. At half-time they were two-up. Robson gave The Clarets a deserved lead in the 22nd minute after combining sharply with Connelly. Lawson then added a second ten minutes before half-time with an acute-angled shot, having been set up by Miller's typically powerful run. After the interval, Burnley were content to soak up whatever pressure United could muster. Their record signing, 'Golden Boy' Albert Quixall managed to reduce the deficit after 65 minutes, prompting a frantic, late, 'Red' assault, but, defying the vociferous 60,000 support, Burnley clung onto their lead tenaciously.

## 28 December 1959

Burnley 1 Manchester United 4
Fulham 1 Sheffield Wednesday 2
Luton Town 0 Arsenal 1
Manchester City 4 Everton 0
Newcastle United 1 Chelsea 1
Nottingham Forest 1 West Bromwich Abion 2
Preston North End 1 Leicester City 1
Tottenham Hotspur 1 Leeds United 4
West Ham United 3 Birmingham City 1
Wolverhampton Wanderers 0 Bolton Wanderers 1

## Burnley 1 v 4 Manchester United

*'Little White Bull'*

Harry Potts made the mistake of recalling Jimmy McIlroy for the return fixture. McIlroy was patently unfit and contributed little to this frustrating defeat. Jimmy recalled: "I was suffering from a deep-rooted groin strain – the type of injury that can handicap a footballer for months, or even a complete season. Playing against Arsenal, the groin first went. Previous to the Arsenal match, I had been on the treatment table daily for five weeks with a pulled muscle and from Highbury I returned to the table for further concentrated treatment. As Christmas approached, I was out of action but it was agreed that I should play in the return game with Manchester United. That match was only five minutes old when I realized I had made a bad decision in electing to play. Burnley came in for considerable criticism for playing me half fit – but here I must make the position clear. Although I played in many matches during the second half of the season when I should really have been resting, at no time did I play against my wishes. The decision was invariably left to me."

As for the game, Dennis Viollet gave United a 20th minute lead but Jimmy Robson produced a superbly headed equalizer eight minutes later prompting a spell of intense Burnley pressure. However, they could not capitalize on their greater possession. Denied by David Gaskell's brilliant goalkeeping and their own profligacy, Burnley were hit on the break with a header from Viollet in the 58th minute and then by two strikes in the final six minutes from their dashing winger and 'Jack the lad', Albert Scanlon. The United players nicknamed Scanlon as 'Joe Friday' after the *Dragnet* TV character on account of his boasts to know the 'ins' and 'outs' of everything. On this grey, misty afternoon, he certainly discovered the 'ins' and 'outs' of Burnley's defence. The locals among the 47,253 crowd returned home very disappointed.

With that the curtain was brought down on 1959. Burnley were still Championship contenders but despite their free scoring abilities (55 goals in 24 games), their defensive vulnerability threatened to undermine them. Up until the New Year they had conceded 40 goals (21 at home), managing to keep clean sheets in just two games. Without greater sturdiness at the back, it was clear that the main prize would elude them.

## First Division

| **31 December 1959** | *P* | *W* | *D* | *L* | *F* | *A* | *Pts* | *Goal average* |
|---|---|---|---|---|---|---|---|---|
| 1. Tottenham Hotspur | 24 | 12 | 8 | 4 | 53 | 30 | 32 | 1.77 |
| 2. Preston North End | 24 | 12 | 7 | 5 | 49 | 39 | 31 | 1.26 |
| 3. BURNLEY | 24 | 13 | 3 | 8 | 55 | 40 | 29 | 1.38 |
| 4. Blackburn Rovers | 24 | 13 | 3 | 8 | 44 | 35 | 29 | 1.26 |
| 5. West Ham United | 24 | 13 | 3 | 8 | 47 | 42 | 29 | 1.12 |
| 6. Wolverhampton Wanderers | 24 | 13 | 2 | 9 | 59 | 45 | 28 | 1.31 |
| 7. Fulham | 24 | 12 | 4 | 8 | 46 | 46 | 28 | 1.00 |
| 8. Sheffield Wednesday | 24 | 11 | 5 | 8 | 45 | 27 | 27 | 1.67 |
| 9. Bolton Wanderers | 24 | 11 | 4 | 9 | 32 | 29 | 26 | 1.10 |
| 10. Manchester United | 24 | 10 | 5 | 9 | 59 | 47 | 25 | 1.26 |
| 11. West Bromwich Albion | 24 | 9 | 6 | 9 | 45 | 39 | 24 | 1.15 |
| 12. Newcastle United | 24 | 9 | 5 | 10 | 47 | 49 | 23 | 0.96 |
| 13. Chelsea | 24 | 9 | 5 | 10 | 46 | 53 | 23 | 0.87 |
| 14. Manchester City | 24 | 10 | 2 | 12 | 52 | 52 | 22 | 1.00 |
| 15. Blackpool | 24 | 8 | 5 | 11 | 34 | 37 | 21 | 0.92 |
| 16. Arsenal | 24 | 8 | 5 | 11 | 38 | 49 | 21 | 0.78 |
| 17. Everton | 24 | 7 | 6 | 11 | 37 | 46 | 20 | 0.80 |
| 18. Leicester City | 24 | 6 | 8 | 10 | 38 | 52 | 20 | 0.73 |
| 19. Nottingham Forest | 24 | 8 | 3 | 13 | 29 | 46 | 19 | 0.63 |
| 20. Leeds United | 24 | 6 | 6 | 12 | 39 | 58 | 18 | 0.67 |
| 21. Birmingham City | 24 | 6 | 5 | 13 | 32 | 47 | 17 | 0.68 |
| 22. Luton Town | 24 | 5 | 6 | 13 | 27 | 45 | 16 | 0.60 |

# JANUARY 1960

In Moscow, President Khrushchev announced that the USSR would cut its armed forces by 1.2 million men over the next two years appealing to the US to begin negotiations on disarmament. President Eisenhower indicated in his State of the Union message on 7 January that Soviet 'deportment and pronouncements suggest the possible opening of a somewhat less strained period in the relationship between the Soviet Union and the Free World', although adding the cautionary note that these 'pleasant promises' needed to be 'tested by performance.' Meanwhile, the US sought to strengthen its defence position in the Pacific by signing a Treaty of Mutual Co-operation and Security with Japan. Eisenhower's caution over arms negotiations was reinforced by a warning issued by his head of Strategic Air Command, General Thomas S. Power, who stated that within two years the USSR would have sufficient long-range missiles to launch a 'massive' attack on the United States.

With Eisenhower's term of office coming to an end, 44-year-old John F. Kennedy decided to run for the American presidency. He had two main obstacles to overcome: his inexperience and his Catholicism but he rejected former president Truman's entreaties to be 'patient for another four years.' Kennedy retorted: 'if all under the age of forty-four were to be excluded from positions of trust and command this would have kept Jefferson from writing the Declaration of Independence, Washington from commanding the Continental Army, Madison from fathering the Constitution and Christopher Columbus from even discovering America.'

The colonial past was catching up with the former Imperial powers. The Algerian crisis had left France on the brink of civil war. President de Gaulle's offer of self-determination for Algerian people favoured the Muslim nationalists more than the French settlers. Led by café owner, Joseph Ortiz, the settlers proceeded to riot and build barricades, killing 14 policemen who were ordered to stop them. Fearing that the army would side with the settlers, De Gaulle sacked the rebellious right wing Algerian commander, General Massu. On 29 January, De Gaulle made his crucial TV appeal, imploring the army not to associate with the rebels. It succeeded. Unit after unit declared its loyalty. The centre of Algiers was cordoned off and the water and electricity supplies shut down. The rebels were isolated.

In Brussels, a month-long conference moved the Congo towards independence with Patrice Lumumba released from prison to act as the senior Congolese negotiator. Our colonial past was coming back to bite us, too, with riots breaking out during Macmillan's visit to Southern Rhodesia (now known as Zimbabwe).

In Bonn, West German Chancellor Adenauer was determined to expunge vestiges of Nazism insisting that offenders in the recent national wave of anti-semitism should be 'thrashed'. The heat that his anger aroused seemed almost lukewarm compared to the political fracas caused by the South African Progressive Party's censure of apartheid.

Meanwhile, Pope John XXIII issued instructions to all Catholics attempting to prevent them from watching 'unsafe' films or TV. Priests were banned from even visiting a cinema or a theatre. Britain's contribution to the moral clampdown was to ban the sale of 'pep pills'.

With the 'new look' shopping centre beginning to take shape, Burnley's Council believed it was time to do something about the town's 'Victorian monstrosity' of a railway station. The British Transport Commission was urged to renovate the dilapidated Central Station building. You could see the Council's point of view. They wanted to present Burnley to new investors as a town of the future not one festering in its past.

For those who still had faith in the future of the textile business, there was the heartening news that the Barden Mill Company was now running double shifts in order to meet the increasing demand for specialist textiles. Nevertheless, the Town Council continued to press for other industries to move to the Burnley. In January they extended an invitation to car manufacturers to move into the area. Although prospective investors were encouraged by the possibility of cheaper labour, the communications difficulties remained as a significant impediment. However, there was reason to cheer when the Government's decided to award Burnley a grant to cover 75% of the cost of constructing a ring road.

*Burnley Central Railway Station in 1959: 'a Victorian monstrosity' [46]*

In mid-January, Burnley had its first substantial snowfall of the winter, with the salt-pocked and yellowing snow clinging to the pavements all week. While the Burnley Co-op offered 20/- (£1) savings on coal an increasing number of central heating providers were moving into the market. The Hudson Heating Company of Jack Bridge asked: 'Oil or toil this winter? Move with the times and change to oil'. Notwithstanding the impact of the Suez crisis, there was a widespread belief that oil would become the staple fuel of the future. After the Yom Kippur War in 1973, that confidence was shaken badly.

During the early fifties, Burnley's atmosphere had often been heavily polluted during the winter months. It was a legacy of its heavy industry, its fossil fuel heating and, of course, its valley location. On dank, still days, dark smoke and grit from its chimneys would combine with the fog to produce dense sulphurous 'smog'. Visibility could then plummet to less than five yards. It was a problem which afflicted most large, built up areas in Britain, causing thousands of respiratory-related illnesses and deaths. The Clean Air Act had been passed in the summer of 1956 in order to address this health hazard. The Act banned the emission of dark smoke from chimneys, trains and industrial furnaces. It also contained measures to limit the discharge of grit into the atmosphere. The Act gave local authorities wider powers to establish smoke control zones. Some emissions would still be allowed but householders were offered grants towards the cost of converting their coal-burning grates to smokeless fuel. Initially, progress was slow because smokeless fuel was more expensive but with more competitive pricing and wider options being offered, including oil or gas fired central heating, habits began to change. As a result the local air quality gradually improved, particularly once Burnley's steam-driven industry began to thin out.

After rationing had been progressively removed during the first half of the fifties, foods such as sugar, butter, cheese, margarine, cooking fat, bacon, meat and tea became more plentiful. Not that this injected much more variety into our standard menus. The legacy of fifteen years of rationing and food shortages meant that most working or middle-class households, that is to say, their women members, were not equipped to go beyond plain cooking.

Up until the end of the decade the standard meal in a working or middle-class home was meat and two veg. It was accepted practice that the Sunday joint should be eked out over three or even four days. After the roast came cold meat and bubble and squeak, made up from the remains of Sunday's vegetables, perhaps accompanied by some chutney or piccalilli for a smidgen of flavour. A shepherd's pie usually provided the joint's final flourish, with the meagre morsels of hand-minced meat heavily supplemented by bread and onion. For variety, macaroni cheese might turn up after the joint had been taken down to the bare bones, though the bones might be sufficient to provide a wisp of taste for some home-made soup bulked out with carrots, potatoes and pearl barley. The joint had another essential by-product – dripping. This was a mass of congealed fat and jelly which was spread onto bread or toast as a snack. It slid down better than Foie Gras. For special occasions a steak and kidney pudding might appear, with the invariably fatty stewing steak encased in suet. It is small wonder that the 'baby boomer' generation was cast as the coronary kids.

Fish commonly appeared on Fridays, and not just for Catholics. The fish was often bought from a delivery man on his 'fish round'. If kippers or haddock were on the menu these were sometimes poached in milk. This was not to everyone's taste. One 'baby boomer' said: 'to this day, I think things poached in milk look like someone's already eaten them'. Nevertheless, Friday was frequently the only day of the week when our hearts were given a break for Saturdays were widely synonymous with sausages. The Saturday sausage was more alliterative than alluring since the fifties' models spat fat with venomous velocity and were, in any event, stuffed with less meat than *KiteKat*. As proof of their blubber-inducing qualities a well-known brand of sausages was advertised by the corpulent actor playing Friar Tuck in ITV's *The Adventures of Robin Hood*. If your house did not have a garden or an allotment, the choice of vegetables was often limited to 'runners', cabbage, peas, onions and carrots. Broccoli and asparagus had not yet been invented.

In the fifties, a cooked dessert was de rigueur. Sunday was essentially a pie day – apple, rhubarb and occasionally gooseberry, when in season. During the week, once the pie leftovers were consumed, the milk pudding reigned supreme, with rice, semolina, farola and tapioca (aka 'frog spawn') puddings to savour. In winter, sponge and suet puddings were popular, providing sumptuous mega-cholesterol feasts of jam or treacle sponges, jam roly polys or spotted dicks, all accompanied by custard with the thick, dark yellow skin. Mind you, this fat-frenzied diet was quite functional. In those days our houses were arcticly cold in winter. Our bodies needed a few tyres of confidence.

Before the emergence of the supermarket towards the end of the fifties, shopping was a laborious and piecemeal process. Quite frequently, housewives would only buy sufficient ingredients for the daily meal with delivery men providing a fresh supply of milk, bread, fish, meat and other groceries. Until the early sixties, *Sainsbury's* sold its butter, cheese, bacon and biscuits to order with queues forming in front of its marble-topped counters. Their shop assistants would use a stretch of wire to cut the cheese from large roundels and wooden spatulas to pat the butter into shape. The bacon was sliced from a large hock and biscuits dispensed from large barrels. The aromas inside their store were heavenly. Meanwhile, the legacy of Empire was retained by grocery shops like *Home and Colonial*. Of course, once fridges became affordable, shopping habits began to change although there was some initial hesitation about frozen foods. These were often seen as inferior to home-grown or – cooked varieties and even considered vulgar in some middle-class households.

It was rare for working class families to eat out except when on a day trip or on holiday. Mostly, these meals were taken at a 'greasy spoon' café or, if in London, at a Lyon's Corner House cafeteria. The food was generally of poor quality. Novelist John Wain described a typical offering in his novel, *Living in the Present*: 'corned-beef rissoles, a spoonful of greens boiled to rags and tasting of soda, and perhaps a chunk of waxy ice-cream to follow.' At a time when TV chefs, including Fanny Cradock and Philip Harben, were championing something better than wartime austerity, there were few defenders of British catering. Outrageously, Egon Ronay claimed: 'what they do in Wales could be called gastronomic rape, except that they don't seem to derive any pleasure from it.' It was left to the Americans and the Italians to show us the way, although Indian and Chinese cuisine was making tentative advances, albeit principally in London. Unsurprisingly, it was an American company which was the first to challenge the cartel of insipid British catering when it opened its first Wimpy bar here in 1954. The Wimpy offered grilled hamburgers, Knickerbocker Glories and milkshakes which had an immediate appeal for teenagers, buoyant with increasing affluence. The Italians delivered their standard Berni Inn menu of prawn cocktail, steak and chips and Black Forest gateau at an affordable price and also won over the teenage market with the Expresso (*as they were then known*) coffee bars. Not that everyone was taken with their glass – cupped coffee as illustrated by a typically lugubrious Tony Hancock in his 1960 film *The Rebel*: 'I don't want any froth! I want a cup of coffee! I don't want to wash my clothes in it!'

School dinners provided children with their principal eating out experience. Just over half of all school children received these in 1950. By 1966 this proportion had risen to a peak of 70%. In the fifties, the meals were usually delivered in huge metal containers over substantial distances, so that the food was already congealed on arrival. With the meat full of gristle, inventive disposals were required to evade the attentions of pinched Stafford Cripps – like school staff on monastic missions to combat waste. Many children's hatred of greens began here for when the container lids was lifted the customary stench was intestinal.

When commercial TV was launched in 1955, the country was introduced to a wider variety of food. The advertising jingles and slogans such as 'Snap, crackle and pop', 'Go to work on an egg', 'Oxo gives a meal more man appeal' gradually became a part of our culture, extolling an image of an idealised nuclear family, which was already becoming anachronistic. These not-so-'hidden persuaders' also helped create a growing child consumer market by touting new confectionery like Wagon Wheels (which were definitely bigger then) and gizmos in cereal packets, such as little submarines that operated with baking powder. With increasing affluence offering housewives greater freedom, faster food became more attractive. Shop-bought cakes began to supplement the home-made variety but it would take most of the sixties to divest ourselves of the disciplines of the austerity years. We did not require instruction on the re-cycling of leftover food we simply reached for our frying pans.

## 2 January 1960

Arsenal 4 Wolverhampton Wanderers 4
Birmingham City 0 Tottenham Hotspur 1
Blackburn Rovers 1 Nottingham Forest 2
Blackpool 3 Fulham 1
Chelsea 2 Leicester City 2
Everton 0 Bolton Wanderers 1
Leeds United 1 Luton Town 1
Manchester City 4 Sheffield Wednesday 1
Newcastle United 7 Manchester United 3
West Bromwich Abion 4 Preston North End 0
West Ham United 2 Burnley 5

## West Ham United 2 v 5 Burnley

*'Way Down Yonder In New Orleans'*

This game was played just two days before Albert Camus's death in a road crash. When asked whether he preferred the theatre or football Camus replied: "Football, without hesitation"; adding: "after many years during which I saw many things, what I know most surely about morality and the duty of man, I owe to sport and learned it in the RUA" (Racing Universitaire Algerios, the club for which he kept goal before succumbing to TB). The novelist remarked: "in the depth of winter I finally learned that there was in me an invincible summer". Unfortunately for West Ham, their invincible summer had turned into susceptible winter after hammerings by The Owls 7-0 and Blackburn 6-2. Things were not about to improve.

As a result of the recent deluges, Upton Park resembled Agincourt. Mud, freshly glistened by the swirling drizzle, stretched from one goalmouth to the other. Only the wings offered a refuge to the thin remaining grass and that's where Harry Potts instructed his team to play. Jimmy McIlroy was still troubled by his groin injury and ruled out. Lawson was restored as his replacement. There was a buzz that long term absentee Colin McDonald might also be brought back in goal having managed a recent 'A' team fixture. Alas, the game was up for the former England keeper. He was unable to claw his way back to full fitness and form and finally left Turf Moor a year later.

*Ted Fenton's West Ham, featuring the young Bobby Moore [47]*

The game was the flip side of the Turf Moor encounter in August. It was a reversal of the Agincourt result, too, with Burnley's fleet footed cavalry triumphing in the East End swamp. True, West Ham managed to exert brief pressure on Adam Blacklaw's goal after Phil Woosnam's fortuitous 12th minute equaliser, but for the most part Burnley were totally ascendant, trampling discourteously all over their hosts. Brian Pilkington and John Connelly destroyed the Hammers on their flanks, leaving the home full backs, Joe Kirkup and Noel Cantwell, frequently floundering in the wingers' spattering wakes.

Benefiting from the impetus of his massive mud slalom, Ian Lawson slid in Burnley's first after 11 minutes. He was then hauled off so that his mudpack could be removed and his sight recovered. Brian Pilkington's brilliant run and chip in the 32nd minute, atoned for Adam Blacklaw's slip before John Connelly's crisp shot just before the break made The Clarets' advantage almost unassailable. Ian Lawson took Burnley out of sight in the 75th minute when he converted Brian Pilkington's towering header, a monumental feat by Burnley's tiny left winger, the smallest player on the pitch. West Ham were gifted a penalty three minutes later, yet another mystifying decision from referee, Stokes, but Burnley brushed this irritation aside with Connelly blasting a swerving drive past Noel Dwyer in the 89th minute to complete a 5-2 rout.

Peter Kinlan of the *Sunday Pictorial* commented: 'who better than Burnley to end West Ham's run of seven home wins in a row? For this was brisk, business-like Burnley turning on a super show … as they darted like demons across the mud to hit the Hammers well and truly on the head … Perky

'Pilky' gave West Ham's right back, Joe Kirkup a rare run – around. 'Crafty' Connelly put on a dazzling display – worthy of the international he is. So pulverising was the Connelly treatment of Eire full back, Noel Cantwell that West Ham had to move him to their forward line in the second half. Accurate and artistic, the Burnley wing twins tore gigantic gaps in West Ham's defence'.This win took Burnley moved up to second place, three points adrift of Spurs. However as Peter Kinlan observed, 'if they go on playing like this they'll soon have nobody above them'.

## 9th January 1960
## Lincoln City 1 v 1 Burnley (FA Cup 3rd Round)

*'Bad Boy'*

With Burnley en route to Lincoln, Egyptian President Nasser prepared to lay the Aswan Dam's foundation stone, signifying that a show of force can prevail even against a more powerful foe. It was in these fenland parts that this country made its defiant show of force against the initially greater power of Nazi Germany. It was called 'reaping the wild wind'. Each night ungainly Lancaster, Stirling and Halifax bombers, gorged with high explosives, would drone across a sombre, corrugated sea, straining for an unenlightened height from which they would exact bloody revenge upon the Ruhr and targets beyond. Blurring the distinction between war and religion, Lincoln Cathedral accorded the Lancaster bomber stained glass immortality. Set on a steep hill, the towering Minster continues to preside dramatically over the City's past and present. So fittingly, its iconic features, set against thunderous skies, were outlined on the front cover of the Imps' tu'ppeny programme, beneath which 'Lincoln City FC' was printed in gothic script. By contrast, Burnley, were left with a prosaic font. If this represented Lincoln's claim for cultural superiority, it is doubtful whether Harry Potts would have felt slighted since Burnley came to Sincil Bank as the second strongest team in the land.

Not that Lincoln were push overs. They were then a middling Second Division side with an impressive record of turning over bigger clubs. Liverpool had been thumped 4-2 at Sincil Bank and 3-1 at Anfield, where inside forward, Bert Linnecor, had scored a hat trick. Derby (6-2), Middlesbrough (5-2) and Charlton (5-3), had been put to the sword by the free-scoring 'Imps'. Their six forwards would share 64 goals over this season with the fast, direct winger, Jack McClelland notching 18 and record scorer, Andy Graver adding another 12 to his 100 plus tally. With tough half back Bob Jackson shoring up the home defence, Burnley had a real fight on their hands. Yet another heavy pitch and a passionate 21,963 crowd made the task even more daunting.

Harry Potts conceded later that this tie had been a struggle. He concluded: "It is true that we had many pulsating moments of anxiety in our first encounter with Lincoln City, but having regard to the fact that the second half found us labouring under a very serious handicap, through John Angus being unfit as the result of a mishap during the game: the additional and very important factor that we were without the services of Jim McIlroy, and also bearing in mind our first half supremacy which was worth at least a two goal lead instead of a one goal lead provided by Ray Pointer (after 29 minutes), I feel we deserved the share of second half luck that came our way in those tense last 20 minutes. And if we had had that extra goal to help our efforts, there is little doubt, I think, that we should have finished winners at Sincil Bank. Admittedly, the fine efforts Lincoln made to turn our difficulties to their advantage undoubtedly entitled them to a second chance."

Although Burnley were the better side in the first half, there was little doubt that Lincoln deserved their draw having laid siege to the Burnley goal for most of the second half. Burnley were forced into a series of desperate clearances as Lincoln mounted one muddy onslaught after another. It couldn't last and it didn't. The Imps' inside forward Ron Harbertson finally equalized in the 65th minute, deservedly earning Lincoln a second chance three days later.

## 12 January 1960
## Burnley 2 v 0 Lincoln City (FA Cup 3rd Round replay)

*'Staccato's Theme'*

The BBC had discovered that half the nation watched TV at peak times, but 35,456 put the box aside on this cold evening to cheer on The Clarets. In those days the FA Cup ties had a higher cache than the League games among supporters. How strange that now seems.

Harry Potts commented: "we did not enter into this second chapter without our pre-match anxieties. There was the question of whether John Angus and Jim McIlroy would stand up to the test. We did not decide to include them without feeling very sure that they were both fit to play again, but fitness tests and other examinations are never so stern as match play itself, and there is always that little bit of uncertainty whether players who have been out of action or under treatment, as they have had to be, will break down inside ninety minutes of football as strenuous as Cup-tie football is. Happily both stood up to the exacting test splendidly, and most certainly that was of great value to our efforts on Tuesday evening. I did not fail to note the shrewdness of my respected fellow manager, Bill Anderson, in putting Angus's fitness to the test. Happily, the result was very gratifying to me for

John met it firmly enough to demonstrate that he had no injury problem on his mind. We benefited enormously too, from the re-appearance of 'Mac' and realised what they had escaped from by what he did on Tuesday without being in top gear." Although not fully fit, Jimmy Mac celebrated his return with a carefully stroked penalty goal and, with Brian Pilkington heading a second from Jimmy McIlroy's free-kick, Burnley cantered to victory.

Jimmy McIlroy remembered: "Influenza kept me out of the Third Round Cup-tie at Lincoln. I was up and about again before the Tuesday replay: or rather I was fit enough to return to the treatment room. I turned out in that replay, despite having to nurse my leg all the time. At a vital stage in the match Burnley were awarded a penalty kick and it was my job to take it. As I placed the ball on the spot, I debated with myself whether to place my shot or blast it. The goalposts seemed to be miles apart, a good omen for me. Feeling certain I would score, I stroked the ball home to put us one goal to the good (after 26 minutes). Our second goal was scored by Brian Pilkington (eleven minutes later), heading in a free kick I had taken from near the right corner flag. The newspapers were most flattering in their descriptions of the accuracy with which I had placed the ball on to 'Pilky's' head ... but I must now be honest and admit that I intended the ball for Jimmy Robson!"

## 16 January 1960

Bolton Wanderers P Luton Town P
Burnley 2 Chelsea 1
Fulham 0 Everton 0
Leeds United 3 West Ham United 0
Leicester City 0 West Bromwich Albion 1
Manchester United 2 Birmingham City 1
Nottingham Forest 0 Blackpool 0
Preston North End 1 Newcastle United 2
Sheffield Wednesday 3 Blackburn Rovers 0
Tottenham Hotspur 3 Arsenal 0
Wolverhampton Wanderers 4 Manchester City 2

## Burnley 2 v 1 Chelsea

*'Why'*

Today winter applied an icy grip in Burnley, too. With only the goalmouths and the field markings cleared of crumpling snow, both teams had difficulty in keeping their feet. Languishing Chelsea were determined to tilt the odds further in their favour by substituting ruggedness for skill. Right-back, John Sillett and midfield enforcer, Stan Crowther, were their worst offenders with

*Chelsea desperately defend their goal against Burnley's forwards [48]*

poor Brian Pilkington their principal victim. With little protection coming from referee Langdale, Burnley's left-winger took a frightful battering, limping off at the final whistle with severe bruising and swelling on his legs and ankle.

Brian recalled: "Chelsea's left-back, Peter Sillett, was a lovely bloke but, his brother, John at right-back could be nasty. We were playing Chelsea. It was right cold with snow covering the pitch. As I went by 'Snozz', he hit me hard on the inside of my knee, bruising the ligament. As I lay there in the snow, he hissed at me: 'that's for taking the p*** at Chelsea'."

However, Pilky refused to succumb, bravely returning to the fray after these outrageous challenges and determinedly running again and again at the flailing Chelsea defenders. It was Jimmy Robson who delivered the vital blows, though. Having opened the scoring in the 38th minute by converting John Angus's precise free-kick, he secured the points after 64 minutes by capitalizing upon Ray Pointer's sliced pass and hammering the ball past Reg Matthews.

*Another Burnley raid on the Chelsea goal as The Clarets run out 2-1 victors[49]*

Chelsea's sole moment of joy was entirely providential. Johnny Brooks guided Peter Brabrook's pass home in the 52nd minute after the Burnley defence had been caught slithering and sliding out of position.

## 23 January 1960

Birmingham City 2 Preston North End 1
Blackburn Rovers 0 Wolverhampton Wanderers 1
Blackpool 0 Sheffield Wednesday 2
Chelsea 1 Leeds United 3
Everton 6 Nottingham Forest 1
Luton Town 4 Fulham 1
Manchester City 1 Arsenal 2
Newcastle United 0 Leicester City 2
Tottenham Hotspur 2 Manchester United 1
West Bromwich Albion 0 Burnley 0
West Ham United 1 Bolton Wanderers 2

## West Bromwich Albion 0 v 0 Burnley

*'Be My Guest'*

In the early 1960s, football journalist Peter Morris described the Black Country, the home of the Albion thus: 'this aptly designated and singularly disfigured tract of industrial conurbation sprawls massively from the north-west boundaries of Birmingham, taking in much of South Staffordshire and the north-eastern fringes of Worcestershire. Squat, grimed houses and cottages are squeezed together here on sooty parade in stiff defiant little rows and squares all along the railway lines, with power cables and the monolithic ranges of waste tips and charred reeking hummocks, wreathed perpetually in the smoke and the dust and the grit of it all; a harsh acreage of pithead, iron foundry and blast furnace. This sturdy environment helped produce the Albion football club and, ultimately, its own brand of spectator. This is a land notorious for hardship and sweated labour, for enterprise, too, and an incredible capacity for hard work which has brought wealth in its wake. There is strength of character in its men and women as resolute as you will find in all the length and breadth of England.' So, there were no easy pickings to be had here, then.

*West Bromwich Albion 1959/60 [49a]*

Actually, the home form of ninth-placed West Bromwich had been erratic thus far with seven League victories but also five defeats. Since the Turf Moor encounter, 'The Baggies' had replaced the departed Maurice Setters with Darlaston lad, 'Chuck' Drury, another tough competitor. Jock Wallace had displaced Ray Potter in goal and the powerful Welsh full back, Graham Williams had taken over from his namesake, Stuart. Andy Aitken, a winger from Hibernian, had been added to the squad but had struggled to make an impact. The West Bromwich line-up for this game was unchanged from that which had just reeled off four victories on the bounce. By contrast, Burnley were not at full strength. Deprived, by injury, of Jimmy McIlroy and Brian Pilkington, two of their main attacking assets, Burnley were then hampered by Ray Pointer's lameness following a strong tackle by West Bromwich defender, Don Howe. Setting aside their misfortune, Burnley battled fiercely to secure both a clean sheet and a point in this stalemate played at the squishy Hawthorns. Regrettably for them, Spurs were able to extend their lead having beaten Manchester United 2-1 and with Wolves winning 3-1 at Ewood Park, the Wanderers were now just one point behind The Clarets.

## 30 January 1960
## Swansea Town 0 v 0 Burnley (FA Cup 4rd Round)

*'Voice In The Wilderness'*

Burnley had another tough visit to negotiate. Like Lincoln, Swansea were a mid-table Second Division side and like Lincoln they had a reputation for scoring and conceding goals with equal facility. Over the previous three seasons they had shipped an incredible 270 league goals. Their keeper, John

King, had been given a spell up front although it was unclear whether this was as a reward or as a punishment. King was back between the sticks, though, when Burnley came to town. Swansea's principal strikers were the combative, niggling Manchester United veteran, Colin Webster, and the small but abrasive Brayley Reynolds, sporting an Elvis quiff. The bustling Reynolds was not exactly blessed with silky skills. A Swansea supporter recalled him once scoring a hat-trick with each goal elbow-assisted. The Swans' main providers were winger, Len Allchurch, brother of the Newcastle inside-forward, Ivor, and former Magpie inside-forward, Reg Davies. At the back they had the commanding young centre half, Mel Nurse.

An unattributed press cutting described the game thus: 'clinging, heavy mud plus the iron will of eleven Welsh heroes almost brought the downfall of much fancied Burnley. Indeed, all Wales was arguing last night about a goal, which everyone claims Swansea scored. It happened in the 65th minute, when the strength-sapping mud was taking its toll. Swansea golden boy, 17-year-old Barry Jones put over a picture centre for Reg Davies to slam home. 'Goal' yelled the 30,000 crowd, but the linesman was waving frantically and caught the eye of referee Powell. The offside decision was a bit of a mystery. Reg Davies protested: "I was behind the ball when it was passed. I couldn't have been offside". Referee Powell explained to me, "Davies was not offside. It was centre-forward Reynolds who was standing in front of the ball". Said Swansea manager, Trevor Morris: "we'll win the replay".'

## First Division

| **23 January 1960** | *P* | *W* | *D* | *L* | *F* | *A* | *Pts* | *Goal average* |
|---|---|---|---|---|---|---|---|---|
| 1. Tottenham Hotspur | 27 | 15 | 8 | 4 | 59 | 31 | 38 | 1.90 |
| 2. BURNLEY | 27 | 15 | 4 | 8 | 62 | 43 | 34 | 1.44 |
| 3. Wolverhampton Wanderers | 27 | 15 | 3 | 9 | 68 | 51 | 33 | 1.33 |
| 4. Sheffield Wednesday | 27 | 13 | 5 | 9 | 51 | 31 | 31 | 1.65 |
| 5. Preston North End | 27 | 12 | 7 | 8 | 51 | 47 | 31 | 1.09 |
| 6. Bolton Wanderers | 26 | 13 | 4 | 9 | 35 | 30 | 30 | 1.17 |
| 7. Fulham | 27 | 13 | 4 | 10 | 50 | 53 | 30 | 0.94 |
| 8. West Bromwich Albion | 27 | 11 | 7 | 9 | 50 | 39 | 29 | 1.28 |

| | *P* | *W* | *D* | *L* | *F* | *A* | *Pts* | *Goal average* |
|---|---|---|---|---|---|---|---|---|
| 9. Blackburn Rovers | 27 | 13 | 3 | 11 | 45 | 41 | 29 | 1.10 |
| 10. West Ham United | 27 | 13 | 3 | 11 | 50 | 52 | 29 | 0.96 |
| 11. Manchester United | 27 | 11 | 5 | 11 | 65 | 57 | 27 | 1.14 |
| 12. Newcastle United | 27 | 11 | 5 | 11 | 56 | 55 | 27 | 1.02 |
| 13. Manchester City | 27 | 11 | 2 | 14 | 59 | 59 | 24 | 1.00 |
| 14. Blackpool | 27 | 9 | 6 | 12 | 37 | 40 | 24 | 0.93 |
| 15. Chelsea | 27 | 9 | 6 | 12 | 50 | 60 | 24 | 0.83 |
| 16. Arsenal | 27 | 9 | 6 | 12 | 44 | 57 | 24 | 0.77 |
| 17. Leeds United | 27 | 8 | 7 | 12 | 46 | 60 | 23 | 0.77 |
| 18. Leicester City | 27 | 7 | 9 | 11 | 42 | 55 | 23 | 0.76 |
| 19. Everton | 27 | 8 | 6 | 13 | 43 | 50 | 22 | 0.86 |
| 20. Nottingham Forest | 27 | 9 | 4 | 14 | 32 | 53 | 22 | 0.60 |
| 21. Birmingham City | 27 | 7 | 5 | 15 | 35 | 51 | 19 | 0.69 |
| 22. Luton Town | 26 | 6 | 7 | 13 | 32 | 47 | 19 | 0.68 |

## FEBRUARY 1960

According to Harold Macmillan, the international political wind was changing. He was referring to the growth of national consciousness and the dissolution of the nineteenth century colonial empires. On 3 February he warned his South African parliamentary audience that the great issue for the remainder of the Twentieth Century was whether the uncommitted people of Asia and Africa would gravitate towards the communist East or to the capitalist West. Not that these portents impressed his South African hosts too much. South African Premier, Verwoerd retorted: 'there has to be justice not only for the black man in Africa but also for the white man.' This was just one month before the Sharpeville massacre.

Macmillan was true to his word. Within three weeks of his policy-defining speech, the Kenya constitutional conference in London reached agreement. Black Majority rule was ensured after universal suffrage was introduced with Black and White voters having equal rights. Finally, a line was drawn under the policy of repression which scarred the latter days of British rule. This had culminated in the brutal beatings and subsequent deaths of 11 Mau Mau dissidents at the infamous Hola Camp. Now in a spirit of reconciliation, the British government, represented by Colonial Secretary, Iain Macleod, offered to buy a million acres of the fertile White Highlands of Kenya for redistribution as smallholdings to Black African farmers.

Whilst South Africa clung to its policy of apartheid, the American South legislated for racial integration but more is required than the force of law to eliminate bloody prejudice and uphold civil rights. This week a bomb was detonated at the home of one of the first black pupils to attend Little Rock Central High School. Here, the winds of change had become whipped up into a savage twister. Meanwhile, Martin Luther King was arrested for perjury in connection with his state income tax return of 1956.

Britain agreed with France to jointly build a supersonic airliner capable of flying at 2,000mph. The estimated cost of each aircraft was put at £5-6 million, but the final purchase cost proved to be in the order of £23 million. Nevertheless, Concorde was about to become a reality.

The sexual morality of young people was also a concern home and abroad. Here, the debate focused upon the liberating impact of the contraceptive pill. A front-page article in the *News of World* described the anger of the Catholic clergy and social workers at the experimental production of the 'penny contraceptive pill'. The social workers feared for the morality of teenage girls while the Bishop of Nottingham said, 'New methods have been proposed to thwart God's purpose in marriage'. Meanwhile in the US, there were increasing worries about the spread of venereal disease. Connecticut reacted by banning the sale of *Playboy* magazines from its news stands.

When it came to protecting women's rights in 1960 Britain still had some way to go. In one reported court case of serious domestic violence, the presiding magistrate, Colonel Leonard Stevens simply suggested that the victim 'make her husband sweep the floor and do some chores'. Her husband assured the court, 'I love my missus, sir, and she's a good cook an' all'.

On 13 February the Town Council were informed that the Board of Trade would not be providing Government funding to help establish new industries in the area. The news was met with 'shock and disappointment.' Representation was made to Reginald Maudling, President of the Board of Trade calling for Burnley's inclusion on the D-Area list, which would enable the area to benefit from development funding. On 27 February Maudling promised to take corrective action 'if unemployment should soar' in Burnley. Since December, Burnley's unemployment figures had risen. 2.5% of its working population were now without employment, which was 0.5% above the national average but 1.5% below the threshold for D-Area assistance. Both MPs for the area called upon the Government to recognise the true employment situation in the Burnley area, issuing warnings about the 'false cotton boom.' Now there was no need to be politically circumspect. Daniel Jones MP pressed for a meeting with Maudling to advance the case for investment in the area.

The economic gloom was not relieved by the weather. On 18 February the town cowered under a day-long blizzard. The roads were treacherous with a

Corporation bus plunging down a 15 foot embankment outside Laneshaw Bridge. The weather was not any better elsewhere. Burnley's game at Birmingham had to be called off. However, there was the consolation that the club had been chosen to represent England in an international tournament in New York during the summer months. Club chairman Bob Lord said: "This is the highest honour we've ever been offered." Bob would change his tune on arrival in America when he and his team were brought face-to-face with the tournament's shambolic organisation.

It was all change in Burnley's market, after the Burnley Chamber of Trade agreed to alter Burnley's traditional market day on a Monday to a Tuesday. It was all change at the bus station too as the futuristic design for the new building was finally revealed.

*'The Vic', Burnley in the early sixties [50]*

## 2 February 1960
## Burnley 2 v 1 Swansea Town (FA Cup 4th Round replay)

*'Reveille Rock'*

Burnley's display at Turf Moor had a pleasing familiarity about it: a familiar show of strength, despite the omission of Jimmy Mac who continued to struggle against injury. His restoration at the wretched Vetch had again proved premature, labouring, as he did, in the oozing mud. With Ian Lawson still incapacitated after the knocks he had suffered against Chelsea and West

Bromwich, Billy White was brought in as Jimmy McIlroy's replacement. Brian Pilkington was back to full fitness, though, having had two weeks to nurse his bruises.

This replay proved to be a tougher proposition than the Lincoln game but Burnley rose to the challenge splendidly, prompting Harry Potts to give the following ecstatic post-match summary. "We read a lot today about what are termed as soccer's missing millions. I don't believe it. My reason for stating this is the attendance we had here on Tuesday evening for our replay with Swansea Town. We could not expect a big crowd from Swansea for a mid-week game. Our gate depended on people from a fairly close radius and when one takes into account that there was another replay tapping the area of support, no more than 20 miles away, an attendance of just over 37,000 was indeed gratifying. But one can go further. Throughout Monday night and all day Tuesday, rain had been falling. Appreciating as I do, this show of interest, I am happy to find that those who braved the conditions to see the match, found it worth their time. As at Swansea, it was another game of thrills and spills in plenty – a rollicking Cup-tie. In spite of nail-biting moments we went through in the closing phase, I consider we deserved our victory. Moreover, our football was good enough to be remembered with satisfaction. Similarly, I am equally sure that all will remember with admiration the fine spirit and endeavour produced by our opponents. They put up a brilliant fight, when all seemed lost, throwing everything to the winds in that last rescue bid. I think it provided very encouraging evidence that we have quite something to go to the market with when it comes to Cup fighting." Thanks to Jimmy Robson's two goals in the 28th and 47th minutes, Burnley had just sufficient protection against Swansea's furious late rally.

Jimmy McIlroy remembered: "missing several League matches, I returned to the team for the Fourth Round Cup-tie against Swansea Town at the Vetch Field. It was an exciting match but not a good one. The pitch was muddy, heavy and wet. On the Sunday my leg was even more painful than it had been after previous outings. I thought this time I was a definite non-starter. I almost said a non-runner but I had been that since Christmas! Watching the replay from the trainer's box, I decided never again to envy spectators their lot at vitally important games. It was agony to watch the Swansea players storming our goal in the closing minutes, besieging our defence after being apparently well beaten'. Swansea's centre half, Mel Nurse, scored in the 83rd minute after being pushed forward in a forlorn attempt to recover lost ground. Jimmy continued: 'But Burnley eliminated Swansea 2-1 and for the third time were drawn away from home. This time Bradford City, who had given Everton a hiding in the previous round, were to be our opponents."

## 6 February 1960

Arsenal 5 Blackburn Rovers 2
Burnley 2 Newcastle United 1
Fulham 1 Bolton Wanderers 1
Leeds United 1 West Bromwich Albion 4
Leicester City 1 Birmingham City 3
Manchester United 0 Manchester City 0
Nottingham Forest 2 Luton Town 0
Preston North End 1 Tottenham Hotspur 1
Sheffield Wednesday 2 Everton 2
West Ham United 4 Chelsea 2
Wolverhampton Wanderers 1 Blackpool 1

## Burnley 2 v 1 Newcastle United

*'Starry Eyed'*

While Burnley town centre was still in the throes of re-development the programme for today's game harked back to the previous decade. Clarkson Bros coal and coke merchants of Manchester Road depot suggested: 'now that coal is off the ration buy your supplies from us', while A. Simon: tailor and outfitter and outfitter insisted that 'the man with taste' smoked a pipe; had a brylcreemed short back and sides hair style; chose a Toplin or Tern non-iron white shirt and a diagonally striped tie and insisted upon cavalry twill flannels finished off with a loosely buttoned Harris Tweed sports jacket. It was not exactly *'Expresso Bongo'*. Meanwhile, P. Eastwood (Burnley) LTD. of 44a, St. James Street prided themselves on their 'Rolls Royce Motor Hearse and Fleet of Austin Cars for Funerals' followed by an underlined statement: 'Wedding and Private Parties a Speciality'. Talk about hedging your bets. Their proudest boast, though, was that they offered the 'Finest Fleet of Sun Saloon and All-Weather Coaches.' Whatever did they mean by *'All-weather coaches'*?! Puffing Billy, anyone?

*Northern Ireland colleagues Jimmy McIlroy and Alex Elder enjoy an away trip on an 'all weather' coach. It looks like a cold ride [51]*

As for the London Midland railway adverts for the forthcoming away games at Birmingham (*ultimately postponed*) and Bolton, these made no mention of weather-proofed carriages so it was probably safe to assume a dry, if absurdly long ride. The excursion to Birmingham, costing 17/6 (73p) was due to leave Burnley Central at 8-15 a.m.! The Bolton trip, a 23-mile journey costing 4/3 (23p), was due to leave shortly after 1p.m. It might have been marginally quicker to cycle to both. It was left to Althams Travel Services of 29, Market Street to confirm that this was the modern world. Althams offered a complete service including: 'steamship passages and cruises to all parts of the world; booking agency for air lines; British and continental holidays arranged. Passports etc. dealt with.' Not to be outdone on the home front, they offered bookings for British holiday camps, too.

As for the game, Jimmy Robson again showed the sceptical Turf Moor supporters what it means to be hot. Jimmy Adamson's astute pass enabled the young Geordie to break from the half way line and, from fully 30 yards out, he left fly with a sizzling drive that flashed past Brian Harvey's desperate dive. Having put Burnley ahead after just four minutes it was left to Robson's forward partner, Ray Pointer, to snatch the points with an exquisite lob in the 67th minute.

In between these two sublime strikes, Burnley laboured to stay in the game as those brilliant inside forwards, Eastham and Allchurch, threatened to dismantle their overstretched defence. Allchurch equalized in the 55th minute after Eastham had created confusion with a typically sinuous run and incisive pass. Had Newcastle's makeshift centre forward, Malcolm Scott, not wasted a gilt-edged opportunity immediately afterwards, Burnley might have struggled to gain a point.

This hard-fought but barely deserved victory was doubled in value when it transpired that Spurs had drawn 1-1 at Preston, allowing Burnley to close the deficit to three points. Wolves also dropped a home point against Blackpool, meaning that they were now two points behind Burnley with an inferior goal average. Interestingly, a crowd of just shy of 27,000 turned up for this critical game, 10,000 fewer than was attracted to the Swansea FA Cup replay.

With the weather ruling out the League fixture at St. Andrews on 13 February, Burnley had a welcome two-week break before meeting Third Division Bradford City in the FA Cup 5th round on yet another quagmire of a surface. In those days all professional footballers needed the constitutions of trench troops. They needed to be tough emotionally as well. Harry used space in his programme notes to reproach the Burnley supporters for their 'sledging' of various members of the team. Both Adam Blacklaw and Jimmy Robson had taken some stick during the season. It seems incredible that a side in sight of the Double should take so much flak when it stumbled occasionally. Alas, moaning in the face of plenty is only too plentiful.

## 13th February 1960

Birmingham City P Burnley P
Blackburn Rovers 2 Manchester City 1
Blackpool 2 Arsenal 1
Bolton Wanderers 1 Nottingham Forest 1
Chelsea 4 Fulham 2
Everton 0 Wolverhampton Wanderers 2
Luton Town 0 Sheffield Wednesday 1
Manchester United 1 Preston North End 1
Newcastle United 2 Leeds United 1
Tottenham Hotspur 1 Leicester City 2
West Bromwich Albion P West Ham United P

## 20 February 1960
## Bradford City 2 v 2 Burnley (FA Cup 5th Round)

*'Pretty Blue Eyes'*

Bradford City had made a poor start to their season, not helped by the loss of their principal striker, John McCole, to Leeds United. Even Accrington Stanley, the Third Division's chopping block, who shipped 70 goals on their travels, still managed to beat City 5-4 at Valley Parade in September. With the club under increasing threat of relegation, City manager, Peter Jackson, converted 21-year-old left winger, Derek Stokes, to the vacant centre-forward position. It proved to be a masterstroke. Stokes' 25 League goals ultimately rescued this young Bradford side, despite losing eight of their last ten games, when Stokes was absent through injury. But The Bantams put together an impressive run of results over the winter period. Prior to this tie, they were unbeaten in 12 League and 6 FA Cup matches.

*Derek Stokes Bradford City [52]*

Despite Stokes' heroics, Bradford had found goals hard to come by. In eleven of their 23 home games they had scored no more than a solitary goal.

However, as so often happens with a team under pressure in the League, a Cup competition provides a source of relaxation and reinvigoration. First Division, Everton, found this to their cost, when they were turned over 3-0 in the Third Round with Stokes applying the final nail. Stokes was even more prolific in the FA Cup than in the League having scored 9 goals in the six games. After moving to Huddersfield in June 1960 for £22,500 he would be capped at Under-23 level for England.

Mud is always a great leveller in unequal football matches and on this dismal day there was mud in abundance. Jimmy McIlroy said: "I am not a soccer snob but when I saw the playing conditions at Valley Parade, I knew that any quality team would be hopelessly handicapped playing there. The ground was too muddy to even allow us to walk out and test it before getting stripped. Shoes, socks and even trousers would have been ruined if we had attempted to set foot on this alleged football pitch. It did not help matters when we had to negotiate a perilous stone staircase leading from the antiquated dressing room to the mud heap. Surveying the pitch from the stands it resembled a sandy beach just after the tide had receded with a glistening sheen stretching across it." Burnley supporter Stuart Barnes remembered that "Harry Potts had to wear wellingtons to carry out a pitch inspection".

In February 1960, Valley Parade had been reduced to a three-sided ground with the formerly elegant Midland Road stand demolished following subsidence. However, over 26,000 were squeezed in, 16,000 more than City's average gate, to watch a pulsating tussle. At first quality told. Jimmy McIlroy continued: "In the first 20 minutes we waltzed through the Bradford City defence whenever we pleased, in fact it was all too easy: we became casual in our finishing. It seemed we could score whenever we wished. After half an hour the pitch had churned up so badly that good football was out of the question. As we ploughed up the soft surface, the game degenerated into a slogging contest involving 22 athletes. The difference in quality between the sides was cancelled out. Obviously the fitter team would win, and with the half time score at 0-0, I had no fears about what seemed to be an inevitable success.

Midway through the second half, our superiority complex was badly shaken as City outside right, Webb, scored the opening goal. This compelled Burnley to throw everything into attack, a policy which cost us another goal, with the prolific scoring Bradford City centre forward, Derek Stokes, breaking away unexpectedly to put us 0-2 down. I looked at the clock in the stand and saw it registering 4-30. With only 10 minutes left, and two goals to be pulled back, Burnley were nearly out of the 1959/60 FA Cup competition. I had to pinch my hand to check whether I was dreaming. I was thinking, we should be murdering this lot.

We swarmed around the home goalmouth. John Connelly ran perfectly through the City defence to side foot our first goal. Seven minutes left. Now there were 21 players in the Bradford half of the field … most of them, indeed, in the penalty area. It was one minute after 4-40. Alex Elder, reckoned that the referee played over 5 minutes extra-time. The referee took a look at his watch, and I looked up at the home goal, which appeared to be completely boarded up. The anguish for the spectators, regardless of their allegiance, must have been unbearable.

Brian Pilkington was fouled on the edge of the penalty area, and took the free kick himself. The ball was headed towards the City goal. It was like an army in that Bradford penalty area, and, as I made a surge forward to try to meet his cross, I was knocked flat. The ball hit the crossbar, and as it came out again, I died a thousand deaths. Then in a fantastic flurry of legs, arms, heads and feet, the ball was somehow scrambled over the line to settle in the net. From my fallen position, in the deep mud between the Bradford's goal posts, I was able to see the ball creep over the line for our equaliser. We were thankful to leave Valley Parade while retaining an interest in the competition. Bradford were gutted, of course. For such a lowly team to come so close to eliminating us must have come very hard. But I doubt whether some of our supporters knew what had happened. I was aware that a number had already left before our late equaliser, having abandoned hope and sought the consolation of catching an early coach home. Remember, in those days the coaches did not have radios. I'm sure these supporters would have arrived back in Burnley convinced that we had lost."

Some of those supporters did not have a comfortable ride home. Stuart Barnes, then a 14-year-old, Burnley Grammar schoolboy said: "I travelled on one of the regular soccer specials and coming home my friend and I had to hunch up in the netted overhead parcel shelves as the football special was packed over capacity." So much for Health and Safety rules in 1960!

Jimmy Robson and John Connelly also recalled the game clearly. Robson said: "the game would not have started if played today. There were pools of water all over the pitch. The conditions certainly favoured Bradford. We could not get our passing game going. What is more, the ball kept sticking on their goal line. Had it run more freely we would have been several goals to the good before they scored. I think we expected this to be an easy victory. With our game at Birmingham on 13 February postponed because of the weather, a number of us travelled over to Bradford to watch them play Bournemouth in a Division Three match. Quite frankly, Bradford were awful. It was a 0-0 draw and none of us felt we would have any difficulty in defeating them. But it is so different when you actually play these teams. It rarely goes like you imagined when you are sat up there watching them. That lesson has been rammed home countless times since. We should have known better. As it was we needed two very late goals from John Connelly to save us. As we shook hands at the end of the game I could see in their eyes that they knew their chance had gone."

Burnley's saviour, John Connelly added: "it's a shame there's no archive film of the game to show people today just what conditions were like in those days. Sandra, my wife, and her family were there to watch. I was only courting then. After the game I asked Harry Potts if I could go home with them instead of on the team coach. I can remember to this day what Harry said. "You can go anywhere," said Harry beaming. I actually lost a boot in the mud that day, it was so deep. It just got sucked off my foot, though I did find it."

## 23 February 1960
## Burnley 5 v 0 Bradford City (FA Cup 5th Round replay)

*'Misty*

If Valley Parade had been a squash, that was nothing compared to the breathless crush that occurred at a frozen Turf Moor this evening. Incredibly, 52,850 pushed, shoved and wriggled their way into the bulging ground. There may have been more squeezed in since the Brunshaw Road gates gave way allowing a host of non-paying supporters to join the throng. The road over the Moss at Colne had to be closed because of the weight of traffic, forcing John Connelly to abandon his car and run to Turf Moor.

Supporter Frank Hill recalled: "I was one of the last people to get in to Turf Moor for the Bradford replay. I looked at the Long Side. There was no chance of squeezing in there so I went round to the back of the Bee Hole End. It was jam packed right to the back, with people stood a couple deep on the downslope behind the back row, so obviously they couldn't see a thing except when the action came down to their end of the field. Then the crowd surged forward and the people at the back could climb up a couple of steps and see the field. But when the crowd eased back again, they were down the back again with nothing to see."

Frank McGhee of the Daily Mirror reported: 'One goal illustrated the vast difference in speed and skill and striking power between the good, solid Third Division side and this Burnley team with its moments of magic and its touch of genius. It happened in the 62nd minute with Burnley two up but still in danger. They grabbed their lead in a furious, frantic start through Ray Pointer (4 minutes) and Jimmy Robson (8 minutes). They had been so much on top for those few blazing minutes that it looked as though they would do to Bradford what Tottenham did to Crewe – humiliate, devastate them. But that old Burnley habit of sitting back whilst the opposition was hitting back let Bradford City into the game again. Inside right David Jackson had a shot screaming for goal, luckily blocked by Alex Elder and drove another only just wide. Centre-forward, Derek Stokes was desperately unlucky to lose his goal-a-game Cup record when he nipped in between Miller and Adamson, the only occasion this pair put a foot wrong, and had a tremendous shot smothered. Burnley looked rattled. Then it happened. Brian Pilkington picked up a clearance well inside his own half and set off. Bradford right back Tom Flockett pounded after him … Even though Pilkington had to cross icy, slippery patches the gap between them opened up inch by panting inch until the winger was far enough in front to cut in and crack the ball across to Pointer. The centre-forward controlled it, slowed it and smashed it in all in one smooth, flowing move. This was the goal that broke Bradford's hearts. This was right out of their class … Two minutes later, Jimmy McIlroy who had an unusually quiet night tapped a typically short corner to John Connelly. The winger tried a lob into the goalmouth. To everyone's surprise including, I suspect, his own, the ball floated over 'keeper, George Stewart and into the net … Just to make sure Jimmy Robson added a fifth in the 68th minute. It was City's first defeat since 24 October.'

Jimmy McIlroy remembered this game vividly, too. "In the replay, also staged in bad conditions with a hard frost making the playing surface treacherous, the ball did at least roll and I am sure it was to Burnley's advantage. It was not a memorable match – the turning point coming when Pilkington had the courage to carry the ball nearly 40 yards on solid ice before passing to Ray Pointer who scored with a wonderful shot." Jimmy also set up Ray Pointer's opening goal by remarkably heading a cross into his path.

Brian Hollinrake, also a Burnley supporter, recalled that the playing surface was treacherously icy, particularly on the Southern flank, where the stand blocked the sun. He remembered Ray Pointer slaloming into the brick surrounding wall, hitting his head hard only to carry on as if nothing had happened. As Brian remarked, Ray was a brave player. "He always chased a cause, even if it was lost."

The only matter of dispute concerned the wretchedly overcrowded conditions and the club's handling of the ticketing arrangements, with children charged at adult rates. Supporter Stuart Barnes recalled: "The chairman Bob Lord became all fatherly by insisting kids should be in bed at that time and removing half charges for kids. Leaving the ground and still on the asphalt terrace, my school mate, Geoffrey Driver, was run over by an invalid car at the Bee Hole End as we shuffled out. His toe was broken!" As for the angry, excluded and heart-broken Bradford City fans, they demanded their money back after being forced to return to their coaches by the local police. A police spokesman said: 'if it had been an all-ticket match the crowd would have been restricted at a 48,000 ceiling but over 52,000 got in.'

Harry Potts addressed his critics, stating: "our gates this season have averaged 27,500. We are aware that Cup-Ties usually pull in more people, which is why important Cup matches are made all-ticket affairs. In this instance we did the next best thing, appealing to people to come early to avoid congestion and chaos by allowing time for effective marshalling. We understand that apparently, and unfortunately, it was around seven o'clock that the big invasion really developed. Outside the ground, in spite of this, everything was kept orderly, but inside the ground many of the gangways and passages became jammed. There were many pockets in the ground which were not full and that if the passages had been kept clear everyone would have been able to reach these sparsely filled POCKETS. WE ARE NOW MAKING EVERY ENDEAVOUR TO ELIMINATE THE POSSIBILITY OF THIS PROBLEM recurring at any future match and will be GRATEFUL for your kind co-operation by way of arriving a little earlier at our games." Fortunately, a potentially dangerous situation did not result in any injuries or worse and the glittering prize of victory was a 6th Round home draw with Blackburn!

## 27 February 1960

Arsenal 1 Newcastle United 0
Blackburn Rovers 1 Tottenham Hotspur 4
Blackpool 0 Manchester United 6
Bolton Wanderers 2 Burnley 1
Everton 4 Preston North End 0
Fulham 5 Leeds United 0
Luton Town 2 Leicester City 0
Manchester City 3 Birmingham City 0
Nottingham Forest 3 West Ham United 1
Sheffield Wednesday 1 Chelsea 1
Wolverhampton Wanderers 3 West Bromwich Albion 1

## Bolton Wanderers 2 v 1 Burnley

*'On A Slow boat To China'*

In those days before crowd segregation, it wasn't always sweetness and light between the groups of home and away supporters, particularly when local bragging rights were at stake. Stuart Barnes recalled: "a trip to Bolton and standing on the embankment taught some of us not to wear our favours as sudden swoops by home fans who stood farther back resulted in hats and scarves being stolen and thrown over the fence and onto the adjacent railway lines." As for Burnley they could only blame themselves for throwing away two points in this frustrating defeat at Burnden Park. Their familiar defensive frailties again cost them dear. At the front of the Burnden Stand roof ran the enscription 'Dine at the Pack Horse Restaurant Nelson Square Bolton.' Burnley would not be dining out on this performance.

*Bolton Wanderers 1959/60 [52a]*

With Robson and Seith absent through injury, Tommy Cummings was restored as centre half, with Adamson slotting into the right half position. Territorial Army squaddie, Ian Lawson, was draughted in to replace Robson. Within two minutes, Burnley were behind as Bolton's right-winger, Brian Birch, punished their disorganised defence with a shot that found goal via a deflection. This setback stung The Clarets into immediate retaliation. Bolton's lead lasted just eight minutes. Following mounting pressure, Connelly seized upon the ricochet from McIlroy's blocked shot to equalize. With Adamson and McIlroy creating the chances, Burnley proceeded to pummel the Bolton box but were unable to convert their superior skill and greater possession into goals.

Although under the cosh for long periods, Bolton counter attacked with speed and menace. They had two 'goals' disallowed and also hit the post. Wingers, Birch and Doug Holden, had outstanding games, pulling Angus and Elder all over the place and creating space in which Freddie Hill and Dennis Stevens could forage. Meanwhile, 'The Trotters' tough defenders proceeded to damage Burnley's supply line, with the dangerous Adamson neutralised with a reckless tackle. But it was Blacklaw's calamitous error, which enabled Bolton to snatch the points. Bolton right back, Roy Hartle, pumped a long and hopeful free kick into the Burnley box. Under little pressure, Adam Blacklaw moved forward to claim the ball only to find that he had misjudged the flight. He tried to correct his misjudgement by backpedalling furiously but was unable to stop the ball plopping into the net behind him. As hard as they tried, Burnley were unable to recover.

## First Division

| 27 February 1960 | P | W | D | L | F | A | Pts | Goal average |
|---|---|---|---|---|---|---|---|---|
| 1. Tottenham Hotspur | 30 | 16 | 9 | 5 | 65 | 35 | 41 | 1.86 |
| 2. Wolverhampton Wanderers | 31 | 18 | 4 | 9 | 77 | 55 | 40 | 1.40 |
| 3. Sheffield Wednesday | 31 | 15 | 7 | 9 | 56 | 34 | 37 | 1.65 |
| 4. BURNLEY | 29 | 16 | 4 | 9 | 65 | 46 | 36 | 1.41 |
| 5. Bolton Wanderers | 30 | 14 | 6 | 10 | 39 | 34 | 34 | 1.15 |
| 6. Fulham | 31 | 14 | 6 | 11 | 60 | 60 | 34 | 1.00 |
| 7. Preston North End | 30 | 12 | 9 | 9 | 53 | 53 | 33 | 1.00 |
| 8. West Bromwich Albion | 30 | 12 | 8 | 10 | 57 | 45 | 32 | 1.27 |
| 9. Manchester United | 31 | 12 | 7 | 12 | 73 | 61 | 31 | 1.20 |
| 10.Newcastle United | 31 | 13 | 5 | 13 | 64 | 62 | 31 | 1.03 |
| 11.Blackburn Rovers | 30 | 14 | 3 | 13 | 50 | 51 | 31 | 0.98 |
| 12.West Ham United | 30 | 14 | 3 | 13 | 58 | 62 | 31 | 0.94 |
| 13. Arsenal | 31 | 12 | 6 | 13 | 53 | 62 | 30 | 0.85 |
| 14. Chelsea | 31 | 10 | 8 | 13 | 59 | 69 | 28 | 0.86 |
| 15. Nottingham Forest | 31 | 11 | 6 | 14 | 40 | 57 | 28 | 0.70 |
| 16. Manchester City | 30 | 12 | 3 | 15 | 63 | 61 | 27 | 1.03 |
| 17. Blackpool | 30 | 10 | 7 | 13 | 40 | 48 | 27 | 0.83 |
| 18. Leicester City | 31 | 9 | 9 | 13 | 48 | 62 | 27 | 0.77 |
| 19. Everton | 31 | 9 | 7 | 15 | 50 | 56 | 25 | 0.89 |
| 20. Leeds United | 30 | 8 | 7 | 15 | 48 | 71 | 23 | 0.68 |
| 21. Birmingham City | 29 | 8 | 5 | 16 | 38 | 55 | 21 | 0.69 |
| 22. Luton Town | 30 | 7 | 7 | 16 | 36 | 53 | 21 | 0.68 |

# MARCH 1960

One of the worst civilian massacres in South African history occurred on 25 March. 56 Africans were killed and 162 were injured when the police opened fire in the black township of Sharpeville. It happened on the first day of civilian disobedience against the hated pass laws. A crowd of 15,000 had converged upon a police station to be met by a line of 75 armed policemen. When stones were thrown and the crowd began to rush forward, the police opened fire. The police commander, Colonel D.H. Pienaar said: "it started when hordes of natives surrounded the police station. If they do these things, they must learn their lesson the hard way." ANC leader Chief Luthuli reacted by launching a pass book burning campaign. Meanwhile the South African Government outlawed all political organisations. This only intensified the struggle with the Government subsequently declaring a state of emergency as 30,000 blacks demanded the release of their leaders. Nevertheless, at the

UN, Britain and France refused to condemn South African actions. So much for the winds of change.

In the Belgian Congo, civil unrest was increasing also, with the fiery Patrice Lumumba leading the fight against the colonial oppressors. Martial law was declared after unrest in which 14 people died. By contrast, in New York, a tentative reconciliation was sought between Israeli leader, David Ben-Gurion and West German Chancellor, Konrad Adenauer, who met one another for the first time. Ben-Gurion explained: "The Germany of today is not the Germany of yesterday. We remember the past not in order to brood upon it but in order that it shall never recur."

In Morocco, first an earthquake, then a tidal wave and finally a fire destroyed the resort of Agadir on 1 March, killing at least 1,000 people including dozens of British tourists. Meanwhile in Montgomery, Alabama, 1,000 black students staged a peaceful protest against segregation just as Martin Luther King was urging President Eisenhower to help defuse the mounting racial tension. Much nearer to home, right-wing Mosleyites attacked an anti-apartheid rally addressed by Labour leader, Hugh Gaitskell.

At Camp David, USA, Macmillan and Eisenhower agreed the proposals they would put to the Soviet Union regarding a nuclear test ban treaty. But this seemed of little significance compared to the press coverage of inane Royal gossip. The 6 March edition of the *News of the World* reassured us that marriage to commoner Antony Armstrong-Jones would rescue the 'gay and vivacious' Princess Margaret from 'shadowy palace solitude'. Reviewing the paper's array of entrapment advertisements, we were left to wonder whether the 'mature' 29-year-old princess had finally found '*Val Pack*', the face cream that 'removes blemishes' and 'pulls men to the altar'. Many adverts still caricatured marriage as a young woman's ideal career move, a dream goal rather than a hopeful beginning. And while we were invited to smirk at the *News of the World*'s coverage of Diana Dors' salacious tales, starry-eyed girls were implored by the same paper not to 'cheapen themselves' in the cause of ambition.

The biggest scandal of the week, though, was said to involve the Met's vice squad who had been accused of taking bribes of 'as much as £600 per week' to allow some Soho booksellers 'to openly display and sell improper books and photographs'.

Concerns about declining moral standards are the stuff of good copy. In 1960, things were no different. One Sunday paper suggested that the solution to crimes of violence was more violent penalties. Sir Charles Taylor MP explained, 'I do not believe that any odd psychiatric tricks are going to turn thugs into Sir Galahads. So let corporal punishment be given quickly, summarily and firmly. If it doesn't reduce crimes of violence within five years then we should have to think again and I will eat my nylon socks.' It is hard not to believe this is not some spoof put out by *Monty Python* or Harry Enfield.

At this time the *News of the World*, Britain's best-selling newspaper (with a 6.6 million readership), ran a comic strip of the *Hardies*. Presumably this fictitious family was seen as a fairly accurate representation of a typical reader's family. They were described thus: 'Dad is Tom Hardie, a 45-year-old factory foreman who is balding a bit but won't admit it. He's keen on his pipe and looks solemn but he's got a twinkle and makes as much noise as the next at the local football match. He never misses the pools or his darts. Mum is Agnes. She's country-wise and a bit superstitious. She brings a sprig of May into the house. She's still nice looking at nearly forty but worries about her figure. She and Dad snap a bit sometimes but they wouldn't change each other for gold. Sheila, their 19-year-old daughter is a secretary. She's always coming home but planning to marry in the Spring. She loves fashion and beauty. Their son, Ken, at sixteen is an apprentice and plays jazz inexpertly. Their youngest daughter, Elizabeth, is the bright, spoilt nine-year-old.' Just try placing these 'Hardies' alongside some stereotypical Sixties swingers. But in understanding what life was like for most families during the so-called permissive revolution, their lifestyles were probably a lot nearer to the 'Hardies' than the 'flower people'.

Life was certainly more akin to the Hardies for the vast majority of Burnley households although the new decade was bringing with it some good news. On 12 March, the *Burnley Express* reported that a 'huge, new factory at Padiham will be ready next month' where spin dryers, washing machines, boilers and water heaters will be manufactured. In its edition a week later, there was further good news headlined with: 'Cotton Firm's Big Expansion.' We were told that John Grey Ltd. had plans for the re-equipping of King's Mill, Harle Syke, including the installation of air conditioning. 100 new jobs were to be created to produce both cotton and rayon products.

There was rising hopes of Burnley FC appearing at Wembley after drawing Blackburn at home in the 6th Round FA Cup tie. The local retailers, Ardal, used the opportunity to advertise their TV rental service. 'On the road to Wembley' ran their advert. Alas, it was to prove premature.

Also on the downside, the North East Lancashire Development Committee's delegation failed to budge Reginald Maudling over funding for industrial diversification. MP Daniel Jones was not prepared to leave it there, though, and proposed to make further representations to him alongside other Lancashire MPs. Even the politicians were not spared the effects of the economic down turn. It was also reported on the 19th March that Alderman Craddock, the Mayor of Colne, had been made redundant by the South Valley Manufacturing Company.

*Burnley town centre 1960 [53]*

However, the biggest controversy of the month concerned the proposed rate (now Council tax) increase of 1/6d. The rate increase was said to be the first in two years. The Tories criticised the Labour administration stating that the rate rise was 'avoidable if the socialists had been more business-like.' The Labour leader of the Council retorted that the rate rise represented 'value for money'. In its editorial section the *Burnley Express* reported that the upward pressure on the rates was largely attributable to salary increases brought about by national settlements. This political set piece could have been played out in any of the ensuing years.

## 1 March 1960

Burnley 2 Tottenham Hotspur 0
Preston North End 5 Blackburn Rovers 3

## Burnley 2 v 0 Spurs

*'Poor Me'*

At the top of the charts, Adam Faith, the nasal Buddy Holly plagiarist, hiccupped through *Poor Me* but there was no room for self pity on this night. Burnley had to beat Spurs to give themselves any chance of overhauling the League leaders' five-point advantage. Although almost 33,000 turned up for this crucial game, it was 20,000 fewer than for the Bradford FA Cup tie!

*Long-time leaders of the First Division, Tottenham Hotspur, were defeated thanks to goals from Pointer and Connelly [54]*

Spurs were formidable opponents. They had tough, muscular defenders with Maurice Norman, Peter Baker and Ron Henry; elegant play-makers with Danny Blanchflower, John White and Tommy Harmer; a midfield tank in Mackay;

and fluidity of movement up front, spearheaded by the bludgeoning Bobby Smith, the predatory Les Allen and the exocet speed of Cliff Jones. If allowed to settle into their stride, they were capable of taking sides apart – home and away.

Ominously, Spurs started this game well. White shirts appeared to be flitting here, there and everywhere. Danny Blanchflower sat firmly on his Northern Ireland team-mate, Jimmy McIlroy, while his midfield partner, Mackay, ably supported by Norman, Baker and Henry, clamped down on the other Burnley forwards, denying them space and blocking their runs. With Burnley's forwards immobilised, Spurs swarmed forward, bewildering the Burnley defenders by their constant positional shifts and sudden switches of attack. In the glare of the Turf Moor floodlights, The Clarets were frequently chasing shadows. Fortunately, Adam Blacklaw had recovered his composure after the calamity at Burnden Park. He needed to be at his best to deny Les Allen and Cliff Jones although he was indebted to Smith for crashing a good opportunity into the side netting and to Jones for scuffing a shot wide from just ten yards. At the other end, Robson's sharp header forced Brown to save brilliantly and a searing drive from Miller flashed past the post. But on balance, Spurs dominated the first half. Burnley were relieved to reach half-time unscathed.

After the interval, the balance of play began to change. Burnley found a means of escape by aping their opponents' tactics. Angus and Elder were instructed to push up to provide more support for their wingmen. Pointer and Connelly began to exercise their characteristic mobility leaving Norman and Henry uncertain about their marking duties. McIlroy, too, started to work closer with his midfield partner, Adamson. Space emerged where there had been none. Significantly, it was the reinforced Adamson – McIlroy partnership which helped bring about the opening goal just past the hour. Taking advantage of the greater freedom, the two of them combined to release Connelly on the right. Connelly sprinted to the by-line and pulled back a sharp, pinpoint cross, which Pointer headed powerfully past Brown. Turf Moor erupted in a frenzy of excitement. Spurs were soon up and back on the offensive, though. The Clarets goal became besieged, as cross after cross fizzed across their area with the Spurs forwards firing in shots from all angles. Blacklaw stood tall and firm as his colleagues threw themselves into a desperate defence of their crucial lead. The Turf Moor lights seemed to intensify the manic activity with the ball pinging back and forth with almost exaggerated speed. But with Spurs committed to all-out attack, they left larger gaps at the back and it was Connelly's pace and thrust which again undid them. With twenty minutes remaining, Connelly grabbed his chance. Racing past Baker, his lone marker, he advanced on goal and flashed a low scudding shot past the diving Brown for the clinching goal. The title was still up for grabs.

## 5 March 1960

Birmingham City 4 Nottingham Forest 1
Burnley 1 Blackburn Rovers 0
Chelsea 3 Luton Town 0
Leeds United 2 Blackpool 4
Leicester City 5 Manchester City 0
Manchester United 0 Wolverhampton Wanderers 2
Newcastle United 3 Fulham 1
Preston North End 0 Arsenal 3
Tottenham Hotspur 4 Sheffield Wednesday 1
West Bromwich Albion 1 Bolton Wanderers 1
West Ham United 2 Everton 2

## Burnley 1 v 0 Blackburn Rovers

*'Delaware'*

Talk about 'After the Lord Mayor's Show'! This dull, sterile clash grated rather than sparked. There was not a hint of the rancorous combat usually associated with these intense derbies. For the most part the 32,000 crowd were quiescent, becalmed as much by the lack of action as by the somnolent spring sunshine. Blackburn started the stronger with England wing half, Ronnie Clayton's shot rattling the post and Derek Dougan's looped header just clearing the bar. They finished the stronger, too, with Ally MacLeod's late fierce drive kicked away by Blacklaw. In between there was little of note apart from Elder's containment of England's international winger, Bryan Douglas. The monotonous success of Rovers' offside trap was breached just once when Jimmy Robson's headed in Connelly's 27th minute corner. It was enough to secure a narrow win. Burnley's 1-0 League victory kept them in third place with 40 points, three points adrift of leaders Spurs.

## 12 March 1960

## Burnley 3 v 3 Blackburn Rovers (FA Cup 6th Round)

*'You Got What It Takes'*

The prospect of a rematch seven days later hardly put a spring in the step of supporters from either side, but then this was an FA Cup quarter-final. Wembley, the glittering holy grail of the entire sporting nation, was in sight and Burnley's prospects of attaining the Double attracted 51,501 to cram into

*Pilkington's shot is too good for Blackburn keeper Harry Leyland [55]*

Turf Moor on a glowering, grey, misty afternoon. The teams, however, did not pick up on the buoyant, expectant mood and during a goalless first half Blackburn were slightly the better of two indifferent sides. However, Adam Blacklaw had to be on top of his game to deny the visitors on a couple of occasions.

Within three minutes of the second half, the game changed dramatically. McIlroy's sweeping cross-field pass found Pilkington unmarked on the left-hand edge of the Blackburn penalty area. Pilkington reacted quickly, half driving, half lobbing the ball towards the top right hand corner of the net. It was too good for Harry Leyland.

Nine minutes later McIlroy engineered the second, too. Finding himself by the right wing corner flag and surrounded by three Blackburn defenders, he managed to wriggle past them and flash a low cross into Blackburn box for Pointer to anticipate the move and glide the ball in.

Burnley's third, in the 61st minute, was conceived on the Gawthorpe training ground. Jimmy Mac explained: "During training sessions, we felt that a long pass beating the full back could give Connelly just the sort of chance he thrived on. It worked like a charm with Jimmy Adamson making the pass." Connelly was alert to the move, accelerating into the open space behind Dave Whelan and slipping the ball past the advancing Leyland.

*Ray Pointer anticipates Jimmy McIlroy's pass to put Burnley two up [56]*

*John Connelly latches onto Adamson's through ball and dinks a shot over Leyland [57]*

*Douglas's controversial penalty goal restores hope for Blackburn [58]*

With 15 minutes remaining, McLeod's innocuous shot flew up and hit Alex Elder on the arm. To the amazement of everyone, referee, Hunt, awarded a penalty and up stepped Bryan Douglas to slot home the gift.

This was the catalyst for Blackburn's revival. Before the penalty award Rovers were resigned to defeat. Afterwards, they had a renewed appetite for the fight and within the next four minutes they had reduced the deficit further when Dobing blasted a lethal drive past an unsighted Blacklaw from 20 yards.

*McGrath's half hit effort finds goal via the far post and Blackburn are level [59]*

Now, Burnley were forced to defend desperately but it took a freak effort four minutes before full-time to confound them. Centre Half Matt Woods' long free-kick floated into the crowded penalty area. Fatally, the ball was not headed clear. The awkwardness of resulting bounce threw the Burnley defenders off balance and allowed Blackburn left-half, Mick McGrath, a snatched chance. Somehow his sliced shot evaded the scrimmage, with the ball having just enough impetus to clip the inside of the far post and roll slowly into the net. Fortunately, time was called shortly afterwards with a re-invigorated Blackburn moving in for the kill. Afterwards, poor Alex Elder was inconsolable. He could not accept that he should have been punished so harshly, repeating again and again to himself: "it was an accident, an accident."

*With the tables turned Blackburn almost win the tie at the death [60]*

## 16 March 1960
## Blackburn Rovers 2 v 0 Burnley FA Cup 6th Round replay

*'Who Could Be Bluer?'*

Despite the disappointment of throwing away a three-goal lead, Burnley were confident they could win the replay. They believed they had the greater class but were undone by two crucial selection errors. Jimmy McIlroy explained: "for months (I thought) I could do my stuff on one leg. The club doctor asked me how the groin felt. I told him 'I wouldn't think of playing if this was a League game. But I'm going to turn out. I've got away with it in seven cup

*Supporters queuing at Ewood Park for the Sixth Round replay [61]*

ties, and maybe I can kid my way through the eighth'. It was not to be … between December 12th and the end of March, I felt fully fit in only one match. Tom Finney's advice depressed me. Tom told me: 'I had exactly the same trouble last season, and like you, I played when I was 50% fit. That nearly put me out of football permanently, so eventually I did the only thing possible. I didn't kick a ball for 14 weeks.'" Jimmy concluded: "(At Blackburn) I had probably my poorest ever game in a Burnley shirt."

Jimmy Robson knew he should not have played, either. He recalled: "I had been sick most of the day. The team assured me 'you'll be right' and mistakenly I believed them. I knew, though, even before we stepped out that I would be in trouble if this game went to extra-time, which of course it did. As it turned out I could hardly offer a thing. I wasn't any help at all."

It was small wonder then, that Blackburn bossed a nervy, physical contest of abysmal quality in front of a crowd of almost 54,000. Amazingly, Burnley survived unscathed in normal time but within 13 minutes of extra time, Dobing's scrambled effort gave Blackburn a decisive lead. Ecstatic Blackburn supporters immediately engulfed the Burnley goal. It took several minutes for the pitch to be cleared and the ball retrieved from the whooping masses. Deflated and misfiring badly, Burnley could not rescue the game as hard as they tried. With six minutes remaining MacLeod secured the tie after heading Clayton's long throw over Blacklaw. Dreams of the Double were crushed. Blackburn duly progressed to a dismal Cup Final defeat by Wolves.

As at the Bradford replay, concerns were expressed about crowd management in the face of such a large turn out of supporters. *The Burnley Express* commented: 'as expected, Blackburn Rovers experienced crowd difficulties at Ewood Park on Wednesday with the "all pay on the ground" decision which brought spectators from all parts of Lancashire and Yorkshire to see the match. Many ticket holders could not reach their entrances and those who held means of admission for the Riverside stand had the utmost difficulty in forcing a way through the ground queues to reach the way in. I have met several who have described it as a most alarming experience on the ground, particularly when they were almost carried into position and were helpless with the swaying of the crowd when they "arrived" near the goal. The police ordered many on to the running track in an effort to relieve the pressure. The return home meant a wait of over one and a half hours for many due to traffic congestion and the difficulty in moving from car parks and side streets.'

## 19 March 1960

Birmingham City 2 Bolton Wanderers 5
Burnley 3 Arsenal 2
Chelsea 2 Blackpool 3
Leeds United 4 Manchester City 3
Leicester City 2 Wolverhampton Wanderers 1
Manchester United 3 Nottingham Forest 1
Newcastle United 3 Luton Town 2
Preston North End 3 Sheffield Wednesday 4
Tottenham Hotspur 1 Fulham 1
West Bromwich Albion 6 Everton 2
West Ham United 2 Blackburn Rovers 1

## Burnley 3 v 2 Arsenal

*'Fings Ain't What They Used T'be'*

Just 20,000 turned up to revitalise their frustrated team and assuage their disappointed hopes. *The Burnley Express* commented: 'many people are making no secret of their feelings about the team's chances of bringing honours to Turf Moor. Expressions such as "the usual slump will set in" and that the players "cannot rise to the occasion" have been heard since Wednesday. It is when "supporters" do not give them a chance that Burnley have developed the peculiar habit of doing the unexpected as far as play and results are concerned. The Tottenham match was a typical example. Few thought that the locals would beat the Londoners, yet it was a stirring encounter crowned by two great goals. There was a sense of keen determination and cold, calculating play in both defence and attack in that game which regrettably was absent on Wednesday night. Luck is not enough. Burnley made their own in the Spurs match. That should be their example for the game today – and for the remainder of the season.'

Once the Army had permitted him to play, Ian Lawson, was drafted in to replace the injured Jimmy McIlroy. Jimmy Robson had recovered sufficiently to be included. Harry Potts made a further tactical adjustment, moving Jimmy Adamson to centre half giving Brian Miller license to push up in support of the attack. This approach had worked well at Highbury and it worked rather well here, too.

Making light of McIlroy's absence, Lawson played in Ray Pointer cleverly for a 7th minute opening goal. Having landed a quick, decisive punch, The Clarets proceeded to batter the Gunners' goal. Arsenal were forced to rely upon hopeful punts upfield in order to relieve the pressure. But instead of turning the screw, Burnley threw the Londoners a lifeline. At the start of the second half a mix up between Adamson, Seith and Elder allowed Arsenal winger, Jackie Henderson, to nip in for an unexpected equaliser. This setback prodded Burnley into action immediately and it was the released Miller who made his mark in the 54th minute. Thrusting himself into the crowded box, Miller connected perfectly with Connelly's corner, sending a firm header past Welsh international keeper, Jack Kelsey.

John Connelly followed this with a trademark goal twenty minutes later. Having beaten Irish full-back McCullough for the umpteenth time, Connelly cut in from the right and drove an unstoppable shot past Kelsey.

This should have signalled game over but another lapse in concentration resulted in Henderson narrowing the gap with five minutes remaining. With the Blackburn debacle fresh in their minds, the crowd became very edgy but this time the defence held firm and the points were secured.

## 30 March 1960

Blackburn Rovers 1 Chelsea 0
Manchester City 3 West Ham United 1
Sheffield Wednesday 4 Manchester United 2
Wolverhampton Wanderers 6 Burnley 1

## Wolves 6 v 1 Burnley

*'Running Bear'*

The previous Saturday, Spurs had lost at Bolton to open up a chink of light for the chasing clubs. But now the second and third placed teams met at Molineux in a midweek game which would shape their destinities. Fresh from their FA Cup semi-final victory over Villa the previous Saturday, Wolves were fired up for this re-arranged fixture. Their humiliating 4-0 European Cup defeat by Barcelona in early March still stung. The British and Spanish pressmen had been unforgiving, contemptuous, even. Wolves had a score to settle.

Ironically, it was Wolves' much villified deficiencies that did for Burnley tonight. Wolves were usually merciless when confronted by vulnerability – a succession of drubbings confirmed that. They had put ten goals past Manchester City over two games this season and nine past Fulham in just one. At their predatory best they would pepper the opposition's half with long balls, with their muscular wing halves, Clamp and Flowers moving up swiftly to support their five voracious forwards. In mounting attack after attack, Wolves would often overwhelm beleaguered defences, crashing over them like raging Atlantic rollers. Tonight, it was Burnley's turn to be deluged. Even the returning Jimmy McIlroy could not alter their fate.

For the first 13 minutes it was 'nip and tuck', then suddenly all hell broke loose. Wolves scored twice within a minute. First, centre-forward Murray prodded home after a lightning break and then fledgling right winger, Mannion, headed in Broadbent's swift cross one minute later. Ray Pointer pulled one back immediately, converting John Connelly's pass but all this did was to prompt a vicious reprisal. Just two minutes later South African left winger, Horne, streaked through Burnley's defence to net Wolves' third. When Peter Broadbent thumped home Wolves' fourth in the 36th minute, it was clear that this contest was now about damage limitation. To that end both Cummings (replacing the injured Angus) and Elder were compelled to make several goal line clearances with Blacklaw well beaten.

There was no let up after the break, either, with Burnley continuing to be run ragged by Wolves' fast, direct, power play. After trapping Burnley on the ropes for twenty minutes, Bobby Mason and Gerry Mannion finally made their domination count, adding further goals in the 65th and 70th minutes. By this time Burnley were totally bemused. At the final whistle several Burnley players left the field uncertain what the final score was.

Whilst Brian Pilkington put this wretched performance down to "just one of those things", Brian Miller believed he had an explanation for Burnley's poor performance. He said: "the truth was that half a dozen of us had just had injections in preparation for the New York Summer tournament we were to be in. We had painful swellings under our arms, felt really ill, and me – I woke up after the afternoon sleep drenched in sweat feeling dreadful. No wonder we lost. The fans often see you lose or hear the score and they don't know the background to it." It was scant consolation for those supporters. It seemed after this humbling that Wolves and not Burnley would be the club fighting it out with Spurs for the League title as the 1959/60 season rapidly approached its conclusion.

### First Division

| 30 March 1960 | *P* | *W* | *D* | *L* | *F* | *A* | *Pts* | *Goal average* |
|---|---|---|---|---|---|---|---|---|
| 1. Tottenham Hotspur | 35 | 18 | 10 | 7 | 74 | 42 | 46 | 1.76 |
| 2. Wolverhampton Wanderers | 35 | 20 | 5 | 10 | 89 | 61 | 45 | 1.46 |
| 3. BURNLEY | 33 | 19 | 4 | 10 | 72 | 54 | 42 | 1.33 |
| 4. Sheffield Wednesday | 34 | 17 | 7 | 10 | 65 | 43 | 41 | 1.51 |
| 5. Bolton Wanderers | 35 | 16 | 8 | 11 | 50 | 44 | 40 | 1.14 |
| 6. Newcastle United | 35 | 17 | 5 | 13 | 76 | 67 | 39 | 1.13 |
| 7. West Bromwich Albion | 35 | 14 | 10 | 11 | 67 | 52 | 38 | 1.29 |
| 8. Blackpool | 35 | 15 | 7 | 13 | 55 | 56 | 37 | 0.98 |
| 9. Preston North End | 35 | 13 | 11 | 11 | 65 | 67 | 37 | 0.97 |
| 10. Fulham | 35 | 14 | 8 | 13 | 64 | 71 | 36 | 0.90 |
| 11. Manchester United | 35 | 14 | 7 | 14 | 83 | 68 | 35 | 1.22 |
| 12.West Ham United | 35 | 15 | 4 | 16 | 67 | 74 | 34 | 0.91 |
| 13. Arsenal | 35 | 13 | 8 | 14 | 60 | 67 | 34 | 0.90 |
| 14. Blackburn Rovers | 34 | 15 | 3 | 16 | 55 | 59 | 33 | 0.93 |
| 15. Leicester City | 34 | 11 | 10 | 13 | 56 | 64 | 32 | 0.88 |
| 16. Chelsea | 35 | 11 | 8 | 16 | 65 | 79 | 30 | 0.82 |
| 17. Manchester City | 34 | 13 | 3 | 18 | 71 | 74 | 29 | 0.96 |
| 18. Nottingham Forest | 35 | 11 | 7 | 17 | 44 | 68 | 29 | 0.65 |
| 19. Everton | 35 | 10 | 8 | 17 | 61 | 67 | 28 | 0.91 |
| 20. Leeds United | 34 | 9 | 9 | 16 | 58 | 82 | 27 | 0.71 |
| 21. Birmingham City | 34 | 9 | 8 | 17 | 50 | 67 | 26 | 0.75 |
| 22. Luton Town | 35 | 7 | 10 | 18 | 41 | 62 | 24 | 0.66 |

## APRIL 1960

South Africa was becoming the focus of the world's concern as racial crimes became daily occurences. In Johannesburg an attempt was made upon the life of the South African Prime Minister, Dr Hendrik Verwoerd. The would-be assassin was not one of the vociferous black protesters but instead David Pratt, a 52-year old wealthy white farmer, who had been refused a visa to visit his second wife in Holland. Meanwhile, England cricketer, Rev. David Sheppard, did what the British Government had so far failed to do, and publicly condemned the South African apartheid regime. Sheppard added that he would not tour the country with an England team whilst the apartheid policy remained in force.

The Easter weekend saw an influx of 5,000 refugees into West Berlin, mostly small farmers from East Germany. This stemmed from the East German Government's enforced collectivisation of small farms. The West German authorities reported that they were struggling to accommodate such large numbers.

At Westminster, there was uproar about the Government's intention to scrap the £65m Blue Streak missile project. Blue Streak had become obsolete, overtaken by the speed of the Cold War arms race. The unpalatable truth was that the UK could only retain its own nuclear deterrent by becoming more dependent upon American technology. That came at the high price of granting the USA the use of military bases in Britain. The question on our lips was: 'would this make the country safer or more vulnerable in the event of a global conflict'?

In Seoul, there was a violent uproar as the dictatorial 'father' of the South Korean Republic, Synghman Rhee, was forced out of office after a week of rioting and 115 demonstrators' deaths. In Mississippi, too, there was bloody discord with 10 blacks shot in the State's worst ever race riot. Meanwhile at home, Formula 1 racing driver, Stirling Moss, lost his licence for dangerous driving. The British Government also decided that Dr Richard Beeching should lead a four-man team to bring about the modernisation of Britain's rail network.

With Easter in sight, the Burnley Palace was showing *The Nun's Story* in which the delectable Audrey Hepburn wrestled attractively with her conscience; her spiritual duties apparently conflicting with her demanding nursing responsibilities in a Belgian Congo hospital. Her long, elegant, polished finger nails probably betrayed her true priorities, though.

There was a bigger struggle going on outside. Tory Alderman Brooks decided to have a pop at Labour MP Daniel Jones for 'meddling in local affairs', maintaining that the management of the local issues 'were best left to the town's representatives'. Jones was not best pleased with this, replying angrily: 'I intend to devote myself entirely to the people of Burnley. The Tories should keep political discussion from the level of the gutter.'

*Massey's Brewery, Burnley [62]*

With the construction beginning on a new coal-fired power station at Padiham 'B', an NCB spokesman cited this when he addressed the Burnley Trades and Labour Council on 16th April, dismissing claims that the coal industry was dying. He pointed out coal's various uses in smokeless zones. Not that many local folk needed persuading. Easter blew in cold and wet, so much so that warnings were issued to cavers to stay away from the Pennine pot holes.

More concern was reported about the unruly behaviour of some local young people after a train from Blackpool arrived in Burnley late on 23 April in a heavily vandalised state.

## 2 April 1960

Birmingham City 2 Everton 2
Burnley 3 Sheffield Wednesday 3
Chelsea 3 Manchester City 0
Leeds United 0 Wolverhampton Wanderers 3
Leicester City 0 Nottingham Forest 1
Manchester United 2 Bolton Wanderers 0
Newcastle United 1 Blackpool 1
Preston North End 4 Fulham 1
Tottenham Hotspur 1 Luton Town 1
West Bromwich Albion 2 Blackburn Rovers 0
West Ham United 0 Arsenal 0

## Burnley 3 v 3 Sheffield Wednesday

*'Fall In Love With You'*

Harry Catterick's Owls had made absolutely sure that this was not to be yet another Yo-Yo season. They had bustled and barged their way into fourth spot coming into today's game. Fortunately, craggy John Angus was fit enough to resume at right-back.

After the midweek Molineux massacre, Wednesday fancied their chances and hit Burnley like a train. Within three minutes Keith Ellis had thumped home their opening goal. With Tony Kay and Bobbie Craig putting themselves about, Burnley were rattled. In order to combat their physical presence, Harry Potts instructed Miller to adopt a rampaging midfield role, with Adamson returning to centre-half. For the first 45 minutes, though, Burnley could not get into their stride. Their neat, one touch passes were making no impression upon Sheffield's 'bump and grind' artists.

After the break, Harry Potts decided to adopt a more direct approach with long balls employed to by-pass the visitors' scrapping midfielders. This gave

John Connelly and Brian Pilkington more opportunity to exploit their speed against the muscular Wednesday defenders. Vindication was swift with Connelly equalizing in the 55th minute. It was a typical Connelly goal – a dash inside his full back, followed by a swift cross shot that evaded the grasp of England keeper, Ron Springett.

Parity lasted a matter of seconds, though. Burnley's defenders lost concentration and Wednesday's lively left-winger, Alan Finney, took advantage, heading in a looping cross to restore the visitors' lead. Worse still, 20 minutes later Bobby Seith stumbled on the ball inside his own box and Bobbie Craig pounced to punish his error.

Burnley did not capitulate, though. Just one minute later Ray Pointer's speed and determination proved too hot to handle. After bursting into the box, England centre-half, Peter Swan, was forced to fell the blonde striker. Jimmy McIlroy nonchalantly stroked home the resultant penalty as if this was just practice. With little time left, Burnley had to go for broke, pushing all forward except Adam Blacklaw. Wednesday's defence began to falter under the intensifying pressure. With all hands grasping the pump, 'The Owls' penalty area was as crowded as Blackpool beach on an August Bank Holiday. But bustling Brian Miller was not to be denied. Charging through Wednesday's reinforced ranks he made perfect connection with a clipped centre to crack home an 88th minute equaliser.

Unfortunately, Burnley's euphoria at having jumped jail was tempered by the bad news that Wolves had won 3-0 at Leeds. Burnley were now four points adrift of both Spurs and Wolves.

This match proved to be Bobby Seith's 211th and last league game for Burnley. The 28-year-old Scot would not know this until the *Burnley Express* announced the team for the following game at Nottingham Forest. Bob was aggrieved at not being told directly. A dispute ensued which resulted in him leaving the club at the end of the season. It was a most regrettable way for his splendid 12-year Turf Moor career to come to an end.

## 9 April 1960

Arsenal 1 Chelsea 4
Blackburn Rovers 1 Newcastle United 1
Blackpool 0 Birmingham City 1
Bolton Wanderers 2 Preston North End 1
Everton 2 Tottenham Hotspur 1
Fulham 1 Leicester City 1
Luton Town 2 Manchester United 3
Manchester City 0 West Bromwich Albion 1

Nottingham Forest 0 Burnley 1
Sheffield Wednesday 1 Leeds United 0
Wolverhampton Wanderers P West Ham United P

## Nottingham Forest 0 v 1 Burnley

*'My Old Man's A Dustman'*

Football correspondent John Macadam was back spurring his hobby horse. He wrote: 'only in this country is grubbiness accepted as part of the natural background of soccer. In Continental and Latin-American countries it is not so. What a differently pleasant prospect Nottingham presents, though! There, Cup-holders and ill-starred County face each other across the calm bosom of the River Trent with its oarsmen and its swans'. A less urbane perspective of Nottingham was presented in Alan Sillitoe's 1958 novel *Saturday Night and Sunday Morning.* His feisty, working class hero, Arthur Seaton, described his life as one of hard graft, hard drinking and hard womanising with the odd scrap or two thrown in. Scrapping was the order of the day at the City Ground, too. Certainly, there was no room for aesthetics. The points at stake had importance at both ends of the table. Burnley travelled without right-winger, John Connelly, who was representing England at Hampden Park. Harry Potts was not prepared to follow Bill Nicholson's lead and hold John back for this vital game. Harry was also without the injured Alex Elder. Debutantes Trevor Meredith and Billy Marshall, replaced them. Jimmy Adamson moved to right half to replace Bob Seith with Tommy Cummings returning as centre half.

1959 FA Cup Winners Forest had endured a difficult season. Only Luton had scored fewer goals in the 36 League games played. Centre forward, Tom Wilson, would be their only goalscorer to break into double figures. Neither Wilson nor Forest's other principal goal scorer, Colin Booth, were fit to play in today's game. Consequently, classy wing-half, Jim Iley was forced to fill in as a makeshift centre forward with Elton John's uncle, Roy Dwight restored to the right wing. Ex-Claret Billy Gray took on Booth's mantle at inside right and Stewart Imlach continued on the Forest's left flank. This was a patched up Forest side and it showed. Burnley's full-backs, Angus and Marshall, had little difficulty subduing Dwight and Imlach. With Adamson and Cummings nullifying any central threat, the home side had hardly a chance.

In truth, this was a dire game played in a turbulent wind on a dry, rutted, grassless surface. One moment of quality settled the outcome and, typically, Jimmy McIlroy, was the provider. With an hour gone, Jimmy Mac received a throw in, shimmied and accelerated past Jack Birkitt and Jim Iley and then crossed crisply for Ray Pointer to power a header past keeper, Chic Thomson. Pointer and Meredith might have added to Burnley's advantage but Thomson just managed to turn aside Pointer's fierce drive and Meredith was denied by the bobbling surface after Miller had put him through on goal. With the ball bouncing awkwardly, Meredith lifted his shot over the bar.

With Wolves game postponed controversially, on account of a plethora of international call ups, this win brought Burnley back within two points of top spot, although for now they remained in fourth position following Wednesday's 1-0 victory over Leeds.

## 15 April 1960

Arsenal 2 Fulham 0
Blackburn Rovers 0 Luton Town 2
Burnley 1 Leicester City 0
Chelsea 1 Tottenham Hotspur 3
Everton 4 Blackpool 0
Manchester City 1 Bolton Wanderers 0
Newcastle United 3 Sheffield Wednesday 3
West Ham United 2 Manchester United 1

## Burnley 1 v 0 Leicester City

*'Theme From A Summer Place'*

After thrashing West Ham 5-0 on Monday night, Wolves restored a four-point lead over Burnley. The Clarets had to put their annoyance aside at Wanderers being allowed to delay playing that vital match until they had their international players back. For this Good Friday fixture they were up against those seasoned travellers, Leicester, for 'The Foxes' had experienced only one defeat in their last ten away games.

Burnley were denied what appeared to be a legitimate opening 'goal' after just three minutes. Leicester keeper, Gordon Banks seemed to have carried Robson's header over his goal line but the referee, L. McCoy, waved aside Burnley's protests. His apparent oversight did not prove costly. As at Nottingham, one moment of quality turned this exacting game. With eight minutes gone, a slick exchange of passes between Brian Pilkington and Jimmy Robson provided the opening for John Connelly to drive the ball home. This one goal was enough to secure the points but it provided scant evidence of Burnley's dominance. However, titles are always won by the sides who can eek out victories against resilient teams.

Cummings' restoration at centre-half had helped tighten the defence and today he kept the dangerous Welsh striker, Ken Leek, firmly in his pocket, while Jimmy Adamson and Brian Miller cancelled out the potential threats of Jimmy Walsh and ex-Claret, Albert Cheeseborough. Alas, the victory came at a heavy price. Connelly sustained a cartilage injury towards the end of the game signalling the end of his season. Nevertheless, Burnley returned to third spot after The Owls were held 3-3 at Newcastle, although Spurs' 3-1 victory at Chelsea preserved their two-point advantage.

## 16 April 1960

Birmingham City 3 Arsenal 0
Burnley 3 Luton Town 0
Chelsea 1 Nottingham Forest 1
Leeds United 1 Bolton Wanderers 0
Leicester City 3 Everton 3
Manchester United 1 Blackburn Rovers 0
Newcastle United 1 Wolverhampton Wanderers 0
Preston North End 4 Blackpool 1
Tottenham Hotspur 0 Manchester City 1
West Bromwich Albion 3 Sheffield Wednesday 1
West Ham United 1 Fulham 2

## Burnley 3 v 0 Luton Town

*'Stuck On You'*

With so much at stake a crowd of 21,000 was very disappointing – there were 3,000 fewer at Turf Moor than at the previous day's game. Perhaps the bracing weather made the Costa Fylde more enticing. However, it was very noticeable that during the 1959-60 season, First Division gates fluctuated considerably according to the perceived quality of the opposition. Having said that, after their invigorating victory at Blackburn, yesterday, Luton were expected to put up a bit of a scrap. They did not. Far from approaching this game as snarling relegation dog fighters they seemed more like whimpering poodles. The game proved to be a very unequal contest.

Luton's determination to win lasted for no more than the opening 16 minutes. Once Ray Pointer's twenty-yard drive eluded former England keeper, Ron Baynham, and found goal, the visitors capitulated deferentially. They seemed utterly deflated, finding no encouragement in having a one-man advantage for most of the game – this followed the enforced withdrawal of Pointer due to injury. As for Burnley, they made light of their loss and proceeded to pummel the Luton goal throughout. The Clarets were denied a hatful of goals only through a combination of desperate defending by Luton's overstretched back line and the woodwork. Tiny Trevor Meredith, who had broken a leg in a reserve game at the start of the season, was in inspired form as Connelly's replacement. Luton's bemused left-back, Ken Hawkes, was turned inside out. There was an end product to Meredith's trickery, too. He laid on the gilt-edged chance for Jimmy Robson to score Burnley's second in the 33rd minute. Jimmy McIlroy wrapped up the 'turkey shoot' with almost 30 minutes remaining by scoring with a spot-kick. The value of this victory was magnified by results from elsewhere. News of Wolves' 1-0 defeat at Newcastle took time to filter through, but was received warmly. Burnley now stood in pole position in the title race, on the same number of points as rivals Spurs and Wolves, but with more games remaining. Could they make them pay?

## 16 April 1960

| | | | Home | | | | | Away | | | | | Overall | | | | | | |
|---|---|---|---|---|---|---|---|---|---|---|---|---|---|---|---|---|---|---|---|
| | | P | W | D | L | F | A | W | D | L | F | A | W | D | L | F | A | Pts | GA |
| 1 | Tottenham Hotspur | 39 | 9 | 6 | 4 | 39 | 22 | 10 | 5 | 5 | 40 | 25 | 19 | 11 | 9 | 79 | 47 | 49 | 1.68 |
| 2 | Wolverhampton W | 38 | 14 | 3 | 2 | 59 | 24 | 8 | 2 | 9 | 38 | 38 | 22 | 5 | 11 | 97 | 62 | 49 | 1.56 |
| 3 | BURNLEY | 37 | 15 | 1 | 4 | 52 | 28 | 7 | 4 | 6 | 28 | 29 | 22 | 5 | 10 | 80 | 57 | 49 | 1.40 |
| 4 | Sheffield Wednesday | 39 | 11 | 7 | 1 | 44 | 16 | 7 | 3 | 10 | 31 | 38 | 18 | 10 | 11 | 75 | 54 | 46 | 1.39 |
| 5 | West Brom A | 38 | 11 | 3 | 5 | 46 | 24 | 6 | 7 | 6 | 27 | 29 | 17 | 10 | 11 | 73 | 53 | 44 | 1.38 |
| 6 | Newcastle United | 39 | 10 | 5 | 5 | 42 | 31 | 8 | 3 | 8 | 40 | 41 | 18 | 8 | 13 | 82 | 72 | 44 | 1.14 |
| 7 | Bolton Wanderers | 39 | 10 | 5 | 4 | 32 | 26 | 7 | 3 | 10 | 20 | 23 | 17 | 8 | 14 | 52 | 49 | 42 | 1.06 |
| 8 | Manchester United | 39 | 11 | 3 | 5 | 43 | 27 | 6 | 4 | 10 | 47 | 45 | 17 | 7 | 15 | 90 | 72 | 41 | 1.25 |
| 9 | Preston North End | 38 | 9 | 5 | 5 | 40 | 33 | 6 | 6 | 7 | 34 | 38 | 15 | 11 | 12 | 74 | 71 | 41 | 1.04 |
| 10 | Fulham | 39 | 10 | 4 | 5 | 37 | 27 | 5 | 5 | 10 | 31 | 52 | 15 | 9 | 15 | 68 | 79 | 39 | 0.86 |
| 11 | Blackpool | 39 | 9 | 4 | 6 | 31 | 31 | 6 | 4 | 10 | 26 | 35 | 15 | 8 | 16 | 57 | 66 | 38 | 0.86 |
| 12 | West Ham United | 39 | 12 | 2 | 6 | 46 | 32 | 4 | 3 | 12 | 24 | 50 | 16 | 5 | 18 | 70 | 82 | 37 | 0.85 |
| 13 | Arsenal | 39 | 8 | 5 | 7 | 34 | 36 | 6 | 4 | 9 | 29 | 38 | 14 | 9 | 16 | 63 | 74 | 37 | 0.85 |
| 14 | Chelsea | 39 | 7 | 5 | 8 | 43 | 45 | 6 | 4 | 9 | 31 | 39 | 13 | 9 | 17 | 74 | 84 | 35 | 0.88 |
| 15 | Leicester City | 39 | 7 | 6 | 6 | 35 | 29 | 4 | 7 | 9 | 27 | 43 | 11 | 13 | 15 | 62 | 72 | 35 | 0.86 |
| 16 | Everton | 39 | 12 | 3 | 5 | 49 | 20 | 0 | 7 | 12 | 23 | 53 | 12 | 10 | 17 | 72 | 73 | 34 | 0.99 |
| 17 | Blackburn Rovers | 38 | 11 | 3 | 5 | 35 | 26 | 4 | 1 | 14 | 21 | 39 | 15 | 4 | 19 | 56 | 65 | 34 | 0.86 |
| 18 | Manchester City | 38 | 10 | 2 | 7 | 44 | 31 | 5 | 1 | 13 | 29 | 47 | 15 | 3 | 20 | 73 | 78 | 33 | 0.94 |
| 19 | Nottingham Forest | 38 | 7 | 5 | 7 | 27 | 28 | 5 | 3 | 11 | 19 | 42 | 12 | 8 | 18 | 46 | 70 | 32 | 0.66 |
| 20 | Birmingham City | 37 | 8 | 5 | 5 | 35 | 28 | 3 | 4 | 12 | 21 | 41 | 11 | 9 | 17 | 56 | 69 | 31 | 0.81 |
| 21 | Leeds United | 37 | 5 | 5 | 9 | 34 | 45 | 5 | 4 | 9 | 25 | 41 | 10 | 9 | 18 | 59 | 86 | 29 | 0.69 |
| 22 | Luton Town | 39 | 5 | 4 | 10 | 21 | 27 | 3 | 7 | 10 | 25 | 42 | 8 | 11 | 20 | 46 | 69 | 27 | 0.6 |

## 18th April 1960

Birmingham City 1 West Bromwich Albion 7
Blackpool 0 Everton 0
Bolton Wanderers 3 Manchester City 1
Fulham 3 Arsenal 0
Leicester City 2 Burnley 1
Luton Town 1 Blackburn Rovers 1
Manchester United 5 West Ham United 3
Preston North End 1 Leeds United 1
Sheffield Wednesday 2 Newcastle United 0
Tottenham Hotspur 0 Chelsea 1
Wolverhampton Wanderers 3 Nottingham Forest 1

## Leicester City 2 v 1 Burnley

*'What In The World Has Come Over You?'*

Leicester's cramped Filbert Street ground was hemmed in by a matrix of red-bricked, terraced streets, four of which bore the names of nuts – Brazil, Hazel, Walnut and Filbert before the planners found the idea too nutty. Pistachio and Cashew never got their chance. Bucking the trend, the entrance to the East stand was made via Burnmoor Street and probably carved out of some poor soul's kitchen. When the ground rocked, so did the surrounding households. There was not room to breathe inside Filbert Street. Overlooked at the back by a vast power station and confined further on its western side by the Grand Union Canal and the Great Central Railway, Leicester's ground struggled to fit in its pitch. The touchlines were practically merged with the lower terraces. Visiting sides had to test their brakes before stepping out.

With injuries mounting and Bob Seith's exclusion decided upon, Harry Potts' reliance upon a small first team squad was causing increasing difficulties. Although Ray Pointer was passed fit to play after the X-Ray on his leg injury showed no fracture, he was not at the races today. Presented with an easy opportunity after just a few seconds of play, uncharacteristically he failed to find the target. He was not the only Claret who was below par, though, for this was a leg-weary, lacklustre performance against a side, which had made five changes after their Good Friday defeat. The injection of new blood did the trick for 'The Foxes'. By half-time they were two up. In the 29th minute, centre-forward Ken Keyworth and winger Howard Riley combined to set up Gordon Wills for a 'twenty yarder' and then eight minutes later Keyworth played Cheeseborough in for a second with the Burnley defenders appealing vainly for offside. Although Trevor Meredith reduced the deficit sixteen minutes before the close, heralding a late rally,

Gordon Banks was at his commanding best in halting Burnley's charge. In fact, Cheeseborough came close to extending Leicester's lead during the frantic final exchanges.

Wolves's victory over Nottingham Forest seemed to have dealt a huge blow to Burnley's chances. There was certainly no charge to the title by any of the contenders. Indeed it would undoubtedly be one of the lowest ever winning points totals. Not that the victors would care.

## 23 April 1960

Arsenal 5 Manchester United 2
Blackburn Rovers 0 Leicester City 1
Blackpool 1 Burnley 1
Bolton Wanderers 2 Chelsea 0
Everton 1 Leeds United 0
Fulham 2 West Bromwich Albion 1
Luton Town 3 West Ham United 1
Manchester City 2 Preston North End 1
Nottingham Forest 3 Newcastle United 0
Sheffield Wednesday 2 Birmingham City 4
Wolverhampton Wanderers 1 Tottenham Hotspur 3

## Blackpool 1 v 1 Burnley

*'Standing On The Corner'*

With Wolves having dropped another point in a goalless draw at Nottingham Forest on the preceding Tuesday and facing Spurs at Molineux on this day, this Lancashire derby took on vital importance. Supporter Stuart Barnes remembered: 'going to Bloomfield Road was usually a pleasure with The Clarets doing generally well there. Walking along the promenade to the ground and buying a copy of *Billy's Weekly Liar* (a spoof newspaper) was a feature of the trip'. Despite Stuart's confidence, this was another ragged, nervous display on a pitch with as much grass as Blackpool sands. A crowd of 23,750 assembled with most supporters housed on the vast sun-drenched Kop with its towering view of the adjoining railway sidings and glimpses of the distant sea. Mid-table Blackpool started strongly with their fast, direct winger, Bill Perry, causing John Angus no end of problems. With steadier finishing, Perry might have put the Seasiders well in front before Burnley recovered their poise. However, prompted by Meredith and Pilkington, their best players on the day, Burnley began to turn the tide before the interval, forcing twelve corners in a period of intense pressure.

*Burnley pressurize Blackpool keeper Tony Waiters [63]*

Fittingly, it was a Pilkington – Meredith combination, which gave Burnley the lead on the half hour. Pilkington's corner was only half cleared and Meredith blasted the loose ball past future Claret, Tony Waiters. The goal failed to steady Burnley's nerves, though, and assisted by their increasingly influential right winger, Steve Hill, Blackpool seized back the initiative. With just six minutes remaining, Hill beat Elder's challenge and crossed to the far post where the lanky Ray Charnley thumped a header past Jim Furnell, who was deputising for the injured Blacklaw. This was a crushing blow but despondency turned once more to flickering hope as news came through of Spurs' fluent 3-1 victory at Molineux. Another twist had just been taken in this alluring title race.

Reverend David Wiseman remembered that: "a very jittery Jim Furnell took the injured Blacklaw's place. Our hearts were in our mouths every time Jim touched the ball (and I don't think he was too happy either!). Jim later went on to play for Liverpool and Arsenal and make over 400 league appearances but he will never forget his debut at Bloomfield Road!"

## 23 April 1960

| | | | Home | | | | | Away | | | | | Overall | | | | | | |
|---|---|---|---|---|---|---|---|---|---|---|---|---|---|---|---|---|---|---|---|
| | | P | W | D | L | F | A | W | D | L | F | A | W | D | L | F | A | Pts | GA |
| 1 | Wolverhampton W | 41 | 15 | 3 | 3 | 63 | 28 | 8 | 3 | 9 | 38 | 38 | 23 | 6 | 12 | 101 | 66 | 52 | 1.53 |
| 2 | Tottenham Hotspur | 41 | 9 | 6 | 5 | 39 | 23 | 11 | 5 | 5 | 43 | 26 | 20 | 11 | 10 | 82 | 49 | 51 | 1.67 |
| 3 | BURNLEY | 39 | 15 | 1 | 4 | 52 | 28 | 7 | 5 | 7 | 30 | 32 | 22 | 6 | 11 | 82 | 60 | 50 | 1.37 |
| 4 | Sheffield Wednesday | 41 | 12 | 7 | 2 | 48 | 20 | 7 | 3 | 10 | 31 | 38 | 19 | 10 | 12 | 79 | 58 | 48 | 1.36 |
| 5 | West Bromwich A | 41 | 11 | 4 | 5 | 47 | 25 | 7 | 7 | 7 | 35 | 32 | 18 | 11 | 12 | 82 | 57 | 47 | 1.44 |
| 6 | Bolton Wanderers | 41 | 12 | 5 | 4 | 37 | 27 | 7 | 3 | 10 | 20 | 23 | 19 | 8 | 14 | 57 | 50 | 46 | 1.14 |
| 7 | Newcastle United | 41 | 10 | 5 | 5 | 42 | 31 | 8 | 3 | 10 | 40 | 46 | 18 | 8 | 15 | 82 | 77 | 44 | 1.06 |
| 8 | Manchester United | 41 | 12 | 3 | 5 | 48 | 30 | 6 | 4 | 11 | 49 | 50 | 18 | 7 | 16 | 97 | 80 | 43 | 1.21 |
| 9 | Fulham | 41 | 12 | 4 | 5 | 42 | 28 | 5 | 5 | 10 | 31 | 52 | 17 | 9 | 15 | 73 | 80 | 43 | 0.91 |
| 10 | Preston North End | 41 | 9 | 6 | 5 | 41 | 34 | 6 | 6 | 9 | 36 | 42 | 15 | 12 | 14 | 77 | 76 | 42 | 1.01 |
| 11 | Blackpool | 41 | 9 | 6 | 6 | 32 | 32 | 6 | 4 | 10 | 26 | 35 | 15 | 10 | 16 | 58 | 67 | 40 | 0.87 |
| 12 | Leicester City | 41 | 8 | 6 | 6 | 37 | 30 | 5 | 7 | 9 | 28 | 43 | 13 | 13 | 15 | 65 | 73 | 39 | 0.89 |
| 13 | Arsenal | 41 | 9 | 5 | 7 | 39 | 38 | 6 | 4 | 10 | 29 | 41 | 15 | 9 | 17 | 68 | 79 | 39 | 0.86 |
| 14 | Everton | 41 | 13 | 3 | 5 | 50 | 20 | 0 | 8 | 12 | 23 | 53 | 13 | 11 | 17 | 73 | 73 | 37 | 1.00 |
| 15 | Chelsea | 41 | 7 | 5 | 8 | 43 | 45 | 7 | 4 | 10 | 32 | 41 | 14 | 9 | 18 | 75 | 86 | 37 | 0.87 |
| 16 | West Ham United | 41 | 12 | 2 | 6 | 46 | 32 | 4 | 3 | 14 | 28 | 58 | 16 | 5 | 20 | 74 | 90 | 37 | 0.82 |
| 17 | Manchester City | 40 | 11 | 2 | 7 | 46 | 32 | 5 | 1 | 14 | 30 | 50 | 16 | 3 | 21 | 76 | 82 | 35 | 0.93 |
| 18 | Blackburn Rovers | 40 | 11 | 3 | 6 | 35 | 27 | 4 | 2 | 14 | 22 | 40 | 15 | 5 | 20 | 57 | 67 | 35 | 0.85 |
| 19 | Nottingham Forest | 41 | 8 | 6 | 7 | 30 | 28 | 5 | 3 | 12 | 20 | 45 | 13 | 9 | 19 | 50 | 73 | 35 | 0.68 |
| 20 | Birmingham City | 40 | 8 | 5 | 6 | 36 | 35 | 4 | 5 | 12 | 26 | 44 | 12 | 10 | 18 | 62 | 79 | 34 | 0.78 |
| 21 | Leeds United | 40 | 6 | 5 | 9 | 36 | 46 | 5 | 5 | 10 | 26 | 43 | 11 | 10 | 19 | 62 | 89 | 32 | 0.70 |
| 22 | Luton Town | 41 | 6 | 5 | 10 | 25 | 29 | 3 | 7 | 10 | 25 | 42 | 9 | 12 | 20 | 50 | 71 | 30 | 0.70 |

## 27 April 1960

Birmingham City 0 Burnley 1
Blackburn Rovers 3 Leeds United 2

## Birmingham City 0 v 1 Burnley

*'Handy Man'*

This was one of Burnley's games in hand over Spurs and Wolves and it was imperative that they made it count. Birmingham were a tougher side than the one that had travelled to Turf Moor in September. They were scrapping with feral intensity to preserve their First Division status and were buoyant after their outstanding victory at Hillsborough on the previous Saturday. Adam Blacklaw was fit enough to return in goal but Jimmy McIlroy, Brian Miller and Tommy Cummings were all carrying knocks. Given the impor-

tance of the fixture, Harry Potts risked all three.

Urged on by a 37,000 crowd, The Blues certainly let Burnley know that they were about. Once again, the Burnley defence seemed jittery until the imperious Jimmy Adamson steadied everyone's nerves. He imposed himself on the frenzied proceedings with authoritative composure, breaking up a succession of Blues' attacks and organising his defence astutely.

Despite their obvious anxiety, Burnley might have taken an early lead. Jimmy McIlroy's powerful free kick was just scrambled away by City 'keeper, Schofield. Then, Ray Pointer had a goal ruled out for a marginal offside decision. Referee, Smith, also waved away claims for a penalty after Trevor Meredith appeared to have been felled inside the City box.

But Birmingham were not on the back foot for long. They were soon probing Burnley's defence. With play switching rapidly from one end to the other, this was anyone's game. The crucial breakthrough came with just nine minutes remaining. Trevor Meredith evaded Brian Farmer's agricultural tackle and nutmegged Dick Neal, giving him the space to send over a sharp cross. Ray Pointer was first to the ball but instead of shooting first time, he flicked it on to Brian Pilkington, whose shot hissed past Schofield.

The last nine minutes were agonising to watch as Birmingham poured forward. The Burnley goal was under almost constant siege. With The Clarets gathered tightly around Adam Blacklaw it was like Rorke's Drift. One thumped clearance followed another. Miller hacked a shot off the line; tackles flew in as the Burnley defenders fought frantically to defend their crucial lead. Adamson, however, remained the 'King of cool', operating as if he was in the eye of a hurricane. Remaining calm and controlled, he seemed almost oblivious to the storm raging around him. There was no disputing the 'man of the match' here.

## 30 April 1960

Birmingham City 1 Blackburn Rovers 0
Burnley 0 Fulham 0
Chelsea 1 Wolverhampton Wanderers 5
Leeds United 1 Nottingham Forest 0
Leicester City 1 Bolton Wanderers 2
Manchester United 5 Everton 0

Newcastle United 0 Manchester City 1
Preston North End 2 Luton Town 0
Tottenham Hotspur 4 Blackpool 1
West Bromwich Albion 1 Arsenal 0
West Ham United 1 Sheffield Wednesday 1

## Burnley 0 v 0 Fulham

*'Sweet Nothin's'*

Depending upon the results elsewhere, Burnley could have secured the Championship on this sunny afternoon. However, first they had to beat Fulham, but without Jimmy McIlroy's inspiration they proved incapable of breaking down the dogged and well-organised 'Cottagers', whose goalkeeper, Tony Macedo, performed magnificently. With Adamson ensuring that the home defence remained impregnable and with Tommy Cummings keeping Johnny Haynes at bay, this turned out to be a sterile stalemate.

The excited 30,000 who had turned up in the hope of witnessing a Champions' display shuffled home disgruntled, sure that The Clarets had blown it. By virtue of winning at a canter at Stamford Bridge (5-1), Wolves had ensured that Burnley needed to defeat City at Maine Road on the following Monday evening to snatch the title from them.

Former Burnley MP, Peter Pike remembered: "I drove up from London in a Ford Prefect with two of my friends, both Fulham supporters. It was a much more difficult journey in those days, driving largely on old roads and having to negotiate a succession of town centres. We also lost our way on the A6 at one point, finding ourselves heading in the direction of Wales but we recovered just in time, arriving in Burnley shortly before kick-off. It was all rather disappointing, too. The game was a poor, boring affair, but there was still a chance of winning the title. That night in Burnley this prospect was the talk of the town."

With the rest of the First Dvision programme having been completed, Burnley now knew their task. They were one short, but treacherous step from immortality.

## 30 April 1960

| | | | Home | | | | | Away | | | | | Overall | | | | | | |
|---|---|---|---|---|---|---|---|---|---|---|---|---|---|---|---|---|---|---|---|
| | | P | W | D | L | F | A | W | D | L | F | A | W | D | L | F | A | Pts | GA |
| 1 | Wolverhampton W | 42 | 15 | 3 | 3 | 63 | 28 | 9 | 3 | 9 | 43 | 39 | 24 | 6 | 12 | 106 | 67 | 54 | 1.58 |
| 2 | Tottenham Hotspur | 42 | 10 | 6 | 5 | 43 | 24 | 11 | 5 | 5 | 43 | 26 | 21 | 11 | 10 | 86 | 50 | 53 | 1.72 |
| 3 | BURNLEY | 41 | 15 | 2 | 4 | 52 | 28 | 8 | 5 | 7 | 31 | 32 | 23 | 7 | 11 | 83 | 60 | 53 | 1.38 |
| 4 | West Bromwich A | 42 | 12 | 4 | 5 | 48 | 25 | 7 | 7 | 7 | 35 | 32 | 19 | 11 | 12 | 83 | 57 | 49 | 1.46 |
| 5 | Sheffield Wednesday | 42 | 12 | 7 | 2 | 48 | 20 | 7 | 4 | 10 | 32 | 39 | 19 | 11 | 12 | 80 | 59 | 49 | 1.36 |

| | | Home | | | | | | Away | | | | | Overall | | | | | | |
|---|---|---|---|---|---|---|---|---|---|---|---|---|---|---|---|---|---|---|---|
| | | P | W | D | L | F | A | W | D | L | F | A | W | D | L | F | A | Pts | GA |
| 6 | Bolton Wanderers | 42 | 12 | 5 | 4 | 37 | 27 | 8 | 3 | 10 | 22 | 24 | 20 | 8 | 14 | 59 | 51 | 48 | 1.16 |
| 7 | Manchester United | 42 | 13 | 3 | 5 | 53 | 30 | 6 | 4 | 11 | 49 | 50 | 19 | 7 | 16 | 102 | 80 | 45 | 1.28 |
| 8 | Newcastle United | 42 | 10 | 5 | 6 | 42 | 32 | 8 | 3 | 10 | 40 | 46 | 18 | 8 | 16 | 82 | 78 | 44 | 1.05 |
| 9 | Preston North End | 42 | 10 | 6 | 5 | 43 | 34 | 6 | 6 | 9 | 36 | 42 | 16 | 12 | 14 | 79 | 76 | 44 | 1.04 |
| 10 | Fulham | 42 | 12 | 4 | 5 | 42 | 28 | 5 | 6 | 10 | 31 | 52 | 17 | 10 | 15 | 73 | 80 | 44 | 0.91 |
| 11 | Blackpool | 42 | 9 | 6 | 6 | 32 | 32 | 6 | 4 | 11 | 27 | 39 | 15 | 10 | 17 | 59 | 71 | 40 | 0.83 |
| 12 | Leicester City | 42 | 8 | 6 | 7 | 38 | 32 | 5 | 7 | 9 | 28 | 43 | 13 | 13 | 16 | 66 | 75 | 39 | 0.88 |
| 13 | Arsenal | 42 | 9 | 5 | 7 | 39 | 38 | 6 | 4 | 11 | 29 | 42 | 15 | 9 | 18 | 68 | 80 | 39 | 0.85 |
| 14 | West Ham United | 42 | 12 | 3 | 6 | 47 | 33 | 4 | 3 | 14 | 28 | 58 | 16 | 6 | 20 | 75 | 91 | 38 | 0.82 |
| 15 | Manchester City | 41 | 11 | 2 | 7 | 46 | 32 | 6 | 1 | 14 | 31 | 50 | 17 | 3 | 21 | 77 | 82 | 37 | 0.94 |
| 16 | Everton | 42 | 13 | 3 | 5 | 50 | 20 | 0 | 8 | 13 | 23 | 58 | 13 | 11 | 18 | 73 | 78 | 37 | 0.94 |
| 17 | Blackburn Rovers | 42 | 12 | 3 | 6 | 38 | 29 | 4 | 2 | 15 | 22 | 41 | 16 | 5 | 21 | 60 | 70 | 37 | 0.86 |
| 18 | Chelsea | 42 | 7 | 5 | 9 | 44 | 50 | 7 | 4 | 10 | 32 | 41 | 14 | 9 | 19 | 76 | 91 | 37 | 0.84 |
| 19 | Birmingham City | 42 | 9 | 5 | 7 | 37 | 36 | 4 | 5 | 12 | 26 | 44 | 13 | 10 | 19 | 63 | 80 | 36 | 0.79 |
| 20 | Nottingham Forest | 42 | 8 | 6 | 7 | 30 | 28 | 5 | 3 | 13 | 20 | 46 | 13 | 9 | 20 | 50 | 74 | 35 | 0.68 |
| 21 | Leeds United | 42 | 7 | 5 | 9 | 37 | 46 | 5 | 5 | 11 | 28 | 46 | 12 | 10 | 20 | 65 | 92 | 34 | 0.71 |
| 22 | Luton Town | 42 | 6 | 5 | 10 | 25 | 29 | 3 | 7 | 11 | 25 | 44 | 9 | 12 | 21 | 50 | 73 | 30 | 0.68 |

## 2 May 1960
## Manchester City 1 v 2 Burnley

*'Cathy's Clown'*

And so the entire season came down to this 90 minutes. Win and Burnley would be champions. Any other result would hand the title to Wolves. The Wanderers manager Stan Cullis was in the stands near the ranks of Burnley wives to see if his side would be crowned champions. Unbeknownst to the Wolves supremo, a number of his players were present in the huge crowd which had come to see the title-decider. Cullis had ordered them to stay away from the game – after all they had an FA Cup final against Blackburn to prepare for.

Peter Burch has vivid memories of the huge scrum outside and inside Maine Road. He said: "I don't think anyone anticipated just how many people would turn up because the traffic piled up before we got anywhere near Moss Side. Our coach was abandoned some distance from the ground. Almost 66,000 crammed into Maine Road on that bright, balmy May evening but many supporters were locked out. One young man climbed over one of the main gates and unlocked them so that others could surge in, carrying a tide of helpless fans up a stairwell and down a terrace gangway, which, amazingly, remained clear."

*Only four minutes gone and Brian Pilkington's cross is diverted in by City keeper Bert Trautmann to put Burnley in the lead [64]*

Peter and his strapping 17-year-old mates managed to gain entrance by masquerading as juveniles – this was the only terrace turnstile to remain open after kick-off. So for one shilling (5p) they too joined the throng. It was incredible that no one was seriously hurt. Today there would have been recriminations about the fans' behaviour as there was at the 2007 European Champions League final in Athens; there would have been an enquiry about the ticketing arrangements and stewardship but this was 1960. Despite the Burnden Park disaster of 1946, in which 33 supporters lost their lives in precisely these circumstances, health and safety matters were less tightly regulated; heaving, uncontrolled crowds were tolerated.

Stuart Barnes added: "being a schoolboy meant that my chances of going were remote especially as money was tight, but that lunch time quite by chance I called in hoping to see my mother who worked at that time at Joseph Lucas' Wood Top Factory. She had lunch on occasions at a nearby café with colleagues. I didn't know if she would be there. Fortunately she was, but as there were several adults sat together I kept quiet. After a few minutes the conversation turned to the match and one of the men said he was going but didn't know the way to Maine Road. I chirped up saying that I did, as my friend and I used to cycle (yes, cycle) to Longsight Sheds to train spot and knew they were not far away from the ground. In fact I had never been to Maine Road but wanted to show off a bit. When asked if I was going to the match I said no, but he offered to take me if I directed him and his mates, (with my mother's permission, of course), but how could she refuse? The match was pay at the gate so YES here we come, and I could hardly believe it. So about 4.30 that afternoon I met up with the group and off we went with some trepidation on my part in case it all went wrong and we finished up lost. As we drove through Whitefield it became obvious that there was going to be no chance of getting lost as the police were already on duty, directing traffic.

We parked miles from the ground and started walking. The whole thing was electric with most Burnley supporters parked in roughly the same area, but by the time we arrived at the turnstiles people were running around all over the place trying to find a turnstile they could use. It was obvious the ground was nearly full. I joined the same queue as my group but kick off came and went and we had hardly moved when someone shouted out that the only way to get in was via a kids' turnstile which was a feature of admission then. I was encouraged to go there but was worried about meeting up afterwards. A few basic directions were given and that was it for me as I bolted towards the turnstile. As I did so a terrific cheer went up and word then quickly spread that Burnley were in front. I charged through the gate and ran up the many steps to the top of what I later learned was the Kippax Stand. This stand was the 'Longside' with standing only and was so full that I could not even pass beyond the backmost row. I wasn't tall so there was no choice other than to stretch and watch on tip-toes which I did for the 80 remaining minutes."

Burnley supporter Gerard Bradley recalled: "Grandad had looked after me on the Turf since I was about six or seven years old, guiding me to the front of the Bee Hole end to the right of the goal. By 1959/60 he was retired and in his late sixties. I was sixteen and by now was looking after him. At Bolton in February 1960 we were narrowly missed by a large lump of concrete attached to a barrier as it gave way under crowd pressure. Grandad decided that next season he would be in the stand! The Manchester City game would be our last match together as from then on I would join my friends on the Longside. We travelled in the back of a *Burnley Express* van, with Dad and another photographer in the front. Traffic was so bad that we abandoned the van some two miles from the ground and hurried towards Maine Road. When we arrived just before kick-off there were long queues at the turnstiles and some were actually closing. We tried several queues and were beginning to lose hope when miraculously a short queue was found and within minutes we had entered as several doors clanged shut. There was a big roar and we had just missed the City equaliser. It transpired that The Clarets had scored early on, long before we had got into the ground. We could not see very much as we joined the back of the crowd and tried to edge our way in. I was tall and soon found a small viewing spot and I gave my old rattle to Grandad to stand on – even so I had to relay a description of most of the action."

Burnley had indeed started this most vital of games with a bang. Four minutes in, The Clarets grabbed a lucky goal. Brian Pilkington beat right-back Ken Branagan but ran the ball too far forward and found himself on the by-line with Bert Trautmann, that famous big cat of a goalkeeper, moving to cut off the cross. Little Pilky did the only thing he could do – he hit the ball across the goal and got the lucky deflection he hoped for – off Trautmann and into the net.

A few moments later, Pilkington had the goal at his mercy and missed. He had cause to regret it before long. In the 12th minute a Ken Barnes free-kick floated over a wall of penalty area defenders and Law flicked the ball to City centre-forward, Joe Hayes, who smashed it in. The Burnley defence appealed for offside, but in referee Hugh Gerrard's book City were level. It was now that Burnley showed the steel behind the silk – particularly Jimmy McIlroy, handicapped by a thigh injury that reduced him to half pace and the battling Clarets had their reward after exactly half an hour.

Craggy City centre-half, Dave Ewing, felled Pointer on the left hand side of the home box with an ugly, clattering tackle. Cummings clipped the resulting free-kick into the penalty area. City's right-back, Ken Brannigan, tried to shove a ball back to Trautmann and watched in horror as it curled away to outside-right Trevor Meredith. The 20-year-old reserve winger had played in only half a dozen League games but took the chance like a veteran, on the volley and Burnley led again. This was the vital, championship-winning goal … though no-one knew it then.

Gerard Bradley recalled: "Burnley were attacking our end of the ground and when Meredith scored a second for The Clarets this produced a crowd surge vastly improving our position and view but leaving my rattle several yards away. (Some kind chap returned it later)."

Supporter Stuart Barnes recalled: "the score stood at 2-1 when half-time arrived and the second 45 minutes have got to be the longest ever, with many

*Trevor Meredith scores what proves to be the Championship-winning goal [65]*

checks of the watch. Every small thing seemed like a massive heart stopping event, from Blacklaw catching a harmless cross to a City shot into the crowd."

*Daily Mirror* journalist Frank McGhee described the action as Burnley clung on with their lives. 'Hayes hooked a great City chance over the bar in the 38th minute; while Jimmy Robson who brought a fantastic save from Bert Trautmann on half-time. But it was Adam Blacklaw who ultimately saved his side. With 15 minutes left he stopped one from Hayes. A minute later he tipped over a powerhouse drive from Barnes, just as Hayes ran in to flatten him. Ten minutes to go – and he saved from Law. With six minutes left it was Hannah. Four minutes left – and it was Barnes. Now Burnley summoned up the strength to attack again. Three minutes left, two minutes, the last minute. One more shot from left-half, Alan Oakes. One more competent save from Blacklaw – and it was all over.'

Supporter Peter Burch recalled the one heart-stopping moment in the final nerve-wracking minutes: "with very little time to go, City centred the ball from the right and there, leaping at the far post, was their recent massive £53,000 signing, the young, combative Scotsman, Denis Law. All studs and elbows, he looked a certain goal scorer, but Adam Blacklaw's stretching finger tips stopped him from wrecking Burnley's dream. I was 25 feet away. I can still see Law's face. For years afterwards my mate would remind me, graphically and laughingly, how my face had turned an instant shade of white."

Law's chance was the last moment for City and the last for Wolves. The referee's whistle heralded The Clarets' first league title for 39 years, and one of the most remarkable ever.

Frank McGhee proclaimed: 'Burnley, the team of quiet men – five of them are part-timers and the whole outfit cost less than (£15,000) – snatched the First Division Championship from the teeth of the famous Wolves ... They proved last night that they have the backbone of steel and nerves of ice as well as football skill ... This was a match that had to be watched with one eye on the clock and with one eye on the titantic struggle that see-sawed its way through 90 minutes that pulsed and throbbed with the roar of 66,000 fans. One point was no good to Burnley. They had to get both.'

After the final whistle had sounded, McGhee observed: 'Brian Pilkington, 5 foot 5 inches Burnley left-winger played himself to a standstill. Just before the end he collapsed on the touchline. While he was being carried to the dressing room hundreds of fans burst onto the pitch to congratulate the Burnley players. Long after the game Burnley supporters were still outside the main gate chanting "we want the Champs!"'

Stuart Barnes continued: "the referee finally blew for full time and all I can recall from that moment on was seeing fans leap over the wall onto the pitch and then feeling very fear struck when I realised that the only way out for the mass below was up the steps to where I was standing and then back down the way I had entered. Thousands of City fans surged upwards towards me so I had no alternative than to run for it."

The *Burnley Express* reported: 'hundreds of the thousands of supporters from East Lancashire who attended the match either joined in mobbing the team as they came off the pitch or waited for them outside Maine Road or

Burnley Town Hall. After the match, a big crowd waited outside the dressing room entrance and main doorway for the team who, on being joined by Mr Lord and Mr Potts, were invited into the main reception room by the City directors.'

The late Harry Potts' wife, Margaret remembered the occasion with great clarity. She told Dave Thomas, author of *Harry Potts – Margaret's Story*; 'They had to close the gates early and lock thousands of supporters out. I heard that the police actually closed some roads in the area. We heard stories that some fans had walked there. Two coaches had left Burnley, one with the players, directors and staff and the second with all the wives and ladies (*except Sheila Blacklaw who was unable to find a babysitter*). The stadium was packed, the colours marvellous, the noise deafening, the atmosphere and sense of expectation like nothing I had ever experienced.

When little Trevor Meredith scored the winner we all just went wild. (Wolves' manager) Stan Cullis still didn't move a muscle in his face. Funnily enough, I thought of his abrupt words to me when Harry worked at Wolves: "we don't cater for relatives here". We counted down the minutes, sat and fidgeted, watched as Jimmy Mac wasted precious seconds and then minutes holding onto the ball by the corner flag. The referee kept looking at his watch but wouldn't blow the whistle. More than just a few Wolves fans were there in their colours to cheer on City.

Mac jigged up and down by the flag again. When was the ref going to blow that whistle, we kept asking each other? The tension was enormous, the Burnley fans were whistling and calling and praying. Harry was in his dugout kicking every ball and willing the time away. We looked at our watches time and time again. Our nerves were at breaking point…and then when he blew that superb whistle and we heard that wonderful cheer of acclamation and relief at the end, we just cheered and clapped and felt so elated. It was a feeling I can hardly describe. Claret and blue was everywhere as the pitch disappeared under a sea of spectators as somehow the players got back to the dressing room. There was no champagne; they celebrated with sherry drunk from old tea mugs. I know for some of them it was days before it really finally sank in.

For a small town and club that people from the south thought was in the back of beyond, this was just an incredible achievement. Burnley gained an identity and a pride that night which lifted it out of the doldrums. It was a town of hardship and job losses with its rows and rows of old industrial housing and ancient mills, which had been closing one by one for three decades. It was a place full of neglect, and buildings that were darkened and stained literally by a hundred years of factory smoke and figuratively by low wages.

From the pictures of Harry during the game, you can see the tension and strain etched into his face, the staring eyes, the furrowed brow, the clenched fists, and the hunched shoulders. For almost 70 minutes he watched as his team hung on to their 2-1 lead. It must have seemed an eternity. I was just so proud of Harry seeing him down there at the end. He had done something magical for this tiny place; he had lifted people's morale and spirits and given them hope. The town and club were well and truly on the map.'

And this author's memories? They came from afar, but are fresh still. I had discovered that the BBC Light Programme was covering the second half. With bedtimes a scarred war zone, I had to smuggle the transistor into my bedroom, muffling its sound under heavy bedclothes. It was a dark wait of sweaty expectancy. There were no progress reports: just dismal dance music, musty balm from another age and no longer in step.

I was unaware that on a bald, bumpy pitch, Burnley had recovered their zest and had taken the lead as early as the 4th minute. City's response was ferocious and immediate. They threw themselves at Burnley as if they were contesting the Championship, too, rather than playing out a final inconsequential fixture. Play ebbed and flowed at a frantic pace.

With City throwing caution to the winds there were chances for Burnley on the break but Trautmann made amends for his earlier error with a couple of fine saves. The importance of this was underlined when Hayes blasted in Dennis Law's miscued flick. Back came Burnley and only Trautmann's brilliant fingertip save denied Robson. However, just past the half hour mark the decisive goal was scored. All of this was made clear to me after a plummy voice finally announced: "we are going to Maine Road, Manchester for Association Football. Raymond Glendenning is the commentator." Although the details of a second half, played almost 50 years ago, are understandably sketchy, the claustrophobic tension of that night remains; wriggling under the covers, arching and flattening the legs, creating stale, warm currents; air conditioning from hell. There were no distractions in the moist darkness while straining to make sense of the play; surfing the ambiguous crescendos; yearning for reassurance and, as full-time crept closer, counting down the seconds; calling them too quickly in trying to repel the mounting anguish. Football is always more frenetic on the radio. There were numerous near misses. Despite the calming control exerted by Adamson and Cummings, most of these seemed to be at Burnley's end. They sounded impossibly close. Finally, that final whistle sounded and with it came the toppling sensations of relief, euphoria and exhaustion but also the hopelessness of sleep.

Former Burnley MP Peter Pike recalled his experience of the game from the distant perspective of south London. He said: "I couldn't go to the City game as I could not get time off work. I also had a problem in attempting to listen to the radio broadcast as I was chairing a Young Socialists meeting in Merton and Morden that evening. That was an obstacle I was able to overcome. At the appointed hour, I produced a pocket transistor radio, which in those days was still somewhat rare and was of novelty interest to everyone at the meeting. In the final phase of the game with Burnley in the lead we seemed under pressure and I kept shouting at the radio for the referee to blow the whistle. It seemed an eternity but it in the end it came. Burnley were champions and into Europe.'

Gerrard Bradley remembered that after the game: "we made our way back to the *Express* van and found Dad waiting. Traffic was very dense so it was nearing midnight when we made our way through Rawtenstall, Crawshaw-booth and the other small settlements along the valley. We were a few minutes ahead of the team coach and people were lining the route. They appeared out of houses in dressing gowns and pyjamas to await the victors. Dad wanted photographs of the coach so we stopped amid a large crowd at the bottom of Manchester Road as the team bus came down past the Town Hall. We arrived home about two in the morning, very happy but sad that days watching The Clarets with Grandad were finally over."

Peter Burch added: "the coach trip back to Manchester was strangely subdued to begin with. It might have been natural flatness, which follows elation or just the fact that it hadn't sunk in. There had been no TV coverage and no presentation of the trophy; the show biz side of football was still a long way off. For example, Ray Pointer was described in the programme as a 'welder by trade'. No porsches there then. As the coach entered Rawten-stall one thing became apparent: people were waiting in their doorways waiting for the team coach to pass. This was Clarets country. A crowd had gathered on Manchester Road outside the Town Hall to meet the surprised players, who were whisked inside to take their bows on the balcony. It wasn't stage-managed, it was just spontaneous."

The *Burnley Express* reported: 'during the return journey supporters in cars and coaches signalled their delight by waving berets and scarves and sounding rattles. However, it was not until they reached Rawtenstall that the team began to realise that various reception committees were awaiting them. Now they found that they were passing groups of cheering people every few hundred yards, with the largest crowd being at Rawtenstall centre. The coach had a police motor cycle escort to the Burnley borough boundary where a patrol car took over. It was at the summit where the first shock of the surprise welcome hit the party. Mr Lord called the attention of the team to the sight ahead and Mr Potts asked them to open the windows of the coach to show their appreciation. The descent into the town was past a stationary line of cars with lights shining and drawn into the near side so that the coach could pass. People were standing four deep on the pavement and, as soon as the team appeared, the car klaxons were sounded and it was cheers all the way.

There was another surprise as soon as the Manchester Road bend by Springhill Road was turned. "Look at this!" called one of the party – and "this" was a tremendous crowd and a tumultuous welcome. As soon as the escort car came to a halt, the supporters swarmed in between it and the coach, cheering wildly. The Mayor (Councillor Miss Edith Utley) was on the steps of the Town Hall, so the captain Jimmy Adamson, followed by Tommy Cummings, Mr R.W. Lord and Mr R. Cook emerged from the coach to join her. The mayor motioned for the remainder of the party to leave the coach, and each member had to run the gauntlet of a police-cleared pathway of back-slapping enthusiasts, Ray Bennion and Billy Dougall being surrounded and unable to join the others for some minutes'

The crowd chanted "We want Mac! We want Mac!" in a continuous roar, but Jimmy McIlroy had left the party near his home off Manchester Road. Jimmy Adamson quietened the cheering throng and thanked them for their warm and unexpected reception. The party were then invited into the Mayor's parlour where Councillor H. Woodcock and members of Brierfield

*Jimmy Adamson, Ray Pointer, Adam Blacklaw and Tommy Cummings taste the fruits of victory [66]*

District Council were waiting. "We were having a meeting," he said, "then we heard the score and decided that the least we could do was to get to Burnley and offer our congratulations. After all, two of the team – John Angus and Jimmy Robson – are in lodgings at Brierfield, and we are all very proud of them.

The Mayor was delighted with the result and insisted that the players go out onto the balcony to the crowd. Adam Blacklaw was one of the first to be called upon by the supporters, and then Tommy Cummings sought out the youngsters of the team who were too embarrassed by the enthusiasm, and if they had not had a 'public appearance' they were seized and hustled to the front where they were laughingly introduced by Mr Lord. And the crowd loved it – their cheers could be heard distinctively as far away as the prairie field. Mr Harry Potts, giving them a vote of thanks, said that it was all very well supporting a consistently winning team. It was when things did not go right that proved a test of loyalty and he felt that the Turf Moor crowd had been behind them. Their loyalty had come to the rescue.

Concerted shouts for McIlroy followed, and it had to be explained that the international had called at home as no-one knew that there was going to be a welcome like that experienced. McIlroy eventually arrived at the Town Hall when most of the crowd had gone and just before the party moved on to Turf Moor. Word had been received that another reception was awaiting the team at the club's headquarters late as it was, but many had departed when the team appeared.

Burnley supporter Gary Roberts had been unable to get to Maine Road because he had a game of his own but due to mistaken identity managed to become caught up in the post-match celebrations. Gary said: "on 2 Monday May 1960, aged 21, I played for Nelson first team away to Skelmersdale United in the Lancashire Combination Division one. I was a second team player and it was my only appearance for the 1st team, only because, the 1st team were being rested for the Combination Cup Final to be played on the following Friday. We were duly beaten 3-0 by a superior side, but we had the pleasure of listening to the last ten minutes of Burnley beating Manchester City 2-1 to win the 1st Division Championship. This was before the Motorway was opened, so the only way back to Nelson was down Manchester Road into the centre of Burnley. Long before we reached Burnley there were thousands of fans lining the pavements eagerly awaiting Burnley's triumphant heroes. The amusing part of this story is that we received a great welcome because the crowds at first thought we were The Clarets."

Two days before Gary Powers' U-2 spy plane was shot down by the Soviets, Burnley's celebrations flowed through the night and the ensuing days. For weeks, the lives of thousands of Burnley fans hovered upon a cushion of contentment. The Everly Brothers' number one hit, *Cathy's Clown*, still marks that time in the memories of all those lucky enough to be present.

The *Burnley Express* reported on the players' immediate reactions: 'after the match was over earlier in the evening, and Burnley's triumph was assured, reactions of members of the team suffered from demonstrations of delight to stunned disbelief. Jimmy Adamson, the skipper, said, "As soon as the final whistle sounded, I let my emotions get the better of me for the first time on a football field. I thought, 'This is it' and threw my arms round someone – either Tommy Cummings or Dusty Miller."

*Burnley's celebration parade [65a]*

Later Jimmy Adamson said: "It is the happiest moment of my football life. I feel very grateful to the boys for playing so well and making our delight possible. It is something we share and will never forget. We owe this success to our manager. He is a wonderful fellow and has worked so hard for our benefit."

Tommy Cummings, one of the senior members of the side, said: "This is a happy club and I think that has a great deal to do with it. I think it is fair to say that we all feel pleased because of our manager. Mr Potts is a grand fellow and it is his triumph rather than ours."

In describing his goal to the *Burnley Express* reporter after the game, Brian Pilkington said: "I intended it for a centre and cut across the ball. It spun off my foot and beat Trautmann. When I saw it cross the line by the far post I let out a whoop. It did not hit anyone on the way."

Reflecting upon his winning goal, modest Trevor Meredith said simply: "I was glad to see it go in. I am very happy'. Speaking on the gnawing tension of the game, Jimmy Robson added: 'I have never known a match in which it was so acute. It was the longest second-half I have ever experienced"

As for excluded wing-half, Bob Seith, he said: "after my disagreement with Bob Lord, I was not involved. I did not go to Maine Road. I did listen to the second half commentary on the wireless at home, though. I was so pleased for my team-mates. It was a terrific effort. As I said, I had no problem with Burnley. Burnley had been good for me."

Billy Dougall, the physiotherapist and former trainer-coach and manager, commented: "It was the best thing that happened to Burnley F.C. when Harry Potts came to Turf Moor." Trainer Ray Bennion said: "this is a hat-trick of training triumphs. I was trainer of the club's 'A' team which won the old West Lancashire League Championship before the war when Harry Potts was a young member of the side. Then I held a similar position with the team which won the Central League title and now the major honour – the Division One Championship."

For his part Bob Lord announced exultantly: "all through this tough season I have thought this young team of ours would win something – and now they've done it. I think the League Championship is a more satisfying success – for it takes skilful football, guts and courage to go through a hard programme of 42 matches and come out on top. And now we can go to New York as the English Champions – that's the way we wanted it. And of course we can have a crack at the top Continental sides in next season's European Cup competition. We have said we will give the public of Burnley – remember the population is only 81,000 – football they can appreciate and this is only the beginning."

Drained, but evidently flushed with pride, Harry Potts confined himself to a few, typically modest remarks: "I'm delighted with all of them and I'm sure there are even better things ahead of us. I'd like to mention Jimmy Adamson's inspiring captaincy but every one of the lads gave everything in this fight."

A Burnley supporter, recording his memory on The Clarets Mad website, wrote: 'I was at the game against City. I remember on my way to work the morning after and buying all the morning newspapers. One thing that sticks in my mind was a picture of Stan Cullis the Wolves manager. He looked like he had eaten a dead rat.'

Actually, Cullis, the fierce competitor but consummate sportsman, did have more to say. Approaching Burnley Chairman, Bob Lord, with a rueful smile in the immediate aftermath, he graciously said: "Good luck, Bob. You've deserved it and I mean every word I say. It was tough. But I guess it was better than seeing your own team go down. It has been a tough struggle all through. We did our best. Unfortunately, it wasn't enough. Congratulations to Burnley, they are a good side."

Burnley supporter Frank Bailey wrote a tribute to another aspect of Burnley's triumph: sportsmanship: 'in the first-half when some of the team seemed jittery, Adamson at all times was cool and resolute in attack and defence. After Burnley had scored and City received an encouraging and almost frightening roar of support, the ball went out of play twice on the Burnley right-wing, and each time Adamson actually ran to collect it when many would have tried a little gamesmanship in order to help retain that slender lead. If we get more sportsmanship of this type, the whole game will improve.'

*Burnley's showpiece Keirby Hotel opens with press claims to be the 'Claridges of the North' [67]*

Burnley was a town celebrating amidst regeneration. The showpiece Keirby Hotel, which had been constructed throughout the preceding year, opened on the 30 April. It would come just in time to honour the Football Club's crowning glory. Healey Royd Mill also demonstrated that there was life after cotton, turning over its production to the manufacture of shoes and slippers and creating 700 new jobs in the process. But as the gleeful Burnley folk greeted their new First Division champions, few would have suspected that this was might be as good as it would get.

But for now the town rejoiced at the club's achievement. Remarkably, Burnley had won the First Division title by taking top spot just once during the entire season – as a result of that victory in their final game at Maine Road. Perhaps Jimmy Greaves best summarises their magnificent legacy. He wrote: 'Even in defeat I wanted to applaud their artistry. In an era when quite a few teams believed in the big boot, they were a league of gentlemen.'

## First Division

| 2 May 1960 | *P* | *W* | *D* | *L* | *F* | *A* | *Pts* | *Goal average* |
|---|---|---|---|---|---|---|---|---|
| 1. BURNLEY | 42 | 24 | 7 | 11 | 85 | 61 | 55 | 1.39 |
| 2. Wolverhampton Wanderers | 42 | 24 | 6 | 12 | 106 | 67 | 54 | 1.58 |
| 3. Tottenham Hotspur | 42 | 21 | 11 | 10 | 86 | 50 | 53 | 1.72 |
| 4.West Bromwich Albion | 42 | 19 | 11 | 12 | 83 | 57 | 49 | 1.46 |
| 5. Sheffield Wednesday | 42 | 19 | 11 | 12 | 80 | 59 | 49 | 1.36 |
| 6. Bolton Wanderers | 42 | 20 | 8 | 14 | 59 | 51 | 48 | 1.16 |
| 7. Manchester United | 42 | 19 | 7 | 16 | 102 | 80 | 45 | 1.28 |
| 8. Newcastle United | 42 | 18 | 8 | 16 | 82 | 78 | 44 | 1.05 |
| 9. Preston North End | 42 | 16 | 12 | 14 | 79 | 76 | 44 | 1.04 |
| 10. Fulham | 42 | 17 | 10 | 15 | 73 | 80 | 44 | 0.91 |
| 11. Blackpool | 42 | 15 | 10 | 17 | 59 | 71 | 40 | 0.83 |
| 12. Leicester City | 42 | 13 | 13 | 16 | 66 | 75 | 39 | 0.88 |
| 13. Arsenal | 42 | 15 | 9 | 18 | 68 | 80 | 39 | 0.85 |
| 14. West Ham United | 42 | 16 | 6 | 20 | 75 | 91 | 38 | 0.82 |
| 15. Everton | 42 | 13 | 11 | 18 | 73 | 78 | 37 | 0.94 |
| 16. Manchester City | 42 | 17 | 3 | 22 | 78 | 84 | 37 | 0.93 |
| 17. Blackburn Rovers | 42 | 16 | 5 | 21 | 60 | 70 | 37 | 0.86 |
| 18. Chelsea | 42 | 14 | 9 | 19 | 76 | 91 | 37 | 0.84 |
| 19. Birmingham City | 42 | 13 | 10 | 19 | 63 | 80 | 36 | 0.79 |
| 20. Nottingham Forest | 42 | 13 | 9 | 20 | 50 | 74 | 35 | 0.68 |
| 21. Leeds United | 42 | 12 | 10 | 20 | 65 | 92 | 34 | 0.71 |
| 22. Luton Town | 42 | 9 | 12 | 21 | 50 | 73 | 30 | 0.68 |

Nine months after the Maine Road triumph, two major changes were to take place in professional football: the abolition of the maximum wage and, thanks to George Eastham's High Court action, the upholding of a player's right to play for the club of his choosing once his contract had expired. In 1960, a player could earn a maximum basic wage of £20 per week no matter where he played, although this payment was between 50-75% more than that given to an average manual worker. Of course, life was much cheaper then. Even luxury goods like a 3lb chicken cost 14 shillings (70p) and a bottle of wine 7 shillings (35p). A 15-day all-inclusive holiday on the Costa Brava cost around £24. However, footballer's lifestyles were not so far removed from many of their supporters. The abolition of the maximum wage began to widen that difference with the better-supported clubs able to attract better players with ever-increasing wages. With that widening of economic opportunity came the narrowing of competition. With the exception of Ipswich in 1962 and the occasional freak Cup final results, such as those by Oxford and Wimbledon during the eighties, Burnley's League victory in 1960 was one of the last hurrahs for the small town club. The memory should be cherished.

Chapter Six

# 'A Taste of Honey':

*Why Burnley's title-winning triumph of 1959/60 was incredible*

## 1. Burnley: the smallest English town to support a League winning team

With a population of just over 80,000, Burnley was the smallest town or city to support an English Premiership or First Division title-winning side. Only two sides have come close to matching this feat before or since; Huddersfield Town, who won a hat-trick of titles in the 1920s and Ipswich Town who won the title in 1962. Both towns were 38% larger, however.

To place the significance of Burnley's achievement in a modern context, try imagining a team from Hartlepool, Selby, Kettering or Hastings competing in the current European Champions League. In 2001, each of these towns had a population of a similar size to that of Burnley in 1961. Of course, Burnley had a number of small surrounding towns, including Nelson and Colne, providing an additional support of around 70,000. But all the top clubs had extended catchment areas, at least of a similar size to Burnley's and, in many cases, larger. For example, in 1961, even remotely-placed Blackpool could call upon 75,000 residents from nearby Fleetwood, Lytham St. Annes and Poulton-le-Fylde to supplement its support, which was derived principally from the town's population of 150,000. Blackpool could also trade on its status as a prime holiday spot, whereas Burnley could not. Unlike Preston, Burnley was out on a limb, apparently on a road and rail 'to nowhere'. That was a bane of its economic life.

Also in 1959, Burnley had to contend with fierce local competition at the turnstiles. Six other First Division teams – Manchesters United and City,

Bolton, Blackburn, Preston and Blackpool – were situated within a 40 mile radius of Turf Moor, Burnley, with five other clubs, from the lower divisions of the Football League – Rochdale, Bury, Accrington, Halifax and Oldham – located nearby, too. Only the London-based clubs faced a similar competition and they all had a far larger city and suburban population to call upon.

## 2. Burnley's share of local support was twice the First Division average

Burnley's population was declining, reflecting the downturn in the town's economic prospects. With its cotton trade dwindling and its coal reserves running down, Burnley's population had reduced by around 20% – a loss of 23,000 residents – since The Clarets last lifted the First Division Championship in 1921.

Although a measure of prosperity was temporarily restored during the early to mid fifties, the town's population continued to fall. But despite having a comparatively small population, Burnley attracted an average crowd of just under 27,000 to its League games during the 1959/60 season. A crowd of 27,000 represented 33% of the town's population. The average share for a First Division club in that season was a mere 12%. Also, despite the substantial loss of population between 1921 and 1961, a greater proportion of the town's total residents watched Burnley in 1959-60 (33%) compared with 1920-21 (31%).

For more details about the comparative sizes of potential support see Appendix 1 *Comparative Strength of Local Support*

## 3. Burnley: the first British exponents of Total Football?

'Total Football' is the description of a style of play in which any player can take over the role of any other in the team. Its refinement, if not its genesis, is attributed to coach Rinus Michels, who managed Ajax and the Dutch national side during the 1970s. Johan Cruyff is often considered to be the most famous exponent of the system. However, this tactical approach did not appear in the early 70s as some kind of 'Year Zero' enlightenment. English manager Jack Reynolds pioneered the idea when he managed Ajax before the Second World War. In the summer of 1960, Hungary's famous coach, Gusztav Sebes said that his Ujpest club was experimenting with a 'circular system', in which every player pulled equal weight, being capable of playing in all positions. This, too, was Total Football. Indeed, the Real Madrid and Brazilian sides of the late 50s could claim that they, too, were early exponents of the system.

Arguably, Burnley's title-winning side were the first British exponents of the approach. Jimmy Adamson explained in 1962: "we like to keep our game fluid. We don't believe in sticking to numbers on our backs. If the full back suddenly finds himself in the momentary role of a winger, then he gets on with it, and someone else takes over his job in the rear. Burnley play their football 'off the cuff'. That best describes the Burnley style. There are few hard and fast rules. Obviously we try to vary our tactics according to the opposition and state of the pitch. But off the cuff fluid football is the aim."

It was this versatility, exercised so fluently within an ostensible VW-type line up, which foxed so many opponents. Even Spurs, who came closest to matching this style of play, tended to keep their full backs at home, at least before their double-winning triumph, because Bill Nicholson was so determined to eradicate his side's defensive errors, which almost brought about their relegation in 1959.

## 4. Burnley: the 'dead-ball' wizards

Jimmy Greaves referred to Burnley's "mesmerising variety of free-kick scams". As demonstrated before, Burnley perfected a wide range of dead-ball ruses covering throw-ins, corners and free-kicks, working hard on these two afternoons per week. As Jimmy McIlroy pointed out the success of their methods was always hard-won, achieved only on the back of hours and hours of practice. Alan Brown and Harry Potts, like Bill Nicholson, realised the tactical importance of such preparations because as Bill said: "statistics have shown that between a third and a half of goals scored by a football team come from re-starts, corners, free kicks or throw-ins."

Burnley's ingenuity in dead-ball situations was capable of flummoxing top continental opposition, such as Rheims, as well as leading English sides. Their inventiveness had respected pundits, like Brian Glanville, purring. But it was not just their extra flair that gave the club important advantages, it was their professional dedication, too. Like Wolves and Sheffield Wednesday, Burnley prepared well for the game ahead, but like Spurs, they were prepared to extemporise during the course of the game. A plan was never a straitjacket.

## 5. Burnley: early prophets of the coaching gospel

When Alan Brown became Burnley's manager in 1954, he instilled a respect and appreciation for the new coaching methods. He also encouraged his players to obtain their coaching badges. Brown was a strong champion of skills improvement and Harry Potts followed suit when he took over in 1958. This was at a time when a number of top club managers and players were sceptical about what coaching could offer. As evidence of Burnley's commitment to professional development, captain Jimmy Adamson emerged as one of the leading coaches in the country, groomed for the role as national coach after the 1962 World Cup finals. The new ideas disseminated by Lilleshall and its invited speakers, including the influential Herrera and Sebes, were readily absorbed by forward-thinking Burnley.

## 6. Burnley: the 'cheapest' Champions of the post war period

Burnley spent just £13,000 in transfer fees in bringing together its title-winning side – £8,000 on inside-forward Jimmy McIlroy in 1950 and £5,000 on left-back, Alex Elder in 1959.

Only Wolves came close to matching Burnley's achievement in assembling a title-winning side on such a small transfer budget. Wolves' manager Stan Cullis paid fees for just three players on his books in the 1959/60 season – £12,000 to Brentford for inside-forward, Peter Broadbent, £3,000 to Millwall for keeper Malcolm Finlayson and £12,500 to Kilmarnock for centre-forward Joe McBride (who was quickly sold to Luton). By contrast, the Spurs double-winning side of 1960/61, which was put in place during Burnley's triumphant season, cost over £150,000. Greaves' purchase in 1961 raised that figure to over £250,000.

Burnley's spending on McIlroy and Elder represented less than one quarter of what Manchester City spent on just one player, Denis Law. It also amounted to less than a third of what both Manchester United paid for Albert Quixall and what Arsenal stumped up for Mel Charles, and half of what Newcastle splashed out on Ivor Allchurch. Burnley's outlay on new players was also much less than that even at a number of struggling clubs. For example, in a desperate attempt to cling onto their First Division status, Everton splashed out around £100,000 on new recruits during the 1959/60 season. In that same season, Nottingham Forest paid over £40,000 for reinforcements, too, while even doomed, cash-strapped Luton mustered £18,000 for centre-forwards, Joe McBride and Harvey McCreadie.

Much has been said about how the Busby Babes represented the flowering of a brilliant youth policy. Whilst it is true that the title-winning Manchester United sides of 1955/56 and 1956/57 were almost entirely home grown, they were also reinforced by a few expensive imports. For example, centre-forward, Tommy Taylor, cost almost £30,000 when signed from Barnsley. Birmingham City were paid £25,000 for right-winger Johnny Berry. Goal-keeper Ray Wood cost £5,000 from Darlington and, just before the Munich disaster, Doncaster were paid £23,500 for Northern Ireland keeper, Harry Gregg. Even Alf Ramsey's frugally-assembled Ipswich side, who won the First Division Championship in 1962, cost over £30,000 in transfer fees. Only one team came close to matching Burnley's homegrown achievement. In 1946/47, the first tumultous season after the War, Stoke City's first team squad had cost them under £250, including the £10 signing on fee for players joining from junior football. Stoke nearly pulled off a remarkable title-winning miracle to match Burnley's, but lost their last game of the season at Sheffield United, when a victory would have given them the title.

## 7. Burnley: the best scouting network in the land?

This is a more contentious claim. Some might argue that Wolves and Manchester United had an equally valid case here. Others might identify additional contenders, such as Chelsea, West Ham, Bolton and Sheffield Wednesday. All of these clubs successfully filled their teams with home-grown players. Arguably, the Burnley scouts had a more difficult task, though. Given that clubs then restricted their talent-spotting to Britain, the Burnley scouts had to operate within a heavily fished pool with fewer selling points, at least in comparison with many of their First Division rivals. Both Manchester United and Wolves had established formidable reputations during the fifties. Arsenal, Newcastle, Chelsea, Blackpool, Bolton, Manchester City, West Bromwich and Spurs were big names, too. They had all won silver-ware during this decade. Their achievements almost sold themselves. Many young lads pursued by the Burnley scouts did not know too much about Burnley, the town. Moreover, once persuaded to visit, their first impressions were not always favourable as several players recalled quite vividly. But they were persuaded they would have better chances of success there.

The Burnley scouts captured an array of glittering talent that not only sustained Burnley's place in the top flight but enabled it to challenge for major honours up until the mid seventies. Until money was allowed to rule, a bulging harvest was repeatedly reaped from under the very noses of their opponents – most notably in the North East of England and in Scotland and Northern Ireland, too. The Burnley's scouts were hard-working, alert, persistent and persuasive, often seeing off their rivals because their club offered a promising lad better prospects of progress. The very fact that Burnley were the 'cheapest' Champions of the post-war period is testament to the effectiveness of the club's highly successful scouting network.

## 8. Burnley: early pioneers of 'Investors in People'

Nowadays, Investors in People is an organisational buzz term. The initiative is designed to provide a framework to help organizations find the most suitable means for achieving success through their people. It rests upon organizations communicating clear aims and objectives to all of their staff; providing regular supervision and relevant training; and engaging 'hearts and minds' in pursuing collective improvement. But long before 1993, when this initiative was launched, with its showy accompaniments, such as the certifying wall plaques, Burnley Football Club was quietly walking the talk.

Young players arriving at Burnley were well looked after. Their digs were carefully vetted. They were well fed and watered. They were inducted quickly into the club's ways – its aims, standards and principles, as illustrated by Bob Seith's early experience with manager, Cliff Britton. With the Burnley managers and their coaches exercising a strong loco-parentis role, no young player was left in any doubt about what was expected of him on or off the field. Trade apprenticeships were sorted out for those new recruits without one. This was to ensure that these young footballers had something to fall back upon should professional football not work out for them. Once serious relationships with girlfriends emerged, the club took steps to ensure that their young men behaved responsibly, liaising with their parents, as appropriate. As managers, both Alan Brown and Harry Potts were responsive to their players' needs at difficult times such as during bereavement. The sensitivity they showed at times of distress was another strong factor in bonding their players to the club. Although the club was efficiently and thoughtfully organised, with careful attention paid to training, tactics, finances, travelling arrangements etc., the human touch remained. New recruits were welcomed as if they were joining an extended family. They quickly formed warm, mutually-supportive friendships and had fun, too, while working hard.

As far as learning the ropes was concerned, the young players were properly coached with an emphasis placed upon building up their skills and confidence. At many clubs the youth players were little more than skivvies, with limited opportunities to improve their game. This is not to say that the young Burnley players were wrapped in cotton wool. Several members of the class of 1959/60 recall clearly the slog of balancing outside daily work with evening classes and training plus the toughness of their inductions on the playing field. However, unlike the practice at many other clubs, each young Burnley player was given an extended period to show what he could do. The attraction of Burnley was that it established a strong reputation as a kindly, happy, responsible club which invested strongly in its young players, giving many of them early opportunities to prove their worth on the big stage. It was small wonder that so few of them wanted to move on.

## 9. Burnley: where careful planning came before 'quick fixes'

At a time when many top clubs tended to rely upon the cheque book, Burnley looked to their reserves. They invested in their young home-grown talent instead, preparing them carefully for the time when they might step up. An important ingredient of their success was the creation of purpose-built, modern training facilities at Gawthorpe in the mid fifties. These facilities included three full-size pitches, a gym and a revolutionary all-weather surface. Although clubs such as Spurs and Leicester had their own training ground, many First Division clubs of the time did not. For example, the facilities at nearby Preston and Blackpool were primitive by comparison. At a number of leading clubs, including Manchester United, impromptu games were often organised on the stadium's cinder car park or underneath the stands. Clubs such as Leeds used the perimeter of the pitch as their training ground, focusing mostly upon fitness routines involving jogs and sprints. Burnley found better ways. The club's investment in Gawthorpe paid off handsomely with a succession of young stars and established players having the right facilities in which they could hone their craft.

## 10. Burnley: a declining town but a leading club

Burnley was a mill town in decline. Despite the gradual arrival of new manufacturing industries, its heyday remained in its Victorian past. Because Burnley was tucked away in a narrow valley at the foot of the Pennines, it was easier to overlook the place. Just as the local politicians claimed, its road and railway connections needed urgent improvement. Burnley was too cut off from everywhere else. And yet this little town, struggling to survive in changing economic times, supported an ultra modern football club, brimming with innovative ideas which put it on a par with the best continental sides.

Looking back, how many football club chairmen have set out their club's vision, policies and manifesto for change in a published book? This is what Bob Lord did in 1962 when he wrote: *My Fight for Soccer*. Whilst Lord sometimes conducted himself like a proud and autocratic Victorian industrialist, he was no stick in the mud. He built for the future, improving the ground and the training facilities and flew his team to away games. Lord foresaw many of the changes that have subsequently taken place in British football. He was determined that Burnley should stay ahead of the game. He supported the abolition of the maximum wage having taken the unusual step, for a club chairman, of canvassing the views of his own players. And whilst his relationships with his managers were not always cordial and sometimes destructive, his prescient ambition has to be applauded. As has been shown, his club was vibrantly inventive and gloriously entertaining on the field and prudent, efficient and well-organised off it. Despite the various tensions and occasional divisions besetting the club, as with Alan Brown's, Bob Seith's and Jimmy Adamson's acrimonious departures, Jimmy McIlroy's shock transfer and the sidelining of Harry Potts, Burnley remained for the most part a close-knit, happy, caring family unit. Wives, husbands and families pulled together. All of the former players and a couple of their wives, interviewed for this book, spoke unhesitatingly of their joyful memories and their warmth and affection for the club. Burnley FC might have been a leading edge outfit but made sure its staff and their families were on board on its forward journey. There were no fancy slogans. Progress rested upon honest, down-to-earth, resourceful efforts. As Sheila Blacklaw stated, "we were not pretentious but happy".

Chapter Seven

# A Team of Artists and a League of Gentlemen

*Burnley's class of 1959/60*

ANY GREAT side comes together over a period of time and Burnley's 1959/60 title winners were no different. Their genesis can be traced back at least a decade. Frank Hill, manager from 1948 to 1954, began to assemble the nucleus of the title-winning side. His first signing of lasting significance was that of 19-year-old Ulsterman Jimmy McIlroy from Glentoran for an £8,000 fee. Jimmy Mac's first appearance was at Sunderland in October 1950. Here he replaced Harry Potts, who had been transferred to Everton to play in Cliff Britton's languishing side. Frank Hill also drafted in another Geordie, 22-year-old Jimmy Adamson at right half for the final eighteen games of the season, having converted Adamson from an inside forward. Hill had toyed with the idea that McIlroy might be more effective at wing half, too. Fortunately, he did not pursue the idea. The creative midfield partnership of McIlroy and Adamson would

*Burnley 1959/60 League Champions: Back row (left to right) Alex Elder, Jimmy Robson, Tommy Cummings, Adam Blacklaw, Brian Miller, John Angus, Ray Pointer. Front row: John Connelly, Jimmy McIlroy, Jimmy Adamson (captain), Brian Pilkington, Trevor Meredith [68]*

provide the fulcrum of Potts' title-winning side.

Peter Fyles, author of *Burnley's Greatest Goal and the Last of the Golden Boys* commented: 'whatever Hill lacked in close relations with his players, he compensated for in football astuteness and determination. He was described by one former player as "a hard little devil of a character". He loved playing five-a-side soccer and often matches would last several hours until his side eventually edged into the lead. Only then would the game end. Hill was a bad loser.'

*Alan Brown (on right), Burnley captain and manager (1954 – 1957) [69]*

Peter Fyles referred to the impact made by Billy Dougall, Hill's trainer. Fyles wrote: 'Dougall would insist upon repetition until flawlessness was achieved. Wingers would run down the line and cross and if the targeted forward had to check or increase his stride, it was deemed unacceptable.' Here was evidence of that professional discipline and attention to detail which marked Burnley out from many of their rivals.

At the start of the 1954/55 season, former captain Alan Brown replaced Frank Hill as manager after Frank had elected to return to Preston, the club he had previously served as trainer. Brown introduced an even greater level of professionalism, applying meticulous detail to training arrangements including the practise of dead ball routines and demanding total application from his players. He also restored defensive solidity. Arthur Hopcraft, author of that masterpiece of sports writing, *The Football Man*, described Alan Brown's later Sheffield Wednesday side as 'intensely industrious, technically capable and only the unusually strong teams or the unusually gifted could beat it with any effort to spare. It was the sort of side which appeals consistently to supporters without ever scraping their nerve-ends. It usually did incisive and resolute things that spectators could admire; it seldom struck the sparks that dazzle, either individually or collectively.' His Burnley model was much swisher, though.

Brown could come across as curmudgeonly censorious, a Protestant ethic warrior, similar in personality to Wolves' Iron Manager, Stan Cullis. As an example he once told Arthur Hopcraft: "people complain there's a shortage of *characters* in football nowadays but when they say that they usually mean *bad* characters. I get an hour's work out of an hour's time. I think I'm known for that." However, there was greater warmth and flair about him than these austere statements suggest.

Brown certainly made an impression on his charges during his three season at the helm. Bob Seith believed that: "the 1959/60 Championship was not won by what happened in just one season. Success was built up over a period of time. The architect of that success was Alan Brown. He was the first coach that Burnley Football Club ever had. Previously, the Club had trainers, of course, but Alan Brown was its first coach. Alan Brown was a tremendous innovator. He brought in many things that had not been thought about before. For example, he devised 'shadow' training where the whole team would attack just the goalkeeper and perhaps two or three defenders – it helped create momentum, instill positional sense and a rhythm to the way we played. We would practise these routines for half an hour or so, may be once or twice a week. I don't want to knock Harry Potts but really he inherited what Alan Brown had created. Harry did introduce a few new ideas but it was Alan Brown who was the main architect of Burnley's success." Brian Pilkington added: 'Burnley's passing game, playing to feet derived from Alan. At that time we were a small forward line so it made perfect sense."

The 1957/58 season was a time of change. With Alan Brown departing for Sunderland, first team trainer Billy Dougall took over as manager, but because of his deteriorating health, his trainer colleague, Ray Bennion was required to deputise until Harry Potts was appointed as a permanent replacement in January 1958. At first, it seemed as if the managerial changes had upset the club's equilibrium. In September, Burnley were tormented by both ex-Claret, Billy Gray and Scottish left-winger, Stewart Imlach in a 7-0 thrashing at Nottingham Forest. This humiliation was then followed by a 6-1 hiding at Chelsea. Despite scoring six times in his first ten games, Alan Shackleton was discarded for the Luton game at Kenilworth Road in favour of the 21-year-old, blond bombshell, Ray Pointer. Again, Burnley lost, dropping into 19th position but Pointer would soon make his point. Ironically, that would come in the very next game, a 6-0 drubbing of Alan Brown's ageing and relegation-bound Sunderland, whose cause was undone by two howlers from ex-Claret, Billy Elliott, then playing as a wing half. Pointer would score again as Leicester were put to the sword 7-3 with both Cheesebrough and McIlroy recording hat-tricks. Pointer notched a third as Portsmouth were beaten 3-1 in Burnley's first league game under the Turf Moor floodlights in December 1957. Before the season was out, John Connelly was blooded as an inside-forward. His meteoric rise as a fast, direct, goal-scoring winger for Burnley and England was about to begin. Meanwhile, Les Shannon's days in Burnley's half-back line were numbered with the title-winning combination of Adamson, Miller and Seith establishing itself.

After that spluttering start, Burnley managed to improve upon their 1956/57 standing by climbing one further place to 6th position, not that the Burnley public seemed too impressed. The average gate at Turf Moor fell to 22,251, the lowest since the War. Of course, the Munich air disaster cast a shadow over the latter stages of the 1957/58 season. At Burnley the gloom was also tinged with controversy, after a much-depleted Manchester United side lost 3-0 at Turf Moor in March 1958. Prior to the game, Burnley chairman, Bob Lord had been criticised for refusing to donate Burnley players to United's cause and was accused afterwards of badmouthing one of their players. With the nation stunned by the tragedy, this accusation fermented quickly into countrywide outrage with some members of the national press fanning the flames.

In his book *My Fight For Soccer* Lord reacted to the charge that he had been unhelpful to United in their time of need. He said whilst Burnley were prepared to help United with players, 'we were not prepared to wreck our First Division side in order to help Old Trafford to regain its feet. Remember that we in Burnley have not the scope surrounding the United of Manchester. Mr Jimmy Murphy, acting manager of Manchester United at that sad time, certainly approached me about the transfer of Cheesebrough and Pilkington, but I had to tell him I could not hold out much hope of those valuable players leaving the club.'

Long-serving Burnley supporter Geoff Crambie recalled: "The game was a bad-tempered affair. I remember Alan Shackleton being felled in the area and reacting by going up to the United 'keeper with his fists raised. I recall, too, that Mark 'Pancho' Pearson, United's inside forward, put himself about with some fierce tackling. I know it caused a stir when Pearson was called a 'Teddy boy' but he did look like one. He had his sideburns, his Tony Curtis quiff and this impressive DA ('Duck's arse'). Coming so soon after the Munich disaster, the game was a very emotional affair. The United team and their supporters were obviously aggrieved by what happened. That's probably why their players went in so hard. The referee seemed to side with them, too, despite dismissing Pearson. It was ridiculous really – he booked four of the Burnley players but said little to the United players who seemed free to go in as hard as they pleased. The Burnley crowd became very angry. Even though we won the game 3-0, four hundred or so Burnley supporters gathered outside Turf Moor at the end, incensed at United's rough treatment of their team, apparently abetted by the referee.

Before the game the United players were happy to sign autographs but afterwards they were ushered away quickly into their coach. As for the referee, he was kept back for a couple of hours until the heat had died down and the crowd had dispersed."

During 1958/59, Harry Potts' first full campaign in charge, the title-winning side began to come together, although it was not until the New Year before its engine really began to purr. A ten-match unbeaten run in March and early April lifted the side from 13th to 3rd place. Only a blip in the final three games reduced Burnley to a final placing of 7th.

Ray Pointer scored eleven of his 27 League goals during this hot streak, which featured eight victories with seven coming on the bounce. During this formative season, Connelly chipped in with twelve goals, having replaced Doug Newlands on the right wing, and Jimmy Robson added ten at inside left. Unfortunately, relegation-bound Aston Villa knocked Burnley out of the FA Cup again. Once more this came as a result of a 2-0 defeat in a 6th Round replay, but this time the venue was Turf Moor. 1958/59 also heralded the sad end of the career of goakeeper Colin McDonald, England's 1958 World Cup hero, although this would not be confirmed until two years later. But just as McDonald's career was ending, so Alex Elder's was beginning. Signed for £5,000 from Northern Irish side, Glentoran, left back Elder would prove to be the final piece in the title-winning jigsaw. Ironically, Harry Potts and Bob Lord had flown to Belfast in October 1958 to watch a centre forward, as they were then uncertain as to whether Ray Pointer would make the grade. Their attention was distracted by the immaculate skills of the young Irish full back. Elder duly signed terms in January 1959 but would not make his first team debut until the following September. With its best team almost in place, Burnley approached the 1959/60 season with confidence.

*Lord of his manor – Chairman Bob Lord at Turf Moor 1959 [70]*

## Chapter Eight

# A Class Apart

*Meet the League Champions of 1959/60*

## The Players

### Adam Blacklaw: goalkeeper – a sturdy last line of defence

Adam Blacklaw was born in Aberdeen on 2 September 1937. Reflecting upon his childhood, Adam told Dave Edwards of the *Aberdeen Press and Journal*: 'the only ambition I had as a youngster was to follow my dad, Jimmy, into football and, thankfully, I was able to make a living from the game. All I ever did as a kid was kick a ball against the wall, and despite the cobbles, me and my pals used to have great fun playing football in the street. The war started when I was a boy, but it didn't really affect me, apart from the fact I used to get a wee bit worried about my dad, as he was a chief petty officer in the Navy, but he returned home safely. My dad worked as a ship's carpenter at Hall and Company in Aberdeen and played centre forward for his work's junior football team, as well as for Banks o' Dee. My dad was a really good footballer, an old-fashioned centre forward.'

Adam played as a centre-forward, too, in his youth, representing Aberdeen schoolboys in this position. However, having been persuaded to adopt the role of goalkeeper, it became clear that he had natural ability 'between the sticks'. Adam commented: 'I knew I had something in me, and at just short of 6ft, I had a reasonable build for a goalkeeper.'

He was soon selected to represent Scotland schoolboys against England schoolboys at Filbert Street, Leicester. Scouts from Burnley and Leicester were at that game but it was Burnley who were the quicker off the mark and Adam duly joined their ground staff in 1954.

*Adam Blacklaw, Burnley and Scotland denying The Owls' centre-forward, Keith Ellis [71]*

Adam added later: "I played schoolboy football for Aberdeen but thought I would probably have to move away to get a chance of a professional career. I came from a working class family. We weren't well off. Aberdeen was not prosperous then. This was before the oil boom. It seemed a long way to Burnley. I didn't know where it was to tell the truth. I knew it was small but I thought I had a better chance of making it through the ranks at a small club. That's what attracted me to Burnley. In those days the gap between the reserves and the first team was not as great. They played in a similar way, too. So, you were able to adjust more easily. Also in those days, when you were an apprentice footballer, you were just that, an apprentice tradesman who also played football. The club put me through my apprenticeship as a bricklayer."

Although Adam signed professional terms later that year he had to wait for two years to make his debut in the First Division as future England World Cup goalkeeper, Colin McDonald stood before him. With McDonald injured, Adam finally made his First Division start at a fogbound Turf Moor on 22 December 1956. It was an auspicious if murky experience as Burnley thrashed visiting Cardiff City 6-2. With Colin McDonald consistently in the immaculate form that helped deny the brilliant Brazilians, Adam did not get much of a look in during the following season. However, following McDonald's tragic injury in March 1959, he was able to seize the senior spot which remained almost his unchallenged possession until March 1965.

Adam remarked: "I missed only two matches in my first six seasons, one because I was on international duty with Scotland and the other when our manager, Harry Potts, rested the whole team in preparation for our European game in Hamburg the following week. I didn't agree with the manager's decision and told him I wanted to play, but he was frightened one of us might get injured and miss the Hamburg game. Harry Potts was a really good manager, while our chairman Bob Lord was a character. He loved the club, but woe betide anyone who said "no" to him.'

During this period he excelled in many games, denying the likes of Everton in September 1959, Rheims in the European Cup in 1960 and Sheffield Wednesday in the FA Cup in 1961 with a series of brilliant performances. Allied to his acrobatic skills was his sturdy presence, his sound positioning and general dependability. It was these qualities which prompted the Scottish FA to select him for representative honours at both Under-23 and senior levels. His second cap was won in a remarkable 6-2 victory over Spain at Real Madrid's Bernabeu Stadium in June 1963. That victory remains as Scotland's biggest away win in Europe, a result made even more remarkable by the fact that just a year later Spain proceeded to win the European Nations Cup in 1964 – their last international success before the Euro 2008 triumph. Unfortunately, Adam's international career would end gloomily in Naples where Italy overpowered a patched-up Scottish side 3-0 to deny them a place in the 1966 World Cup final competition.

Adam had good reason to remember Naples since it was there, in February 1967, where he was approached at gunpoint by an Italian policeman. Adam's supposed crime was to have gone to the aid of first choice goalkeeper, Harry Thomson, who was on the receiving end of some rough treatment from the disappointed Napoli side. Burnley had just eliminated the star-studded Neapolitans from the European Fairs Cup competition and the Italians were out for revenge.

Adam recalled: "I was reserve goalkeeper that night, but my replacement, Harry Thomson, had a great game, pulling off save after save to deny the Italians in a 0-0 draw, taking us through 3-0 on aggregate. At the end of the game, when Harry went to shake hands with Alberto Orlando, the Italian spat in his face and threw a punch at him. That was enough for me and I leapt to Harry's aid, only to be set upon by about half a dozen Italian players and stadium staff. But I was a big fella and could handle myself, as I had been a boxer in my younger days in Aberdeen. As I was getting up off the ground, I was able to throw one guy over my shoulder and down a flight of steps, but when I saw a policeman with a gun, I decided to head for the safety of our dressing-room and join the rest of my team-mates. We were later escorted to the airport by an armoured lorry and nine military jeeps." As a pitch-invading Blackburn fan once found to his cost, you didn't mess with Adam.

After contesting the number one position with Harry Thomson for two seasons, Adam moved onto fierce local rivals, Blackburn in 1967 where he played 96 times before moving on to Blackpool and making his final league appearance in 1970.

Adam finished his playing career in the Northern Premier League with Great Harwood, alongside former Blackburn Rovers stars Bryan Douglas, Ronnie Clayton and Roy Vernon. From there Adam moved over to Clitheroe Town where he was manager for a brief spell in the early seventies. He then ran a paper shop in Burnley for seven years and became steward at the Burnley Cricket Club, whose ground is next to Turf Moor, before running the Cross Keys pub for several years and working as a caretaker-handyman at Nelson and Colne College.

Looking back on his career Adam said: "We had some wonderful players, lads like Ray Pointer, Jimmy Adamson, who later went to manage the club, and, of course, Jimmy McIlroy. McIlroy was maybe the best of the lot, and just like the rest in a squad packed full of internationals, Jimmy Mac wasn't the least bit big-headed. We had no real stars, but we worked hard for each other. If any of us was having an off day, everyone else would dig in even deeper to help them through it. We played for each other – that was the secret of our success. I would like to be remembered as a member of the team which took the First Division championship to the town of Burnley for only the second time in the Club's history."

Adam made 383 senior appearances for Burnley over a ten year period and for five seasons was virtually ever present.

## John Angus: an ultra cool right back

John Angus was born in Amble, Northumberland on 2 September 1938. He played for his local boys' club before being signed by Burnley as an amateur in 1954. A year later, he was signed as a professional on his 17th birthday.

Angus played his entire club career between 1956 and 1972 as a right-back for Burnley. He also made a single appearance for England in Vienna in 1961 in the unaccustomed position of left-back. National coach, Walter Winterbottom, described John's performance as one of the finest debuts he had seen. However, John had stiff competition from two of England's finest right-backs, Jimmy Armfield and George Cohen, whilst on the left there was the immaculate Ray Wilson. Neverthless, John won 7 Under-23 caps between 1959 and 1962 and also represented the Football League. Jimmy McIlroy reckoned John would have secured more representative honours if he had been more inclined to travel. John replied: "I was never one for travelling. I'd always preferred to stay around home. I had lots of opportunities – trips to Europe with club and country and to the USA, and Canada, too, when Burnley took part in the twin summer tournaments of 1960, staged in New York and Montreal. To be honest I don't remember much about these trips – I can still remember where we stayed in New York, just off Times Square but apart from the outing to Niagara Falls, very little has remained. It's a shame. Obviously, it was an honour playing for your country and travelling opened your eyes to how different people lived but for all that I still wasn't keen on going abroad. I didn't like travelling to away games much, either."

*John Angus, Burnley and England [72]*

At the start of his Burnley career, John struggled to win a place in the reserve team with the quality of players then available at Turf Moor and was less than a week away from his 18th birthday before he made his reserve team debut. A week after that debut, however, he was called into the first team after the Club was hit with a number of injuries. He was up to the task, though, performing well in a 2-1 victory against Everton on 3 September 1956 and giving Republic of Ireland international winger Tommy Eglington, the 'Eire Express', a difficult time. John completed that season with an unbroken run of 25 appearances in League and FA Cup games, displacing the young, versatile full back, David Smith. Although Smith regained the right back slot in the following season, John enjoyed an extended run of games in the 1958/59 campaign under new manager, Harry Potts, with Smith moving to left-back.

*Daily Mirror* reporter Frank McGhee reckoned that John's performance against the crack French side, Rheims, in the home leg of the European Cup tie in November 1960 was one of his best. Frank wrote then: 'Angus, the man who made this game after a late fitness test, was always decisive in the tackle and once the ball was his he always used it devastatingly. He showed the confidence of real class'. Frank repeated the compliment after the home leg with Hamburg S.V. in the next round. He wrote: 'John Angus was supreme. Outside left, Gerd Dorfel, rated by the Germans as their greatest winger in years, found that trying to trick Angus was futile…' Unfortunately, the one occasion when Dorfel did escape Angus's attention a goal resulted which would help Hamburg to overturn a 3-0 deficit and win the quarter-final tie 5-4 on aggregate.

Angus was a cool, classy defender. He only missed one game during the 1959-60 season. Significantly, it was on the night that Wolves tore a below par, innoculation-hampered Burnley apart at Molineux. He acquitted himself as a defender of the highest calibre during Burnley's European Cup campaign of 1960/61 and was a regular when Burnley were runners-up in both the League and FA Cup in 1961/62.

John remarked: "I've always been composed. Whatever game you are playing if you lose your temper you've had it. Yes, I could keep my head when we were under pressure. I was quite comfortable playing in front of 60,000 plus crowds. It wouldn't bother me. It wasn't as if I was totally cut off. I could still hear the supporters mouthing off but it never got to me. I didn't suffer with nerves.

I wasn't much of a dribbler but as a defender I would always try to find a team mate with a constructive pass. We were a passing team. That's not to say we didn't play hard. As a full-back it was important that you went in with a tough challenge on your winger, early on. It needed to be fair, though. You needed to let him know you were there. If they had something about them they'd not be put off by this. They'd come back at you. But those who were not up to a physical battle would then give you an easier time. So those early exchanges were important in deciding who was to be on top. The referees were more lenient then. For example, you could tackle from behind. But they'd still pick you up if you went over the top.

We started as out-and-out defenders. Our job as full backs was to stay with our winger, to stop them playing but as time moved on so we moved up more, with us having more of an attacking role.' John emphasised this by providing the crosses for all three of Burnley's goals in their 3-1 away leg victory over Lausanne-Sports in the European Fairs Cup tie of 1966.

John retired at the end of the 1971/72 season having failed to recover from tendon damage. He played in a total of 439 league games for Burnley and with Cup games totaled 521 appearances, scoring 4 goals.

John reflected: "The team would have held their own against any of the modern sides for skill counts in any era. Our Championship side had players in every position who always wanted to win by playing good football and that always made us a very hard team to play against. As to the details, though, I can't remember much about that Championship year. It seems such a long time ago. It was a good time but you move on. I rarely think about those days. In fact, I rarely talk about football now. I sometimes catch a bit of an Arsenal or Manchester United game on TV and can see how attractively they play. I see similarities between the way Arsenal play the game and the way we used to play. But to be honest I'm more interested in golf or walking or fishing.'"

Long-standing Clarets supporter and author, Reverend David Wiseman, commented in his book '*A Case of Vintage Claret*': 'John Angus, though strong and a hard man to play against was cool, a competitor to respect, and a polished player. How often have the likes of myself and my mates shouted "Get rid!" when he has put his foot on the ball in his own goal area, looked around, dribbled it seems along the goal line, to distribute the ball in an entirely opposite direction from the obvious one!'

## Alex Elder: a barnstorming left-back

Alex Elder was born in Glentoran on 25 April 1941. He was one of just two members of the Championship-winning side who were bought from another club. Burnley paid Glentoran £5,000 for his signature in January 1959. The fee was just £3,000 less than they paid the same club for Jimmy McIlroy's registration, nine years previously. He quickly established himself as a first team regular during the Championship-winning season after being selected to mark legendary Tom Finney in the derby game at Preston, on a hot September evening in 1959. As club historian Ray Simpson commented in his book *The Clarets Collection*: '[Alex's] hard, solid tackling and accurate passing became trademarks of his game, as did his barnstorming runs at opposition defences. He missed only one Burnley game that season to enable him to win his first full international cap in a 3-2 defeat for Northern Ireland at Wrexham in April 1960. He was still only 18 and went on to become virtually a fixture in his national side for almost a decade. He forged a formidable partnership with John Angus and the two were almost inseparable until Alex Elder broke an ankle in pre-season training in August 1963 … He took over from Brian Miller as Club captain in July 1965 and led The Clarets to a European Fairs Cup place at the end of the season.'

Alex made 330 senior appearances for Burnley, scoring 17 times. His first goal came in an FA Cup tie with Queen's Park Rangers at a cold, foggy Turf Moor in January 1962. A *Sunday Pictorial* reporter recorded in the occasion: '…none of the cheers were as loud as the one that greeted the first ever goal by Alex Elder. Alex tripped through the entire Rangers' defence to crack home a rocket shot. Alex used to be a forward and occasionally he likes to show that he has as much talent in attack as he has in defence.'

Alex eventually moved on to Stoke in August 1967. Unfortunately he suffered persistent knee problems whilst with the Potters and made just 80 appearances before moving to Leek Town in 1973. Afer leaving football, Alex became a brewery salesman before successfully establishing his own business. He now lives in Spain.

The following extracts are taken from an interview he gave to Burnley supporter and author Phil Whalley during the 1990s when he was still living in Lancashire. Phil has kindly given his permission for these extracts to be included here.

Alex recalled: "I was fortunate as a young boy, coming into a side with so many great players – and I mean great in the proper sense of the word. We were, in those days, a great family club – the young members of the side and of the reserve side babysat for the more experienced players, looked after the kids and so on, and that's the way we were. And that's why we were called the family club. We all went out and had meals together, the wives – well, we all lived in and around the town, so they all knew one another and we all met each other during the week and socialised. They even went shopping together. So all this meant that when you were out on the park, you did your best not to let your team mates down. Obviously, this is a lot different from today, where I don't think any of the players live in the town, they've got to get out to get home, so there's not the same camaraderie, I wouldn't have thought, as there was in those days.

*Alex Elder, Burnley and Northern Ireland [73]*

I was very fortunate. I played for my country in my first full season. I made my debut for Burnley in September 1959 and I made my International debut in the April of 1960 against Wales at Wrexham – a Home International as they were in those days. I had played for the B team, an Irish B international against France in the January of that year and I was reserve twice, but made my debut against Wales against the great Cliff Jones. I got the runaround against Cliff Jones as well! But I kept my place in the side, so perhaps having a hard game to start with was good for me."

## Jimmy Adamson: 'Spider' – an elegant wing half

Burnley FC historian, Ray Simpson, wrote: "Jimmy Adamson was born on 4 April 1929 in the mining community of Ashington, the sixth child of a colliery worker. Like thousands of football mad youngsters in the north-east of the 30s, the narrow ill-lit alleys forming murky corridors between the terraced houses were the first football pitches the young Adamson knew. His ball skills were finely honed during endless hours of constant practice on the uneven cobbled surface. At school Jimmy Adamson was a centre half and his ability and undoubted class would have won him many honours at schoolboy level but for the war. After leaving school he joined Ashington YMCA and switched from centre half position to inside forward. It was while playing for East Chevington juniors that he was spotted by Turf Moor scout Jackie Dryden, an ex-Claret who was as shrewd a judge of natural talent as they come and the young Adamson was soon on his way to East Lancashire."

*'Theme From A Summer Place': Jimmy Adamson (right) with Brian Pilkington at Gawthorpe training ground, September 1959 [74]*

Jimmy initially suffered homesickness and made a quick dash for home but he was enticed back and signed his first professional contract in January 1947 when aged 17 years. His early years were difficult as he struggled to master the inside forward role he had been assigned. Manager Frank Hill saw the problem and converted Jimmy into a right half where he blossomed. It was in this position that he made his debut at Bolton in February 1951 replacing club stalwart, Reg Attwell. Although Jimmy never was the fastest of players, his lovely control and his superb reading of the game eventually brought him selection in an England 'B' team against Scotland 'B' team. He had an excellent game.

Dennis Signy and Norman Giller commented in their book *Golden Heroes: Fifty Seasons of Footballer of the Year*: 'From the same district as Bobby and Jack Charlton… (Adamson) was always a composed and authorative figure as a defensive anchorman. His job was to win the ball and then pass it to playmaker Jimmy McIlroy who would in turn feed it to the striking force that included England internationals Ray Pointer and John Connelly…Jimmy was so highly rated as a tactician that he was appointed England coach for the

1962 World Cup finals while still a Burnley player. He declined the chance to take over as England manager from Walter Winterbottom, so leaving the way for Alf Ramsey to be appointed. The rest, as they say, is history.'

Jimmy was awarded the Player of the Year trophy for 1961/62 but his playing days were rapidly reaching an end. He pursued his coaching career with the dedication and shrewdness of his earlier mentor, Alan Brown and having obtained his certificates he joined the Burnley coaching staff in 1964, having made 486 senior appearances for Burnley and scoring 18 goals. Jimmy went on to manage Burnley for five years before taking on similar positions at Sunderland and Leeds. Despite his imprudent boast that his young Burnley side of 1970 would become the 'team of the seventies' (*they were relegated from Division One at the end of the ensuing season*) there was a period during the mid-seventies when his remark seemed possibly prophetic. These were the last days of 'the golden boys'; a smooth, fluent, skilful side comprising the likes of Alan Stevenson, Martin Dobson, Mick Docherty, Jim Thomson, Leighton James, Keith Newton, Peter Noble, Doug Collins, Colin Waldron, Geoff Nulty, Frank Casper, Paul Fletcher, Brian Flynn and Ray Hankin. Alas, the club was unable to both balance the books and keep their young stars and, with the conveyor belt of youthful talent seizing up, Jimmy's dream or prophecy was left in tatters. Jimmy left Burnley in acrimonious circumstances in January 1976 and according to those who remained in contact with him, he found difficulty in recovering from that bitter experience. He left football for good in 1980 having resigned from his managerial post at Leeds after his team had made a poor start to the season. But without doubt he remains as one of Burnley's greatest footballers and arguably their most influential captain.

## Bob Seith: 'the artistic' half-back

To his family and friends, he is known as 'Bob'. To the Burnley faithful, he is known as 'Bobby' but originally he was known as 'Rab', that was, before his Burnley re-christening. Bob Seith was born in Coatbridge on 9 March 1932, the son of a former Scottish League player. Encouraged by his father, Bob joined The Clarets as an amateur in 1948. He had previously been playing for Monifieth, a Dundee Junior Club. Monifieth was where Bob spent most of his youth. Although Blackpool were interested in signing him, Bob said: "Jimmy Scott, the Burnley scout was the first one in and the most persistent. Besides my father thought that Burnley offered better prospects because they had more reserve sides. In Scotland, there were fewer reserve sides. As a result so many players were passed over because they were not given a full opportunity to show what they could do."

Bob settled well at Burnley and was duly invited to sign professional terms in March 1949. He recalled: "Cliff Britton was the manager then. Although he was a Bristolian, he was utterly dedicated to Burnley. He made that clear to me at the very start of my career. One day he took me aside and asked me to accompany him to the top of the hill above Turf Moor. There, we peered down through the industrial haze upon the numerous mills and stone built terraces. With a broad sweep of his arm he impressed upon me, 'these are hard-working folk who graft hard for five and a half days each week. It is our *duty* to entertain them, to take them out of themselves for 90 minutes.' Although a generally dour man, Cliff Britton's passionate conviction has stayed with me."

Bob graduated to the first team, replacing Jimmy Adamson at right-half against Manchester United at Old Trafford on 3 October 1953. He was then aged 21 years having served two years national service in the RAF. It was there, as a member of the medical corps, that he began his chiropodist training. He obtained his chiropody qualification in 1955 and state registration in 1970.

When Bob began his career at Burnley, Alan Brown was still the centre-half and captain of the first team. As an inspirational leader, both as Burnley's captain in the late forties, and as the Club manager, between 1954 and 1957, Brown made a lasting impression upon the young Bob Seith with "his superb coaching, man management and motivational skills".

In the 1955/56 season, Bob Seith staked his claim for a regular place in the Burnley side, playing 39 times at right half, replacing the injured Jimmy Adamson and playing alongside Tommy Cummings at centre-half and Les Shannon at left half. When Adamson returned in late February 1956, Tommy Cummings was moved to right-back to accommodate him.

Bob became a fixture at right-half between 1956 and 1959. However it all started to go wrong for Bob following a 3-3 draw at home to Sheffield Wednesday in April 1960. He made an error during the game which led to 'The Owls' third goal. Bob was dropped for the following game at Nottingham Forest. He said: "I knew nothing about it until I read about it in the evening paper. I think Harry Potts really should have told me first." However, Bob said: "I had no problem with Burnley. They were generally very good to me. And, in any event that's where I met my wife, Jean."

The row between player and manager led to him being ostracised. "I didn't get to see the final games of the Championship season," Bob said. "They didn't play me in the reserves. I was not involved. But I did listen to the radio coverage of the final part of the game at Maine Road. I was so pleased for my team mates. It was a great achievement. After the season ended, I came back to Dundee. During that summer of 1960 a friend suggested that I should approach 'The Dark Blues' about joining their training sessions, just to keep fit. The Dundee manager, Bob Shankly (brother of Bill) agreed that I could take part and after seeing me perform in a practice match, he told me that he wanted to sign me on permanently. There was a snag here because Bob Lord had lined me up for a move to Stoke. I'm not sure what the connection was but Bob Lord seemed to be very close to Stoke – Jimmy McIlroy went there, so did Alex Elder and Doug Newlands. But I had no intention of going there. They were a Second Division side then. The Blackpool manager, Ron Suart, told me that he would have liked me to join them but said that Bob Lord wouldn't hear of it. Dundee were not prepared to meet the asking price that Bob Lord had agreed with Stoke so there was a problem. I ended up talking with Bob Lord over the phone. I told him straight that I wouldn't be pushed into a move to Stoke or Liverpool – another second division club who had offered a fee for me. If he wasn't prepared to let me go to Dundee, I said I would leave football. In those days the club held your registration so they could determine where and whether you played football.

*Bob Seith, Burnley's defensive wing half [75]*

Anyway, I had another string to my bow. I had my chiropody qualification so I thought I would turn to that if I couldn't play professional football. He realized then that he wouldn't get his way and let me go to Dundee for £7,500. But he wouldn't let me have a Championship medal. I had to wait until 1999 to receive that."

Bob continued: "funnily enough, many years later some friends of ours bought Bob Lord's former house. Sensing my possible unease in visiting them at the house, they told me, 'it's alright, we've had the place exorcised.'

Bob's unjust deprivation of a Championship medal was rectified after the writer Ian Ross uncovered this omission many years later. Following Ross's contact with the Professional Footballers' Association and with the current Burnley Chairman, Barry Kilby, Barry readily agreed to present him with one. Bob reflected: 'as Jimmy McIlroy pointed out, it was worth the wait. While he and the rest of the team had their medals doled out by Bob Lord in the dressing room, I received mine in the middle of Turf Moor in front of 12,000 appreciative fans'. Bob received the most fantastic ovation from the Burnley supporters as he walked around the pitch perimeter after the presentation. He was clearly overwhelmed by the reception. It was a fitting way to put the record straight and accord him the credit he rightfully deserved.

Bob played in a great Dundee side which reached the semi-finals of the European Cup and then, after finishing as a player, he joined the coaching staff at Dundee and later moved to Rangers in a similar role. Here he worked under the legendary Scott Symon. One of his final contributions at Ibrox was to help re-focus Alex Ferguson who was incensed at Symon's sacking in 1967. Bob said: 'it must have worked because Alex went out and scored a hat-trick.' He, too, was disillusioned with Rangers' decision to remove Symon and consequently returned to Lancashire in 1968, to manage Preston North End, although they were a club in decline.

After Preston were relegated to the Third Division in 1970, Bob left to become the manager of the Scottish national youth team. This role was short-lived as he moved on to take charge of Hearts in November of that year. The Maroons improved under his charge and in 1973/74 topped the League for several months following a 13-match unbeaten run. However, an inconsistent finish saw them narrowly miss out on European qualification and, following a 10 games win-less streak at the beginning of 1974/75, Bob resigned. He became Chief Chiropodist with Dundee District of Tayside Health Board in 1977 and remained in that position until his retirement.

For Clarets of a certain age he is fondly remembered as a fine defender, strong in the tackle and accurate with the ball. It is gratifying that he finally received his just reward for his fine contribution to Burnley's Championship success in 1960. In an illustrious career with The Clarets he played 238 games, scoring 6 goals.

## Tommy Cummings: centre-half – a swift stopper

Tommy Cummings was born in the Castledown area of Sunderland on 12 September 1928. He played initially for Hilton Colliery Juniors. This side created quite a stir because they were invited to represent Great Britain at a European junior tournament in Strasbourg in 1947. From that point Tommy Cummings was placed prominently in the shop window. Spurs were interested. Middlesbrough were interested. Huddersfield were interested. Blackpool were interested but it was Burnley who signed him in October 1947 with a £10 fee passing his way. Tommy's father liked the sound of Burnley once Burnley manager, Cliff Britton, made him an offer he was disinclined to refuse: a guaranteed job for Tommy at Bank Hall Pit. Tommy duly became a part-time mining engineer and, once he had been promoted to the first team, he took home £8 per week as a Burnley part-timer, too.

Tommy told Mike Prestage author of *Burnley: The Glory Years Remembered*: "My father was a miner and he said that football was a short life and he wanted me to have a trade to fall back on. Middlesbrough couldn't find me a job but Cliff Britton said there would be no difficulty in finding me work as a mining engineer. That satisfied my father and he signed there and then. I didn't know where Burnley was at that time, but we were aware of the club and knew they were very strong. They already had a reputation for finding players in the North East. In fact there used to be a joke that when we played in Newcastle, there were always a lot of spare seats on the coach home because of the number of players from the North East who stayed up for the weekend."

*Tommy Cummings, Burnley's centre-half [76]*

Tommy made swift progress through the ranks and made his debut at Maine Road, Manchester in December 1948. The result was a 2-2 draw. Tommy did well, so well, in fact, that he was chosen to fill Alan Brown's boots, following the departure of Burnley's inspirational centre-half and captain to Notts County.

Tommy remembered: "I knew I needed a good game and I had one. I was a bit quick in the tackle that day."

For the next seven seasons, Tommy was a fixture in the number 5 shirt, missing just 14 league games. During this period he was selected for the England 'B' side on three occasions and also represented the Football League in 1950. Unfortunately, he never gained the international recognition his fast, skilful play deserved simply because Billy Wright was always ahead of him. The nearest he came to selection for the senior England side was when he was summoned to join the Northern Ireland ferry at Liverpool. Tommy was quite star struck. He said: "my name was being shouted so I looked up and there was Stanley Matthews shouting for me. But it was Billy Wright who got the nod, so I was left on the bench with Jackie Milburn who also failed to get into the team that day. We seemed to be in the way. There were people in the Windsor Park crowd getting angry with us because they reckoned we were blocking their view. Then they started to throw stones at us. I was struck on the head by one. Jackie was really annoyed and was all for throwing the stone back but I stopped him. It was just as well as I'm sure there would have been a riot had he done so."

Burnley author Peter Fyles observed in his book *Burnley's Greatest Goal and the Last of the Golden Boys*: 'Back in 1948, Cummings was the youngest centre-half in the First Division. Any striker hoping to take advantage of his inexperience was out of luck. For not only was he quick on his feet but he was quick to read the game and was quite happy taking the ball out of the danger zone by himself. Like most defenders at the time, Cummings was tough. Tommy explained: "if I went to clear a cross, it was well understood between me and Jimmy Strong our goalkeeper, that it was best if I sent him flying into the back of our net or that he punched me in the face, rather than be uncertain and let in a goal".

In reflecting upon the goal that is described in Burnley folklore as 'Burnley's greatest', Tommy told Burnley authors, Geoff Crambie and Nathan Lee: 'my greatest game for Burnley has to be the Newcastle game in 1952. Fans still come up to me and say it really was the best goal they had ever seen. My memory brings back beating captain, Joe Harvey and then big Frank Brennan the centre-half on the edge of the box and then I just hit it as hard as I could past Ronnie Simpson.' Tommy was probably being modest. Harry Potts thought Tommy beat eight players, if 'keeper, Ronnie Simpson is included.

Tommy's career was put on hold as he suffered a serious cruciate ligament injury to his right knee at the end of the 1955/56 season. It would take two seasons for him to fully recover. It is a testament to his great determination and dedication that he managed to overcome what was, in those days, usually a career-ending injury. Tommy said: "I was sidelined for two years. I remember trying to get back, working in training only for the knee to break down again. At one point my right leg was an inch longer than the left. This was due to the build-up of muscle because of all the training I was doing with the injured leg. It was heartbreaking at times but I was determined not to give up."

When he returned he faced stiff competion from young Brian Miller. Nevertheless, Tommy proved himself to be resilient and flexible, able to apply his talents at full back also. So well did Tommy recover that Derek Wallis of the *Daily Mirror* picked him out as the man who 'wrecked Manchester United's Championship hopes' in March 1959. After Burnley had defeated 'The Reds' 4-2 at Turf Moor on a bright Easter Saturday in March 1959, Wallis wrote: 'Bulldog Tommy played with such poise and skill that there was hardly a chirp out of United's close-harmony inside forward trio. This was the Cummings of four or five seasons ago before his career was threatened by a serious knee injury'. During the Championship-winning season Tommy played at full back eight times but he was back in his best position for the night of glory in May 1960. He was at the centre of the action as Burnley clung onto their narrow lead tenaciously.

Tommy played his last first team game with Burnley in August 1962, giving way to the emerging John Talbut. He then moved on to become Mansfield Town's player/manager guiding them to promotion from Division Four and almost taking them up another rung two years later. After a brief and unsuccessful period as Aston Villa's boss he returned to Burnley and moved into the licensed trade as several other ex-Burnley players have done. He also became the Chairman of the Professional Footballers' Association taking over from Jimmy Hill in December 1961 after Hill had successfully campaigned for the abolition of the maximum wage eleven months before. Journalist Ivan Sharpe considered that Tommy was well suited to the role commenting: 'he has a quiet, interceding way: it will serve him well in office.' This was Tommy – an unshowy, unassuming man with an equable temperament. But he possessed a fiercely competitive drive and an indefatigably determined spirit, too, which saw him recover his career at Burnley, not only following his cruciate injury but also when he re-claimed the centre half position during the 1961/62 campaign. After retiring Tommy continued to live in Burnley until his death in July 2009.

## Brian Miller: a powerhouse at wing half or centre half

Burnley FC historian, Ray Simpson, wrote: 'Brian Miller first arrived at Turf Moor as a 15-year-old amateur in 1952. He was brought up in Hapton (Burnley) and had been spotted by a Burnley director playing in a schoolboy cup final in Blackburn. He was soon recruited to the office staff and made steady progress through the junior teams before signing as a professional in 1954. He made his debut at wing-half, deputising for Les Shannon during the FA Cup marathon with Chelsea in February 1956. Over the next few years his rugged, hard-tackling style was a key factor in the team's success and he played in every League and Cup game during the momentous championship season of 1959/60. His consistency was further rewarded that summer with three England Under-23 appearances, the first a 4-1 win in Berlin against East Germany.'

Burnley author, Dave Thomas interviewed Brian in 2005 and kindly gave his permission for extracts of his interview to be included in various parts of this book. In recalling his early days at Burnley, Brian said: 'Several of us worked at Bank Hall Pit at the same time as playing football. That was instead of doing National Service – serving your time in the army, which is what everybody had to do until it was abolished sometime in the sixties. Tommy Cummings, John Angus, myself, John Connelly. Jimmy Robson all served our time there and it was about the same time as we won the Championship, although by the time of the Championship we had stopped work at the pit. We worked at Bank Hall 'til 4.30 every day and then trained in the evenings. There were a few of us had to do that. Can you imagine that ... we worked for the NCB all day, above ground, either as joiners, electricians or bricklayers and then played First Division football. Spurs players didn't do that. That's another reason why it was such an accomplishment for a small town team like Burnley to do so well. If there was a night game we got the afternoon off but then when I moved to Thorny Bank Pit there was an understanding manager there who gave me time off in return for tickets. It helped if the manager was a Burnley fan."

*Brian Miller, Burnley and England [77]*

Brian made his senior England debut in Vienna in May 1961 alongside team-mate, John Angus. Both players were selected out of position – John at left-back and Brian at right-half! England's manager at the time, Walter Winterbottom, would undoubtedly have rewarded Miller on many other occasions, but for the remarkable consistency of Wolves' Ron Flowers within what was a very settled side. Even at schoolboy level, Miller's path to international honours was blocked by an exceptional talent. Brian recalled: "I made the final trial, North v South, and it was between a lad called Duncan Edwards and myself for the left-half position. He was such a great player . . ."

During the early and mid-sixties, Brian was almost ever-present in the Burnley side missing just 20 League games in eight seasons. He was a veteran of both the European Cup campaign of 1960/61 and the European Fairs Cup competition of 1966/67. He was a regular member of the side that almost gained the Double in 1961/62. Regrettably, Brian's playing career ended in April 1967 after having sustained a twisted knee at Burnley's bogey ground, Villa Park. Trainer, George Bray thought initially it 'was summat and nowt' but the injury was much worse than George thought. It was a cruciate injury. Brian was aged 30 years and had made 455 senior appearances scoring 37 goals over his 12 seasons with the club.

After his playing days were over, Brian joined the coaching staff and graduated to manager in 1979, replacing Harry Potts whose side had made a disastrous sart to their Second Division season. He was unable to stop Burnley's relegation to the Third Division in May 1980, a new low for the club. Nevertheless, in reaping the last full harvest of young Burnley talent, he duly led the likes of Trevor Steven (a future England star), Brian Laws, Mickey Phelan, Vince Overson, Andy Wharton and Kevin Young to the Third Division championship just two seasons later, assisted by canny imports such as Billy Hamilton (Northern Ireland's centre forward), Steve Taylor, Paul McGee, David Holt and Tommy Cassidy and bolstered by veteran keeper, Alan Stevenson and the immaculate Martin Dobson. Unfortunately, a poor run of league results in 1982/83 led to his dismissal. Sensationally, it came on the day of the League Cup quarter-final at First Division Spurs, which Burnley won 4-1! It was also his 46th birthday. He was replaced by Frank Casper, a Burnley star of the late sixties and early seventies, but Frank had no greater success and despite progressing to the semi-final of the League Cup and the quarter-final of the FA Cup, Burnley returned to Division Three.

Brian turned to keeping shop, a job which he carried out with easy-going, personable charm. When a floundering, almost bankrupt and desperate Burnley FC came calling once more in 1986, many men would have turned their back – not Brian, though. Despite the hurt he must have felt about his dismissal in 1983, he was prepared to pick up the managerial reins once more. This time he had at his disposal; a useful winger; a few kids; too many cast offs; a crocked centre-half and veteran Leighton James to keep Burnley in the Fourth Division. In Brian's prime he played in front of a 50,000 crowd at Turf Moor. Now his team was sometimes drawing less than 2,000. By May 1987, the club was facing relegation from the Football League and almost certain extinction. The media attention was so overwhelming, it was ghoulish – how Britain loves its falls from grace! Over 15,000 turned up at Turf Moor for the final game against Orient. Many had come to see a burial for Burnley had to win to survive. With the creditors sharpening their claws, relegation implied extinction. It was the last chance saloon.

Brian remained manifestly calm, controlled and courageously resolute. He deflected the publicity from his struggling team, relaxing them with his composed, practical advice enabling them to focus fully on their essential task. The pressure upon him must have been enormous but it did not show. Burnley's gnawingly tense, narrow victory on that sunny afternoon was as much due to him as it was to his team. Subsequently, Burnley were given a little breathing space in terms of time and money and he used the reprieve well. His subsequent skill in re-assembling the team from free-signings and bargain basement acquistions led to a Wembley appearance just twelve months later. It came in the Sherpa Van trophy final against Wolves in front of 80,841 supporters – the full England side had drawn a fraction of that support in the previous game played there. Talk about from bust to boom! Shortly before that Wembley appearance Brian was asked, if given the opportunity, would he have swapped the Wembley show for promotion from the Fourth Division. His reply was typically pragmatic. "In some ways the answer must be yes and I'm sure any manager would say the same in my position. But what really matters is the long-term future of the club and, if I'm totally honest, I would have to say that Wembley could be better for us. In my book, if you're going to move up from one division to another you have to be ready for it. There's no point in going up to come straight down again. I'm not saying that would have happened to Burnley but I know deep down we needed to be stronger for the Third Division. As it is, our profit from Wembley should enable me to go out and buy three or four new players in the summer; the type of players who can help us to become genuine promotion contenders. Don't forget, this club nearly died. It was almost the end (*said with obvious feeling*). Fortunately, I was able to bring in eight new players to make sure we didn't get ourselves into that situation again."

Sadly, Brian passed away in April 2007 following a short illness. He will be remembered with both warm gratitude and huge respect not only as a magnificent powerhouse of a wing half who performed superbly at the very top of his profession but also as the thoroughly decent, down-to-earth and brave man who helped save his beloved club from oblivion and nudge its fortunes back into the sun.

## John Connelly: 'The Flash' – a criss cross whizz right-winger

John Connelly was born in St. Helens on 18 July 1938. He was serving his apprenticeship as a joiner and playing for St.Helens Town in the Lancashire Combination when Burnley signed him in November 1956.

John told a reporter from *Charles Buchan's Football Monthly* in 1960: 'most youngsters on a month's trial with a big League club scarcely expect to be offered professional terms after only seven days. Yet that is what happened to me at Turf Moor in 1956. I had been taken there by Mr. Alan Brown – then Burnley's manager – from St. Helen's Town, where I had played as an inside left, after service with St. Teresa's school and then the school Old Boys F.C. I immediately began with Burnley's 'B' team, and the club fixed me up with a part-time job as a joiner at Bank Hall Colliery. That was my trade and I was anxious to carry on with it, in case I did not make the grade as a footballer … I persuaded the Burnley management to let me carry on with my joinery job, and I still work there as a part-timer. In fact, I was at work at the Bank Hall pit when I learned of my selection for England against Wales!'

John was initially self-conscious about his small stature. His Burnley landlady even remarked: 'it's a shame little lads like you should leave home!' But John remarked: 'with the intelligent training given me at Burnley it didn't take long to add to my weight and strength'.

With such strong competition from Brian Pilkington, John only managed eight first team appearances during his first two seasons at the club. But after Harry Potts' appointment as manager, John was given his chance and he seized it with both feet – scoring 12 goals in 37 appearances during the 1958-59 season.

John recalled: "my first real chance came when our brilliant left-winger, Brian Pilkington, was playing for England ... I was called on to play at outside-left in the Central League team. After that I kept my place in the reserves, and when Pilkington was again called up for a representative match I made my League debut against Leeds United. After returning to the reserves, I appeared at inside-left against Bristol City but I was soon restored to the left-wing. I was beginning to think I was going backwards ... when one day, manager Harry Potts asked me if my right foot was any good. Well I've always been two-footed and so I said "yes". He wanted to experiment with me as a right-winger. That was my big chance. I went into the League side soon afterwards.

*Joiner John Connelly hears of his England selection while working at Bank Hall Colliery in October 1959 [78]*

At school I had been fairly good at athletics and the speed I developed has since stood me in good stead in a position where pace is an absolute 'must' – especially in First Division football. It was been said that I like to cut inside my full-back and roam into the middle. That's because at Burnley we forwards usually switched about quite a bit and, of course, I looked for similar opportunities when I was in the England attack."

John's rise, thereafter, was so meteoric that he was selected for the full England side within a year – playing against both Wales and Sweden in the autumn of 1959. John proceeded to represent England 20 times between 1959 and 1966 with 8 appearances for the Football League and 1 Under-23 Cap.

He also won League Championship medals with Burnley and Manchester United as well as experiencing European Cup action.

According to club historian Ray Simpson: 'John Connelly ranks alongside the very best wingers Burnley FC has ever produced – electric pace, ball control and a fierce shot coupled with a goal scoring record that speaks for itself (105 goals in 265 senior appearances). No wingman since the war has scored more goals for The Clarets and, in the Club's entire league history, only the celebrated Louis Page has found the net on more occasions from the flanks.' Although John enjoyed an illustrious career at the very top of English and international football, like his Burnley contemporaries, this never turned his head. He was content to remain in his native Lancashire and, in fact, never played for a club outside his home county.

In 1964 John left for Manchester United where he stayed for two years, featuring in England's 1966 World Cup squad and starting the opening game of the tournament, the 0-0 draw with Uruguay.

Connelly continued to enjoy his football despite dropping down the divisions with first Blackburn and then Bury where he played alongside former Burnley team-mate, Jimmy Robson.

John was not just a swift, twinkling performer with an eye for goal, he was a really tough competitor, too. Bobby Charlton referred to this side of his game in his autobiography *My Manchester United Years*. Bobby said: 'in those days there was a small group of talented wingers who had learned that in an increasingly physical game they could not afford just to take knocks, brush themselves down and return to the action. They had to make their presence felt as ruthlessly as they could and Connelly elected himself to this tough group of survivors which included Terry Paine of Southampton and Johnny Morrissey of Everton. In my view, though, Connelly was the best in this category. He wasn't afraid to leave his foot in and this was never a secret; it produced instant respect in any marker. Connelly was perfectly equipped for this survival game. He was strong and quick who was happier to take on the challenge of unnerving a full back. He could beat a man well enough, but he was never inclined to stay around to admire his handiwork. If he had a chance to move on goal he was not reluctant to do so, as his scoring showed eloquently enough. His greatest contribution, however, given the finishing potential of his forward colleagues was to get to the by-line and cross accurately.'

## Jimmy McIlroy: Burnley's creative genius at inside-right

During the fifties and early sixties, Jimmy McIlroy, was Burnley's and Northern Ireland's creative genius. He played 497 times for Burnley in all competitions and scored 131 goals (116 in League games), a very high strike rate for a midfielder. He made his debut in October 1950 at Sunderland and within a year he had gained his first cap for Northern Ireland.

Even when hampered by injury, as he was for most of the 1959/60 season, he was irrepressible, continually pulling the strings in midfield, threading killer passes through bewildered defences and dumbfounding markers with his characteristically deft footwork, his trademark shimmies, feints and sudden changes of pace. Although not the fastest of Burnley's fleet-footed forward line, few could match his speed over ten yards and from a standing start. He had the art of creating space for himself and others in the most crowded parts of the field, frequently evading challenges from a cluster of defenders detailed to hem him in at the corner flag, nutmegging their heavy challenges and flitting along the touchline with the sureness of touch to set up chances for the inrushing Ray Pointer or Jimmy Robson.

*Jimmy McIlroy, Burnley and Northern Ireland [79]*

A typical example of his skill in tight situations was described by Ken Jones of the *Daily Mirror*. Jones was reporting upon Burnley's 2-1 victory over Fulham in the FA Cup semi-final replay with Fulham in April 1962. He wrote: 'Fulham were really beaten in one glorious moment of soccer skill by Jimmy McIlroy ... half fit and ineffective for most of the match (he) went strolling down the left wing with the ball. He slowed to a walking pace. Then to a stop, and kidded Fulham left half, Eddie Lowe, into standing in front of him. Then from a standing start he burst into a fantastic sprint to the near post and pin-pointed a pass for Robson to blast home his second goal. It was as carefree and casual as so many of the moves Burnley plan. Eddie Lowe said later, "I held off tackling McIlroy in that fatal moment. It was no good getting in because Jimmy is unbeatable in that sort of tight situation. I've never seen him stopped."'

Jimmy was born in the village of Lambeg near Belfast on 25 October 1931. As a junior he played for the Craigavad club near Bangor and was signed by Irish League club Glentoran in early 1949 aged 17. By the time he turned 18 a few months later he had already established himself in the Glentoran first team. With his first team struggling to score goals, Burnley manager, Frank Hill, began to scour Northern Ireland for suitable talent. His eyes were originally set upon an unnamed centre forward but he was dissuaded on account of the high asking price. Then, on March 15th 1950 Burnley manager Frank Hill saw Jimmy McIlroy play a starring role in Glentoran's 4-1 away win over Distillery, a match in which Jimmy also scored. Frank liked what he saw but Glentoran were less impressed with Burnley's initial offer. Obviously, Frank was both very keen and persuasive because within six days of watching Jimmy McIlroy's stellar performance, Jimmy was at Turf Moor having signed for a fee of £8,000.

Jimmy has a vivid memory of starting life with Burnley: "I remember distinctly the day I signed for Burnley. I was walking along this unlit Irish lane when my sister cycled up to me. She said that there were some men from Burnley who wanted to sign me. Almost without thinking I grabbed her bike to cycle home leaving her to trudge back in the darkness!

When I got to Burnley I stayed in a hotel in the middle of town. As I woke on the Monday morning, they were clearing away the rubbish and rotting fruit and vegetables left over from the Saturday market. The smell was awful. I thought then what sort of God-forsaken place had I come to. Danny Blanchflower's first view of the town was no different. We were later standing together outside Turf Moor before a home match with Spurs. As he watched this crowd of men in cloth caps and mufflers shuffle across the greasy cobbles, he exclaimed: 'how can you live in a place like this!' But Burnley was a perfect town for someone who had been living in a tiny Irish village. I soon felt at home here. I think I would have been bewildered by the size of the place had I moved to London. Although others have made fun of it, this is my home.

There were occasions when I might have moved abroad. Sampdoria, the Italian Serie A club, were interested in signing me during the early sixties. It looked an attractive proposition. I said to my wife: 'how would you like to live in a villa, by the Mediterranean Sea with our children attending an international school'. She was not convinced, though, exclaiming: "what do we want to leave Burnley for"!

Jimmy McIlroy was essential to Burnley's success. Indeed for much of the 1959/60 season he was not fully fit, but still played. For a long period he suffered from a deep-seated groin strain and early in the season he had to contend with a shoulder injury. But he was regularly strapped up and sent out to do battle as if he was Turf Moor's *El Cid*.

Throughout his time at Burnley he retained an instinctive grasp of how to forge telling openings for his team-mates, how to stay one step ahead of the opposition. As gifted as Jimmy was, it seemed to come as something of a surprise to him that he could compete with and triumph over the best international players – both with Northern Ireland and also with Burnley during their 1960/61 European Cup campaign. He was that modest. He was intensely conscious that it was a huge honour for the small town of Burnley to be representing England in the European Cup, remarking that it was only prior to the European Cup games that he had felt really nervous, acknowledging the weight of responsibility that this status and expectation conferred.

However, as modest as he was, he certainly knew his own mind. For example, he was openly critical of the arrangements made for the summer tournament held in New York after Burnley had won the Championship in 1960. He commented: "it was a very excited team that gazed upon at the famous Statue of Liberty and sailed up the Hudson River into New York's magnificent harbour. We thought we should soon be seeing the bright lights of Manhattan, but instead we found ourselves in a dingy hotel in Brooklyn so we kicked up a fuss about it. Luckily we were soon moved to a better hotel but as soon as the competition began we realised that it was almost impossible to take the games seriously. The crowd had come to enjoy themselves and what the players were doing was often of little interest to them. Before the games started an announcer would tell them: 'ladies and gentlemen the ball game has started' and would proceed to give a running commentary on the whole match. If the whistle sounded he would yell: 'it's hands, folks!' or 'that means a corner shot for New York'. Often he would interpret the referee's decision quite wrongly but most of the crowd didn't know any better so they were quite happy about it. When a goal was scored he would announce: 'scorer number nine with an assist by number ten' and in the final minutes of a game would produce a countdown worthy of a space-rocket launching. It was all very amusing but hardly helpful for playing soccer."

Jimmy set out his stall for the improvement of English football in his 1960 book *Right Inside Soccer*. It was a wide-ranging critique. Jimmy had little time for the petty bureaucracy he considered to be perpetrated by football's governing bodies. He was particularly damning of the restrictions imposed upon wage levels and upon clubs who wished to provide coaching to schoolboys. He had little patience with their decision to impose a ban upon football shown on TV as a means of arresting the decline in attendances. Here he was on more controversial territory vis-a-vis his club chairman. Jimmy dismissed a banning order as 'an easier way out than discovering *why* football is less attractive than television and remedying its faults (*for example, with better ground facilities*). The ban is the lazy man's way of dodging a fight.'

Jimmy was arguably the best player at Burnley not only during his time at the club but at any time in the club's history. His team mates recognised his remarkable skills, so did his opponents and as for the Burnley supporters, they generally regard him as the greatest Claret of all time. Burnley author Dave Thomas commented: 'the day after Jimmy McIlroy made his debut in the Burnley reserves side in March 1950 the *Burnley Express* greeted his arrival with maybe 6 inches of column space. When he departed 13 years later the same newspaper treated it as though there had been the death of a reigning monarch'. Jimmy's departure to Stoke in March 1963 prompted outpourings of grief and anger among the Burnley supporters. Some turned their backs on the Club and never returned.

Jimmy explained: "I went into Harry Potts' office and he told me straight out that the board of directors at a special meeting had decided on his recommendation to place me on the transfer list. I asked him why and he said he was not satisfied with my playing efforts. In fact, he said he was disappointed in me and that there was nothing more to it." Jimmy said he could not understand this logic, pointing out that normally when players were underperforming they were demoted to the reserves. Harry Potts told the Burnley Express: 'the only person responsible (for his departure) is Jimmy himself'."

Burnley's loss was Stoke's gain as McIlroy helped them win promotion back into the top flight in his first season at the Victoria Ground. After completing three years with Stoke, Jimmy turned his attention to football management with Oldham Athletic, where he pulled his boots back on in a vain attempt to assist his charges improve their fortunes. He wrote a regular column in the Burnley Express and still lives in the town today.

No greater accolade can be given to Burnley's finest than that which Sir Matt Busby gave in 1960: 'Jimmy undoubtedly possesses something which is shared only by the all-time greats. Subtlety dominates his game, and this allied to the ability to read a match, and find the open space in a flash, makes him a foe to be feared by all opponents. It should be stressed, too, that Jimmy McIlroy, denied the advantage of physical strength, has reached his present eminence by employing sheer skill, and skill alone.'

## Ray Pointer: 'Mr Perpetual Motion' – the 'blond bombshell' centre forward

Ray Pointer scored 133 goals for Burnley in 270 League and Cup appearances, a highly impressive hit rate. His final League tally of 118 goals in 223 games made him the club's second highest goal scorer in the Football League. Only George Beel's pre-World War Two record of 178 League goals surpassed him.

Ray epitomised the modern centre-forward. He was constantly in motion. He would bewilder defenders with his rapid movement across the line, frequently exchanging positions with wingers, John Connelly and Brian Pilkington and, after Brian's departure in 1961, with Gordon Harris, too. Repeatedly criss-crossing one another's paths, Ray and his wing partners followed well-rehearsed moves as if part of an experienced dancing trio, but they were prepared to improvise, also.

Ray would frequently track back to pick up passes well within his own half; harrying the opposition's attack, when possession was lost. He was always on his toes, ready to make a lightning break from deep positions, in order to create space for others as well as to capitalise upon scoring opportunities himself. On the run he had a slightly hunched bearing, his head thrust forward as if intently nosing out the opportunities. Centre-halves would rarely follow his runs. He was too mobile. In this respect, Ray represented the 'new wave' of British centre forwards, which emerged at the end of the fifties. These were more influenced by the continental artists such as Di Stefano, Kopa and Albert than by the more traditional hurly burly, bustling, battering ram centre forwards as typified by Nat Lofthouse, Dave Hickson, David Herd, Bobby Smith, Keith Ellis and Alex Dawson.

*Ray Pointer Burnley and England [80]*

Although not a physically imposing leader of the line, Ray was as equally brave as the more battling, bruising breed of British centre forwards. This was exemplified when he almost negligently brushed aside the sharp pain he must have felt when colliding headlong with the surrounding fence at Turf Moor during the icy Bradford City FA Cup replay in February 1960.

Ray was not big in stature (he was 5′ 9″ tall and 10 stone 10lb in 1959), but he was a capable header of the ball. It was his header which eluded the grasp of goalkeeper Schnoor and enabled Jimmy Robson to score Burnley's third against Hamburg SV, in the muddy European Cup tie in January 1961. But Ray's greater strength was on the ground. Being two footed, Ray could shoot sharply from all angles. Portugal would suffer the fierceness of his shooting at a bright, gusty Wembley in October 1961, as he helped England qualify for the Chile World Cup Finals at their expense. Unfortunately for Ray, this game proved to be the last of his international appearances. Having scored twice in his three games for England, with both goals coming in World Cup qualifiers, he was replaced in Chile, initially by the disappointing Gerry Hitchens of Inter Milan, but also by the able, though injury-prone, Alan Peacock of Middlesbrough.

Despite being such a prolific goal scorer for Burnley, Ray was never a selfish striker. He remained a committed team player; a thoughtful provider as well as a reliable taker of goals. He would dutifully and tirelessly fetch and carry in the team's cause. His exchanges with Connelly and Pilkington did not diminish his menace for he was dangerously probing on the flanks and could cross crisply from either wing, even when closely shepherded. With so much on offer, Ray was rarely out of any game for long. With his quiffed, almost impossibly blond hair, his greyhound speed and predatory finishing, he would brighten up the bleakest of grey winter afternoons.

It was Ray's brilliant versatility that caught the eye of a *Sunday Pictorial* reporter in October 1960. He described Ray's performance in a 4-1 League win at Blackburn thus: 'Never on the field of football conflict have so many men been bewildered by one man. He was a ray of sunshine in this grim tangle. And he lifted a dreary local derby from the depths with a sizzling one-man show. The number nine on his back was just a decoy because if Rovers expected him to hang about waiting for service, then they were sadly mistaken. Take the way he made Burnley's first two goals…from the right wing touchline, hammering across precision centres with the hit-me-quick look. Take the way he chased both Blackburn's raw young full backs, Mike England and Fred Pickering, into the ground. You have got to hand it to Pointer, the man who all Burnley thinks should be lined up opposite club mate, Jimmy McIlroy, in the Belfast international. Ray didn't stop at the full backs. He went along and teased Blackburn's usually sure-footed backline of Clayton – Woods – McGrath into more mistakes than they are likely to make for the rest of the season. And at the end, when jittery defenders were wearing their tempers on their shirt sleeves, Ray sapped up some lethal tackles without a murmur.'

Ray was born in Cramlington, Northumberland on 10 October 1936. At the age of eleven he represented Blyth boys as a right winger. Ray became a centre-forward after graduating to Cramlington Secondary Modern School. Ray recalled: "I was small, even for a schoolboy, but goals came largely through my speed and this led to my selection for the Northumberland County Schools side. After leaving school I began to learn the trade of welding but I never missed a game for Dudley Welfare Juniors, a team which brother, Bill used to run. I thought my big break had come when Sunderland took an interest in me but as I was only 5′ 6″ tall they thought I was too small to play centre-forward and that was the only position I wanted to play. It was

Bill who persuaded Burnley to have a look at me. Before Burnley became interested, I had spent six weeks at Blackpool, and took part in several trial games. At the end of the six weeks, I went back home to Cramlington, not knowing what was in the wind. Having seen me play for Dudley Welfare, Burnley scout, Charlie Ferguson, then asked me if I would go to Burnley for a trial. Feeling Blackpool had forgotten about me, I went.

Burnley kept in touch while I was doing my National Service with the Royal Horse Artillery, and were keen on my playing for them any time I got leave. That made a nice change from Belsen. Yes, that was where I was stationed, not far from the notorious concentration camp. I turned professional after my 'de-mob' in the summer of 1957. Although I started with Burnley in 1957, I went on to complete my apprenticeship as a welder. I did my welding in the mornings and trained in the afternoon."

*'Staying out for the Summer': Ray Pointer (on right) and Tommy Cummings, at Turf Moor during September 1959 [81]*

After spending just eight weeks at Burnley and playing five reserve games, Ray made his first team debut at Luton on 5 October 1957, five days before his 21st birthday, but the occasion did not provide him with much of a present. Burnley lost 3-2, their fourth defeat on the bounce. Ray recalled: "I didn't score and felt pretty raw in the company of players like Jimmy Adamson and Jimmy McIlroy. But I was determined to learn all I could from these great footballers and soon I began to feel I could hold my place in the side."

Despite making his debut during Burnley's poor run of form, fortunes improved thereafter for Ray and his club. Burnley eventually finished the season in 6th place and Ray managed to score 8 goals in 22 League appearances. He netted his debut goal in his second match, a 6-0 hammering of Sunderland at Turf Moor, and added a further goal in the 7-3 trouncing of Leicester City in November, which featured Jimmy McIlroy's only hat trick in a League game for Burnley. Although Ray contributed two FA Cup goals during that 1957-8 season, Burnley were surprisingly eliminated by middling Second Division side, Bristol Rovers, after a 4th Round replay at Turf Moor, having held 'the Pirates' to a 2-2 draw on a squelching cow pasture at Eastville.

At the end of the following season, one in which Ray netted 27 goals in 37 League games, he was selected for the England Under-23 side. Ray recalled:

"the match was against Italy and took place in Milan. The day before, the full international sides met at Wembley and drew 2-2. We were determined to do better than that – we did. Ray Parry gave us the lead mid way through the first half and soon afterwards he hit the post with a fine shot. The ball rebounded to me and I banged it in the net. A soft goal but I enjoyed scoring it just the same. In the second half we got another and we won 3-0. I wonder if the Italian scouts noticed the player on my right? It was Jimmy Greaves.

After our Championship victory in May 1960, I was chosen to go on tour with the England Under-23 team to East Germany, Poland and Israel. In Berlin we begun with a 4-1 win and followed this up with a 3-2 victory against Poland in Warsaw. But we came unstuck in Tel Aviv. We were the first representative side to visit Israel and they put out their full international side against us. In a temperature of nearly 90 degrees we missed many opportunities in the first half and then faded away in the second. We were well beaten 4-0."

Thereafter, Ray was too old to be selected for the Under-23 side and his chances of making his full international debut were limited by the form of Bobby Smith and Gerry Hitchens. However, he was finally selected for the World Cup qualifier against Luxembourg. Ray commented: "England had already beaten Luxembourg away 9-0 and many people thought the return game would be a walk over for us. I didn't. I know those matches where the other side is supposed to have no chance. I've played in plenty of them in the FA Cup against Third and Fourth Division sides. If your opponents have nothing to lose it seems to give them added strength and determination. That's what happened against Luxembourg. They defended stoutly from the start and it was half an hour before we could break through their compact defence. Then Bobby Robson pushed the ball through to Bryan Douglas on the right wing, and from Bryan's accurate centre I put the ball into the net from close range. In the next ten minutes we got two more ... Three goals up at half-time made us feel pretty pleased with ourselves. But in the second half we lost our touch, passes went astray and every move seemed to break down in midfield. The Highbury crowd did not help. They began to jeer us and cheer every time Luxembourg got away. It was almost like playing in a foreign country. When Luxembourg scored from a free-kick mid-way through the second half they got more applause than we had done for any of our three goals. British crowds like to think that they always support the underdog and I didn't mind the cheers for gallant Luxembourg. But I didn't care for the booing when we made mistakes. Bobby Charlton scored again in the 80th minute to make the score 4-1, and received some ironic cheers for his trouble. We won comfortably enough but I think if I had my choice I would have rather made my debut in a game that was not considered a victory before it started."

By 1961/62, Ray had peaked as a prolific goal scorer. In September 1962, Andy Lochhead began to lead the line with Ray moving to inside right, where he played a more supporting role, particularly after Jimmy McIlroy's controversial transfer to Stoke City in March 1963. Ray told local reporter, Keith McNee in March 1963: "I am playing neither as a second centre-forward nor as an orthodox inside forward. My game is somewhere between the two for the simple reason that it suits us best. I don't have any definite instructions before a game. I just go out and play it as it comes."

An ankle injury sustained at Nottingham Forest in April 1963 began to deplete Ray's powers and subsequent first team appearances became more spasmodic. He moved onto Bury in 1965 and thereafter to Coventry and Portsmouth, where he operated as a midfielder.

Ray impresses as someone who overcomes personal disappointment well, someone who is keen to make the best of things. With his considerable ability he was destined for stardom but he has worn the celebrity mantle with humility if not with reluctance. Fittingly, Ray was given a rousing ovation on his return to Turf Moor in March 1973 with his Portsmouth side; the applause and cheering continued from the moment he emerged from the tunnel until the moment he reached the centre circle.

## Jimmy Robson: Burnley's hunter and gatherer inside-left

Jimmy Robson was Burnley's inside-left during the late fifties and early sixties. In 242 first team appearances he notched exactly 100 goals (79 in Football League games) and had the distinction of scoring the 100th FA Cup final goal at Wembley in 1962. He might have scored the 102nd too, but was denied by a hair-line offside decision – a crucial moment in the game. He opened his account in the 80th minute of his debut game against Blackpool in October 1956. He was then just 17 years old. It was a cracker of a goal and enabled Burnley to salvage a point in a 2-2 draw. Jimmy established himself as a first team regular during the 1958-59 season when he played 33 League games and scored 10 goals. His form was such that he was capped for the England Under-23 side in May 1959. He marked his international debut also with a goal. This one helped secure a 2-2 draw for England, too, in the friendly with West Germany, played in Bochum. The Club were also sufficiently impressed with his development during the 1958-59 campaign that it felt that Albert Cheesebrough, his rival for the inside left position, could be sold to Leicester.

Thereafter, Jimmy made the number 10 shirt his own until the emergence of Andy Lochhead during the 1962/63 season. Among his 18 League goals he scored during the Championship-winning season included five he put past Nottingham Forest, then a Club post war record. But his best strike rate was achieved in the 1960-61 season when he netted 37 goals in all competitions, including three in the European Cup. Remarkably, he scored 24 League goals in his first 25 matches that year! He added 15 more League goals in the following season as Burnley narrowly failed to follow Spurs' example and secure the Double. In the succeeding seasons, Jimmy's strike rate declined as did his first team appearances. In 1965 he was transferred to Blackpool for £10,000, spending two and half seasons at Bloomfield Road as 'The Seasiders' struggled and ultimately failed to cling onto their First Division status. Nevertheless, he scored 14 goals from 60 starts for Blackpool, a respectable return for a club which was finding goals hard to come by. He completed his career, first at Barnsley, helping them to promotion from the Fourth Division, and then at Bury where he teamed up with ex-Burnley colleague, John Connelly. After concluding his playing career at Bury in 1973, Jimmy undertook coaching responsibilities at Burnley, Huddersfield and Rochdale.

*Jimmy Robson, Burnley and England Under-23 [82]*

Jimmy McIlroy said of his fellow inside forward: "Jimmy Robson was very under-rated by the Burnley fans. It amazes me. He was one of the best goal scoring forwards I played with. His goals were not often rocket shots or bullet headers but he was so often there to apply the final touch. I recall, though, that in one game he scored with a fantastic long range shot – so different from his customary prod or toe poke – and he turned to me with a modest grin saying: 'I score all sorts, me'." Ray Pointer added: "Jimmy Robson was so hard working. He would rarely dribble with the ball. He looked for the simple passes and left it to Jimmy Mac and the rest of us forwards to take the defenders on."

By 1959/60, clubs were encouraging at least one of their inside forwards to develop more as a striker. Jimmy Greaves, Peter Dobing, Dennis Viollet and Jimmy Robson were all strong cases in point, although some, like Jimmy Robson, would continue to play supporting roles. The centre forward was no longer simply the main striker. As Ray Pointer explained, centre forwards had to 'fetch and carry' too. During the title-winning 1959/60 season, Pointer, Connelly and Robson almost equally shared 57 League goals, two-thirds of Burnley's total.

Jimmy himself added: "It was true that the role of the inside-forward was beginning to change then – you had several players in that position who were becoming more like a centre forward but we hadn't got to the point where we had twin strikers like now. The inside forward's job was still to fetch and carry and make for goal from deeper positions than the centre forward. With a fast, mobile centre forward like Ray there was more variety in the role – we would both try to work the defenders, to move them around and create space but I was still clear what my basic task was.

Our success was based on a number of advantages. We had excellent players in all positions, of course, but in Jimmy McIlroy we had a true legend. That term is often over-used. I would put Tom Finney and Stanley Matthews in that category, too. With Jimmy he had this ability to find you with a pass whatever the situation. He needed so little space in which to thread through a really dangerous ball. I had no problem with him becoming our highest paid player after the maximum wage was abolished. He was our best player. The team had a good balance of youth and experience, too. I think this balance was crucial to our success. We had good role models like Jimmy Adamson. He had such a will to win. His example was an inspiration to us all. Quite frequently we would pull back from a two-goal deficit – once at Spurs we pulled back a four goal deficit! That said a lot about our determination and people like Jimmy Adamson were so important in leading that fighting spirit."

Jimmy McIlroy maintained that Jimmy Robson was very under-rated by his own fans and the same comment could be applied to the press, who seemed equally slow to appreciate his worth. It seemed that whenever his performances merited press plaudits any praise he received was qualified by some mention of his alleged shortcomings. For example, after he scored five goals in Burnley's 8-0 thrashing of Nottingham Forest in November 1959, the *Daily Mirror* reporter stated: 'Robson, a second prong of Burnley's double thrust centre-forward plan, had only scored six goals in fourteen games and was low down on the public list of Turf Moor heroes. But after his wonder show the stand rose to applaud him off the pitch.' In a similar vein, Edgar Turner of the *Sunday Pictorial* wrote after Burnley's Cup Final defeat by Spurs in 1962: 'straightaway, I must give a pat on the back to the man I have hammered most at Turf Moor – Jimmy Robson. For me, this was his best game of the season.' Turner had clearly overlooked the fact that it was Jimmy Robson's two goals that had helped Burnley squeeze past Fulham in the semi-final replay. Roger Hunt would also be damned with faint praise whilst performing a work horse role in Alf Ramsey's World Cup-winning team. When a group of Scots supporters derided Hunt's worth to Ramsey, Sir Alf retorted: 'Roger Hunt scores 25 goals a season, every season. Yes, Roger Hunt is a poor player!' A similar retort about Jimmy Robson's value could have been made to the carping members of the press. But perhaps Jimmy, a quiet, unassuming man, preferred to be left out of the limelight whilst he went about what he was exceptionally good at – setting up and scoring important goals for Burnley.

## Brian Pilkington and Trevor Meredith: Champion performers on the wing

Trevor Meredith and Brian Pilkington played on the right and left wings, respectively. After replacing hard man Billy Elliott, Brian became a regular first team performer, missing just 26 League games between August 1953 and March 1961, when he was surprisingly transferred to Bolton, hot on the heels of a triumphant European Cup display against Hamburg SV – a game in which he scored two stunning goals.

*Brian Pilkington, Burnley and England [83]*

Because of the consistent brilliance of English international, John Connelly, Trevor found it more difficult to break into the first team. Nevertheless, he deputised superbly for the injured Connelly during the vital run in to the 1959-60 season, laying on the match winner at Birmingham, scoring a point saving goal at Blackpool and, most crucially of all, netting the Championship-winning goal at Maine Road, Manchester. Brian and Trevor were the twin 'Champagne Charlies' of Burnley on that glorious May evening, as a Burnley Express photograph testifies, having both scored in the 2-1 victory.

Neither Brian nor Trevor said that they were nervous or apprehensive about the crucial final game at Manchester. Brian insisted: "no, we weren't nervous. We were confident that we could win. In that last match of the season at City, Connelly was injured, Mac played with his leg strapped up, and Trevor played and was outstanding, so we had people who could come in and play to standard, so yes, we had a very good squad really. We fancied our chances."

Trevor said: "we had a hiccup over the weekend with the draw against Fulham, but by the Monday we were positive we could get the result we needed. And, of course, we had that fantastic start. After just three minutes we were a goal up when Brian's shot beat Bert Trautmann in the City goal. That really lifted us. Then they equalised. Hearts thumped and glances were exchanged. There was just a brief moment of anxiety but it didn't last. We just pressed on. Then came my chance. I think one of their defenders miscued the ball. Anyway it fell to me and I just whacked it. I can't remember too much else, apart from the crowd and watching the clock tick down. It all went so quickly. Being the scorer of the winner was a bit embarrassing, because I'd only come into the team for about seven or eight games at the end. But yes ... it was a bit embarrassing in a way."

*Trevor Meredith, scorer of Burnley's Championship-winning goal [84]*

Brian and Trevor reflected briefly on City's goalkeeper that night, Bert Trautmann. He almost signed for Burnley but Manchester City just beat them to gain his signature. During the earlier part of his career Bert took a lot of stick from away crowds on account of being a former prisoner of war. Trevor remarked: 'we used to have POWs working on our farm. They would do short rotations so they didn't have time to settle. We used to think that the Germans were the hardest workers and that the Italians were lazy. I'm sure it was a generalisation but Bert certainly worked hard to establish himself in English football. He was a great goalkeeper.'

Brian and Trevor are of identical height, at 5′ 5″ but their relative smallness did not diminish their impact. In fact, they proved to be a real handful for defenders. It was Brian's scintillating debut performance against Spurs and England right back, Alf Ramsey, in September 1952, which convinced Burnley manager, Frank Hill, that he could transfer the crowd pleasing Billy Elliott to Sunderland, knowing that he had a ready replacement.

Both Brian and Trevor were blessed with pace and tricky ball skills and, as their scoring records indicate, they knew the way to goal. Brian scored 67 times for Burnley in 300 appearances, with a career total of 87 goals in almost 500 senior appearances, taking in his subsequent clubs, Bolton, Bury and Barrow. As evidenced in the Hamburg game, Brian could shoot as fiercely with his right foot as with his favoured left. For a small man, he was also mightily spring-heeled as he proved at a swampy Upton Park in January 1960 when he produced a towering header, from a right wing cross, to set up T.A. 'squaddie', Ian Lawson, for his second and Burnley's fourth in a runaway 5-2 victory.

Although his first team opportunities were more limited, Trevor showed he had a keen eye for goal, too. Spread over five seasons with Burnley, he scored 8 times in 37 games but it was following his transfer to Shrewsbury in 1964 that he began to demonstrate his finishing power more visibly. Trevor scored 42 times in 229 starts for 'the Town' before retiring from the game in 1972. As with Brian, Trevor could shoot with both feet. In the Championship-winning game at Maine Road, Trevor's critical goal was 'whacked in' with his less favoured left foot.

Brian represented England in a full international against Northern Ireland in 1954 and also gained two England 'B' caps to add to his brace of Football League representative appearances. Besides winning a Championship medal with Burnley, Brian completed his career by helping Barrow achieve promotion from the Fourth Division in 1967. Hailed by one national paper as 'the new Stanley Matthews', after his brilliant display in a 3-0 victory over Luton in April 1960, Trevor proceeded to win two Reserve Championship medals with Burnley and helped the club to three successive Lancashire Senior Cup wins between 1960 and 1962.

Trevor said: "I originally had no thoughts of becoming a professional footballer. Although I played for Kidderminster Harriers, it wasn't until I was undertaking my National Service with the RAF at Catterick in the mid fifties that the opportunity arose. Before that, my family had expected me to go to Loughborough College where I was to qualify as a PE instructor. I had remained at home on the farm in Shropshire until I was 18 years having attended a local Grammar School. At Catterick, I met up with Walter Joyce who was already on Burnley's books. There, I was recommended to the club who offered me a trial. I then started as a professional with the club in November 1957, just as new, young players were coming through to replace some of the older, more established First Team players."

Brian recalled: "I joined Burnley in March 1951. I came from Leyland Motors, who were then in the Lancashire Combination. I attracted Burnley's interest after playing at Padiham. Although we lost 4-3, I scored a hat trick. I was still employed as an apprentice coach painter. That was a seven-year apprenticeship taking me through from 14, when I left school to when I became 21. So, after signing for Burnley in April 1951, I continued with the apprenticeship for another 3 years. It made sense, given that football was not a secure profession. You only had these year-to-year contracts. The club were quite okay about me doing this. They saw the sense of it, too. However, soon after my 21st birthday, I had been picked for England at 'B' and senior level, so I was feeling more established by this time. I was fortunate in a way. I represented England, I represented the 'B' team, I represented the Football League a couple of times, I represented Young England, I represented the FA XI a couple of times. So on the whole, I had a nice career."

Brian, too, joined the RAF as part of his national service. By then he was a Burnley first team regular. "It was brilliant," said Brian. "They offered me a choice of stations so I could continue to turn out for Burnley. I chose Kirkham because it was the nearest. In fact, I only missed two matches while I was doing my national service and that was because I was asked to represent the RAF. I suppose the station commander saw it as something to be proud of. I thought the RAF was great. I got to go places like Gibraltar that I'd never seen before. Some of the other lads at Burnley did their national service with the coal board – John Connelly, Ray Pointer and Adam Blacklaw, I think. They weren't expected to go down the pit, just work on the surface. They continued to turn out for Burnley, too."

Both Brian and Trevor thoroughly enjoyed their time at Burnley. Brian said: "it was absolutely top drawer. It was always a family club. They looked after you well."

Trevor added: "after my daughters were born, Harry Potts, the manager, came round with some little dresses that he and his wife had bought for them. They were really good like that. They tended to hold onto their own, too. Many ex-players became coaches. Oh it was absolutely brilliant, there was a superb family atmosphere and they just looked after us so well – first class travel, first class hotels. The players that came to the club stayed with the club. It wasn't until maybe a decade later that players started going out to bring income into the club. When I started, the players who came into the club tended to stay. The whole club was just a happy club. It was brilliant."

## They also served: the other Burnley players appearing in the Championship-winning side of 1959-60:

### Ian Lawson

Ian Lawson was another Burnley recruit from the North East being a schoolmate of Jimmy Robson. His early career showed enormous promise. He was spotted whilst turning in outstanding performances for the Durham schools side. He was invited to join Burnley as a junior, turning professional on his

17th birthday in March 1956. He was blooded at centre-forward in January 1957 by manager, Alan Brown following Peter McKay's departure. His debut created quite a stir – a four goal haul against Chesterfield in the FA Cup competition of 1956/57. He followed this up with another hat-trick against New Brighton in the next round, prompting the media to hail him as the 'new Tommy Lawton'. But despite representing England Youth, Ian struggled to make his mark thereafter. During the succeeding two seasons he did not make a single first team appearance. His best return came during the 1959/60 title-winning season when he was also in the Territorial Army. In deputising for the injured Jimmy McIlroy on eight occasions, Ian managed to score three important goals – the winner in the 2-1 Boxing Day victory at Old Trafford and a brace in the Upton Park mud. After making several more deputizing appearances during 1960/61, Ian was transferred to Leeds in 1962 for £20,000, where he won a Second Division Championship medal. However, his subsequent moves to Crystal Palace, Port Vale and Barnsley proved to be disappointingly unproductive. Perhaps too much was expected of him too soon, particularly after his spectacular opening shots?

## Billy White

Billy White was another understudy at inside-forward, who filled in for the absent Jimmy McIlroy and the briefly out-of-sorts Jimmy Robson. He scored two goals at home against Manchester City to secure a narrow victory but despite impressing with his neat footwork and accurate distribution he was unable to secure more than seven senior appearances during the title-winning season and none thereafter. After representing the Burnley first team just 12 times in his seven years at Turf Moor, Billy moved onto Wrexham in 1961 where his manager was ex-Clarets star, Billy Morris.

## Gordon Harris

Gordon Harris was just embarking upon a highly successful career with Burnley when he was called upon twice to fill the left wing berth during the 1959/60 season – once at Blackburn, when John Connelly was representing England (Brian Pilkington was shifted to the other flank) and once at the Hawthorns after 'Pilky' had suffered some rough treatment in the previous home game. Gordon's time would come, though, once Brian Pilkington was transferred to Bolton in early 1961.

## Jim Furnell

Jim Furnell was a fine goalkeeper who served other clubs – Liverpool, Arsenal, Rotherham and Plymouth – with distinction. At Burnley, however, he had major competition, first from Colin McDonald and subsequently from Adam Blacklaw. Jim made only one appearance in the 1959/60 campaign. It came in a 1-1 draw at Blackpool where he deputized for the injured Blacklaw. This was not one of his stronger performances, though, as nerves appeared to get the better of him causing palpitations among many of the traveling Clarets.

### Billy Marshall

Northern Irish left-back, Billy Marshall, made just one appearance in the 1959/60 season, deputising for Alex Elder in the 1-0 away victory at Nottingham Forest. Despite showing considerable promise in his early years, Billy found it hard to make the grade at Burnley and eventually moved on in August 1962. He enjoyed one season of success at Oldham when, during the 1962/63 campaign, he became a regular member of The Latics side which won promotion from the Fourth Division. However, he stayed only one more season at Boundary Park before completing his career with Hartlepools United.

## The management, trainers and coaches

### Chairman Bob Lord: 'the John Bull of football'

Chairmen of football clubs were not usually headline figures in the fifties and sixties. Bob Lord was different. For a start he wrote a book about football. It was titled *My Fight for Soccer* and sets out clear manifesto for managing a modern football club at the start of the sixties. It is partly pragmatic, partly conservative but also partly visionary. The book was published just a few years after Len Shackleton left a blank page in his autobiography to indicate how much he thought an average football director knew about football. Bob Lord was wise enough to know his limitations and upon whom he should rely.

Bob Lord made many friends but made many enemies, too, particularly when his blunt, outspoken manner strayed into crass insensitivity. Lord was deeply troubled by the impact of television coverage of professional football upon clubs' finances. As chairman of a small town club with a declining population and dwindling gates he was right to be concerned. But this justifiable concern led him into making a clumsy and wretchedly offensive remark during an after dinner speech in March 1973. He said: "we have to stand up against a move to get soccer on the cheap by the Jews who run television." It is almost certain that he was using the term 'Jew' in the old-fash-

*Burnley Chairman, Bob Lord (on left), Vice-Chairman, Reg. Cook and Burnley Mayor, Edith Utley toast Burnley's League Championship victory, May 1960 [85]*

ioned sense to denote meaness, rather than making a racial slur since he had Jewish friends, but among those who were incensed by his statement was the, then, chairman of Leeds United, Manny Cousins, who was a Jew. Lord apologized subsequently. This was 'a hell freezes over' moment for Bob Lord was rarely apologetic for his blunt remarks. He told a BBC journalist in 1965: "People often expect me to repent after I have made some controversial statement but I never do. I say what I think and stick to it. Nobody gets any shilly-shally from me."

Lord also allegedly remarked that Manchester people had too much sentiment about Manchester United after Munich. As the current London Mayor, Boris Johnson, found in his derogatory comment about Liverpuddlians' alleged predeliction for 'victim status', this is not the sort of comment to win friends or gain influence, particularly given the wave of national sympathy expressed over the Munich disaster. Because he was no stranger to controversy, he may have had remarks attributed to him that he did not make. The alleged controversial denunciation of Manchester United as 'teddy boys' was apparently made by a fellow director.

Nevertheless, Bob Lord had strong supporters both within Burnley FC (former winger, Steve Kindon, was a big fan) and outside. Former BBC television commentator Kenneth Wolstenholme regarded himself among Lord's admirers. In his *Book of World Soccer* 1962, Wolstenholme posed the rhetorical question: 'is (Bob Lord) really the tyrant and dictator he seems to be, the sort of man who bans newspaper reporters from the Turf Moor ground if he doesn't like their stories? In actual fact, Bob Lord is nothing like that. He is a fair man who will listen to the other fellow's point of view. He is a man who believes that no one will ever make any progress unless everyone is willing to thrash out all the problems frankly. Away from football he is a successful butcher, and he still works the sort of day that would make younger men wince. Early in the morning he is up and looking after his butchery business. Then he is off to see his second love – Burnley Football Club.'

As a six-year old, Bob Lord stood outside the Burnley Town Hall in 1914 and watched club captain Tommy Boyle bring home the FA Cup to Burnley for the first time. Bob Lord was a supporter of the club for almost 40 years before he became a director in 1951. By then he had become a wealthy businessman with ownership of a chain of butcher's shops. He was intensely proud of his business achievements. He explained: "as a lad, a local butcher employed me for a pittance. When he refused me a rise I started hawking meat around the town from a cart. As soon as I made £300, I went back to him. 'Sell me your shop', I said 'or you'll be out of business anyway.' The deal was done and this small corner shop, bought in 1927, became the first in my chain."

His first bid to join the board failed but Lord was put up for election a few months later after a director died. He said: "when the votes were cast I put my hands over my eyes so that I would never know who was for me and who against." He became Club chairman just four years after his election to the board but made it clear that he never used a casting vote. He explained: "If it became necessary for me to wield the power of the chair, I would resign. If you cannot win an argument by persuasion, you'll never win it by using the big stick."

In his book *The Football Man* Arthur Hopcraft wrote of Bob Lord: 'since he won the chairmanship he has resoundingly refused to canvass or ingratiate to retain his position. He said to me, "I say to our directors every year, Look, if you don't want me again, that's alright by me." But then he added, "I think those who lifted me out of the chair might find they had a fight on their hands." He is certainly not a chairman to be shifted by gentle persuasion. Lord is a passionate partisan of his town and his football team. He said, "Ask anyone who works for me whether I pay good wages, and they'll tell you 'yes'. Then ask them whether I make them work hard, and they'll tell you I'm a slave driver. I don't think I'm that, but I expect something back for my money.'

In his book *My Fight for Football* Bob Lord insisted it 'has always been my policy to get the best men and pay the highest possible wages.' In November 1960, he was persuaded by the arguments put forward by Jimmy Hill that the abolition of the maximum wage represented a just cause. He reflected 'deep down most of us felt that McIlroy and indeed other Burnley players were not being paid according to their ability or anything like their value to the club.' Bob Lord took the view that increasing rewards would help attract better talent into the game and thereby raise standards. In forming this view, he took the unusual step, at least for a club chairman of the time, of canvassing the views of his own players. This may conflict with the self-opinionated image many have of him but supports Kenneth Wolstenholme's view.

Lord was withering in his criticism of the 'amateur' legislators of the Football League, whose limitations were sorely exposed during the negotiations with the Players' Union. He was no less tolerant of the Football Association's alleged mismanagement of the England football team and, for that matter, the ticket allocation policy for the FA Cup final, believing that the tickets should be largely divvied up between the two competing clubs. Lord was clear that 'the England team manager should have sole control and the responsibility that goes with it. He should be given freedom to choose his own staff of spotters, coaches and trainers. That's what I wish for Alf Ramsey, the man now appointed to the task.' He expressed the same view about the role of the Burnley manager, too, although he never truly granted one a carte blanche.

Lord believed in professionalisation at a time when some club directors felt they were entitled to give their teams half-time instruction. Lord suggested that he had no intention of buying a dog and barking himself. In his book he recounted an uncomfortable experience when, as a director, he was asked by the Burnley board to look at a player at Crewe. He emphasized: 'the only people to judge a workman in a job are the people who have done that job. Scouting by directors was cut out at Burnley immediately I became chairman of the club, and has been carried out by the experts ever since. This accounts for the good youngsters we pick up? This accounts for the fact that Burnley cost about a fortieth of the amount of money poured out by some of our leading rivals in the First Division today? You, sir, can supply your own answers.' Several years after Burnley won the title, Lord added: 'apart from match days, I am never (at Turf Moor) at the same time as the players. Harry Potts, the manager, is the professional appointed to run the club and I believe in letting him get on with it without interference. In my opinion, he is the best in the Division.' Of course, Bob Lord's principles began to waver as Burnley's power as a football club declined during the later sixties. For example, Lord felt compelled to choose between the rival claims of Potts and Adamson for the managerial position. But that is another story.

Bob Lord was a great believer in the 'grow your own' policy but was worried that if freedom of contract was granted this might allow young, talented players to move to other clubs without the host club being adequately compensated. He was convinced that refereeing standards would be improved by greater professionalization. Lord made the point: 'referees have to be physically fit to keep pace with trained athletes and this under the strain of crowd effects, which aggravate their duties. They may be in charge of approximately £1 million worth of footballers in a match and have to decide whether to send a £65,000 man off the field. They have to say whether a goal shall or shall not count and this perhaps when the decision settles which of the two teams shall proceed into the Cup Final at Wembley. They may have to call upon the police to deal with unruly spectators. They have to travel many miles in order to do all this ... All for a fee of seven guineas. Work it out: a road sweeper receives as much.'

Bob Lord was particularly concerned that referees should afford greater protection to skilful players pointing out that it was only through the promotion of skill that English clubs and national team could hope to compete against the best of continental talent. He said: "stopping the other fellow pays off sometimes, unfortunately, and we all know it. If English soccer is to call back the crowds, however, we have ALL got to concentrate on scientific football. We have ALL got to develop the positional play they've studied and produced abroad.' Lord stated that he agreed with the views of an un-named long-standing supporter who observed that 'the continentals aim at a more controlled style of play than most English teams. They do less long-kicking. Their methods are less speculative. Wingmen do not run down the touchline and bang the ball across goal. They double back more, and prefer to draw the defence and make a scoring opening by a shorter pass."

Notwithstanding his many forward-looking ideas, Bob Lord was diametrically opposed to increasing the competition for places in the First and other divisions through expanding the number of promotion and relegation places. He justified this on the grounds that this would only enhance the 'fear factor' among First Division clubs producing more safety first football. This sounds like a case for a cartel.

But when it came to the subject of football stadia, he was much more a man of the future. He was committed to improving football ground facilities at a time when many clubs preferred to invest in transfer fees while their pre-War grounds became increasingly ramshackle. He was highly critical at the standard of facilities at many grounds and picked out Wembley as 'more like a dungeon than the Number One enclosure of English football.' Having been impressed with the quality of Bilbao's stadium during a pre-season tour in the mid fifties, Lord was determined to recreate that vision at Turf Moor. His prioritization of football ground development would arouse increasing controversy among Burnley supporters during the early seventies when the Club was forced to sell off its family silver in order to meet the rising cost of ground improvements. Even with these ambitions, Lord's attentions were still drawn to the bottom line. He said: "we had plans to build a new double decker stand to give all round cover but how could we dare when the crowds failed to come?"

Under Lord's control, Burnley created more covered accommodation than the ground had ever known. However he wasn't just concerned with improving facilities for supporters. Prodded by Alan Brown, he secured a modern training camp just outside the town, with an up-to-date medical room, a gymnasium, three full-size pitches and a revolutionary all-weather surface.

The paradox about Bob Lord's dedication to improving supporters' creature comforts was that he had little time for supporters clubs or the contributions of individual supporters. He once blanked a young supporter who had the audacity to give him a Christmas greeting and when the small boy stepped onto the coach, where Lord was seated, to repeat his message of goodwill, mistakenly believing that the Club chairman hadn't heard him, the boy was sent packing with a flea in his ear. Bob Lord did suffer with deafness, though, but as former centre forward and current Club chief executive, Paul Fletcher, pointed out, Lord tended to use his deafness as a blocking strategy. Fletcher remembers that prior to signing for Burnley in 1971 he was prepared to demand the best terms he could. As it happened, Lord presented his terms, removed his hearing aid and announced: 'say what you like. I can hear bugger all!'

The title of his book *My Fight For Soccer* is instructive. He said: 'everything I've ever had in life I've had to fight for. I've got a maxim in life. If ever someone beats me in a battle, I don't blame them. I blame myself for letting them do it. Then I say, "where did I go wrong?" He was not the sort of man who took on a job he thought he could not do well. To the manager he gave a large measure of control but he expected results. He insisted: 'I want Burnley to be the best, not the second best.' It was some challenge, but one, for that 1959/60 he, and his club, undoubtedly won.

Most of the Burnley players interviewed for this book felt they were well treated by Bob Lord. A number of them remarked upon the swanky hotels they were put up in and the first class travelling arrangements. Lord flew his team to a number of away games at a time when this was highly unusual. He also supplied them with regular choice cuts of steak. He liked to show that his boys were well looked after.

John Connelly certainly thought well of Bob Lord. John said: "he was a wonderful man who'd do anything for his players and looked after us financially. When I got married in 1960 I'd arranged to hire a car and was supposed to collect it the day before. But then the hire firm decided I couldn't have it. It was in the summer and Harry Potts was away on holiday so I rang Bob Lord for help. Actually, I rang Club secretary, Albert Maddox first who said 'see Bob'. So I went to see him at his Lowerhouse meat factory. There he was in his white coat and cap. 'What can I do for you?' he said. I explained about the wedding and honeymoon and the car. 'Well what do want me for?' he asked. 'Well,' I said, 'if you can't help me nobody can.' And that was exactly the kind of thing to say to Bob Lord to set him in motion. People who made demands got nowhere, but appeal to him like that, and he rose to the occasion. You had to set him a challenge. 'Tell your lass not to worry there'll be a car for you if you come down the day before you marry,' he said. So down I went and there was the biggest Wolseley you've ever seen and I thought 'I'll never drive that. It's enormous.' Anyway I did and we went down to Newquay for the honeymoon thanks to Bob Lord. I think it took me two days to drive it there. There's so much that he did for people that no-one knows about."

Whatever Jimmy McIlroy thought of Bob Lord at the time of his traumatic departure from the club in 1963, there was a time when he, too, was a fan. Writing in his 1960 book, Jimmy gave the opinion: 'Mr Lord is an amazing character. No believer in half-measures, he tackles everything with tremedous zest. He openly confesses that his knowledge of football is not comparable with that of professional men; a director has to be a pretty big man to admit that. His sole apparent aim is to make Burnley FC a great name in soccer.' Jimmy's Northern Ireland team-mate, Danny Blanchflower was less impressed, once sniping: "[Bob Lord] is a self-made man who worships his creator." The legendary, late Bill Shankly was probably a better judge, though. He said of Bob Lord: "controversial he may be. But he is no hypocrite. Everything he has done has been with the interests of Burnley FC at heart. He is Burnley through and through. If you think of the club you think of him. The two are inseparable."

## Manager Harry Potts: the avuncular enthusiast

Harry Potts arrived at Burnley as a boy of 16 in 1937 from his home in Hetton-le-Hole. By the start of the first post-War season he had become first choice centre-forward, having served in the Far-East and was a member of Burnley's 1947 FA Cup Final team which was so unlucky to lose 1-0 to Charlton Athletic in extra-time after Harry had hit the crossbar. Harry joined Everton in 1950 and five years later became chief coach at Wolves and then manager of Shrewsbury Town before returning to Burnley in 1958 as manager in succession to Alan Brown. After the glory of 1960, his team came desperately close to winning the double in 1962 but lost the League championship to Alf Ramsey's Ipswich Town and were beaten in the Cup final by Spurs. He remained as Burnley's manager until February 1970.

What made Potts special was his relationship with his players and staff. Trevor Meredith commented: "Harry Potts was a track suit manager. He would take the pre-season training and lead the exercises on the training ground. He was enthusiastic and softly spoken and very rarely blew up. Harry just handled things nicely. He was a very, very positive and a happy sort of fellow. He'd encourage you rather than blow his top if things went wrong. He was really good. However, he did not give us much tactical instruction. That was left more to the senior players, Jimmy Adamson and Jimmy McIlroy. They would organise the dead ball routines, for example, although there is much more emphasis placed upon tactics now than there was then."

Jimmy Robson added: "Harry Potts was such an approachable man – such an enthusiast. He would lead the cross-country runs and participate with such enthusiasm in the five-a-side games. He was a good man manager."

Brian Miller continued: "in the dressing room Harry didn't rant or rave, bully or shout. If he did it was a very rare occasion and it would soon pass if he lost his rag with one of us. If we were losing he didn't need to lose his temper with us. But he did get himself worked up during a game and on a Saturday he was a very different chap to the weekday Harry Potts. Before a game he'd go through routines and free kicks, quietly remind people of their jobs. Let's just say he had a way of getting you to respond without throwing teacups around. He didn't need to. He'd certainly come in red faced and worked up at half time and sometimes full time. You could never say he was calm but most of the time on a matchday he kept himself under control."

As Brian Miller, former club secretary, Albert Maddox and Harry's wife, Margaret, have all pointed out, Harry could get *very* worked up during a game, as he did at Rheims in the European Cup tie. Harry objected so strongly to the French side moving their free-kick forward by several yards, that he ran on and grabbed the ball and put it back where the offence had occurred. This action brought about his expulsion from the bench amidst much angry jostling by the home crowd. Brian Miller remembered: "Harry could not abide cheats or cheating and that's why he did it. But after the game he was just so delighted and excited we had gone through to the next round, he wasn't at all bothered or worried about what he had done on the pitch or that the French had been thumping him, throwing bottles at him and jostling him as he was led off."

The late Albert Maddox, who started work at the club in 1947, remembered the Rheims game. He said: "After that incident Harry was made to move from the touchline and made to sit in the stand next to me. By the end of the match I was black and blue as he fidgeted and thrashed about, metaphorically kicking every ball."

*Burnley's 'track suit' manager, Harry Potts enjoying a joke with his first team players at Gawthorpe during September 1959 [86]*

Margaret Potts told Dave Thomas author of *Harry Potts – Margaret's Story*: "when I went to watch a game, I could see Harry opposite me in the dugout … He would be up and down, gesticulating, getting far too worked up defending his players. I had a lucky gold charm bracelet I used to hang onto while I used to worry he'd go too far and get himself into trouble."

Brian Miller continued: "the only time I ever saw an example of Harry's touchline misbehaviour, though, was during a game at Stoke and Alan Ball senior was a coach there. I don't think Harry liked him and something happened to annoy him during the game so he and Alan Ball sat there throwing stones at each other. There was this red grit stone stuff round the perimeter so there they were throwing it at each other."

However, as Brian indicated: "there were a few games when you might have expected him to be angry but he wasn't. At Ipswich in a later season we were beaten 6–2, that was a major shock in Burnley but that was on a night so hot and humid we were knocked out and Harry just put it down to that. There was no great inquest or fuss made. It was simply 'ah well, let's get on with the next game.' So we won the next 7 games and scored 27 goals. That was Harry – just go out and score more than they do. Same with the Cup Final defeat, we lost, but we didn't play badly, we enjoyed it. There was deep disappointment of course, bound to be, but at the Café Royal in the evening we had a great time – Harry loved his food."

Brian Miller confirmed a widespread view held among Burnley players of his and later generations when he said: "as a man-manager Harry was so good. You could relate to him, trust him, you knew it hurt him just as much to drop a player as it was to be dropped. He was never a man to walk past you without a greeting or a word or a conversation. He could never walk past you and blank you or ignore you. He cared about the private and personal welfare of players. You knew he was genuine and honest. So when I had a broken little toe I still wanted to go out and play for him so I cut a small hole in the boot to take the pressure and tightness off and played on with a broken toe."

In reflecting upon what impact Harry Potts had upon his career as a footballer, trainer and manager, Brian Miller said: "Harry had a great influence on me personally. When I became a manager myself I'd sometimes find myself asking what would Harry have done in such and such a situation, or I'd remember Harry would have done this or that in situations that I found myself in. He taught me that players respond to a manager who makes them feel they are looked after and protected. He showed me that nice guys could win things and that you don't need to bully players and throw teacups. At our peak he had this knack of making us feel that we could go out and win. He'd simply say just go out and score more than they do. Or if we were losing, he would say just make sure you score the next goal and not them. There was always a chance if you could pull one goal back. If I had to summarise him I'd say simply this. He always got the best out of his players. With just rare exceptions all his players loved to play for him and that was because he tried to do all he could for them. His methods were similar to Matt Busby and his achievements in matching Manchester United, Wolves, Spurs and the big city teams in the Sixties were immense. He will always be remembered for the great contribution he made to the history of Burnley Football Club. He was a great man and with his wife Margaret, they were just a smashing couple."

Former Burnley, Spurs, Leyton Orient and England midfielder, Ralph Coates reflected: "what made him a gentleman? His consideration for others, like the way he took me home to Hetton when mam died, or the visit he made to the hospital. He was honest, reliable; you could take any problem to him. He helped me settle in at a time when I was so homesick I just wanted to go back home. He was just so sociable and friendly. There was always a greeting, a comment if you passed him 'how are you?', 'Is everything OK?' But there were two sides to him. At Gawthorpe or on a matchday he had such energy and showed such emotion and if I had to choose one word to describe him during a game it would be 'passionate'. In the dugout he'd kick every ball, head every ball, make every tackle. He'd sit there and make the movements instinctively. I've sat with him while he's done it. If you've seen a boxer shadow boxing that's what Harry was like except it was football. He wore his heart on his sleeve, what you saw was what you got. At Gawthorpe he was a motivator rather than a coach or a tactician. He wasn't a manager who took groups for specific skills training or set routines, he left that to the coaches but he did join in the 5-a-sides. He gave you such confidence. Before a game he'd say to me: 'Ralph, 100% effort. Go out and do the job, you know what you have to do, go out and do it'. Another thing he'd say was: 'don't come back in and say if only I'd done this or done that.' After a game, even a game that we had won he was always so wound up. If he wanted to talk to us he'd shut the door and say: 'right sit down I want to talk to you', but because he was so passionate and almost fanatical on a matchday he found it hard to talk to us calmly or analytically immediately after a game. But that was just Harry because he was so worked up. It was a sort of uncontrolled Harry. The senior players would sometimes question him or disagree and he didn't cope too well with that but that was only because he was just so wound up in the game and that he hadn't detached himself enough from it and his passion was still running high."

In comparing Alan Brown and Harry Potts as managers, Brian Miller concluded: 'they were different characters. Alan was the Iron Man, strict on discipline, took no nonsense, if you got a rollicking from him you just felt like melting but at the same time there was a relaxed side to him when there needed to be. Alan once told us we had a plane to catch once at 7 in the morning for a summer tour abroad. But it wasn't at 7 in the morning it was 7 at night. But all he did was have a laugh at himself when we got there and out came the cards. Alan was a very fine coach and a brilliant motivator of the players. Harry was different, there was a gentler, softer side to him; he didn't need to shout or bully to get players to play for him. You wanted to win *for* him, not *because* of him. You'd never have called Harry the Iron Man. His philosophy was simple, and that was to go out and play, move forward, get onto the attack, and if the others scored we just had to score more than them. We didn't shut up shop and go for a 1–0 win we just wanted to score as many as possible. That's why there were so many high scoring games and why we came back and drew games like the 4–4 game at Spurs when we were losing 4–1 at half-time.'

## 'A man for all seasons': Billy Dougall: team physiotherapist and so much more

Burnley's remarkable title-winning triumph in May 1960 required the collective efforts of some remarkable men. Billy Dougall was one such man. The club summed up his outstanding contribution thus: 'William Dougall's career with Burnley spanned five decades and he was one of the club's finest-ever servants as player, trainer, coach, physiotherapist and manager.' There is an impressive list of testimonials as to Billy's admirable qualities stretching from the former Club chairman, Bob Lord to illustrious former players like Jimmy McIlroy. Billy was highly respected by all on account of the breadth and depth of his professional expertise, his shrewd intelligence, his personal integrity, his unswerving loyalty and his accumulated wisdom. Trevor Meredith, the title–winning goalscorer described him as a "wise owl – a kindly man. He was a bit like a counsellor. He would take you into his physio treatment room not just to sort out your injuries but also to help sort out things that were on your mind – what was going well and what wasn't."

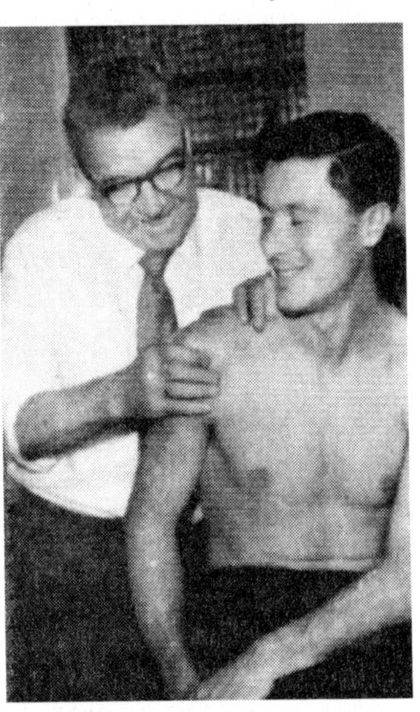

*Healing hands: Jimmy McIlroy kept physiotherapist, Billy Dougall very busy during the 1959/60 season [87]*

Billy's daughter, Mrs Ella Heap, remembered that he was "a good psychologist. If a player was not performing very well, through no obvious fault of his own, my father could be comforting but he also knew which players needed firing up, too."

Ella's son and Billy's grandson, John Heap, added: "Mum regularly tells of his knowledge of players – which ones needed to be bullied and which ones needed an arm round the shoulder, for example – some 30-40 years before sports psychology became widely recognised as a worthwhile discipline." John recalled that: "[Billy] might change, or even pretend to change, the studs of a player who had a poor first half in order to let the player blame external conditions and go out for the second half prepared to play better!' Jimmy McIlroy also referred to Billy's qualities an excellent man manager, saying that Billy knew instinctively which players needed taking down a peg or two. Jimmy remarked that if Billy came across a player who was too full of himself after a good performance, he would make a gently deflating comment like: 'so exactly how many accurate passes did you make today then?' It was just enough to keep your feet on the ground."

*Putting the tea into team work. Harry Potts with his faithful assistants – Billy Dougall (centre) and Ray Bennion (right) [88]*

Ella said that her father had a very tough start to his working life. She explained: "He went down the pit in Scotland when he was only 12 years old. He couldn't have liked that much. He later became a professional footballer first with Falkirk and then with Burnley."

John continued: "Grandad wasn't the only one to find success on the football field. His brother Peter played for Arsenal, and his younger brother Jimmy played for Preston. In fact, the family has produced a number of good footballers. My Mum's older brother, Neil, played for Burnley before being transferred to Birmingham, and later moving on to Plymouth. He was a Scottish international, as well, though I'm not sure whether that was when he was with Burnley or with Birmingham. He went on to manage Plymouth in the late 50s, I think. Uncle Jack – one of Mum's two younger brothers – played top-flight amateur football for a team named Pegasus! He, too, was an international – at amateur level but for England!!"

As a 31-year old wing-half, Billy was transferred to Burnley in February 1926 for what was then a fairly substantial sum of £3,000. There, he played 63 first team games, all at First Division level, between February 1926 and Boxing Day 1927 when he sustained severe cartilage damage during a game at Leicester. Ella recalled that her father kept the surgically-removed cartilage in a jar.

With his playing career over, Billy enrolled on a physiotherapy and masseur qualification course at Glasgow University. This was a remarkable step for someone who had experienced only a relatively short period of formal education. Ella said: "My father educated himself. We always had a lot of books in the house. There were the medical and physiotherapy ones but also other children's reference books, too. We had the complete works of Shakespeare and Bernard Shaw. He was very well read. When we were at school we didn't need the library to help with our homework. We had so much in the house including a set of encyclopedias. He used to read the newspaper from cover to cover. He was well up on current affairs. But he made little of his achievements. He was sociable but quiet. He would never take the floor. He wouldn't take over. He didn't say a lot but he thought a lot.' Billy seemed ideally suited, temperamentally, for the 'faithful lieutenant' role which he adopted so successfully with a line of Burnley managers."

After a brief stint in London, Billy returned to Burnley as reserve team trainer in 1932, graduating to the first team position two years later. It was then he met up with Ray Bennion and the two of them went on to form a partnership that was a major influence in the resurgence of the club in the post-war years. From 1935, when manager Tom Bromilow resigned, until the outbreak of the Second World War, Billy was part of a joint team selection committee, also comprising the Club chairman, Tom Clegg, and Club secretary, Alf Boland. He was also appointed by the Lancashire County FA as their official coach to the Lancashire schools.

Billy helped introduce the revolutionary short corner routine at Burnley. Manager and former club captain Alan Brown is credited with this innovation but John Heap said: "my dad told me that it was grandad that invented the short corner, and that it was such a revolutionary idea that it led to many goals in the first half of the season it was introduced (until we'd played each team once and they had learnt about it)." It seems clear that if the original idea did belong to Billy he would have been the last to crow about it.

Jimmy McIlroy added: "[Billy] had such an influence on both myself and Harry Potts. What he didn't know about football wasn't worth knowing. He was full of wisdom and knowledge and always telling us to look for the perfect ball. He taught me how to shield the ball. When we were drawing or were a goal in front and there was little time left, we would waste time by holding the ball at the corner-flag and keep collecting corners, throw-ins and, if the defenders got frustrated, free-kicks, too. We could use up ten to fifteen minutes at the end of a game doing that, particularly when playing away. That was a tactic Billy developed and instilled in us. He set such high standards. If you were practicing crosses, they had to be inch-perfect before you got a word of praise. If they weren't then you had to keep practising until you got it right. His simple philosophy was always do what the opposition doesn't want you to do. And when Harry became manager he turned to Billy Dougall such a lot. Billy often knew what we were thinking before we even thought of it. He was a master of psychology before it became part and parcel of the game. Looking back he was the greatest motivator I have ever known."

In 1957, when Billy was aged 61 years, he was invited by chairman, Bob Lord, to take over as manager after Alan Brown had resigned to take up the Sunderland job. Although not in good health, Billy agreed. Unfortunately, his health deteriorated further. After it was clear that he required hospital treatment he arranged for the managerial responsibility to be handed temporarily to his trainer colleague, Ray Bennion, before Harry Potts was appointed as a permanent replacement in January 1958. Billy then became the club physiotherapist, a position in which he remained until his 70th year in 1965.

Jimmy McIlroy was in a good position to judge Billy's skills as a physio since he spent so much time in Billy's treatment room during the title-winning season. Jimmy recalled: "I sometimes wondered how much electricity went into that troublesome left thigh of mine, particularly when Billy Dougall, who mended the players injuries so expertly, told me, 'Residents in town are complaining that you cause interference on their TV sets whenever you take a walk'."

Jimmy and Brian Pilkington both remarked on Billy's uncanny ability to detect and treat a muscle injury. They both recall Billy squeezing their damaged muscles and saying "Hmm this is a ten-day job or this is a six-day job." They both confirmed that Billy was invariably right. It was a terrific testament to his abilities as a physiotherapist, that he helped keep the smallest first team squad in the Division largely fit and active during the triumphant 1959/60 season. Football was very rugged in those days and players regularly received nasty knocks and, of course, there were no substitutes. Billy helped hugely in keeping his team fighting fit, even strapping Jimmy Mac up in a sling after he had sustained a bad shoulder injury in the home game with West Bromwich in September 1959. Although it would not be heard of today, Billy not only enabled Jimmy to continue, he helped him return to the fray with sufficient strength to turn the game decisively in Burnley's favour. Ella, his daughter, confirmed what the players had already indicated, that her father had "magical, healing hands".

When Billy became club physiotherapist, his responsibilities did not begin and end on the treatment table. As Jimmy McIlroy suggested, Billy had a wide brief. He acted as a consultant on team affairs and tactics; he contributed his knowledge on coaching; he had responsibility for ensuring that the players had the right boot studs to match the pitch conditions. He also sorted out the travel arrangements, including overnight hotel stays, when they traveled to London, and the curfew arrangements, too! Ella said that her father was rarely home before 6pm each night, irrespective of whether this was a weekday or weekend. Given his sweeping job description, that comes as little surprise.

According to Ella, Billy was a strongly principled man. He abided by a sure moral code. Although he was devoted to his family he would have no qualms about enforcing discipline where necessary. Ella said that it distressed her father when he saw others 'cheapening' themselves. She recalled his disdain at young soldiers during the Second World War who attempted to ingratiate themselves by buying drinks for everyone. Having been wounded in the First World War (he had shrapnel lodged in his leg), he was very conscious of the sanctity of life and of the importance of self respect. He was often troubled by pain as a legacy of his war wound, but when afflicted he was loath to display this. Ella said that if he was in pain while walking home he would choose a back route so that he would not be observed.

Sadly, Billy's period of retirement was very short. According to Ella, he never drew his club pension. Having left the club in 1965, Billy only survived a further year. Increasing health problems, culminating in the amputation of his left leg above the knee, brought about his premature death not long after England's World Cup victory. The club continued to invite Billy to team training sessions after the removal of his leg, but he seemed uncomfortable about being seen in public with his disability and as a result began to lose contact with the club he had sustained so loyally and so expertly for almost forty years. However, he is remembered with huge respect and affection by the players he supported so well.

Chairman Bob Lord said on hearing of Billy's death: "there is no doubt that Bill Dougall has been a most capable, devoted, loyal and conscientious member of Burnley Football Club during the whole of his forty years at Turf Moor. Many players have passed through his fingers, so to speak, and all of them have cause to thank him very much. He was endeared by all who were privileged to know him and he will surely never be forgotten. He was a great player and as a trainer-coach was also absolutely outstanding. Personally I have lost a great and close friend, a man who could always be relied upon. He set our pattern for success and I am sure our present staff will carry it on. His death, though, is tragic and we extend our deepest sympathy to his widow and relatives."

Jimmy McIlroy concluded: "Billy was one of the great unsung heroes of Burnley football club." Truly, he, along with his ever dependable colleagues, Ray Bennion and George Bray, were men for all seasons.

## Ray Bennion: first team trainer – the ever dependable assistant

Ray Bennion was born on 1 September 1896 in Wrexham. In his early life, he played for Gwersyllt School. He then had successful spells at Ragtimes and Chrichton's Athletic (Saltney) before joining Manchester United in April 1921. His debut for United came on 27 August 1921 against Everton at Goodison Park. While at United, he played at right-half. After scoring three goals in 301 appearances for the club and representing Wales on 10 ocassions, he moved to Burnley in November 1932. Here, he played for two more seasons before joining the Turf Moor coaching staff. Moving up the ranks, he was in charge of the reserve side that won their first Central League championship in 1949. His thirty years with Burnley's coaching staff was inextricably linked with Billy Dougall. Between them they provided the astute, faithful backroom support to successive Burnley managers as the Club made its post-war resurgence.

Chairman, Bob Lord regarded the pair as 'my staunchest friends in football – honest, capable friends'. Each Burnley manager would turn to the pair for wise counsel. Whether leading training sessions, undertaking pre-match relaxation routines, pitching in with tactical ideas or sorting out the kit for away games, Ray, like Billy, was an ever-willing contributor to the cause. At Billy's passing in 1965, Ray said of his close work partner of over 30 years: "Bill had been my friend and colleague since the early thirties. I will miss him more than I can say. He had so many fine qualities and he knew football from top to bottom. In fact what he didn't know about football wasn't worth knowing. We travelled a long and often tough path together and his passing leaves a great gap." Ray only survived Billy by two more years, dying shortly before another generation of young Burnley stars won the FA Youth Cup of 1968. It seemed a fitting valedictory moment given the contribution that both Ray and Billy had made to supporting the Club's youth policy.

The BBC Sportsview Soccer Annual for 1965 made the following observation: 'The backroom boys follow the Turf Moor tradition to a man. Adamson and George Bray, his coaching assistant, have known no other club and both won losers' medals in Burnley's two post-war appearances at Wembley; Bill Dougall the physiotherapist, has served the club for 40 years as player, trainer, coach and manager; Ray Bennion, a Welsh international of the twenties was trainer for more than 30 years before retiring in 1964. Even then he came back to look after the players' boots and equipment. "It's impossible to stay away from Turf Moor," Ray said.'

Tommy Cummings concluded: "As a raw teenager I learned a lot from Bill and Ray in a very short time. They were good coaches. They wouldn't pass the exams needed today but to us they were great motivators.'

# Appendix One

## *Appearances, Goalscorers & Attendances*

**League appearances:** Adamson, Miller, Pointer 42; Blacklaw, Angus 41; Pilkington 40; Robson 38; Elder 35; Connelly 34; McIlroy 31; Seith 27; Cummings 23; Lawson 8; Meredith 7; White 6; Harris 2; Furnell, Marshall 1.

**League goalscorers**: Connelly 20; Pointer 19; Robson 18; Pilkington 9; McIlroy 6; Lawson, Miller, Meredith 3; White 2; Adamson 1; Douglas (own goal).

Burnley won the title with the fewest number of League players representing them (18) compared with an average of 24 for other First Division clubs. Only Manchester United rivalled them by fielding just 19 players in league games during that season, although Burnley played five more FA Cup ties. Burnley played 50 competitive fixtures in 1959/60: a massive workload for such a small squad.

Burnley also won the title with one of the lowest Post War point tallies (55) and one of the smallest goal differences (+24), although superior to the records of Chelsea in 1954/55 & Derby in 1974/75. In conceding 61 goals, they had one of the worst defensive records among title-winning sides, only topped by Ipswich in 1961/62. Burnley actually achieved a better overall First Division record in 1965/66 when they finished third. Two thirds of The Clarets' 85 League goals were scored by just three players: Connelly, Pointer, and Robson, emphasising the importance of these three in finishing what Jimmy McIlroy so often created. It was testament to Trevor Meredith's nerve and ability that he had managed to make light of Connelly's absence during those crucial final games.

Even in this triumphant season, Burnley's attendances were low by comparison. Their average gate was almost 27,000: riches indeed by today's standards but the eighth lowest in the Division, some 20,000 behind Spurs and Manchester United. Burnley's feat in 1960 is perhaps not as regarded as significant as, say, Ipswich's League success in 1962 and yet given the size of the town and the intensity of local opposition, Burnley's achievement is arguably greater. It is possibly not recognised as readily simply because of the strength of expectation that the Club had built up since the War. Unlike Ipswich their success was not a one-season wonder. It had been established on the back of a strengthening Post War reputation, founded over 13 seasons of increasing success and sustained for a further 10 campaigns, albeit with dwindling results in the latter sixties.

## Comparative strength of local support

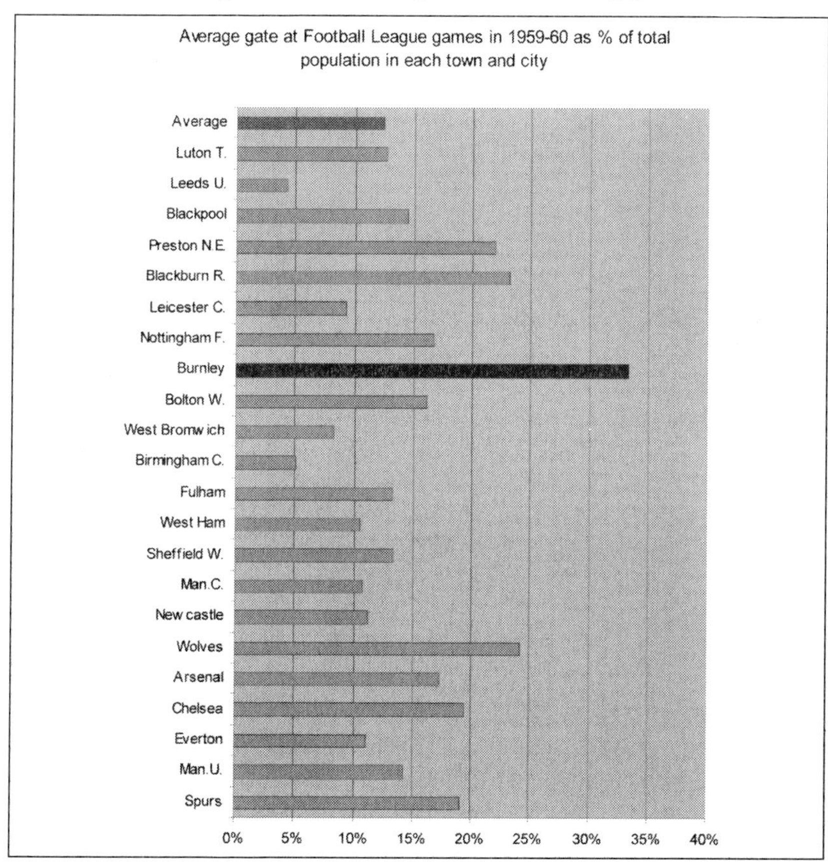


Sources: Office of National Statistics & Empire News & Sunday Chronicle Football Annual 1960-61

## Average gates in 1959-60 (population figures taken from 1961 Census)

| | *Av gate* | *population* | | *Av gate* | *population* |
|---|---|---|---|---|---|
| Spurs | 47,864 | 250,000 | Birmingham C. | 27,689 | 550,000 |
| Man. U. | 47,137 | 330,000 | West Brom. A. | 27,310 | 330,000 |
| Everton | 40,788 | 370,000 | Bolton W. | 27,104 | 168,215 |
| Chelsea | 39,744 | 205,000 | Burnley | 26,869 | 80,559 |
| Arsenal | 39,508 | 228,345 | Nottingham F. | 26,000 | 155,000 |
| Wolves | 36,354 | 150,000 | Leicester C. | 25,389 | 275,000 |
| Newcastle U. | 35,751 | 320,000 | Blackburn R. | 25,061 | 108,000 |
| Man. City | 35,347 | 330,000 | Preston N.E. | 24,530 | 112,000 |
| Sheffield W. | 33,265 | 250,000 | Blackpool | 21,770 | 150,000 |
| West Ham U. | 28,245 | 270,000 | Leeds U. | 21,690 | 500,000 |
| Fulham | 27,830 | 210,000 | Luton T. | 16,423 | 130,000 |

Populations apply to current municipal boundaries in which teams are located e.g Haringey for Spurs, Newham for West Ham, Islington for Arsenal. Where two teams are located within one municipal area e.g. as in Manchester, Birmingham, Liverpool, Sheffield, Nottingham the local population is halved for each team.

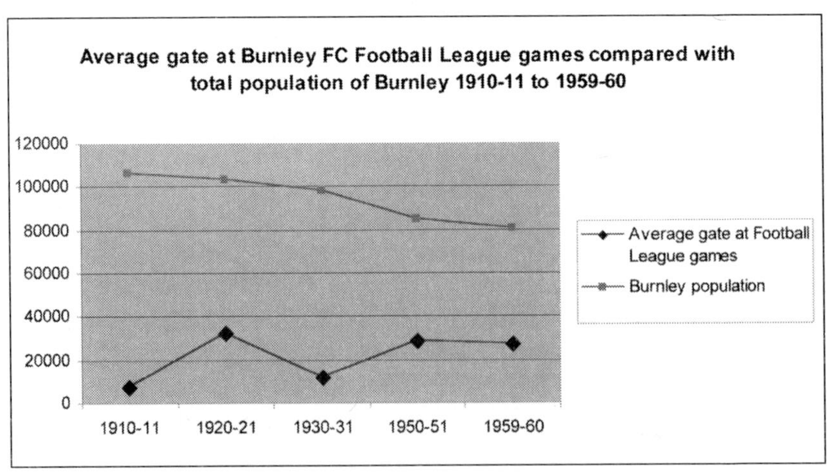

## Burnley's remarkable share of the support over time in the face of population loss

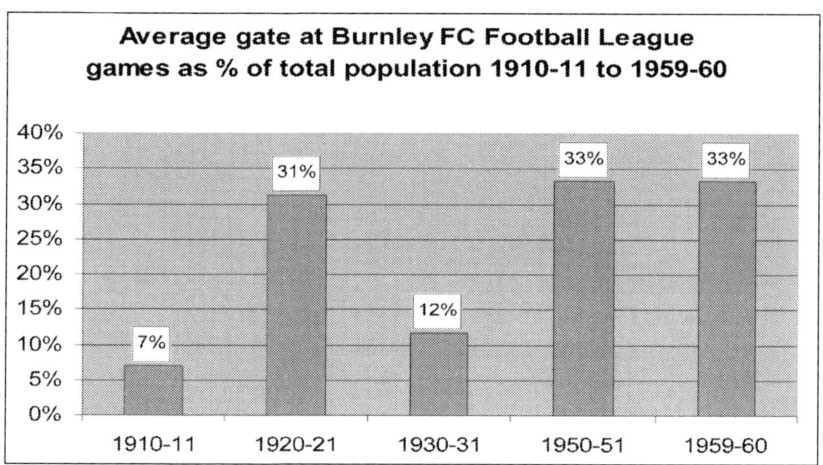


Sources: Office of National Statistics (1961) and Burnley Football Club records

**NB:** that Burnley was a Second Division club in 1930/31. Their loss of First Division status in the previous season combined with the impact of nationwide economic depression reduced their average gate substantially at the start of the thirties.

# Appendix Two

*What the 'soccer slaves' earned in 1959*

During 1959, Danny Blanchflower, captain of Spurs and Northern Ireland, and Jimmy Hill, Fulham's inside-right and Chairman of the Professional Footballers' Association, appeared on British television claiming that their contract and conditions of employment rendered them as virtual slaves to their 'masters', the Football League clubs. The League clubs responded by presenting the following details of players' wages and entitlements in their matchday programmes.

## Basic wages

*Maximum:* £20 a week in the season; £17 a week in the summer
*Minimum:* For a full-time player of 20 years-old £8 a week all year round

## Friendly Match

£2-3 an appearance plus £2 if the game is televised

## League bonuses

£4 a win, £2 a draw

## FA Cup bonuses (half amounts paid in event of drawn matches)

| | | | |
|---|---|---|---|
| First Round | £4 | Fifth Round | £8 |
| Second Round | £4 | Sixth Round | £10 |
| Third Round | £5 | Semi-Final | £20 |
| Fourth Round | £6 | Final | £25 |

## Talent money (paid to First & Second Division clubs)

| | | | |
|---|---|---|---|
| First | £1,100 | Fourth | £440 |
| Second | £880 | Fifth | £220 |
| Third | £660 | | |

## Talent money

| (paid to Third Division clubs) | | (paid to Fourth Division clubs) | |
|---|---|---|---|
| First | £550 | First | £330 |
| Second | £440 | Second | £220 |
| Third | £330 | Third | £110 |
| Fourth | £220 | Fourth | £55 |

## FA Cup (paid to clubs)

| | | | |
|---|---|---|---|
| Winners | £1,100 | Defeated in Round 6 | £440 |
| Runners-up | £880 | Defeated in Round 5 | £220 |
| Defeated semi-finalist | | £660 | |

## European Cup (paid to players for each appearance)

| | | | |
|---|---|---|---|
| First Round | £10 | Fourth Round | £30 |
| Second Round | £20 | Semi-final | £40 |
| Third Round | £30 | Final | £50 |

## Benefits

£150 a year during the first 5 years and £200 a year for succeeding years of service with the same club.

## On tour

£2 a day out-of-pocket expenses

## On transfer

Removal expenses and a sum of up to £300 if transferred at the club's request

## Provident Fund

A sum of equal to 8% of a player's total earnings is put aside each season and is paid to him, free of Income Tax, on the 1st January following his 35th birthday or following his retirement from League football, whichever is later.

## Vocational training

The League pays whole or part of the expenses and fees of players studying for another trade or occupation.

## Coaching

The FA pay fees to over 200 players who have qualified as coaches

## Representative matches

Fees are paid for appearances, up to £50 for a full international.

## Average wage in 1959

£11 2s 6d

## Rewards for top international players

Billy Wright, England's captain with over 100 international caps, estimated that he earned around £2,000 per year from club and country. On top of that commercial opportunities were beginning to emerge. For example, Johnny Haynes advertised *Brylcreem*, Tom Finney *Shredded Wheat* and Jimmy Greaves *Bovril*. Wright, too, had considerable earnings outside the game. By contrast the average Third Division player would earn about half of what Wright drew in basic wages. The Maximum wage did create an artificially level playing field but that by no means meant that everyone earned the same.

How times have changed, though. According to the Office of National Statistics, the average wage for a male in full-time employment in 2007 was £498 per week. In 1959, Billy Wright was earning in excess of four times the national average wage. If that ratio is applied to the 2007 average wage, Wright's earnings would amount to around £2,000 per week or £104,000 per year. A number of Premiership players are earning more than that per week!

# Appendix Three

*How the game has changed since the Fifties – a statistical account*

Some aspects of how the game of football is played have changed markedly in the last 50 years. For example, the top teams of 1959 scored and conceded many more goals than their Premier League counterparts. However, the top teams of today appear better equipped to defend a lead. The leading modern strikers are probably more ruthless in converting chances into goals despite having a slightly inferior ratio of goals to games than their predecessors of 1959/60, but are not blessed with the open spaces afforded to the forwards of fifty years ago. They have to contend with massed, tactically astute defenders. Nevertheless, the figures presented here suggest that some features of our game have remained largely unaltered. For example, a vast majority of goals are still scored from attacks comprising three or fewer passes. Also, between a quarter and a third of goals arise from dead-ball situations – penalties, corners, free-kicks, throw-ins. It seems that one message, in particular, bears repetition: 'break quickly and shoot as soon as the opportunity arises.'

## 1959-60

56% of league games in 1959-60 featured four goals or more with only 4% of games resulting in a 0-0 draw (*Rothman's Football Yearbook 2002-3*)

## Noughties – 1999-2000

41% of league games in 1999 – 2000 featured four goals or more with 9% of games resulting in a 0-0 draw. (*Rothman's Football Yearbook 2002-3*) do 2008/09

## 1959-60

The average number of League goals scored by a First Division side at home was 2 compared with 1.5 for the away team. (*Empire News Football Annual 1960-61*)

## Noughties – 2007-8 do 2008/09

The average number of League goals scored by a Premiership side at home was 1.5 compared with 1 for the away team. (*Sky Sports Football Yearbook 2008-9*)

## Leading League goalscorers – First Division 1959/60 and Premiership 2008/09

| *1959/60* | *Gls* | *Gm* | *Ratio* | *2008/9* | *Gls* | *Gms* | *Ratio* |
|---|---|---|---|---|---|---|---|
| Dennis Viollet (Man Utd) | 32 | 36 | 0.89 | Nicolas Anelka (Chelsea) | 19 | 37 | 0.51 |
| Jimmy Greaves (Chelsea) | 29 | 40 | 0.73 | Cristiano Ronaldo (Man Utd) | 18 | 33 | 0.55 |
| Jimmy Murray (Wolves) | 29 | 40 | 0.73 | Steven Gerrard (Liverpool) | 16 | 31 | 0.52 |
| Len White (Newcastle) | 28 | 40 | 0.70 | Robinho (Man City) | 14 | 31 | 0.45 |
| Derek Kevan (WBA) | 26 | 42 | 0.62 | Fernando Torres (Liverpool) | 14 | 24 | 0.58 |
| Bobby Smith (Spurs) | 25 | 40 | 0.63 | Darren Bent (Spurs) | 12 | 33 | 0.36 |
| John McCole (Leeds) | 22 | 33 | 0.67 | Kevin Davies (Bolton) | 12 | 38 | 0.32 |
| Billy McAdams (Man Cit) | 21 | 30 | 0.70 | Dirk Kuyt (Liverpool) | 12 | 38 | 0.32 |
| John Connelly (Burnley) | 20 | 34 | 0.59 | Frank Lampard (Chelsea) | 12 | 37 | 0.32 |
| Cliff Jones (Spurs) | 20 | 38 | 0.53 | Wayne Rooney (Man Utd) | 12 | 30 | 0.40 |

36 hat tricks were scored in 1959/60 season (Division One only

6 hat tricks were scored in the 2008/09 season (Premiership only)